MANAGING PROJECTS
With Microsoft® Project 2000

For Windows™

Gwen Lowery
Teresa Stover

JOHN WILEY & SONS, INC.

New York Chichester Weinheim Brisbane Singapore Toronto

This book is printed on acid-free paper. ♾

Library of Congress Cataloging-in-Publication Data:

Lowery, Gwen, 1950-
Managing projects with Microsoft Project 2000 / Gwen Lowery, Teresa Stover.
p. cm.
Includes index.
ISBN 0–471-39740-7 (pbk. : alk. paper)
1. Microsoft Project 2000. 2. Industrial project management--Computer programs. I. Stover, Teresa S. II. Title.

HD69.P75 L688 2000
658.4'04'02855369--dc21

00–068611

10 9 8 7 6 5 4 3 2

Contents

Acknowledgments

The authors wish to acknowledge and thank those fine individuals who have made substantial contributions to this edition of the book:

Tony Brady, for his painstaking technical review of much of the book, offering up his special insider knowledge and experience, along with cool techniques and shortcuts.

Carolyn Thornley, for the handsome production of this book, and for being extraordinarily responsive, willing to go that extra mile when needed.

Rob Ferrara, who contributed to the previous edition.

Introducing Microsoft Project 2000

A friend of mine, Allen, was the lead engineer in a highly creative team of computer chip designers. Allen reveled in the give-and-take of team brainstorming sessions and immersed himself in the design and development process of each new product. But despite loving his job, he'd often grumble, "I wish someone else could handle the management part and free me up for the engineering."

One day Allen got his wish—or very nearly. He stopped by my office to pick me up for lunch and saw me working with some extraordinary tables, charts, and graphs on my computer. "What's that?" he asked. I gave him a brief demonstration.

I showed Allen how to use the program to easily create a project schedule, assign people to tasks, track progress, communicate task information among team members, and even how to access project data on the World Wide Web. When the demonstration ended, Allen exclaimed, "This is it—I've finally found someone to manage my projects for me!"

The "someone" that Allen found to manage his projects is Microsoft Project 2000.

Using Microsoft Project is like having your own project management assistant. It helps you create project plans of any size, track progress, identify problems before they wreck the deadline or the budget, and communicate project information efficiently.

If you are a professional project manager, Microsoft Project is designed with the phases of your discipline firmly in mind, so you'll find it a good fit for your project. But even if all you know is that suddenly you're responsible for managing a project with specific tasks, people, and a budget, Microsoft Project will help you learn what you need to know and guide you through the process.

If you've never used Microsoft Project but are familiar with other Microsoft programs, such as Microsoft Excel and Microsoft Word, you'll have a head start getting up and running with Microsoft Project.

What's New in Microsoft Project 2000

Microsoft Project 2000 includes a number of new features and enhancements that enable you to manage projects more easily and effectively than ever. This section covers these new features, which are grouped into the following categories:

- Scheduling tasks and tracking progress.
- Managing resources for better task scheduling.
- Working with the new Network Diagram view.

- Managing tasks and resources across a workgroup.
- Working faster and smarter.

Schedule Tasks and Track Progress with Ease

Microsoft Project has been redesigned so you can more accurately model your plan to how you actually schedule your project. You also have more control over how you view and compare schedule information.

- **Schedule According to Task Calendars.** Just as you can set working and nonworking time with project and resource calendars, you can now create task calendars to specify working and nonworking time on a specific task. With task calendars, you can create a special schedule for one or more selected tasks, independent of the project calendar, and intersecting with or independent of the calendars of resources assigned to them.
- **Be Alerted to Deadline Dates.** If you want Microsoft Project to mark and alert you to a deadline but don't want to make it a date constraint, you can do so with deadline dates. The deadline date is shown as a marker on the Gantt Chart, and Microsoft Project alerts you if a task is scheduled to finish after its deadline.
- **Enter Estimated Durations.** You can enter a task duration as an estimate. This is particularly useful when first setting up a project, while you're still waiting for duration feedback from resources and modeling your schedule. Estimated durations are shown with a question mark in the Gantt Chart and other task views.
- **Use Months as a Unit of Duration.** Along with minutes, hours, days, and weeks, Microsoft Project now supports months (abbreviated as "mon") as a unit of duration. By default, a month is defined as having 20 working days.
- **Clear Baseline or Interim Plans.** While you can create a single baseline plan and several interim plans to use in comparing and tracking progress, you can now also clear the baseline and interim plans in one easy step. This lets you start over with a new baseline or new interim plans, especially useful when your project has made a shift in direction and you want a different basis of comparison.
- **Calculate a Single Critical Path in a Master Project.** When using a master project with subprojects, you can now choose whether Microsoft Project calculates an individual critical path for each subproject or the overall critical path for the entire master project.

Manage Resources for Better Task Scheduling

Effective resource management is essential for a successful project outcome. Microsoft Project provides new methods for flexibly and accurately managing your resources.

- **Vary Resource Availability Throughout a Project.** You can set when a resource joins and leaves a project, if the time is different from the start or end of the project itself. You can also indicate varying available resource units throughout the project.
- **Distinguish Material Resources.** With Microsoft Project 2000, you can now specify consumable resources used in a task, such as concrete or soil. You can differentiate these material resources from work, or human, resources, and assign them to tasks. Material resources are tracked with material units, such as tons of steel or cubic yards of dirt.
- **Set Task Priorities for Resource Leveling.** Microsoft Project now has 1000 priority levels, with 1000 the highest and 0 the lowest priority. Previous versions had nine levels. When leveling overallocated resources, tasks with lower priorities are delayed or split sooner than those with higher priorities.

Graphically Model Your Project with the Network Diagram View

The new Network Diagram view in Microsoft Project 2000 replaces the PERT Chart view of previous versions. New features in the Network Diagram view provide for more flexible information viewing and formatting.

- **Filter Tasks in the Network Diagram.** Apply filters in your Network Diagram to see only those tasks that meet a specified condition.
- **Expand and Collapse Outline Levels in the Network Diagram View.** You can use the familiar outlining symbols to hide or show the subtasks under a summary task.
- **Specify Content for Network Diagram Nodes.** Specify both the number and contents of fields you want to display in each Network Diagram node. You can specify up to 16 fields for each node. You can also label the cells within the nodes.
- **Format Your Network Diagram Nodes.** You have greater control over the look of the Network Diagram nodes. You can set the formatting styles for how different task types are displayed in the Network Diagram. These styles include node shapes, row heights of the cells, and font. You can also format individual nodes independent of their task types.

Manage Tasks and Resources Across a Workgroup

Microsoft Project Central is a new licensed companion product that significantly builds on the Web-based workgroup capabilities in Microsoft Project 98. Microsoft Project Central provides for collaborative planning among workgroup members and project managers. All individuals involved with the project can review, work with, and exchange project information on a Web site. Only the project manager needs to have Microsoft Project. Workgroup members use Microsoft Project Central.

If you choose not to use Microsoft Project Central, you can still send and receive task messages with an e-mail workgroup system.

- **Review Personal Gantt Charts.** Workgroup members can see their tasks in their own Gantt chart. If they're involved with multiple projects, they can see all the tasks for all their projects in a single Gantt Chart.
- **Review the Entire Project.** If the Microsoft Project Central administrator grants access, workgroup members can view information for the entire project. This shows their tasks in the full project context.
- **Create Tasks.** Many project managers prefer to set up the big picture of a project and have leads and resources complete the details for the individual tasks. With Microsoft Project Central, workgroup members can create tasks and send them to the project manager for approval and inclusion in the project plan.
- **Filter, Sort, and Group Tasks.** Workgroup members can filter out information they don't need to see. They also sort or group tasks by a selected field.
- **Delegate Tasks.** Workgroup members can delegate tasks to other workgroup members. For example, the project manager can send tasks to a team lead who can then assign the task to individual resources. This allows for more accurate reporting and increased flexibility. This feature is enabled by the Microsoft Project Central administrator.
- **Send and Receive Reports.** Task assignment and update messages can already be exchanged between the project manager and workgroup members. Now the project manager can also set up a narrative status report format, request reports, receive them from workgroup members, and then compile them into a single project status report.
- **Submit Reports for Different Audiences.** You can set up custom reports in Microsoft Project, then use Microsoft Project Central to make these reports available to different audiences. You can set permissions to allow different sets of users to review different reports, even across different projects.
- **Set Message Rules.** Project managers can establish rules for the update messages they receive from workgroup members. They can specify whether and what kind of updates are automatically accepted and incorporated into the project plan.

Work Faster and Smarter

New and improved features in Microsoft Project 2000 provide greater flexibility and power in your project. These enhancements also make it easier for you to work with your project and to model information in your plan to what's really going on in your project.

- **Jump-Start New Projects with Templates.** Microsoft Project includes a number of comprehensive templates on which you can base your new project. Templates include construction, engineering, new business, new product, and software development projects.
- **Group Tasks and Resources.** In addition to sorting and filtering, you can now group tasks and resources by a field you choose. For example, you can group tasks whose finish date is approaching, or group resources that are overallocated.
- **Use Your Own WBS Numbering and Formatting.** In addition to using Microsoft Project's default work breakdown structure (WBS) numbering scheme, you can create your WBS numbering scheme and apply it to your project. Your WBS format corresponds with your project's outline structure. Use this to align your project plan with your company's WBS conventions.
- **Set Up Custom Outline Codes.** In addition to WBS codes, you can create custom outline codes that are independent of the outline structure. Use an outline code, for example, to specify company accounting codes for tasks or job codes for resources. You can then sort or group by your outline codes. This helps you provide for better tracking and reporting through your project plan.
- **Use Value Lists, Formulas, and Graphical Indicators in Custom Fields.** You can now create value lists for consistent data entry and better reporting. You can define your own formulas for calculating your custom data. You can also use graphical indicators to represent data in a custom field.
- **Directly Edit and Format Your Plan.** You can now edit information directly within the cells of a sheet as well as up on the edit bar. You can directly select the outline level where you want your tasks. You can also set individual rows to varying heights by dragging the row line. Fill handles are now included on sheet views to help speed up copied or consecutive data entry.
- **Switch Between Multiple Projects.** If you have several project plans open, they now all show as separate buttons on the Microsoft Windows task bar. Switch between different projects by clicking their button on the task bar, or by pressing ALT+TAB.
- **Take Advantage of Improved Hyperlinks.** You can now select a hyperlink from a list of previously viewed links. You can also customize the hyperlink's ScreenTip.
- **Have Microsoft Project Automatically Save Your Work.** You can set Microsoft Project to automatically save your work every few minutes at intervals

you define. You can also specify whether you want Microsoft Project to save the current project, all open projects, and whether you want to be prompted.

- **Print with More Flexibility.** More fields are now available for your headers, footers, and legends in your printed views and reports. Paper size settings are now retained, and print scaling is improved.
- **Use COM Add-Ins with VBA.** The Microsoft Project Visual Basic for Applications (VBA) works with changes to the Microsoft Project object model. It now also supports Component Object Model (COM) add-ins.
- **Get Good Help.** Microsoft Project includes a new dynamic HTML-based Help system with an improved Project Map that guides you through the project management process. You make interactive choices that reflect your current task or situation to see only what you need. There are also comprehensive tutorials and more reference information for fields, dialog boxes, troubleshooting, and VBA.

What's Covered in This Book

Managing Projects with Microsoft Project provides concise and in-depth coverage of topics for using Microsoft Project to assist with your important project management efforts. It includes procedures for the tasks you're most likely to perform, from the beginning of the planning stage to project completion. Organized the way you work, this book will help you quickly find the information you need to complete your project planning efficiently.

Think of this book as the expert at your side, telling you not only how to accomplish project planning tasks with Microsoft Project but also enlightening you on the tips, shortcuts, and details you should know to be most successful in developing and maintaining your plan.

The following parts are included in *Managing Projects with Microsoft Project*.

Part 1: Your Project Takes Shape

A good project management strategy combined with a project management tool such as Microsoft Project can be a potent partnership for success. The trick is in knowing how best to apply the software to your strategy. To help you make the most effective use of Microsoft Project, Part 1 explains the project management process, the ways Microsoft Project helps you manage projects, and how to begin a project by using Microsoft Project.

Part 2: Creating and Refining Your Project

A project plan is the key to guiding a project to a successful conclusion. Because of this, Part 2, which explains how to create and refine a project plan, is the heart of this book. In Part 2, you'll learn how to set project goals, create a task list, estimate how long each task will take, put tasks in a logical sequence, show dependencies between tasks, and assign people and other resources to tasks. Lastly, you find out how to refine your project plan so that it's as streamlined and efficient as possible while still accurately modeling your project's realities.

Part 3: Tracking and Updating Your Project

After you create and refine your project plan, the project begins. That's when the power of your project plan is demonstrated. By using your project plan to track actual progress, you improve your ability to make the changes and decisions that keep your project on schedule and within budget. Part 3 explains how to track project progress, collect data, and set up and use a workgroup communications system on an e-mail system, an intranet, or the World Wide Web. You use the workgroup communications system to request and confirm task assignments, send updated task assignments to the workgroup manager, and incorporate updated information into the project plan.

Part 4: Reviewing Project Information

Though Microsoft Project can store thousands of pieces of information, you're probably only interested in viewing a subset of that information at a time. And when you're viewing project information, you might want that information to have a certain look. Occasionally, you'll want to share particularly useful—and well-formatted—project information with team members, upper management, or clients. Part 4 explains how to display exactly the project information you want, change the appearance of project information, and print project information.

Part 5: Using Other Projects and Programs

Work in projects and in companies is increasingly team-based and highly collaborative. You might find yourself managing multiple interrelated projects at once, managing a master project while others manage subprojects, sharing resources, or exchanging or linking information with other software programs. Part 5 explains how to share information among projects and among the different programs people use during a project.

Part 6: Customizing Microsoft Project Tools

Microsoft Project is like a desk filled with tools. Those tools help you perform the many detailed tasks required to manage projects and work with project files, such as menus and menu commands, toolbars and toolbar buttons, and forms and dialog boxes. Part 6 describes how to customize these tools so you can work with Microsoft Project as efficiently as possible, and in your own way. It also explains how you can automate repetitive tasks that you perform with Microsoft Project.

Glossary

The Glossary is a list of many of the important terms that appear in this book.

Part 1

Your Project Takes Shape

How well you manage a project has a direct effect on that project's outcome. While many factors contribute to successful project management, the process and your tools for supporting this process are two of the most important elements. Part 1 defines the project management process, the ways Microsoft Project helps you manage projects successfully, and how to begin a project using Microsoft Project.

Chapter 1 defines projects and project management. It reviews widely accepted project planning methods, and how these methods help you manage projects more effectively. The four phases of a project are explained, as are the four components balanced in project management: tasks, resources, time, and money.

Chapter 2 explains the major ways that Microsoft Project assists you in each phase of your project. It focuses on ways you can use Microsoft Project to meet your specific project management requirements.

Chapter 3 shows you how to use Microsoft Project to begin your project. It tells you exactly what information is essential to beginning your project plan. With step-by-step instructions, you actually begin to build your plan.

1

The Elements of Project Management

Project management means different things to different people. To some project managers, it means directing the troops ever forward until the project goal is attained. To others, it means empowering the individuals who carry out the project tasks, mediating disputes, and keeping the project team informed. Between the fully centralized and fully distributed approaches to project management lies a broad spectrum of intermediate methods.

Nonetheless, all approaches have certain elements in common: They strive to achieve project goals as efficiently as possible, they follow a set of steps to achieve project goals, and they prescribe methods for managing tasks, resources, time, and budget.

This chapter describes those elements of project management common to virtually all approaches to project management. It explains a tried-and-true four-phase project model as well as the main project components you need to manage in order to complete your project on time and within budget.

What Is a Project?

A *project* is a one-time endeavor that ends with a specific accomplishment, such as the development of a unique product or service. It originates when something unique is to be accomplished. A project has the following characteristics:

- A set of nonroutine tasks performed in a certain sequence leading to a goal.
- A distinct start and finish date.
- A limited set of resources that might be used on more than one project.

A project is distinguished from everyday operations. While operations and projects are both performed by people and constrained by limited resources, operations are ongoing while projects are temporary. Operations are repetitive while projects are unique. Furthermore, projects often need tracking and status reporting, while operations typically do not.

A project is completed when its objectives have been met. Operations have ongoing objectives and are a part of everyday business.

Examples of ongoing operations include preparing a weekly payroll or manufacturing a number of units every month. While these operations might or might not have deadlines (end of the week or end of the month, for example), their processes are defined and repetitive, as are the outcomes.

On the other hand, examples of projects include building a home, developing a new product, starting up a business, moving a company or department to another building, deploying a new computer system, running a publicity campaign, and putting on an event. These are unique accomplishments that have a prescribed time span.

What Is Project Management?

Project management is the defining, planning, scheduling, and controlling of the tasks that must be completed to achieve your project goals. *Defining* and *planning* are necessary so you know what you will do. *Scheduling* is important so you know when you will do it. And *controlling* is important because things never work out exactly as planned, so continual monitoring and adjustment are required.

To meet your project goals, it's important that you be on top of changes. This means tracking and rescheduling as the project progresses. You're successful when you satisfy the requirements of your client or management and when you meet your project goals on schedule and within your budget.

A Four-Phase Project Model

A *project model* represents the way real projects proceed in the real world. A number of project models are used in the realm of project management, especially as they apply to specific industries. But generally accepted across different industries is the four-phase project model. The four phases, which are part of nearly every project, are:

- Defining your project.
- Creating and refining your project plan.
- Tracking your project and updating your plan.
- Closing your project.

Defining Your Project

Project definition is the phase in which you set project goals, scope, limitations, and assumptions.

The project *goals* determine the purpose of the project. In the goals, you articulate what you want to accomplish—your ultimate outcome. For example, the project goal might be to build a new house.

There are two types of *scope*, both of which are part of your project definition. The *product scope* consists of the features and functions that are to be included in the product or service. For example, if the project goal is to build a house, your product scope might include that the house is to have two stories and a single fireplace. The product scope is sometimes referred to as a *product specification*.

The *project scope*, on the other hand, specifies the work that must be done to deliver the product or service with the specified features and functions. The project scope determines which tasks do and do not need to be performed to satisfy the product scope and achieve the project goals.

Limitations are constraining factors that affect your project. Because most projects don't have an infinite amount of time for completion, or unlimited funding, deadline and budget are two predominant limitations in any project. It's important during the project definition phase to establish these and any other limitations, especially because they affect your options regarding scope, staffing, level of quality, and more.

Assumptions are educated guesses of those factors assumed to be true for the sake of planning. For example, to create your project plan, you might need to establish the assumptions that your house building project will be delayed by rain no more than 15% of the time, that certain resources will indeed be available from April through June, and that the lead time for ordering lumber is no more than 30 days. By establishing your assumptions, you can plan for potential risks to your project and the associated contingencies.

Creating and Refining Your Project Plan

A *project plan* is the model of your project that you use to predict and control progress. It shows what will get done, when it will get done, and by what means. You create a project plan before the project gets under way.

The most important part of your project plan is the task schedule, which you create in three steps. First, you specify *what* you are going to do by defining the tasks that must be completed to reach your goals. Then you specify *when* by determining how long the tasks take, any required task sequences or dependencies, and any milestone dates that must be met. Then you specify *how* by defining your resources and budget, and then assigning people, material, equipment, and costs to the tasks.

It's best if you don't make all these determinations on your own. You will have a better schedule and more support for the project if you involve the project team in this planning process.

Once you get these details into your project plan, you're able to extract valuable information. If you're trying to figure how long the project will take, this plan will now show it. Once you have resources and time assigned to tasks, you can see the potential costs. If you already have specific deadlines, this plan makes it clear whether you're going to hit them. If you already have a specific budget, the plan helps you calculate whether you're going to meet or exceed it. Furthermore, after reviewing this first version of your plan, you can evaluate your task and resource lists to see whether you've created the best plan to fit the situation.

At this point, you can start making adjustments to refine your schedule. If the project, as planned, is taking too much time, you can add resources or cut scope, often by cutting tasks, reducing task duration, or decreasing quality. Likewise, if it's costing too much, you can cut resources or obtain less expensive resources, decrease quality, reduce scope, and more. On the other hand, if you find yourself with the fortunate predicament of having extra time or extra budget, you can either increase scope and quality, or you can be a hero to upper management or your clients by coming in well ahead of schedule or under budget.

You can use a project plan and its schedule to:

- Communicate to others in your organization what you're going to do.
- Gain approval for the project or justify the need to management.
- Show a customer how you'll deliver a product or service.
- Demonstrate the need, availability, and use for staff and other resources.
- Order material resources in the appropriate quantities.
- Determine cash flow needs.
- Win support from project team members.
- Predict resource workloads throughout the project.
- Communicate progress and highlight potential problems.
- Have a baseline against which you check the progress of your project.
- Keep a historical record of what happened on the project, to be compared to the original plan, and to be used as the basis of future schedules for similar projects.

Having a plan helps everyone see who needs to do what and when they need to do it. It helps communication, makes everyone aware of deadlines, and reduces uncertainty. By tracking the actual progress of the project and comparing it to your original schedule, you can see deviations from the plan, anticipate problems, and correct delays before they become severe. With a plan, you have a better chance of completing your project successfully.

Tracking Your Project and Updating Your Plan

After you've completed the planning phase, you and your team can get on with the real work of the project. To know what's really happening in your project—whether individual tasks and the project as a whole are on schedule—you need to track your project. Your project plan provides reference points against which you can track progress. With these reference points, you compare your original estimated task start and finish dates, task durations, costs, and other such values to what is actually taking place.

When you track project progress, you can pinpoint aspects of your plan that are floundering and devise a strategy for keeping your project on schedule. Tracking will tell you, for example, which tasks need more resources assigned to them, which tasks are under or over budget, which resources are overallocated, and which resources are available for more work.

You can accurately track project progress as long as you accurately update your plan by adding actual values for task durations, start and finish dates, costs, and so on. As time progresses, you can compare your original values to the actual values to determine whether your project is on schedule and within budget.

Closing Your Project

After you've achieved your project goals, you can close the project. Closing a project might be as simple as sending an e-mail message to your manager reporting that the project is now completed. Or, it could involve a more complex process.

For example, you might conduct an extensive postmortem to analyze what went right and what could have been improved. You can record what you and your team learned from the just-finished project and use that information to manage future projects more effectively. The close of one project can be instrumental to the beginning of the next project.

Managing It All: Tasks, Resources, Time, and Money

The success of a project depends on how well you manage tasks, resources, time, and money, which are the primary components of project management. In some projects, you might need to manage only one or two of these items. For example, the project budget might be someone else's concern; while your responsibility might be to concentrate on the tasks being completed.

Even if you aren't directly responsible for all four components in every project you manage, you'll manage more effectively if you understand them all and their impact on your project plan.

Tasks are the specific actions that need to be carried out to achieve the project goals. Examples of tasks required to build a house are digging the foundation, installing the plumbing, and painting the walls. You manage tasks by scheduling them, tracking their progress, and keeping them on schedule.

Resources are the people, materials, equipment, and facilities that are required to fulfill the tasks. You manage resources by assigning them to tasks, making sure that their assigned work time matches their available work time, and tracking resource costs.

Time is how long it takes to complete an individual task or the project as a whole. You manage time by analyzing how long each task takes to complete, adjusting task scope or project scope, assigning more or fewer resources to a task, adjusting the start or finish relationships between tasks, and understanding the deadlines for important milestones.

Money, of course, covers the costs of tasks, resources, and materials. Without funding, there's no project. You manage money by keeping tasks on schedule, using the least expensive resources possible, adjusting task scope and project scope, and tracking costs.

At any point during your project, you might need to focus on only one of these items: tasks, resources, time, or money. But you'll keep your project under control best when you understand the relationships among them.

A Question of Balance

The components you manage in a project—tasks, resources, time, and money—are interdependent. Rarely can you change one without affecting at least one other.

You manage a project effectively by keeping tasks, resources, time, and money in balance from the beginning to the end of the project. Typically, one of these components is fixed and the other three might vary.

For example, if you have an immovable deadline (time is fixed) and the project scope is large (that is, the project consists of many tasks or a small number of long, complex tasks), you might need a large number of resources to complete the project on time. The more resources you add, the more the project will cost.

On the other hand, if you have a fixed number of resources (or a fixed budget), you might need to decrease the project scope or increase the amount of time required to complete the project.

If you absolutely must complete each task in your project plan in order to achieve your project goals (scope is fixed), then you can adjust resources, time, or both. Which you adjust depends on whether you have more resources or time available.

After a project gets underway, it's almost inevitable that the balance you so carefully established at the beginning of the project will totter to one side or the other. For example, if tasks take longer than expected, you might need to add more resources, lengthen the project deadline, or cut project scope. Your client might impose a new goal on the project, thus increasing scope, so you might need to add resources or extend the deadline.

Effective project management requires constant vigilance over the balance among tasks, resources, time, and money. Maintaining this balance, and knowing the priorities among them, is the best way to ensure project success.

Your Main Tasks When You Manage a Project

When you manage a project, your chief obligation is to achieve project goals on time and within budget. Your chief strategy for doing this is to keep tasks, resources, time, and money in balance. The main tasks you need to perform in order to achieve project goals are:

- **Define the project.** Set the project's goals, scope, limitations, and assumptions. Make sure that the goals are measurable, and describe a definite end to the project.
- **Create a project plan.** List all the tasks required to achieve the project goals, put those tasks in a logical sequence, and establish start and finish relationships between tasks. You'll also need to set a start date and assign resources to tasks.
- **Refine the project plan.** The first draft of your plan might contain all the pieces, but then it's time to whittle them down, reorganize them, maybe delete or add a few. Remove unneeded tasks, make sure no resource is overworked, and check that the project can realistically finish on time and within budget.
- **Track project progress.** Understand the current status of your project and know how and when tasks and scheduled. Compare actual project data to your original estimates. Make adjustments to the schedule that are necessary to keep on track. Remember to keep tasks, resources, time, and money in balance.
- **Close the project.** Analyze the project and apply what you learn to the next project.

2

How Microsoft Project Helps You Manage Projects

How do you know when you need to use Microsoft Project? And how, specifically, does Microsoft Project help you manage your project?

You can probably manage a small project without using a project management program. But what determines project size? A project's size and complexity are defined by the:

- Number of people and other resources, such as materials and equipment, involved in the project.
- Number of tasks required to achieve the project goals.
- Schedule length.
- Difficulty of meeting a project deadline.
- Size of the project budget.

These are inherently subjective factors. A project that one person can track in his or her head might completely overwhelm another person. Ability may have nothing to do with this difference. The first person might be managing only one project at a time, and the second person, four or five.

As a rule of thumb, however, many project managers find that they need to use a project management program when the project meets at least one of the following conditions:

- Involves more than five resources. A project management program aids in coordination and communication.
- Includes more than 50 tasks. This number could be smaller, especially if your organization is managing multiple projects, all using the same set of resources.

- Takes longer than 30 days. However, the project could be as small as three days in duration, particularly if a large number of resources or tasks are involved.

In general, if you need to communicate the project plan with others, track project details such as tasks or costs, or use shared resources, a project management program will definitely make your job easier. Remember that the bigger the project, the more details you need to track. With a project management program, you can organize, store, calculate, analyze, and communicate project information in a more complete and automated fashion.

Microsoft Project provides the flexibility to help you manage a project in a manner that closely reflects the way you and your team really work. For example, if you empower team members to be responsible for accomplishing their tasks, you can use the Microsoft Project workgroup feature to request and track task assignments. If you decide to track task progress and not costs incurred during the project, you can update task information only.

Furthermore, Microsoft Project:

- Provides essential assistance in building and tracking your project.
- Calculates your dates, costs, and other project information.
- Completes many fields automatically as you enter or change plan information.
- Stores project information in a powerful database.
- Displays and prints project information in different views and formats.
- Enables you to exchange task information with team members.
- Supplies the tools to share project information with other programs.

Assists You in Most Project Phases

Most successful projects have four phases:

1. Define project goals.
2. Build the project plan.
3. Track the project.
4. Close the project.

While project management software programs can't provide much help with the first and fourth phases, Microsoft Project significantly assists you with the second phase. With a little maintenance on your part, Microsoft Project also handles most of your work in the third phase, presenting the information you need so you can respond and make decisions as issues arise.

Define Project Goals

Your project goals determine the purpose of the project—what you want to accomplish. Though only you can define your project goals, Microsoft Project can store those goals with your project plan. You can refer to them at any time during the project to make sure your project stays on course.

Build the Project Plan

The project plan is a model of your project that tells what tasks are going to be done, by whom, and when. Like any model, it's only as accurate as the information you put into it.

You figure out the best way to achieve your project goals. Then you enter project information, such as tasks, task durations, project start and finish dates, milestones, resources, and costs, into Microsoft Project. Using the information you enter, Microsoft Project calculates and creates your project schedule.

You analyze the results of the schedule and make sure it accurately models your vision for how the project will run. You also fine-tune tasks, dates, and costs as necessary to ensure that your limitations are being met, particularly those regarding deadline, budget, resources, and scope.

Track the Project

When you track your project, you can see your current progress in the plan and compare where you stand with the tasks remaining to be done before the finish date and project completion. You can also identify problems early, before they adversely affect your schedule.

If you use baselines, you can compare your original estimates to actual values to see if your project can achieve its goals within your original time and cost estimates. You compare original and actual values for task start and finish dates, task length, costs, and more. This way, you can make any adjustments necessary to complete your project goals on time.

Close the Project

During the final project phase, you gather and analyze information about the project to determine what went right and what could have been improved. You can then use this information to help you plan and implement your next project.

If you save your original plan information in Microsoft Project, you can compare this information to the way the project actually progressed. You can store your project analysis with the plan, save the plan, and apply what you've learned to succeeding projects.

Calculates Your Schedule Automatically

One of the most powerful and timesaving aspects of Microsoft Project is its ability to calculate a schedule. You enter the raw information, and then the schedule Microsoft Project creates indicates important dates, provides cost information, helps you identify risks and potential problems, and more.

As part of entering this raw information, you:

- Set the project start date, which is the earliest date tasks can begin.
- List all required tasks in the approximate order in which you expect to do them.
- Estimate the amount of time each task will require. Your time estimates are important, as they form the major basis for the schedule that Microsoft Project calculates. The more accurate your duration estimates are, the more accurate the schedule calculated by Microsoft Project.
- Indicate how tasks relate to each other. In other words, if one task can start only when a previous task finishes, you specify this dependency between these tasks. This is another important factor in Microsoft Project calculating your schedule.
- Assign resources to tasks. You tell Microsoft Project which people or equipment will work on which tasks, or how much material will be consumed. You don't have to assign resources to tasks to create a schedule. But if you do, Microsoft Project can factor resources into your schedule and track costs. You can also analyze whether any resources are overallocated or underutilized.

When calculating your schedule, Microsoft Project:

- Schedules tasks immediately as you enter project information.
- Calculates the task start and finish dates, durations, and other values.
- Calculates the project finish date.
- Calculates and summarizes resource and task costs.

As you enter new information or change existing information, Microsoft Project recalculates task start and finish dates, durations, and so on. You see the impact of your changes immediately.

Fills In Many Fields for You

You start building your project plan by entering tasks into a task sheet, which is similar to a Microsoft Excel spreadsheet. Microsoft Project automatically completes other fields now associated with your new task. Some are default values, likely placeholders for information until you enter your real information. Other fields contain information that Microsoft Project calculated from other information you entered.

For example, suppose you start a new project and specify the project start date. You enter your first task in the Task Name field. Microsoft Project automatically enters an estimated duration of 1 day in the Duration field. It calculates a start date for this task based on the project start date you entered, and then it calculates a finish date for this task based on the task duration, which is one day later than the start date. If you change the duration from 1 day to 5 days, the finish date is recalculated to five days after the start date.

Three types of fields are used in Microsoft Project:

- **Entered.** Only you can enter information in this field. Microsoft Project will never complete an entered field for you, even with an estimate or a default value. Examples include the Task Name field and the Resource Name field, because only you have the knowledge to enter tasks and resources.
- **Calculated.** Only Microsoft Project can enter information in this field. Because Microsoft Project is calculating the value for this field from other values you have entered, the information would become unreliable or meaningless if you then entered something different. An example is the Variance field, which displays the difference between an original baseline value (such as cost or start date) and an actual value.
- **Entered or calculated.** Either you or Microsoft Project can enter information in this field. Microsoft Project enters an initial value, either a default value or one calculated from other values you've entered. If you change it, you take over responsibility for that piece of information. Examples include the Duration and Finish fields.

Displays Exactly the Project Information You Want

A project of almost any size is likely to generate hundreds, even thousands, of pieces of data. There are start dates, finish dates, task durations, task dependencies, critical tasks, resource names, e-mail names, group names, working times, actual work, remaining work, baseline cost, fixed cost, cumulative cost, and total cost—just to name a few.

Without a structure, these bits of project data are just a useless conglomeration; they tell you nothing meaningful. But present the right pieces of project data together in an organized format, and you can easily determine the status of your project. With Microsoft Project views, tables, and filters, and by sorting and grouping, the broad collection of project information in the database is arranged so you can work with it, get useful information, and make informed decisions.

Views are the organized formats Microsoft Project uses to display project information. Each view displays just a portion of the total information stored in Microsoft Project. A view displays a particular set of information about tasks or resources in one of several kinds of familiar formats: Gantt chart views, graph views, form views, and sheet views. You enter, edit, and display project information in views.

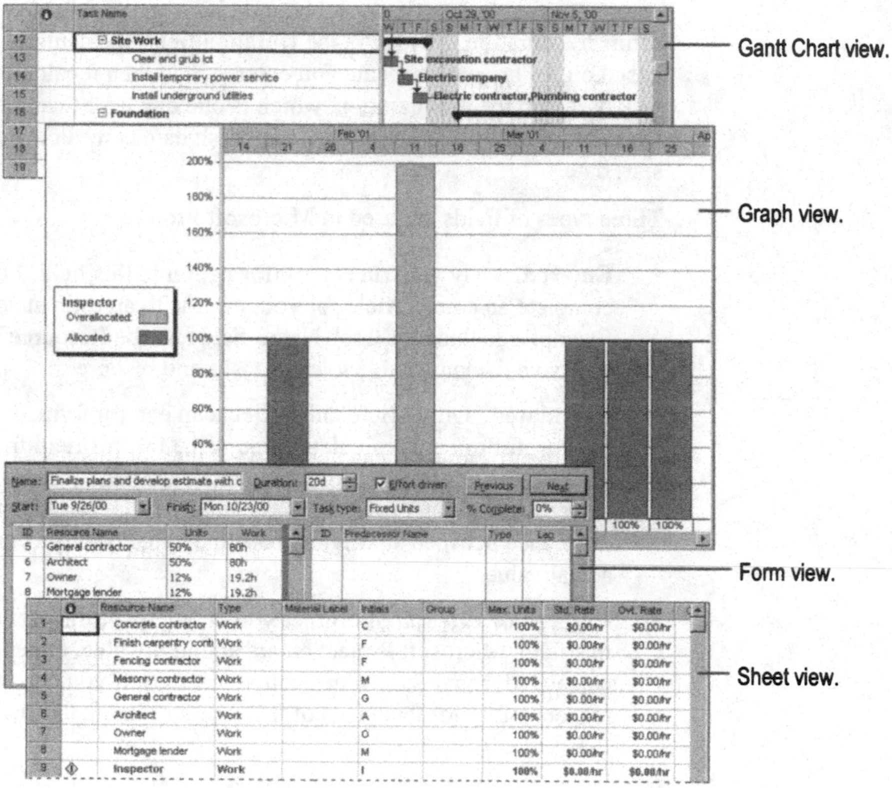

Tables are sets of information arranged in columns that you display in sheet views, which are like spreadsheets. Apply a different table to review a different set of information. For example, to view or edit cost information, apply a cost table to a sheet view. A cost table might consist of columns of information such as total cost, actual cost, and remaining cost. By applying a work table next, you replace (and hide) cost information with information such as total work, percent of work completed, and remaining work.

	Resource Name	Cost	Baseline Cost	Variance	Actual Cost	Remaining
1	Concrete contractor	$10,080.00	$0.00	$10,080.00	$0.00	$10,080.00
2	Finish carpentry cont	$1,536.00	$0.00	$1,536.00	$0.00	$1,536.00
3	Fencing contractor	$400.00	$0.00	$400.00	$0.00	$400.00
4	Masonry contractor	$5,760.00	$0.00	$5,760.00	$0.00	$5,760.00
5	General contractor	$6,400.00	$0.00	$6,400.00	$0.00	$6,400.00
6	Architect	$6,600.00	$0.00	$6,600.00	$0.00	$6,600.00

Sheet view with cost table applied.

	Resource Name	% Comp.	Work	Overtime	Baseline	Variance	Actual	Remaining
1	Concrete contractor	0%	336 hrs	0 hrs	0 hrs	336 hrs	0 hrs	336 hrs
2	Finish carpentry cont	0%	48 hrs	0 hrs	0 hrs	48 hrs	0 hrs	48 hrs
3	Fencing contractor	0%	16 hrs	0 hrs	0 hrs	16 hrs	0 hrs	16 hrs
4	Masonry contractor	0%	128 hrs	0 hrs	0 hrs	128 hrs	0 hrs	128 hrs
5	General contractor	0%	128 hrs	0 hrs	0 hrs	128 hrs	0 hrs	128 hrs
6	Architect	0%	88 hrs	0 hrs	0 hrs	88 hrs	0 hrs	88 hrs

Same sheet view with work table applied.

Filters consist of a set of criteria that tasks or resources must match in order to be displayed or highlighted. Whereas a table typically displays a set of information for all tasks or resources, filters enable you to display only the particular tasks or resources that share a specific set of characteristics. For example, you can use one filter to view only completed tasks, another to view only incomplete tasks, and yet another to view only those tasks assigned to a particular resource. Like views and tables, filters don't delete any information. They show only certain information and hide the rest while it remains stored in Microsoft Project.

Furthermore, you can *sort* information to see data in the order you want. You can also *group* task or resource information by different fields.

Publishes Project Information to Suit a Variety of Needs

A project manager once said that the project plan doesn't actually exist until it's been shared with others. After you finish building your project plan and at regular intervals during the tracking of the project, you'll probably need to share project information with team members, supervisors, clients, and contractors.

Microsoft Project provides a full range of features for printing project information that suits the needs of any recipient. You can print what you see on the screen in a view. You can also print predefined reports. Just as in a view, each report contains a set of information about a specific aspect of your project. Examples include task reports, resource reports, and cost reports. You can print the view or report that contains the information required by the recipient.

In addition to printing hardcopy views and reports, you can also provide project information online in a number of ways. You can:

- Publish project information in Microsoft Project Central.
- Save project information as web document and publish it as a Web page.

- Copy project information as a picture in another program or Web page.
- Route project status information in an e-mail message.
- Post a project to a public folder.
- Send a project as an e-mail attachment.

Not every recipient of project information needs the same level of detail. Supervisors and clients might need overview information only, while team members might require detailed task and resource information. Using Microsoft Project, you can tailor views to display just the level of detail you want or pick a report that already has the right amount of detail. If none of the predefined views or reports meets your requirements, you can easily create a custom view or report.

After you've decided on the right view or report, add your professional flair. Adjust page layouts, add headers and footers, change text to bold or italic, customize page elements, and much more. You can publish effective and polished project documents with ease.

Puts You at the Hub of a Project Communications Network

Communicating project information efficiently among team members is essential to achieving your project goals. Whether your team members are at the same location or dispersed around the world, Microsoft Project can be the center of your project communications network.

Linked within a communications systems based on e-mail, the World Wide Web, or an *internal network* that resembles the World Wide Web—called an *intranet*—Microsoft Project becomes a versatile communications hub. It enables you to assign tasks over a network, receive task updates, and incorporate up-to-date task information into your project plan without having to type it in. You can coordinate many of your team's activities by sending (and receiving responses to) Microsoft Project messages that are specifically designed to exchange task information.

If you're using the Internet or an intranet, Microsoft Project Central is your base of project communication operations. Otherwise, you can use your company's e-mail system for automated communication, task updates, and status reporting.

Shares Project Information with Other Programs

Microsoft Project might not be the only program you and your team need to use to store, edit, display, or print project information. For example, you or your accounting department might use a spreadsheet program to break down project costs in detail. In addition, clients and contractors who need to review project information in electronic form might not even have Microsoft Project, only a word-processing program.

In these and many other situations, Microsoft Project extends a friendly hand with the capability to share project information with different kinds of programs. These include word-processing programs, spreadsheet programs, database programs, earlier versions of Microsoft Project, and other project management programs.

You can exchange text or graphic information between Microsoft Project and other programs in several ways, choosing the way that best suits your needs as well as the requirements of the other program. You can copy and paste, link and embed, and import and export project information.

3

Starting a Project

When you start a project, your first and most important step is to set project goals. This is when you decide what you want to accomplish, when it has to be finished, and how much money you can spend. Well-defined, concrete goals help the project team and clients grasp the project's purpose. They also enable you to determine when the project is complete.

As you list the project goals, consider the project scope, any limitations, and your assumptions. The scope defines the project's parameters. For example, you might decide to build a one-story house instead of a two-story house. Limitations are your constraints, and usually take the form of a specific deadline or finite budget, although there are other types of limitations as well. Assumptions are your expectations or educated guesses you must make to move forward with scheduling the project.

Goals, scope, limitations, and assumptions are interdependent. For instance, if an assumption proves wrong—let's say, the price of certain essential building materials skyrockets shortly after house construction begins—this might cause a budget overrun and you might need to adjust your goals by building a smaller house than originally planned. Or, if the client wants to add another story to the house, you might need to increase scope by adding tasks and resources in order to achieve the expanded goals, but this might affect your schedule or budget limitations.

To ensure that you, your project team, upper management, and clients pull together from the beginning of the project to the end, it's best to set project goals, define the scope, identify limitations, and develop assumptions as early in the project-planning process as possible. Work with project team leaders to analyze and define the project, refine your limitations and assumptions, and ensure that the goals and scope are realistic. By including others in the planning, you solidify their commitment to the project, and the result is a more accurate plan.

Once you've determined project goals, scope, limitations, and assumptions, you can enter some general information about your project into Microsoft Project. For example, you can record the project start date, project title, company name, and project manager. You can also enter notes about the project, including these goals, scope, limitations, and assumptions.

Setting Project Goals, Scope, Limitations, and Assumptions

As you develop the project goals, make sure they state clearly what you're trying to accomplish. You can analyze the clarity and effectiveness of your goals in several ways:

- Think about what you want to achieve or where you want to be at the end of the project. What is the end product?
- State the goal in user or client terms. What does this person want?
- Decide how you'll know when you're finished.
- Analyze your goals to determine if others might be more appropriate.
- Think of other ways to state your goals to be sure you're pinpointing the project's purpose.

Once you've determined your goals, test them by answering the following questions:

- Are the goals measurable and specific in terms of time, cost, quality, quantity, and the end result?
- Are the goals realistic and achievable?
- Are the goals stated clearly so they are understandable and unambiguous to everyone working on the project?

If the answer to any of these questions is no, restate the goals so that they pass the test.

Defining the Project Scope

By defining scope, you define the work that needs to be done as well as the work that shouldn't be done. Explicitly stating the scope helps you and your team focus on the project's purpose and the steps necessary to complete the project. As the project progresses, any changes in scope will be easy to identify and justify. Even if you're not sure of the scope, getting your best guess down on paper gives you a starting point.

You define scope by stating what is and what is not part of the project. For example, you could decide that a house you're building will have one story and not two. If it's later decided that the house should have two stories, it will be obvious that the scope has changed, and that the original budget, resource requirements, and schedule no longer match the scope.

Defining scope is especially important when working with outside contractors. If you don't accurately define scope, the work they do might be either inadequate or overdone and can adversely affect your schedule and budget. If you assumed a contractor understood the scope, you might be charged for work you considered part of the project but the contractor considered extra.

Specifying Project Limitations

An important part of your project definition is identifying the project's limitations. Knowing your limitations at the outset, and the priorities among them, help you decide how to adjust the project as conditions change.

One limitation is often the project deadline—when the product or service developed in this project is required to be finished. Another typical limitation is the project budget.

Related to deadline and budget are limitations having to do with the number and types of resources available, project scope, and level of quality. There can be other limitations related to the geographic area in which the project is being implemented, and more.

Usually one limitation has more flexibility than others, and often, one overriding limitation is a driving force. For example, your project might have an absolutely fixed budget of $250,000, but while the client is hoping for the project to be completed by the end of next quarter, this date is more flexible. In this case, you'll make project decisions that favor saving money rather than saving time.

When you specify these limitations in your project definition, your clients not only understand the limitations you're working under, they can see that you understand their requirements and priorities. Furthermore, if your team members know the project limitations, they can better focus on project priorities and understand the basis for some of the tough decisions you might have to make as the project progresses.

Stating Assumptions About the Project

When you plan a project, you need to make assumptions. Stating your assumptions at the beginning of the project-planning process helps you identify when conditions affecting your project have changed—and which assumptions must change to keep the project on track. It's important to state assumptions clearly and concisely so everyone knows the premises on which your goals and the schedule are based.

Some of your assumptions might turn out to be inaccurate. What's more important than the accuracy of your assumptions, though, is that you're aware of them. By stating assumptions clearly, you'll be able to zero in on changes when they occur and their likely impact on the schedule.

Suppose, for example, you're assuming that an outside contractor will be available to install the house's electrical wiring. You state this up front, so everyone understands that achieving your goals depends on this assumption being true. If the contractor isn't available, your assumption becomes false, requiring a change in the plan.

If incorrect assumptions could dramatically affect your schedule, be sure to put together a contingency plan or risk management plan. For example, if your outside contractor is not available to install the electrical wiring, what will you do instead? If you plan for this contingency before the project begins, you'll know exactly what to do if it occurs, and you'll lose the least amount of time in the schedule.

How do you decide which assumptions to make? Use the following questions as a guide.

- What are you assuming will have been done before you start?
- What external factors, outside your control, can have a major impact on your schedule? The weather? Materials that must come from an outside vendor? Inflation, which might drive your costs over budget?
- What are you expecting to happen at the end? Do you consider, for example, that the project will be finished when the house's yard has been landscaped?

After you've prepared your goals, scope, limitations, and assumptions, share them with other members of your team. You might end up repeating the goal-setting process several times until you have the agreement and support of both your management and the rest of the project team, but taking the time to secure this agreement will save time and ensure success in the long run.

Entering Basic Project Information in Microsoft Project

When you create a new plan in Microsoft Project, you first enter the project start date and other date information. These dates form the basis for your project schedule. If you want, you can also enter general project information such as the project title and company name.

A crucial element of the planning phase of your project is developing your goals, scope, limitations, and assumptions. You can do this before or after you create your Microsoft Project file, and you can record this information in Microsoft Project or in another program—just as long as you do it. If you keep your project goals, scope, limitations, and assumptions at hand as you develop your project plan, you'll have a better chance of building a realistic plan that meets your requirements.

Start a New Project and Enter Project Date Information

In Microsoft Project, a project is the file where all the information for a project plan is entered, stored, calculated, and edited. The first step to creating your project plan is to start a new project.

When starting a new project, you can:

- Create an entirely new project from scratch.
- Base a new project on a previous project you or someone else created.
- Base a new project on one of the Microsoft Project templates.

The Microsoft Project templates include project plans for construction, engineering, new business, new product, software development, and other types of projects. These are more than just examples; they're comprehensive project plans typical for the associated industry or activity.

As soon as you start a new project, a dialog box appears in which you can specify the date you want Microsoft Project to use for scheduling the project. By default, Microsoft Project sets today's date as the *project start date.*

Enter a project start date when you want Microsoft Project to schedule tasks forward from a particular date. As you enter tasks, Microsoft Project schedules them to begin on the project start date by default. As you enter more information about each task, such as dependencies on other tasks or date limitations, Microsoft Project calculates new task start dates.

If it better suits your project, you can specify that you want the project to be scheduled from the finish date and then enter the *project finish date,* which is the latest date on which you want your project to end. If you enter a project finish date, Microsoft Project schedules backwards from this finish date, with each task finishing as late as possible while achieving the finish date. Specify a project finish date if you want Microsoft Project to calculate the latest possible date that you can start and still make the schedule.

Entering a project start date and scheduling forward enables Microsoft Project to schedule tasks flexibly from that date forward. If you enter a project finish date and schedule backwards, you lock in the finish date and limit Microsoft Project's ability to schedule remaining work if tasks run late.

Because of this, schedule from the finish date when you're working toward a date that absolutely cannot change, such as a New Year's Eve celebration, a wedding, a grand opening, or other such date-specific event. Otherwise, you typically get better results to enter a project start date, add tasks, let Microsoft Project schedule the tasks, and then see if the end date calculated by Microsoft Project meets your needs. If it doesn't, you can edit the schedule (reduce the scope, shorten task durations, add more resources, and so on) until your targeted finish date is achieved.

To start Microsoft Project

1 Be sure that Microsoft Project is installed on your computer.

2 On the **Start** menu, point to **Programs**, and then click **Microsoft Project**.

Microsoft Project starts and is displayed on your screen.

To start a new project

New

If you are prompted to insert the Microsoft Project CD to install the templates, do so and follow the instructions.

Open

If you don't enter a date, Microsoft Project inserts the current date as the project start date.

To enter a finish date and schedule backward, click Project Finish Date in the Schedule from box, and then enter the finish date for your project in the Finish date box.

1 In Microsoft Project, click **New**.

To use a template to start a new project, click **New** on the **File** menu, and then click the template you want to use on the **Project Templates** tab.

To base your new project on an existing one, click **Open**, locate and open the project you want to use, save the project with a new name, and then click **Project Information** on the **Project** menu.

The Project Information dialog box appears in front of a blank project.

2 In the Project Information dialog box, enter a project start date or a project finish date.

To enter a start date and schedule forward, enter the date on which you want to start your project in the **Start date** box.

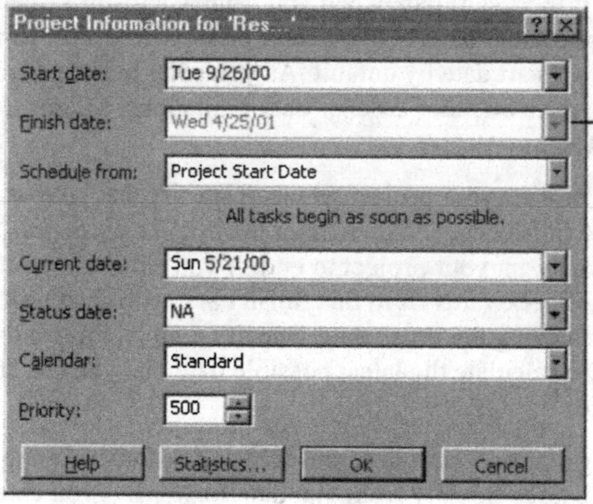

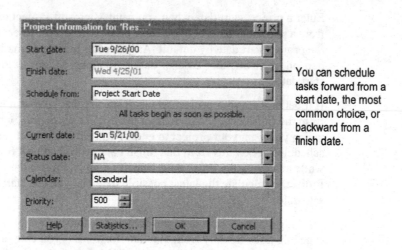

You can schedule tasks forward from a start date, the most common choice, or backward from a finish date.

After you click OK in the Project Information dialog box, a project file appears, ready for you to add or adapt project information. By default, the Gantt Chart view is displayed.

To change your project information at any time, click Project Information on the Project menu.

Enter Project Goals, Scope, Limitations, and Assumptions

Once you've determined your project goals, scope, limitations, and assumptions, you can include them in your project plan. Incorporating them into the project keeps you focused as you develop the plan. After your project has begun and you start tracking progress, you can easily refer to your original goals, scope, limitations, and assumptions should you need to reevaluate them.

To enter project goals, scope, limitations, and assumptions

If you don't see the Properties command on the File menu, click the arrow at the bottom of the menu.

1. On the **File** menu, click **Properties**, and then click the **Summary** tab.
2. In the **Comments** box, type your goals, scope, limitations, and assumptions.

   You can enter any other project notes here as well.
3. Fill in other boxes as appropriate, such as the **Title**, **Manager**, **Company**, and **Keywords** boxes, and then click **OK**.

Entering keywords here can help you find this project later with the Text or Property box in the File Open dialog box.

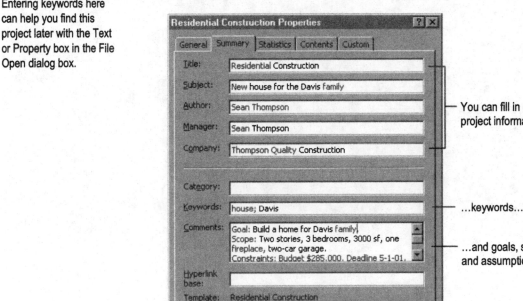

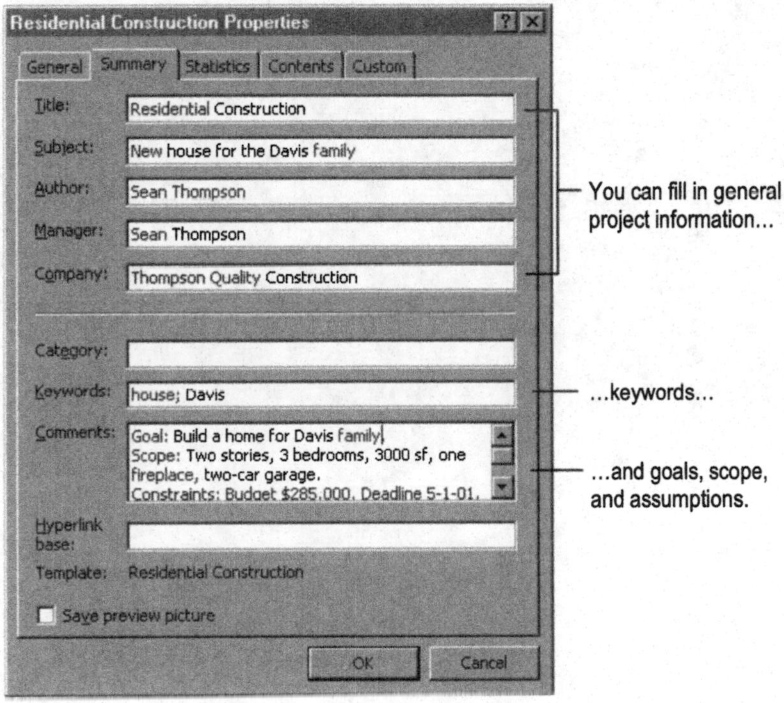

Save Your Project

When working on a project, make sure you save your work frequently.

To save your project

Save

You can have Microsoft Project automatically save your project every few minutes. On the Tools menu, click Options, and then click the Save tab. Set the options you want under Auto Save.

- Click **Save**.

  If this is the first time you've saved the project, the **Save As** dialog box appears. Type a name for the project in the **File name** box, and then click **Save**.

  If you haven't set a baseline for your project, the **Planning Wizard** dialog box appears, prompting you to save a baseline. A baseline is a set of original, planned project information that you can save and compare with actual information as your project progresses. The Planning Wizard continuously monitors your actions as you work and offers suggestions. Typically, you don't set a baseline until you've completed and refined your project plan, so at this time, select **Save without a baseline**.

Part 2

Creating and Refining Your Project

Continuing in the planning phase of your project, you're now ready to identify your tasks and resources. This is the key step for having Microsoft Project create your schedule. You can then refine the details to adjust dates and track costs. Part 2 focuses on how you can enter information about your tasks and resources to model your schedule accurately and get the results you're looking for. This includes:

- Creating a task list, including phases, milestones, and summary tasks, covered in chapter 4.
- Identifying dependencies and key dates with which the project should be scheduled, defined in chapter 5.
- Setting up resource information and assigning resources to tasks, outlined in chapter 6.
- Assigning costs to resources and tasks, described in chapter 7.
- Shortening the schedule, resolving resource overallocations, and reducing costs, explained in chapter 8.

4

Entering and Structuring Your Tasks

After you've determined your project goals, scope, limitations, and assumptions, your next step is to create a list of all those tasks that must be accomplished to meet your goals. Creating a comprehensive task list is essential. If any required tasks are missing from the list, you might not achieve all your goals. The more comprehensive your task list, the more important it is to organize those tasks. You can organize the task list into phases or create an outline structure showing the hierarchy of tasks. This hierarchy can also reflect a work breakdown structure.

With your tasks in place and organized, you can specify information that will affect scheduling. One fundamental piece of scheduling information is the duration of each task, or the amount of time the task is expected to take. By entering task durations, you lay the groundwork for creating a workable and realistic schedule.

Creating a Task List

The task list is the heart of your project. Microsoft Project uses your task list to create the schedule—perhaps your primary reason for using project management software. After you enter the task list, you can add associated information such as task duration estimates, assigned resources, and costs. When the project begins, you can use your task list to keep track of task progress.

The bulk of your task list will consist of regular tasks. However, identifying different types of tasks help you organize and track the tasks in your project.

- A *task* is a specific activity that must be completed to achieve your project goals. A task is typically associated with a duration, cost, and resource requirement.
- A *recurring task* is a task that repeats at regular intervals—for example, a quarterly client meeting, or a monthly status report.

- Think of a *phase* as a "super-task" that includes a group of logically related tasks. For example, a phase could represent a distinct time period, an intermediate goal, a major deliverable, or some other logical division within a project. If your project consists of relatively few tasks, you might not need to group them into phases. For larger projects, however, phases can visually break a long task list into fewer, more manageable chunks and give you an overview of the major steps toward reaching your project goals.
- A *milestone* is a task you use to indicate important events in your schedule, such as the completion of a major deliverable or project phase. It often (but not necessarily) has a zero duration. While milestones are optional, including them builds in an effective checklist of the most important events in your project. Milestones make it easier for you to tell when you've completed a major step toward your goals and whether your project is progressing on schedule.

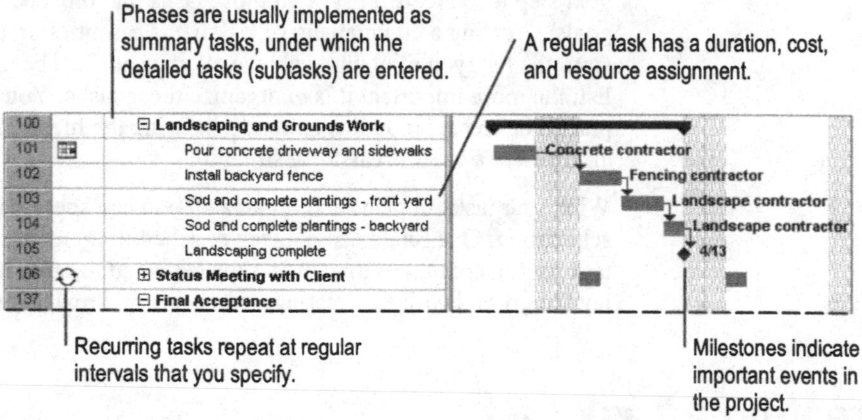

Phases or Tasks First? Two Approaches to Creating a Task List

When creating your task list, you can use one of two basic methods. The top-down method indicates major phases of the project first, with the detailed tasks coming later. The bottom-up method lists all the tasks, then organizes them into phases later.

Enter Major Phases First

Using the *top-down method*, you identify and enter the major phases first, then enter the tasks and milestones within each phase. You continue breaking tasks into smaller and smaller units until you reach the level of detail you want.

For more information about delegating tasks to workgroup members using e-mail or the Web, see chapters 10 and 11.

One advantage of this approach is that you have a high-level version of the plan as soon as you identify the major phases. You can then distribute this version to the appropriate managers or leads and have them work with their teams to create the detailed schedules. You can even use your e-mail system or the Web with the companion product Microsoft Project Central to delegate phases to resources in your workgroup. They can then add the detailed tasks, duration estimates, and send them back to you for automatic incorporation into the project.

For example, suppose your project goal is to build a house. Major phases might include "Lay the foundation," "Put up the frame," "Construct outer walls and roof," and so on. The lead responsible for each phase can work with the appropriate team members to create the individual task lists for each phase. With this method, team members doing the work are more likely to agree with the project tasks and duration estimates, as they developed them in the first place.

Enter All Detailed Tasks First

Using the *bottom-up method*, you list all possible tasks first; later, you organize them into phases. For example, you could brainstorm and identify all possible tasks across all disciplines that go in to the development of a new product. Later, you can move the tasks and group them under logical phases, such as the procurement phase, the manufacturing phase, and the marketing phase.

Specifying Your Tasks and Milestones

How do you determine which tasks and milestones to include in your project? One of the most effective methods is to have each person who will perform or manage the work submit a list of the tasks and milestones for which he or she is responsible. Once you have tasks and milestones from the responsible resources, you can enter them into Microsoft Project.

The input you get from different individuals is going to vary in the level of detail and even in the wording. Because tasks and milestones provide the basis for the rest of your plan and for tracking the progress of your project, it's important that the task list be detailed, clear, and consistent. As you enter the tasks and milestones into Microsoft Project, word them clearly and remove any possible ambiguity. This way, those using the project know exactly what's to be accomplished by each task or milestone.

The following sections provide guidelines for establishing tasks and milestones, setting the appropriate level of detail, and making them consistent.

Guidelines for Specifying Tasks

A task:

- Has an identifiable start and end.
- Usually requires people, materials, or equipment to complete it.
- Is specific enough to permit both intermittent progress and the final result to be measured.

For example, the task "Pour the concrete" calls for resources: one or more people to do the work, a concrete mixer, and a quantity of concrete. Progress on the task can be measured by comparing the number of foundation sections that have been poured with the total number of sections required. When all the sections have been poured, you know that the task is complete.

Use the following guidelines when determining how to enter the tasks in your project.

- Identify tasks as precisely as possible. Each task should be short compared to the overall project duration. For example, if you plan to put up a frame house, you might want to break the "Put up the frame" task into three or more tasks, one for each part of the house (outer walls, inner walls, roof). This helps you make a more reliable estimate for the time and resources required to complete the task.
- Tasks must also be significant enough to be included in the plan. Insignificant or non-schedule–related tasks only clutter your project task list. Take the "Pour the concrete" task, for example. While mixing the concrete is an important part of completing the task, it can be assumed to be done as part of the "Pour the concrete" task. If a task is not significant or discrete enough to affect how other tasks are scheduled, it should not be included as a separate task.
- The level of detail in your list of tasks should be appropriate to the amount of planning and control you want. For example, if you're hiring an outside consultant to do a study, you might be interested in when the consultant starts and when the study will be in your hands, but you are less likely to be interested in the detailed tasks performed by the consultant. In your list of tasks, you'd include one task for the study, showing the duration for the whole, rather than many tasks indicating each step in the study.

  However, if you're doing the study internally and managing the resources responsible for the study, the separate steps in completing the study are crucial to you. Your list of tasks would include every step necessary to do the study.
- When you list your tasks, keep in mind the scope of the tasks and the assumptions on which the tasks are based. This helps you identify changes and measure progress.
- Be complete. Remember to include reports, reviews, and coordination activities in your list of tasks. And remember to include tasks for anticipated rework or modifications after a task has been completed, such as revising a manual or reworking and retesting a new product.

- Name a task using a verb and noun, such as "Pour the concrete," "Build the outer wall frame," and "Shingle the roof." Make the names as explicit as possible, and keep the style of the names consistent throughout. This consistency will help others understand each task in your schedule.
- If you have different phases that include identical task names, distinguish the task names in some way. For example, suppose you have the "Conduct product review" task under three phases: "Market evaluation," "Technical evaluation," and "Concept evaluation." In some views, you see only the task names and not the phases under which they're organized, and therefore this wouldn't provide useful information. Consider some way to distinguish the task names—for example, "Conduct market review," "Conduct technical review," and "Conduct concept review."

Guidelines for Specifying Milestones

A milestone is a task that indicates the end of a phase or the completion of an interim goal. Typically, it requires no work and has a duration and cost of zero. For example, if an interim goal of your project is to lay the foundation for a house, the actual tasks might include "Dig the foundation" and "Pour the concrete," and the milestone might be "Foundation complete."

When you place your milestones appropriately, they can help you measure the progress of your project and increase the motivation and productivity of team members as they achieve short-term goals and successes. Furthermore, a missed milestone date can alert you to the possibility that your project might not finish on time. This provides an early opportunity to take corrective action and recover the schedule.

Use the following guidelines when determining how to enter the milestones in your project.

- Put a milestone at the start and finish of a series of tasks to stress the importance of beginning and completing the tasks by a certain time. For example, at the start of the "Lay the foundation" phase, you could include the milestone "Foundation phase begins" and at the end, "Foundation phase complete."
- Because milestones serve as checkpoints to help you track and control the schedule throughout the project, include milestones only down to the level of detail you want to monitor. If it's not important to you when the foundation phase starts, don't include the milestone.
- Be sure that milestones are related to tasks so you know when the milestone is achieved. For example, the milestone "Foundation phase complete" is directly related to the completion of the tasks preceding it. It will be obvious when you reach the milestone because the tasks in the foundation phase will be complete.
- Include milestones that represent events outside your control if they influence your schedule. For example, include a milestone showing when you must have a bank loan to proceed with a building project. As you approach the milestone, you can check on the loan to ensure that it will be available when needed.

- Name a milestone in a way that makes it clear when the milestone is reached. Use a noun and a verb, such as "Walls complete," "Funding request due," or "Loans approved." Make the names as clear as possible. The style of the names should be consistent throughout. This consistency will help others understand each item in your schedule.

Enter a Task

After you decide which tasks need to be accomplished to achieve your project goals, enter those tasks into your project. Entering tasks is the first and most important step in creating the schedule. After you enter information about each task, Microsoft Project uses that information to calculate task start and finish dates as well as the project finish date.

By default, Microsoft Project gives each task an estimated duration of 1 day and a start date that's the same as the project start date.

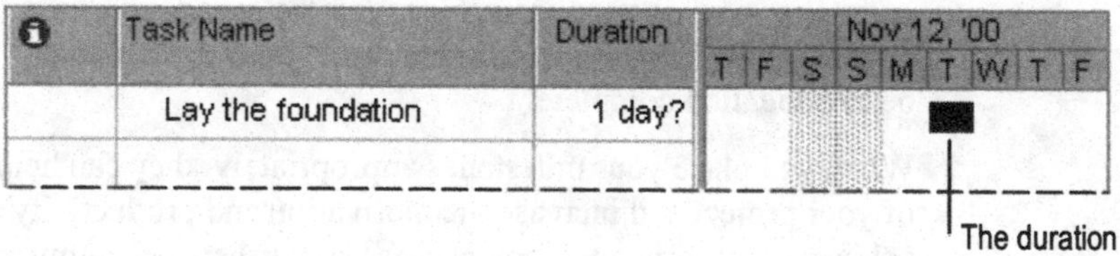

The duration is illustrated by the Gantt bar.

To enter a task

1 On the **View Bar**, click **Gantt Chart**.

2 In the **Task Name** field, type a task name.

3 Click **Enter** or press ENTER.

For maximum clarity, use a verb and a noun to name tasks. For example, say "Wire the outlets" rather than just "Wiring" or "Outlets."

If you already have a list of tasks created in a spreadsheet or database program, such as Microsoft Excel or Microsoft Access, you can import this list into Microsoft Project. For more information about importing project information, see "Importing and Exporting Project Information" in chapter 18.

Enter a Milestone

The completion of a major phase, the deadline for distributing an important project report, and the date of a crucial meeting with clients and upper management are examples of significant events worthy of milestone tasks. To visually distinguish significant events from regular tasks in your schedule, you can turn those events into milestones.

In the Gantt Chart, a milestone is listed along with other tasks in the task list. But because the purpose of a milestone is to indicate a significant event and not necessarily work that needs to be accomplished, you give the milestone a duration of zero. Microsoft Project automatically represents any zero-duration task with a diamond-shaped symbol instead of a Gantt bar in the bar chart portion of the view. By scanning for diamond shapes, you can quickly identify milestone events.

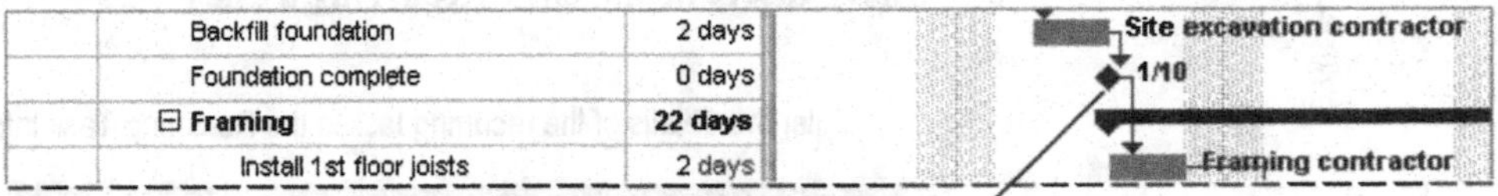

The default milestone symbol.

If you use milestones to mark the completion of project phases, they can help you track progress. A milestone reached on its targeted date can assure you that you're on schedule. A milestone reached after its targeted date can warn you that the project finish date is threatened before it's too late to take corrective action.

To change a task to a milestone

1 On the **View Bar**, click **Gantt Chart**.

2 In the **Duration** field of the task you want to change, type **0**.

3 Press ENTER.

Because milestones usually have zero duration, whenever you enter a task with zero duration, Microsoft Project automatically makes it a milestone task. However, there might be times when you want to use a regular task with a nonzero duration as a milestone marker. In Microsoft Project, you can make any task, with any duration, a milestone.

To change a task with a nonzero duration to a milestone

1 On the **View Bar**, click **Gantt Chart**.

Task Information

2 In the **Task Name** field, select the task you want to change, and then click the **Task Information** button.

3 Click the **Advanced** tab, and then select the **Mark task as milestone** check box.

The milestone marker appears instead of a Gantt bar at the milestone's start date.

Enter a Recurring Task

You might have some tasks that occur repeatedly throughout a project—for example, preparing a monthly status report. Tasks that occur repeatedly at regular intervals are called *recurring tasks*. To automate the entry of recurring tasks in your project, you can enter information about the recurring task once—information such as the task name and the frequency of occurrence. Microsoft Project then adds all occurrences of the task to the project at the frequency you specify.

To enter a recurring task

1 On the **View Bar**, click **Gantt Chart**.

2 In the **Task Name** field, select the row above where you want to insert the recurring task.

3 On the **Insert** menu, click **Recurring Task**.

Enter the details of the recurring task in the Recurring Task Information dialog box.

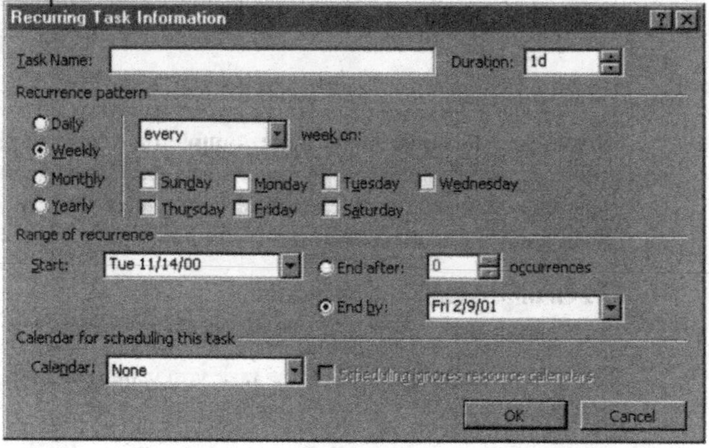

4 In the **Task Name** box, type the recurring task name.

5 In the **Duration** box, type the duration of a single occurrence of the task.

6 Under **Recurrence pattern**, click the interval at which the task will recur: **Daily**, **Weekly**, **Monthly**, or **Yearly**.

The interval you click determines which options are displayed on the right. By default, Weekly is selected and the Weekly options are displayed.

7 Under **Daily**, **Weekly**, **Monthly**, or **Yearly**, specify the task frequency.

For example, if you clicked **Daily**, you might specify every third workday. Or, if you clicked **Monthly**, you might specify the last Friday of every other month

8 Under **Range of recurrence**, enter the start date for the recurring task in the **Start** box and the finish date in the **End by** box. Or, you can enter the number of times the task will occur in the **End after** box.

If you don't enter a date in the **Start** box, the project start date is used.

The recurring task appears as a *summary task*, with the individual recurring tasks displayed as individual Gantt bars along the summary task row. To see the individual recurring tasks, you can expand the recurring summary task by clicking the plus sign next to the recurring task name.

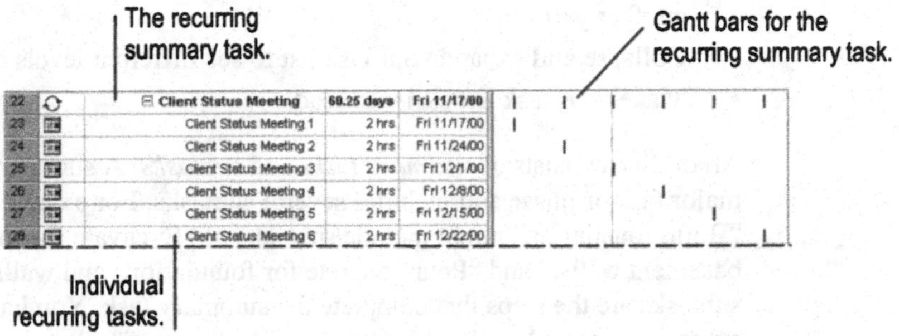

If needed, you can modify an individual recurring task. For example, you can adjust the start date of a monthly status report if it needs to be completed earlier than usual because of a vacation.

Delete a Task

For a number of reasons, you might want to delete a task from your project. Maybe you decided that the task isn't significant enough, or that it's too broad and needs to be broken down into smaller tasks. Perhaps you need to cut costs, eliminate some project goals, or reduce the project scope, each of which could result in some tasks no longer being necessary.

To delete a task

To delete a task, you can also simply select the task and then press DELETE.

1 On the **View Bar**, click **Gantt Chart**.

2 In the **Task Name** field, select the task you want to delete.

3 On the **Edit** menu, click **Delete Task**.

Organizing Your Task List

If you list 10 or 15 tasks in a logical order, your team members can probably understand the purpose and relationships of the tasks without much effort. But if your list contains dozens or even hundreds of tasks, you'll need to structure your list to show phases, hierarchies, and relationships. In Microsoft Project, the main way to structure your task list is by *outlining* it. You can use outlining to:

- Group your tasks into phases, to make it easier to track progress.
- Reorganize your task list by moving groups of tasks from one part of the list to another part.
- Collapse and expand your task list to see different levels of detail.
- Make your task list easier to read.

An outline consists of *summary tasks* and *subtasks*. A summary task often represents a major task or phase and includes several subtasks. For example, a summary task of "Build foundation" might include subtasks of "Excavate for foundation," "Form basement walls," and "Pour concrete for foundations and walls." In other words, the subtasks are the steps that complete the summary task. You have to complete all of the subtasks to complete the summary task. A summary task can also include other summary tasks, for multiple outline levels.

As its name suggests, a summary task summarizes the information of its subtasks. For example, the duration of a summary task is the total time between the earliest start date and the latest finish date of its subtasks. If you're tracking costs, the summary task shows the total for all task costs.

In Microsoft Project, a summary task appears bold and its subtasks are indented beneath it.

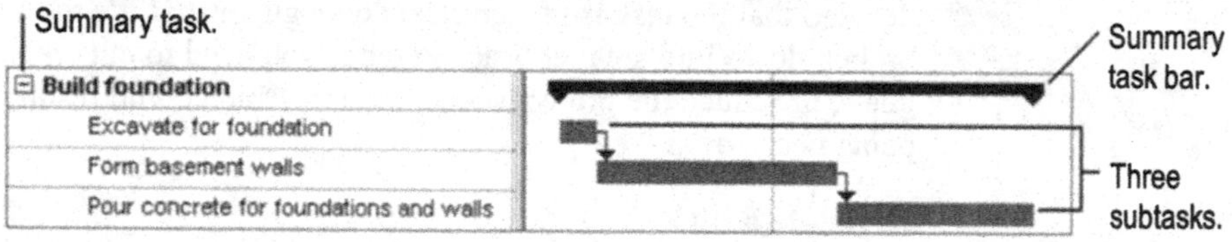

With outlining, you can choose the appropriate level of detail to share with different audiences. For example, with customers or other stakeholders, you might share the top-level summary tasks. For the same project, with the construction manager you might share the main top-level summary tasks as well as all the detail tasks for which the construction crew is responsible.

Add Tasks

You create an outline the same way you create a task list: by using either the top-down method or the bottom-up method. With the top-down outlining method, you can list the major phases first—summary tasks—and then add the detailed tasks required to fulfill the goals of those summary tasks. With the bottom-up outlining method, you can list the detailed tasks first and then group them under summary tasks.

To add a detailed task or summary task for the outline

1 On the **View Bar**, click **Gantt Chart**.

2 Select the task above which you want to insert a new detailed task or summary task for your outline.

3 On the **Insert** menu, click **New Task**.

4 In the new row, type the name and any other information for the new task.

Outline Your Tasks

In Microsoft Project, the way to outline your task list is by *indenting* and *outdenting* tasks. When you indent a task one level with respect to a preceding task, the preceding task appears bold, indicating that it has become a summary task. The indented task becomes a subtask.

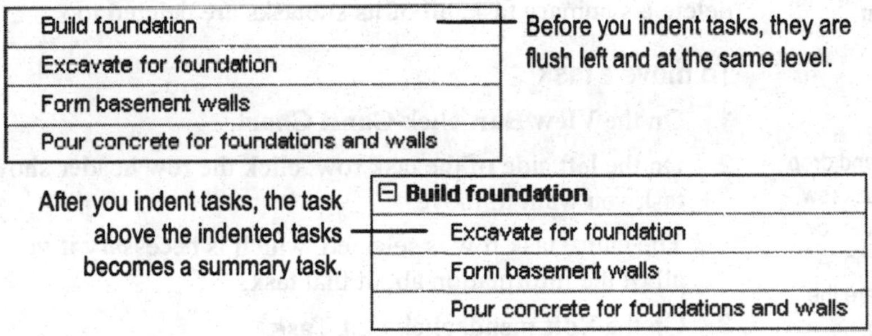

You can outline tasks in all task views except the Calendar view.

To create an outline

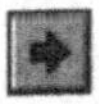
Indent

Outdent

1 On the **View Bar**, click **Gantt Chart**.

2 In the **Task Name** field, select the task you want to indent or outdent.

3 Click **Indent** to indent the task or **Outdent** to outdent the task.

If the Outline Buttons Don't Work

The outline buttons, which are located on the Standard toolbar, work in any task view except the Calendar view. If you're using one of these task views and the outline buttons still don't work, try one of the following:

- Check to see if you're in the middle of entering a new task name or other task information. Until the task information is entered, the outline buttons are not available.
- On the **Tools** menu, click **Options**, and then click the **View** tab. Under **Outline options**, make sure the **Show summary tasks** check box is checked.
- On the **Project** menu, point to **Sort**, and then click **Sort by**. If the task list is not sorted by ID, either select **ID** in the **Sort by** box or select the **Keep outline structure** check box to maintain the outline structure in the sorted project. Click the **Sort** button.

Reorganize Your Outline

You might also move tasks to put them in the proper sequence for when they'll be done, an important step for making tasks happen in the right order and at the right time, as you'll see in chapter 5.

Your outline might not be perfect the first time around. You might, for instance, decide that a task belongs under a different phase, or that you don't need some tasks after all. You can adjust and reorganize your outline by moving and deleting tasks.

In addition to moving and deleting subtasks, you can also move and delete summary tasks. When you move a summary task, all of its subtasks move with it. When you delete a summary task, all of its subtasks are deleted too.

To move a task

You can also drag and drop a task. Select the task row. Click the middle of the row header, and then drag. A gray bar shows where the task will be inserted. Release the mouse button and the row is inserted between tasks where indicated by the gray bar.

1. On the **View Bar**, click **Gantt Chart**.
2. On the left side of the task row, click the row header showing the ID number of the task you want to move.

   The entire task row is selected, which is necessary if you want to move a task and all of the information about that task.
3. On the **Edit** menu, click **Cut Task**.

   The Cut Task command appears on the Edit menu only if an entire task row is selected (that is, by clicking the row header and ID number of a task).
4. Click the row above where you want to insert the task.
5. On the **Edit** menu, click **Paste**.

Show and Hide Subtasks

In your outline, you can show or hide the subtasks of one summary task or all summary tasks. For example, you might want to hide all subtasks to display only the highest-level summary tasks, then print that view in a summary report. Or you might want to display every subtask so that team members can see a comprehensive list of their tasks.

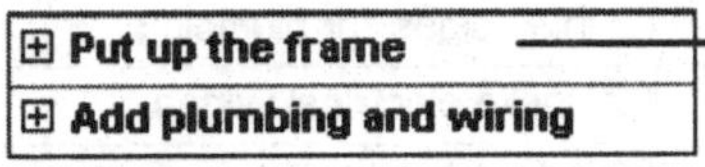

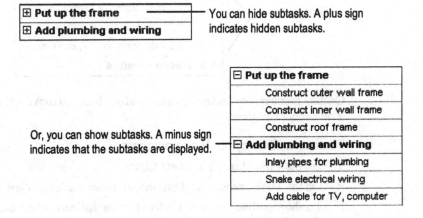

You can hide subtasks. A plus sign indicates hidden subtasks.

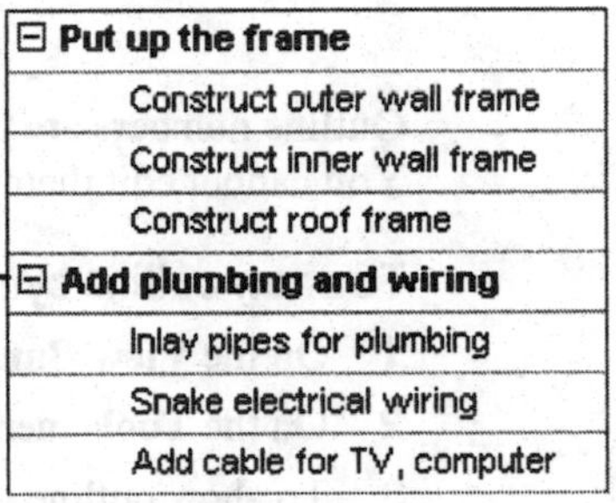

Or, you can show subtasks. A minus sign indicates that the subtasks are displayed.

To show and hide subtasks

1 On the **View Bar**, click **Gantt Chart**.

Show Subtasks

2 In the **Task Name** field, select the summary task containing the subtasks you want to show or hide.

Hide Subtasks

3 Click **Show Subtasks** to show the subtasks or click **Hide Subtasks** to hide the subtasks.

Show

To show all subtasks, click **Show** and then click **All Subtasks**.

Show Outline Symbols and Numbers

Outline symbols are the plus and minus signs that appear next to summary tasks. They indicate whether the subtasks of a summary task are hidden (plus sign) or displayed (minus sign). By clicking an outline symbol, you can quickly show or hide subtasks.

Outline numbers indicate the level of a task in an outline. For example, 1, 1.1, and 1.1.1 indicate tasks of the highest level, the second-highest level, and the third-highest level respectively. These numbers also show that task 1.1 is grouped under task 1 and task 1.1.1 is grouped under task 1.1. Outline numbers can help you keep track of a task's place in the outline hierarchy.

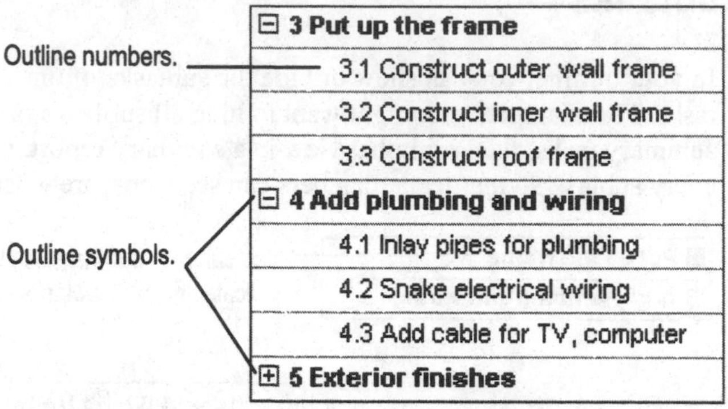

Outline numbers are updated automatically when you move a task in your schedule. You cannot edit them.

To show outline symbols and numbers

1 On the **View Bar**, click **Gantt Chart**.

2 On the **Tools** menu, click **Options**, and then click the **View** tab.

3 To show outline symbols: Under **Outline options**, select the **Show outline symbol** check box.

To show outline numbers: Under **Outline options**, select the **Show outline number** check box.

Estimating the Time for a Task

All tasks (except for milestones) will take some time to accomplish. The amount of time required to complete a task is called the *task duration*. When you include each task's duration in your project, Project can start to calculate your schedule.

For more information about task dependencies, delay, and overlap, see chapter 5.

Then, when you add information about *task dependencies*—for example, which tasks must be completed before the next task begins—Microsoft Project can really build a realistic schedule and estimate your project's finish date.

Because of the importance of task durations and how they work with task dependencies, the calculation Microsoft Project does of the project length will only be as accurate as your duration estimates. To estimate a duration as precisely as possible, analyze the task and gather evidence to support your estimate. You can also approximate a duration based on three estimates: an optimistic estimate, a pessimistic estimate, and an expected estimate.

Use the following sources to estimate task durations accurately:

- Learn how long similar tasks took in past projects. When you use historical data, note any differences between the new task and similar tasks in the past. Take these differences into account when you estimate the duration for the current task.
- Estimate the duration based on how long you'd take to do the task. If you're experienced at this task, assume it would take an average resource longer. If you're not experienced at this task, assume an average resource could do it faster.
- Let those who will actually do the work estimate how long the task will take. Input from someone who's had hands-on experience with a similar task will likely be the most precise.

Microsoft Project makes a distinction between durations and estimated durations. Whenever you enter a new task, the default is a 1-day estimated duration, as noted by a question mark in the Duration field. When you enter an educated or confirmed duration, the question mark goes away. However, if you enter a duration followed by a question mark, this is interpreted as an estimated duration. You can sort, filter, or group on estimated durations. This can help you see which of your durations are confirmed and which are still guesses.

PERT analysis is not related to PERT charts or the Network Diagram view.

For many projects, you can make a single duration estimate for each task and wind up with an accurate schedule. But if you want a greater degree of confidence in your duration estimates and you want to see how optimistic, pessimistic, and expected task durations each affect the resulting schedule, you can perform a PERT analysis (also known as *what-if analysis*). In Microsoft Project, you carry out PERT analysis using predefined variations of the Gantt Chart and the PERT analysis toolbar.

Microsoft Project doesn't include nonworking time, such as weekends and the time between the end of one workday and the beginning of the next workday, in a task's duration. For example, a 2-day task scheduled to begin on a Friday will occur on Friday and Monday.

If you want a task duration to span a continuous period of time, including any nonworking time, you can specify an *elapsed duration*. If you use an elapsed duration, then a 2-day task that begins on a Friday will occur on Friday and Saturday. For example, you can use an elapsed duration to indicate the drying time of a concrete wall.

You can specify a duration in the following time units: minutes (m), hours (h), days (d), weeks (w), months (mo). Let Microsoft Project do the work for you. Unless a task must start or finish on a specific date, don't enter a date. By entering just the duration, you give Microsoft Project the information needed to schedule tasks flexibly and to calculate the most efficient overall schedule possible. Otherwise, you might pin the task to certain fixed dates and prevent Microsoft Project from scheduling tasks in a realistic sequence.

To change a task duration

1. On the **View Bar**, click **Gantt Chart**.
2. In the **Duration** field for the task duration you want to change, type the duration.

   To specify that a duration you're entering is still an estimate, follow the time unit with a "?" question mark. For example, to indicate an estimated duration of two weeks, enter "2w?".

   To specify elapsed duration, precede the time unit with the letter **e** (for example, eday for elapsed days).
3. Press ENTER.

You can change the definition of day, week, and month for your durations. For example, if you want "1d" to mean six hours rather than eight, or if you want "1w" to mean seven days rather than five, you can change these settings.

To change duration options

1. On the **Tools** menu, click **Options**.
2. Click **Calendar**.
3. Specify the various options to reflect the starting day of the week, default start and end times, hours per day and week, and days per month that you want Microsoft Project to use in scheduling the tasks in your project.

Use the Calendar Options dialog box to change duration options.

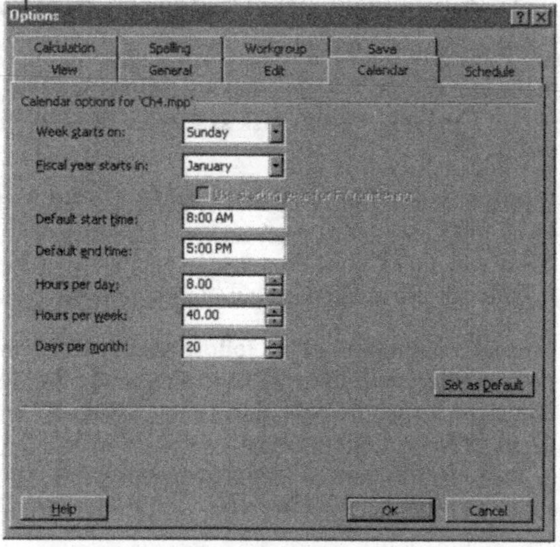

Estimate Durations Using PERT Analysis

How will variations from your estimated task durations affect the project length? What will the schedule look like if tasks take longer than you expect? What will it look like if tasks take less time than you expect? With the Microsoft Project PERT analysis tools, you can create and look at three scenarios, one based on expected duration estimates, another on optimistic duration estimates, and a third on pessimistic duration estimates. The PERT analysis tools not only enable you to generate three schedule scenarios but they also provide you with a sophisticated way to calculate a single duration that's based on expected, optimistic, and pessimistic estimates.

To use the PERT analysis tools, you enter the expected, optimistic, and pessimistic durations of the tasks in your schedule. After you specify how much weight to give to each of the three durations, Microsoft Project calculates a single duration estimate from the weighted average of the three durations.

To estimate durations using PERT analysis

1 On the **View** menu, point to **Toolbars**, and then click **PERT Analysis**.

PERT Entry Sheet

2 On the **PERT Analysis** toolbar, click **PERT Entry Sheet**.

3 For each task, enter the optimistic, expected, and pessimistic durations in the **Optimistic Dur.**, **Expected Dur.**, and **Pessimistic Dur.** fields.

If there's a task duration that you don't want Microsoft Project to calculate, enter the same duration in all three fields.

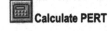

Calculate PERT

4 To calculate the estimated durations, click **Calculate PERT**.

Microsoft Project calculates a single duration estimate based on a weighted average of the three duration values and enters this duration in the Duration field.

By default, Microsoft Project gives the optimistic duration estimate a weight of 1, the pessimistic duration estimate a weight of 1, and the expected duration estimate a weight of 4 (the weights must always add up to 6). If you have reason to believe that the three durations should be weighted differently, you can change their weights.

To change the weights given to your duration estimates

1 If not already showing, on the **View** menu, point to **Toolbars**, and then click **PERT Analysis**.

PERT Weights

2 On the **PERT Analysis** toolbar, click **Set PERT Weights**.

3 Enter new weight values for the three duration estimates.

The three values must add up to 6. Because the default weight values represent standard deviations for PERT probabilities, changing the defaults might make the estimated duration less accurate.

Calculate PERT

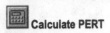

4 To calculate the new durations, click **Calculate PERT**.

After Microsoft Project calculates your estimated task durations, you can view the optimistic, pessimistic, and expected durations—and the resulting schedules.

To view the three schedules resulting from your PERT Analysis estimates

Optimistic Gantt

Expected Gantt

Pessimistic Gantt

- On the PERT Analysis toolbar, click Optimistic Gantt, Expected Gantt, or Pessimistic Gantt.

  These tools present views in which you can see an optimistic, an expected, and a pessimistic schedule and project finish date.

Using a Work Breakdown Structure

Outlining the task list might be all you need to organize the tasks in your project. However, if you or your clients prefer, you can use a *work breakdown structure* with Microsoft Project.

A work breakdown structure, or WBS, is a tree-type structure based on deliverables. Tasks are grouped according to deliverables that are the result of every phase, subphase, and task. The WBS looks like an organizational chart for tasks. Each level of the WBS depicts the project at a different level of detail—the lower the level on the WBS, the more detailed the definition of the task. Depending on the complexity and detail of a project, projects typically consist of three to five levels.

At the lowest level of the WBS is the *work package*, which constitutes the deliverable. This is the point where the actual work is done and the resources are assigned.

When you create a WBS, you start with the project goals, then divide and redivide tasks until you get to the level of detail you need. This ensures that all required tasks are logically identified and grouped. The upper divisions could be project phases, work units (engineers, programmers, production line, and so on), financial cost codes, departments (marketing, accounting, lab, and so on), or major product units (engine, transmission, body, suspension, and so on).

Use WBS Codes

In a work breakdown structure, each task is associated with its own code, such as a number. A task's code can indicate its place in the overall task hierarchy, the department responsible for completing the task, or any other means you might use to organize your work breakdown structure and its code.

You can use WBS codes for sorting and filtering tasks to look at a specific segment of the project information. For example, if a department code is part of the WBS code, you could filter the task list to display only those tasks that include a certain department code.

By default, Microsoft Project uses outline numbers as the WBS coding system. If you want to organize your tasks in a WBS, you can do one of the following:

- Use the outline numbers as your WBS coding system.
- Create and assign your own custom WBS format. Even if you create custom WBS codes, Microsoft Project retains the outline numbers it assigned to the tasks.
- Manually type in the WBS code for each task, independent of the outline numbers or a code mask.

If you create custom WBS codes, Microsoft Project automatically generates new codes for new or rearranged tasks based on the WBS format you defined and the task's location in the outline structure. You can still type in your own values, as long as they conform to the WBS format you defined.

Create and Assign a Custom WBS Code Format

You don't have to create an outline to use a WBS coding system. However, if you want to use outlining features, such as showing and hiding subtasks, the hierarchy in your WBS coding system should match the outline hierarchy. Despite the WBS number you enter, the tasks must be entered at the appropriate level in the outline. In other words, all tasks at the same WBS level should be entered at the same outline level.

If you or your client uses a specific WBS code format, you can create a custom *code mask* that Microsoft Project will then use to assign WBS codes to tasks in line with the tasks' place in the project's outline hierarchy. Your WBS code can be especially helpful if you're working with multiple projects, as the code can include a project code prefix to help you identify the project with which a code is associated. While you can define only a single set of WBS codes per project, you can create up to ten custom outline code formats.

To create custom WBS codes

1 On the **View Bar**, click **Gantt Chart**.

2 On the **Project** menu, point to **WBS**, and then click **Define Code**.

3 To specify a project code prefix that distinguishes the tasks in this project from tasks in other projects, type a prefix in the **Project Code Prefix** box. This can be especially helpful if you manage multiple projects, or if you're working with a master project and subprojects.

For more information about master projects and subprojects, see "Managing Several Projects in One Project File" in chapter 17.

4 To specify the code format for first-level tasks, click the first row in the **Sequence** column, click the arrow, and then click the character type you want for this level.

5 In the **Length** column, click the first row, and then enter a number for the number of characters needed in the first-level code string. For example, type 4 to require four characters at this level of the WBS code. A WBS code can be as long as 255 characters.

6 In the **Separator** column, click the first row, and then enter a character to separate the code string for one level from the code string for the next level. By default, the separator character is a period.

7 Repeat steps 4–6 to specify a code string for each level of indented tasks in your outline.

Use the WBS Code Definition dialog box to specify your WBS code format, or mask.

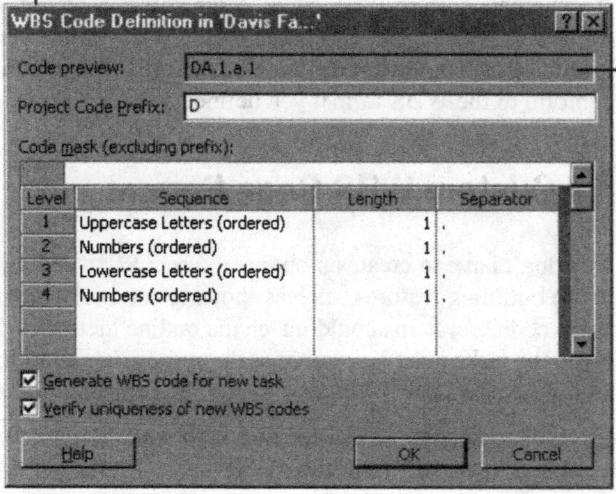

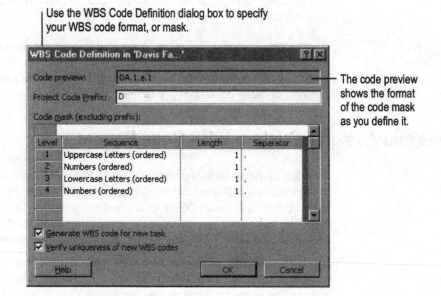

The code preview shows the format of the code mask as you define it.

To review WBS codes

1 On the **View Bar**, click **Gantt Chart**.

2 Click in the column to the left of where you want the WBS column to appear.

3 On the **Insert** menu, click **Column**.

4 In the **Field name** box, scroll to and click **WBS**.

The WBS codes appear in the column with their corresponding tasks.

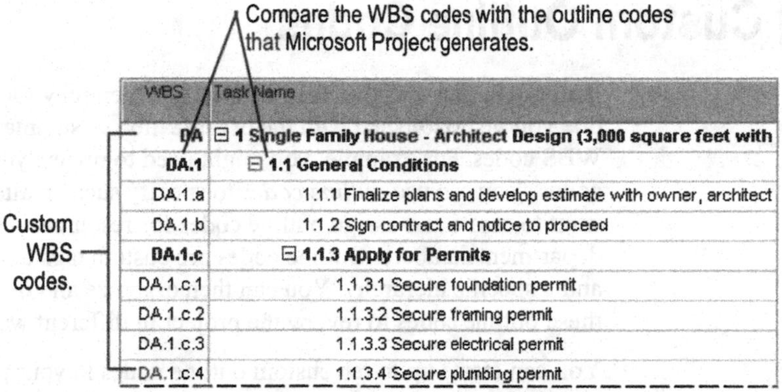
Compare the WBS codes with the outline codes that Microsoft Project generates.
Custom WBS codes.
WBS
Task Name
DA
1 Single Family House - Architect Design (3,000 square feet with
DA.1
1.1 General Conditions
DA.1.a
1.1.1 Finalize plans and develop estimate with owner, architect
DA.1.b
1.1.2 Sign contract and notice to proceed
DA.1.c
1.1.3 Apply for Permits
DA.1.c.1
1.1.3.1 Secure foundation permit
DA.1.c.2
1.1.3.2 Secure framing permit
DA.1.c.3
1.1.3.3 Secure electrical permit
DA.1.c.4
1.1.3.4 Secure plumbing permit

If you create a custom WBS code format and later add, move, or delete tasks, you can have Microsoft Project renumber the WBS codes according to your WBS format and the task locations in the outline structure.

To renumber WBS codes

1 On the **View Bar**, click **Gantt Chart**.

2 On the **Project** menu, point to **WBS**, and then click **Renumber**.

Manually Enter WBS Codes

If you want, you can enter WBS codes manually—that is, without a code mask. You can enter WBS code either in the WBS column in a task sheet or in the Task Information dialog box. However, if you do enter WBS codes manually, remember that Microsoft Project cannot automatically generate or renumber WBS codes for you.

To manually enter WBS codes in a task sheet

1 On the **View Bar**, click **Gantt Chart**.

2 In the **Task Name** field, select the task to which you want to assign a WBS code.

3 On the **Insert** menu, click **Column**.

4 In the **Field name** box, scroll to and click **WBS**.

5 Enter the WBS codes next to the appropriate tasks.

To manually enter WBS codes in the Task Information dialog box

1 On the **View Bar**, click **Gantt Chart**.

2 Click the task to which you want to add the WBS code.

Task Information

3 Click **Task Information**, and then click the **Advanced** tab.

4 In the **WBS Code** box, type the code you want to assign to the task.

Using Custom Outline Codes

You might find that you need to specify a hierarchy for your project in addition to the one you've established with the organization of summary tasks and subtasks or with WBS codes. For example, you might need to review your tasks by accounting cost codes. You can use *outline codes* to specify such an alternate structure. Or, you might want to create and assign outline codes for resources—for example, for job codes or department numbers. Outline codes are custom tags that share specific characteristics and a specific hierarchy. You can then organize and display your tasks according to these outline codes to review the project in different ways.

You can create up to ten custom outline codes in your project to display unique tags for each task based on its level in your custom outline code hierarchy. To view these custom outline codes, you can add a column to your task sheet view. Once you have assigned outline codes to the tasks, you can group or sort your tasks by the outline codes to review them according to this hierarchy.

Outline codes are similar to WBS codes in that they allow you to apply a custom code format to your project that in turn allows you to group, sort, or filter project information in different ways. However, outline codes go further than WBS codes in the following ways:

- A task can have only one WBS structure, while you can define up to ten custom outline codes.
- WBS codes are applied only to tasks, while you can have outline codes for resources as well as tasks.
- The WBS structure usually corresponds with the task outline structure of summary tasks and subtasks. Custom outline codes are not tied to the task outline structure.

To create custom outline codes

1. On the **View Bar,** click **Gantt Chart.**

   If you're creating outline codes for resources, display a resource sheet view.
2. On the **Tools** menu, point to **Customize**, and then click **Fields**.
3. In the **Type** box, click **Outline Code**.
4. In the box, click the outline code you want to define—for example, **Outline Code1**.
5. Click **Rename**.
6. In the **Rename Field** dialog box, type a name for the custom outline code you want to create, and then click **OK**.
7. Click **Define Outline Code**.
8. Click the first row in the **Sequence** column, and then click the character type for the outline code format you want to create.

9 If you want to apply a particular code length or a separator character between the characters of the different outline levels, enter this in the **Length** or **Separator** column.

If you specify a length, this indicates that this segment of the code must be exactly that length (rather than up to that length) to be valid.

10 Click the second row, and then enter the format for the second level of the outline code.

11 Repeat steps 8–10 until your outline format is created.

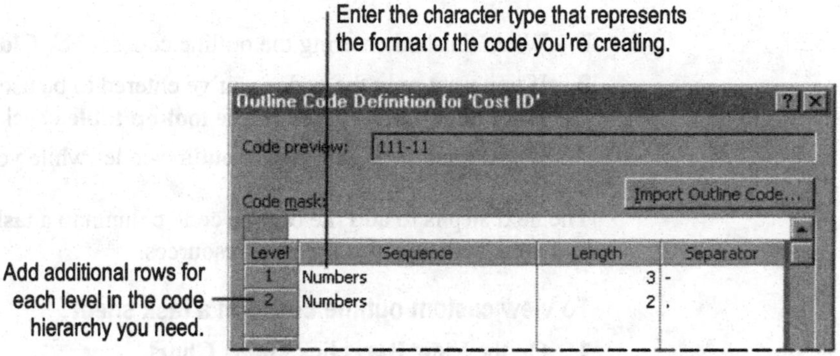

After defining your outline code format, you can create a lookup table for the specific outline codes. If you don't want to set up a lookup table ahead of time, you can enter code values in the task sheet itself, thereby creating your lookup table as you work.

To create a lookup table for outline codes

1 Create your outline codes as described in the previous procedure.

2 With the Outline Code Definition dialog box still open, click **Edit Lookup Table**.

3 In the first row, under **Outline Code**, type your first outline code, following the format you have established for your outline codes (numbers, characters, and so on).

You cannot enter a code that does not follow your format.

4 In the **Description** field, type a description for this outline code.

5 Repeat steps 3 and 4 until all your outline codes are entered.

Indent

6 To indicate the hierarchy of an outline code, select the code, and then click **Indent**.

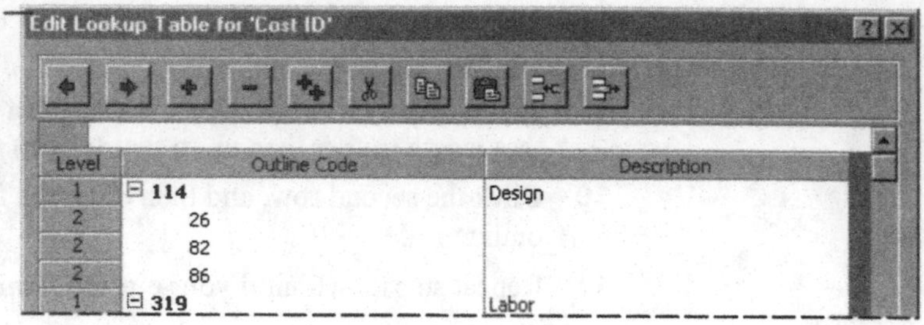

Use the Edit Lookup Table dialog box to enter actual code values you can pick in a task sheet.

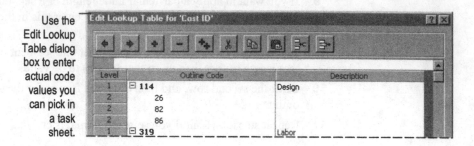

7 When finished entering the outline codes, click **Close**.

8 If you want only the codes you've entered to be used in a task sheet, select the **Only allow codes listed in the lookup table** check box.

If you want to be able to add outline codes while you work, clear this check box.

The next step is to add the outline code column to a task sheet so you can enter, change, and view outline codes for your resources.

To view custom outline codes in a task sheet

1 On the **View Bar**, click **Gantt Chart**.

2 Click the field to the right of where you want to insert a column for the custom outline code. For example, click the Task Name field if you want the outline codes column to be inserted to the left of the task names.

3 On the **Insert** menu, click **Column**.

4 In the **Field name** box, scroll to **Outline Code**, and then pick the outline code you have defined.

The name you gave the outline code appears in parentheses. This is the name that will appear as the new column's header.

To assign custom outline codes to tasks

1 Display a task sheet view that includes the outline code column.

2 Click the outline code field for the task to which you want to assign an outline code.

3 Type an outline code or select it from the list.

As you enter outline codes, the values for each level become part of the dropdown list for the column.

You can group, sort, or filter by outline codes.

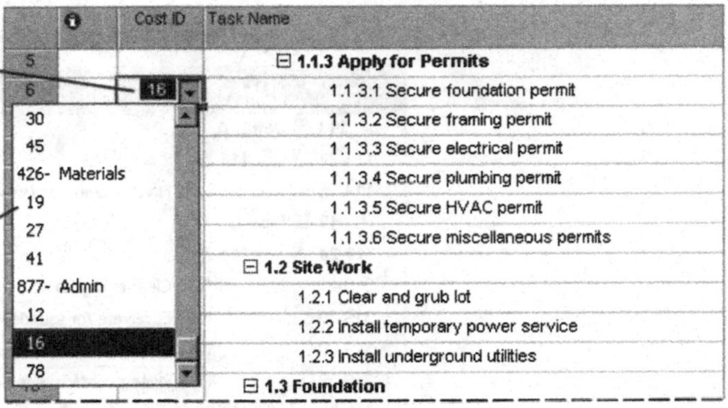

Outline codes provide more information to help you manage your tasks.

To group tasks by outline code

For more information about grouping, filtering, and sorting, see chapter 12.

1. Have a task sheet view displayed, including the outline code column and assigned outline codes.
2. On the **Project** menu, point to **Group by**, and then click **More Groups**.
3. Click **New**.
4. In the **Name** box, type the name you want for the group definition—for example, "Cost ID."
5. If this is a grouping you're going to use frequently, select the **Show in menu** check box.
6. In the **Group By** row under **Field Name**, select the outline code field you used—for example, Outline Code1.
7. Under **Order**, specify whether you want the grouping to be alphabetical in ascending or descending order.

To remove the grouping, on the Project menu, point to Group by, and then click No Group.

8 Click **OK**, and then click **Apply**.

The tasks are grouped by their outline codes.

Cost ID	Task Name
114	**Design**
114-26	**114-26**
114-26	1.1.1 Finalize plans and develop estimate with owner, architect
319	**Labor**
319-20	**319-20**
319-20	1.2.1 Clear and grub lot
319-20	1.3.1 Excavate for foundations
319-20	1.3.5 Strip basement wall forms
319-20	1.3.6 Waterproof/insulate basement walls
319-30	**319-30**
319-30	1.2.2 Install temporary power service
319-30	1.2.3 Install underground utilities
319-30	1.3.2 Form basement walls
319-30	1.3.3 Place concrete for foundations & basement walls
319-30	1.3.8 Backfill foundation
319-30	1.4.1 Install 1st floor joists
319-30	1.4.2 Lay 1st floor decking
319-45	**319-45**
319-45	1.4.3 Frame 1st floor walls
319-45	1.4.4 Frame 1st floor corners

5

Making Tasks Happen at the Right Time

As soon as you enter durations for each task, Microsoft Project has the first piece of scheduling information needed to create your schedule. But by default, Microsoft Project schedules each task to start on the project start date. Because most tasks occur in a particular sequence, more information is needed to create an accurate scheduling model for your project. For example, first you dig a hole, then you pour the foundation for a house. Or, first you determine a new product's specifications, then you develop a prototype. These tasks cannot start at the same time because the second task can't be done until the first task is completed.

To specify these task dependencies, you link tasks in a particular way. Microsoft Project can then schedule according to the task durations and your task sequencing and linking. Task durations and dependencies form the basis for the majority of your task scheduling.

Once these are in place, you can fine-tune the scheduling even more by specifying that certain tasks should have an amount of delay or overlap between them.

Finally, while it's not recommended for the majority of tasks, in certain very specific circumstances, you might need a task to begin or end on or near a particular date. In such cases, you can enter a date constraint. A more flexible method for targeting specific dates is to set a task deadline that acts as a reminder rather than a fixed scheduling control.

With durations, you direct how much time should be scheduled from a task's start to its finish. With links, you indicate the dependencies between tasks and the time frame within which each task will occur. By specifying overlap, delay, and task calendars, your schedule more accurately reflects when tasks should be done. And with the constraints, task deadlines, and default start date, you can ensure that tasks occur at exactly the right time.

Sequencing Your Tasks

To schedule your tasks so that they occur in the right order and at the right time, you first need to determine the task sequence. The *task sequence* is the order in which your project tasks are to be done. Once you set the task sequence, you can start to link tasks to indicate the type of dependency they have with each other.

To decide task sequence, answer the following questions for each task or group of related tasks:

- Does this task depend on another task? Most likely it does, but not all tasks do. For example, making a copy of the house blueprint to save in your files is something you can do at any point in the project.
- If this task does depend on another task, what is it? In other words, which tasks must start or finish before this task can start?
- Which tasks depend on this task? That is, which tasks cannot start or finish until this task starts or finishes?

To put tasks in their proper sequence, use either the Cut Task and Paste commands or the drag and drop method, as described in chapter 4.

Building Your Schedule Using Task Dependencies

A *task dependency* is the logical connection, or link, between two tasks. In many cases, one task can't begin until the previous task is completed (the hole must be dug before the foundation is poured). But some tasks can be done simultaneously. For example, the chimney can be built while the outer walls are going up.

A task whose start or finish depends directly on the start or finish of another task is called a *successor* task. The task that a successor task depends on is called a *predecessor* task. For example, pouring the foundation is the successor task to digging a hole, which is the predecessor task.

You specify dependencies between tasks in your project by linking them. A *link* specifies the type of dependency that exists between two tasks. The most common type of dependency is one in which one task starts as soon as its predecessor is completed: the finish-to-start link.

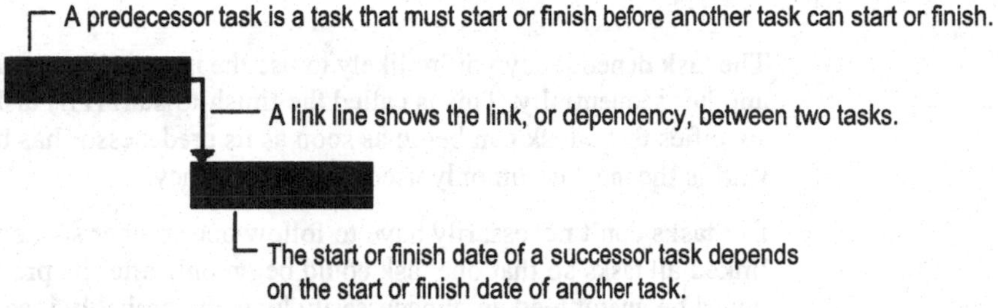

A predecessor task is a task that must start or finish before another task can start or finish.
A link line shows the link, or dependency, between two tasks.
The start or finish date of a successor task depends on the start or finish date of another task.

When you identify the predecessors for a task, specify only those tasks that the task depends on directly. For example, because you must build walls before you can paint them, building walls is a predecessor to painting walls. But, although the house frame must be built before the walls can be painted, building the frame is not an immediate predecessor to painting.

Dependencies do not nail down task start and finish dates. Instead, they form a flexible time framework that indicates when each linked task should start or finish relative to the start or finish date of another task. Once two tasks are linked, the successor's start and finish dates are contingent on the predecessor's start and finish dates. For example, if the successor can't begin until the predecessor is completed, and if the predecessor slips, then the start date of the successor will slip by the same amount of time. By linking tasks, you let Microsoft Project calculate the start and finish dates of tasks as well as the overall project finish date.

For more information about tracking actual progress, see chapter 9.

Task dependencies provide for the most flexibility in scheduling and fewest potential scheduling conflicts. Once your project begins and you start tracking task progress, Microsoft Project can recalculate task dates as you enter actual start and finish dates for tasks that have started or finished earlier or later than your original estimates. You see the effects of schedule changes immediately.

For example, suppose you have identified a task dependency that has a successor task beginning immediately after its predecessor is completed. If Microsoft Project calculates the predecessor's finish date to be February 10, then the successor's start date is February 11. But suppose the predecessor task actually takes two days longer than estimated. When you enter the task's actual duration, Microsoft Project recalculates a finish date of February 12 for the predecessor task and, subsequently, a start date of February 13 for the successor task.

To develop most schedules, start by linking tasks. This framework of linked, dependent tasks forms the backbone of your schedule. Once this backbone is in place, you can modify portions of it, if necessary, by overlapping or delaying tasks, or by applying specific date constraints.

The Types of Task Dependencies

The task dependency you're likely to use the most is the one in which one task follows another sequentially. This is called the finish-to-start (FS) task dependency, which specifies that a task can begin as soon as its predecessor has been completed. Finish-to-start is the most commonly used task dependency.

But tasks don't necessarily have to follow one another sequentially. In fact, if you linked all tasks so that one task could begin only after its predecessor was completed, you'd be guaranteed an unnecessarily long and probably inaccurate schedule. Sometimes, for instance, two tasks need to start at the same time. This start-to-start (SS) dependency can definitely shorten the schedule.

Likewise, you might need two tasks to finish at the same time—for example, if these tasks must both be done in time for a conference. You can link them with a finish-to-finish (FF) dependency to ensure they're scheduled accordingly.

In addition, some tasks might not have any dependencies at all and can be done whenever the rest of the schedule allows.

After you decide task sequence, you can link tasks as necessary. Each link can specify one of the four kinds of dependencies described in the following table.

To specify	Link the tasks with this task dependency type	How it looks on the Gantt Chart
A task starts after its predecessor is completed	Finish-to-start (FS)	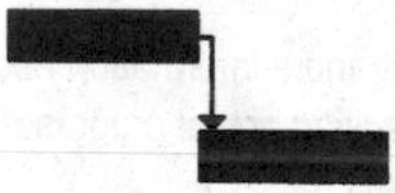
A task starts as soon as its predecessor starts	Start-to-start (SS)	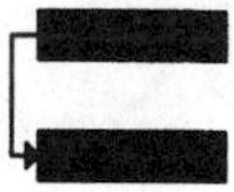
A task must be completed as soon as its predecessor is completed	Finish-to-finish (FF)	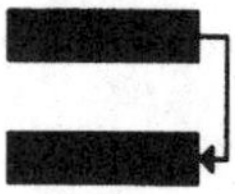
A task is completed after its predecessor starts (this is rare)	Start-to-finish (SF)	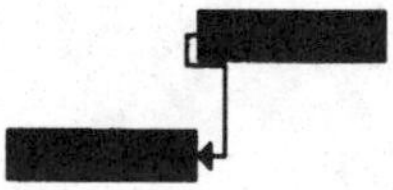

Create a Task Link

After you've determined how the start or finish date of one task depends on the start or finish date of another task, you're ready to link those tasks.

You can link tasks in two ways. Because the finish-to-start (FS) link is the most common link used, Microsoft Project provides you with a way to quickly link two or more tasks with an FS link. If you want to link tasks with other than an FS link, you use a different method. Whichever method you use, you can change a link from one type to another.

You can create an FS link between summary tasks as well as between subtasks. When you create an FS link between summary tasks, the start of one group of tasks depends on the completion of another group.

To link tasks in a finish-to-start (FS) dependency

1 On the **View Bar**, click **Gantt Chart**.

2 In the **Task Name** field, select two or more tasks you want to link.

Select nonadjacent tasks by holding down the CTRL key while you select the task.

Select the tasks in the order they should be linked. For example, the first task you click becomes the predecessor and the next task becomes the successor, regardless of their sequence in the Gantt Chart.

Link Tasks

You can also create an FS link by clicking the predecessor Gantt bar and dragging it to the successor Gantt bar.

3 Click **Link Tasks**.

A link line connecting the two tasks appears in the Gantt Chart. When you use the Link Tasks button, Microsoft Project automatically creates an FS link between the selected tasks.

To link tasks in a start-to-start, finish-to-finish, or a start-to-finish dependency

1 On the **View Bar**, click **Gantt Chart**.

2 In the **Task Name** field, click the task you want to link to a predecessor.

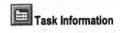

Task Information

3 Click **Task Information**.
The Task Information dialog box appears.

4 Click the **Predecessors** tab.

Another method is to create an FS link in the Gantt Chart, double-click the link line, and then modify the link type.

5 In the **ID** field, type the ID number of the predecessor task.

ID numbers are assigned automatically when you enter tasks and are shown in the row header for each task in the Gantt Chart table.

6 In the **Type** field for the row, select the link type you want.

Change or Remove a Task Link

If a link doesn't accurately reflect the dependency between two tasks, you can easily change the type of link that connects them. If you later decide you don't want a link between particular tasks, you can remove that link.

To change a task link

If the Bar Styles dialog box appears instead, close this dialog box and try it again, being more precise with the mouse.

1 On the **View Bar**, click **Gantt Chart**.
2 Double-click the link line you want to change.
  The Task Dependency dialog box appears.
3 In the **Type** box, click the task link you want.

To remove a task link

1 On the **View Bar**, click **Gantt Chart**.
2 Double-click the link line you want to remove.
3 In the **Task Dependency** dialog box, click **Delete**.

Use this box to change the link.

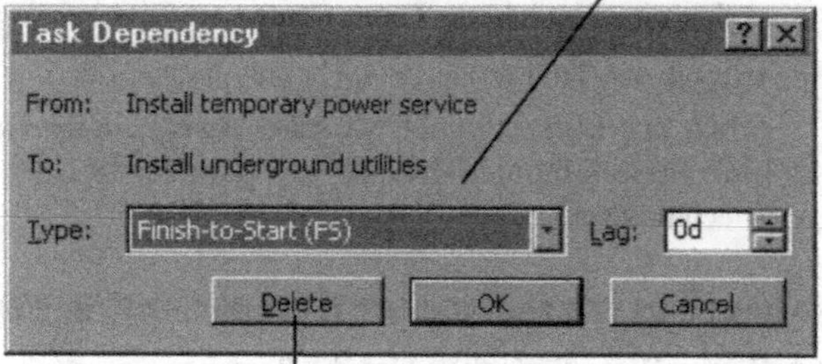

Use this button to delete the link.

You can also double-click the successor task, click the **Predecessors** tab, and then change or delete the task dependency.

Fine-Tuning Task Scheduling

When you identify task durations and dependencies, your project starts to form a reasonable schedule. Because some tasks might have special requirements or exceptions, you can use Microsoft Project to fine-tune this schedule for even more accuracy. You can:

- Specify an amount of delay between linked tasks by adding lag time.
- Add an amount of overlap between linked tasks using lead time.
- Schedule a task independently of or in conjunction with the project or resource calendar.

You can also plan for an interruption or time gap in the scheduling of a task by splitting the task. For more information about splitting a task, see "Interrupt Work on a Task" in chapter 8.

Overlap or Delay Tasks

When you link tasks, not only do you establish the task dependency, you also establish a flexible time framework in which one task starts or finishes relative to the start or finish date of a predecessor task. If a task starts earlier or later than planned, all the succeeding linked tasks start earlier or later.

For many linked tasks, the link alone sufficiently specifies the entire relationship between two tasks. In most cases, you probably want one task to start immediately after its predecessor is completed. But what if you need some time to pass between the finish and start of the two tasks? For example, suppose you have a predecessor task of "Paint the walls" and a successor task of "Put up molding"? You'd probably want to delay putting up the molding for a few days so the paint can dry.

With *lag time*, you can specify a waiting period, or delay, between the finish of a predecessor task and the start of a successor task. For example, if you need a three-day delay between painting walls and putting up molding, you can link these tasks with a finish-to-start dependency and then specify a three-day lag time.

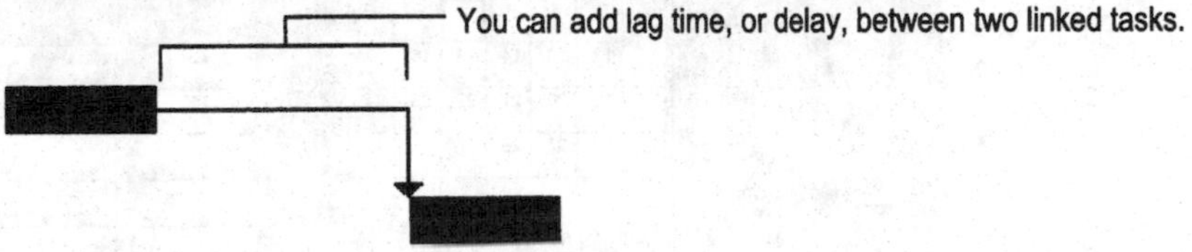

You can add lag time, or delay, between two linked tasks.

On the other hand, by using *lead time*, you can specify an overlap between linked tasks. For example, if you can start painting the walls after half the walls have been put up, you can specify a finish-to-start dependency with a lead time of 50% for the successor task.

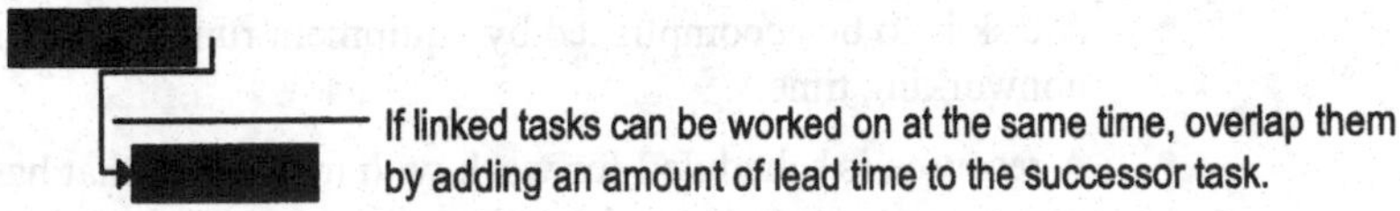

If linked tasks can be worked on at the same time, overlap them by adding an amount of lead time to the successor task.

To overlap or delay linked tasks

Task Information

1. On the **View Bar**, click **Gantt Chart**.
2. In the **Task Name** field, select the successor task to which you want to add lead or lag time, and then click **Task Information**.
3. Click the **Predecessors** tab.
4. In the **Lag** field for the predecessor, type the lead time or lag time you want, as a duration or as a percentage of the predecessor task duration.

   Type lead time as a negative number or as a negative percentage, and type lag time as a positive number or as a positive percentage.

Quickly add lead or lag time by double-clicking the link line.

Schedule with Task Calendars

For more information about project and resource working time calendars, see chapter 6.

Microsoft Project typically schedules tasks using the working times on the *project calendar* which shows the working days and hours for your entire project. Default working times are Monday through Friday, 8:00 A.M. to 12:00 P.M. and 1:00 P.M. to 5:00 P.M. You can customize the project calendar for a project's need, and create *resource calendars* to reflect working times for individual resources.

All tasks are scheduled according the project calendar unless a task calendar is applied.

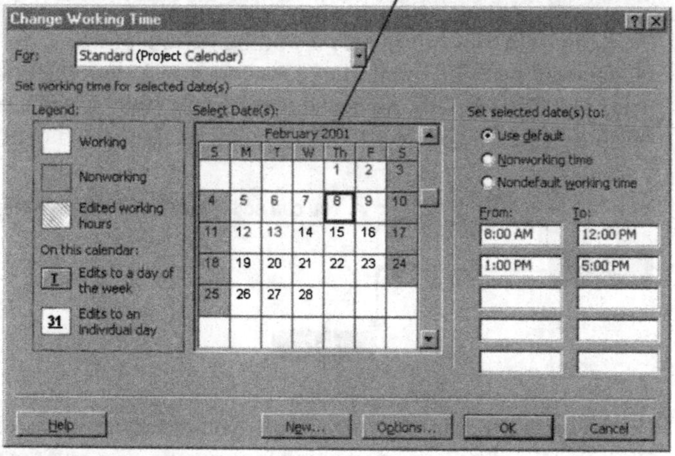

Occasionally, you might have a task that needs to be scheduled so differently from normal working times that it needs its own calendar. Examples include:

- A task is to be accomplished by equipment running during normal nonworking time.
- A resource is scheduled for work with machinery that has regularly scheduled preventive maintenance downtime during normal working time. You want to make

sure that the resource is scheduled for tasks on the machine only when the machine is available.

- A technician needs to work on a special task that can be done only on the weekend, which is normal nonworking time.

You can account for such working time exceptions for tasks by creating and assigning a *task calendar*.

With a task calendar, you can specify a work schedule for the task which might be either independent of or overlap with the project or assigned resource's calendar.

To set up a calendar for a task

1 On the **Tools** menu, click **Change Working Time**.
2 Click **New**.
3 In the **Name** box, type a name for your new calendar.
4 To begin with a default calendar, click **Create new base calendar**.

   To create a new calendar based on an existing calendar, click **Make a copy of**, and then click the calendar name in the calendar box.

5 Click **OK**.
6 Change the calendar to reflect the task scheduling you need:

   To change the calendar on specific days, select the days you want to change on the calendar.

   To select nonadjacent days, hold down CTRL and click the days.

   To select adjacent days, hold down SHIFT and click the first and last day for the calendar change.

   To change a day of the week for the entire calendar, click the abbreviation for the day on the top row of the calendar.

7 Under **Set selected date(s) to**, click **Use Default**, **Nonworking time**, or **Nondefault working time**.
8 To change **Nondefault working time**, type the times you want work to start in the **From** boxes and the times you want work to end in the **To** boxes.

To assign a calendar to a task

1 On the **View Bar**, click **Gantt Chart**.
2 In the **Task Name** field, select the task to which you want to assign a calendar.

Task Information

3 Click **Task Information**, and then click the **Advanced** tab.
4 In the **Calendar** box, click the calendar you want to use for the task.
5 Select the **Scheduling ignores resource calendars** check box to have the task calendar ignore the resource calendars of any assigned resources.

If you choose to have Microsoft Project ignore resource calendars, the task will be scheduled according to the task calendar, even if it's during nonworking time for the assigned resources.

If you choose not to ignore resource calendars, the task will be scheduled where the task calendar and resource calendar have overlapping working time.

Scheduling Tasks for Specific Dates

By now you understand that Microsoft Project typically uses task durations and dependencies to develop your schedule. While you can fine-tune the scheduling of tasks with techniques such as lead and lag time and task calendars, the scheduling is still flexible. By default, tasks are scheduled to be done as soon as possible within the limits of the durations, dependencies, and other exceptions you have specified.

But suppose you need tasks to start or finish by specific dates? While you want to keep your scheduling as flexible as possible, sometimes you need the schedule for a task to be governed by a specific date, such as the date of an event like a wedding or conference. To better control the start and finish dates for tasks, you can:

- Have tasks start and finish on or near specific dates.
- Apply different types of task constraints.
- Specify task deadlines that can serve as reminders rather than controls.
- Change the default start date for new tasks you're entering.

Start or Finish Tasks On or Near Specific Dates

You'll get a more effective, automated, and flexible schedule if you first enter durations, then link tasks, and then allow Microsoft Project to calculate the start and finish dates for each task. This approach lets Microsoft Project calculate dates from the outset. Later, Microsoft Project automatically recalculates dates as you update the schedule.

If you enter dates yourself, you might prevent Microsoft Project from automatically moving task dates forward or backward in time in response to changes in the schedule. In this case, you'd have to continually change the task dates yourself to keep the project current.

However, in certain very specific circumstances, you might really want a task to begin or end on or near a specific date, regardless of how dates for other tasks might change. An example of such a task is a conference to discuss project progress with a client. Regardless of how late or early tasks preceding the conference might be, the conference date needs to remain fixed. You can use an inflexible *date constraint* to tether a task to a specific date.

Every task has a constraint. There are three categories of constraints:

- Flexible constraints.
- Moderate constraints.
- Inflexible constraints.

A *flexible constraint* allows a task's dates to change as the schedule changes. The default constraint, As Soon As Possible, is an example of a flexible constraint. When first created, all tasks in a project scheduled from the start date are assigned the As Soon As Possible constraint. Likewise, all tasks in a project scheduled from the finish date are assigned the As Late As Possible constraint.

With the As Soon As Possible constraint, a task is scheduled to begin as soon as the schedule allows. For instance, suppose a task starts 2 days earlier than planned and it's linked to a successor task with a finish-to-start link. Microsoft Project reschedules this task to start "as soon as possible." In this case, that means 2 days earlier also.

A task that's scheduled to start as soon as possible is flexible: its start and finish date can change if other tasks start or finish earlier or later than planned.

On the other hand, an *inflexible constraint* ties a task to a specific date. The Must Start On and Must Finish On constraints are the two inflexible constraints. Apply an inflexible constraint for those very specific instances when you need a task to start or finish on a particular date.

Between the flexible and inflexible constraints are *moderate constraints*. These constraints, such as Start No Earlier Than or Finish No Later Than, provide date guidelines but can be scheduled with more flexibility than a Must Finish On constraint. A moderate constraint allows a task's dates to change until the specified date and condition are reached.

By entering task durations and dependencies and by keeping the default constraint of As Soon As Possible (or As Late As Possible), you give your schedule maximum flexibility and make it easier to work with. You allow Microsoft Project to automatically recalculate task start and finish dates as the schedule is updated. Only when you definitely need to model a real-world or external date on a task should you apply an inflexible or moderate date constraint.

Types of Task Constraints

Microsoft Project features eight constraint types. These are described in the following table and are ranked in order from most flexible to most inflexible.

Constraint	Flexibility	Description
As Soon As Possible (ASAP)	Flexible	Starts a task as soon as links and other factors in the schedule allow. This is the default for all tasks in a project scheduled from the project start date.
As Late As Possible (ALAP)	Flexible	Starts a task as late as possible without delaying the project finish date. This is the default for all tasks in a project scheduled from the project finish date.
Start No Earlier Than (SNET)	Moderate	Starts a task on or after the date you enter. For projects scheduled from the start date, this constraint is applied when you type a start date for a task.
Finish No Earlier Than (FNET)	Moderate	Finishes a task on or after the date you enter. For projects scheduled from the start date, this constraint is applied when you type a finish date for a task.
Start No Later Than (SNLT)	Moderate	Starts a task on or before the date you enter. For projects scheduled from the finish date, this constraint is applied when you type a start date for a task.
Finish No Later Than (FNLT)	Moderate	Finishes a task on or before the date you enter. For projects scheduled from the finish date, this constraint is applied when you type a finish date for a task.
Must Start On (MSO)	Inflexible	Starts a task on the date you enter.
Must Finish On (MFO)	Inflexible	Finishes a task on the date you enter.

Change a Task Constraint

With a flexible constraint (As Soon As Possible or As Late As Possible) applied to a task, Microsoft Project can recalculate the task start and finish dates if the schedule changes. If you apply an inflexible constraint (Must Start On or Must Finish On) to a task, then Microsoft Project will calculate the schedule to exactly hit the task's dates. If you apply a moderate constraint (such as Start No Later Than or Finish No Earlier Than), Microsoft Project will recalculate the task's dates only until the specified date is reached.

You can also change the default constraint options. These options specify the start time and end time for any date constraints you specify. If you specify a Must Finish On constraint for August 22, these options can specify whether this means 8:00 A.M. or 5:00 P.M, for example.

To constrain a task to start or finish on or near a specific date

1 On the **View Bar**, click **Gantt Chart**.

Task Information

2 In the **Task Name** field, select the task you want, and then click **Task Information**.

The **Task Information** dialog box appears.

3 Click the **Advanced** tab.

4 In the **Constraint type** box, click a constraint type.

5 If you selected a constraint other than **As Late As Possible** or **As Soon As Possible**, type or select a constraint date in the **Constraint date** box.

In a project scheduled from the project start date, if you type a start date for a task or drag a Gantt bar to change the start date, Microsoft Project sets a Start No Earlier Than (SNET) constraint based on the new start date. If you type a finish date for a task, Microsoft Project automatically assigns a Finish No Earlier Than (FNET) constraint. Likewise, in a project scheduled from the project finish date, if you type a start date for a task or drag a Gantt bar to change the start date, Microsoft Project sets a Start No Later Than (SNLT) constraint based on the new start date. If you type a finish date for a task, Microsoft Project automatically assigns a Finish No Later Than (FNLT) constraint.

To change constraint options

1 On the **Tools** menu, click **Options**.

2 Click **Calendar**.

3 In the **Default start time** box, specify the time you want to be scheduled for start date constraints such as Must Start On, Start No Earlier Than, or Start No Later Than.

4 In the **Default finish time** box, specify the time you want to be scheduled for finish date constraints such as Must Finish On, Finish No Earlier Than, or Finish No Later Than.

Resolve Scheduling Conflicts

If there's ever a conflict among the requirements of a task's duration, dependencies, and inflexible constraint, you'll see a message that presents choices for resolving the conflict.

You can also choose whether the constraint or task dependency typically takes precedence in the event of a conflict.

For example, Task A is a 5-day task with a finish-to-start link to Task B, a 3-day task with a Must Finish On constraint on day 8. What would you want to happen if Task A runs late, taking 7 days? Do you want the Gantt Chart to show Task B still finishing on day 8 and honoring the constraint? Or do you want Task B to maintain the finish-to-start link, which would mean the task would now be scheduled for finishing on day 10?

You can control the typical scheduling under these conditions with the **Tasks will always honor their constraint dates** check box.

To handle scheduling conflicts between dependencies and constraints

1. On the **Tools** menu, click **Options**.
2. Click the **Schedule** tab.
3. Select or clear the **Tasks will always honor their constraint dates** check box.
   By default, this check box is selected.

Specify Task Deadlines

Deadline

Suppose you want to keep a task deadline in mind but you don't want to lock your schedule by setting an inflexible constraint. Instead, you can set a *deadline*. Microsoft Project continues to update the schedule as needed, keeps track of deadline dates, shows them on the Gantt Chart, and displays a deadline indicator if a task finishes after its deadline.

To specify a task deadline

1. On the **View Bar**, click **Gantt Chart**.
2. In the **Task Name** field, click the task for which you want to set a deadline.
3. Click **Task Information** and then click the **Advanced** tab.
4. Under **Constrain task**, type the deadline date in the **Deadline** box.

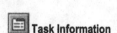

Task Information

Change the Default Start Date for New Tasks

When you first add a task to a project scheduled from the start date, by default, Microsoft Project sets the task's start date as the project start date. If you want, however, you can change the default start date for new tasks to the current date—that is, the date when you create the new task.

If you do this, tasks you entered before you made the change aren't affected (their default start date is still the project start date). The same holds true if you change the default start date for tasks back to the project start date.

To change the default start date for new tasks

1. On the **Tools** menu, click **Options**, and then click the **Schedule** tab.
2. In the **New tasks** box, click **Start on Current Date**.
   This setting causes a Start No Earlier Than constraint to be placed on any new tasks you create, with the date being the date you create the task.

6

Assigning Resources to Tasks

Resources are the people, equipment, and materials required to accomplish project tasks and goals. You can assign resources to the tasks in your project, indicating specifically who or what will be responsible for the completion of the task.

There are two types of resources: *work resources* and *material resources*. Work resources are the people and equipment that accomplish the work of a task. Material resources are the consumable supplies that are used up in the performance on a task. Examples include concrete, steel, and soil.

You can manage a project and achieve your goals with a plan that contains just tasks and no assigned resources. However, identifying and assigning resources gives you more information and therefore more control. It also allows you to collect more accurate cost data, as most costs in a typical project are associated with resources. And if resource management is an important aspect of your project management, which is increasingly the case for many project managers, you'll definitely want to use Microsoft Project to create your resource list and assign resources to tasks. By including resources in your project plan, you can:

- See who is working on which task and when.
- Fine-tune task duration by assigning more or fewer resources to a task. Microsoft Project can calculate a task's duration based on the number of resources assigned to it and whether they're working on the task full-time or part-time.
- Identify resources who are overworked or underworked, then distribute the workload more evenly.
- Track the cost of each resource throughout the project, and therefore the cost of specific tasks or phases of the project.
- Keep project scope, time, budget, and resources in balance. For example, if the project scope increases because your client wants to add another room to the house but still wants the house completed by the original deadline, you can compensate by adding more resources.

You can also employ workgroup capabilities using e-mail instead of the Web. See "Exchanging Information with Resources Using E-Mail" in chapter 10.

If you use Microsoft Project Central, you can use the Web to more effectively automate the resource management aspects of your project. Resources in your workgroup can create detailed tasks, estimate durations, and send them to you for incorporation into your project. You can send new task assignments to resources. You can receive task progress updates and status reports. You can more accurately track the progress of all the resources and identify costs and any possible overallocations. For more information about workgroup capabilities with Microsoft Project Central and the Web, see chapter 11.

The first step toward using resources effectively in your project plan is to create a *resource list*, which contains the name of the resources available to your project. If you want, you can also include additional details about the resource, such as cost, skill set, and availability.

The next step is to set the calendars specifying the working days and times when your resources are available to be assigned to tasks. You set working and nonworking days and hours in a *project calendar*, which shows the working days and hours for your entire plan. You can also create *resource calendars* for the working days and hours for each individual resource. Microsoft Project uses the information from these calendars to calculate task schedules and durations.

The third and final step is to assign those resources to tasks.

You can assign one or more resources to a single task. You can also assign resources part-time to a task. After making the assignment, you can later make changes by adding, removing, or replacing resources as needed. How resources are assigned, and whether they are work or material resources, significantly affect how tasks are scheduled.

Assembling Your Resources

Whether or not you include resources in Microsoft Project, as a project manager, you need to estimate the types and quantities of resources you'll need to accomplish the project goals and individual tasks. You determine what kinds of people, equipment, and materials you need. You also calculate the quantities of resources based on the tasks and the project duration. You typically need accurate task duration estimates to reliably estimate resource needs.

After you make these resource estimates, you can build them into your project by creating the resource list. If necessary, use placeholder names for those specific resources not yet identified.

Your Microsoft Project resource list can be a simple list of names or roles. However, if you want to track detailed resource information, you can add vital information regarding resource costs, availability, and more.

Estimate Resource Needs

When you use resources in your project plan, think about the needs of the individual tasks as well as the needs of the project. To satisfy the needs of an individual task, you'll want to assign resources with the ability to accomplish the tasks swiftly and skillfully. You do this by matching resource skills to task requirements.

At the same time, to satisfy the needs of the project as a whole, be sure to assign enough resources to accomplish your project goals on time. Note that the number of resources needed to complete the project on schedule might change as the project progresses.

So, how many work resources does your project require, and what skills do those resources need? Will you be using material resources? If so, what quantities are needed, and what characteristics should the materials have? You can best answer these questions by estimating the resource needs of each task. One way to analyze the resource requirements of a task is to check similar tasks from past projects. Another way is to develop accurate task duration estimates, then figure resource requirements based on those durations. Or, you can ask someone knowledgeable about the task to estimate the resources needed.

When estimating work resource needs, consider the following questions:

- What skills are required to accomplish the task?
- What level of skill is required to achieve the desired level of quality?
- How many resources are needed to accomplish the task in the time allotted?
- Can a resource work on more than one task, or perhaps more than one kind of task?
- What is your budget, and how are resource choices affected by cost?
- During what point of the project are the resources needed, and when are they available?

When estimating material resource needs, consider these questions:

- What materials are required to accomplish the task?
- What manufacture, quality, or grade of material is needed to accomplish the task as well as fulfill the goals of the project?
- How much material is needed?
- Is material dependent on task duration?
- Are the same materials needed for different tasks?
- How are your material choices affected by your budget?
- When are the materials needed, and how long does the procurement process take?

As you estimate resource needs, you might find that breaking a task into smaller tasks improves your ability to predict the resources needed for the task. If so, once again enter the new tasks, estimate the durations, and add the appropriate relationships with other tasks so the new tasks fit appropriately into the schedule.

Create a Resource List for Your Project

After you've determined which resources you need and how many, add them to your project plan by creating a resource list. A resource list tells you who is on your project team and includes important information about your resources that indicate how they are to be scheduled. If you like, this can also include information about the resources' costs and skills.

Although you can add resources one at a time as you assign them to tasks, it's more efficient to first add all resources to your plan at once, then assign them to tasks. In addition, with the complete resource list, you can see all your resources before assigning them, making it easy to pick the most qualified resource for each task.

Your resource list should include the name of the resource, which can be a person, a piece of equipment, materials, or a group of interchangeable resources, such as painters. For work resources, the resource list should also specify whether a resource is available full-time or part-time.

If resources with the same skills are going to work together on the same task, you can group them into a resource set, then give this set a name that represents all resources in the set. For example, the resource name "Painters" could represent two or more painters.

To create a resource list

1 On the **View Bar**, click **Resource Sheet**.
2 On the **View** menu, point to **Table**, and then click **Entry**.
3 In the **Resource Name** field, type a resource name.
4 In the **Type** field, indicate whether the material is a work resource or material resource.
5 If it's a material resource, complete the **Label** field to indicate the unit of measurement for the material—for example, tons, yards, or linear feet.
6 If you want to track resource costs, enter cost information in the cost fields.
7 Change the default information in the remaining fields as appropriate.
8 Repeat steps 3–6 for each resource you're adding.

For more information about entering cost information, see "Setting Costs" in chapter 7.

Enter the names, or even just placeholder names, to represent your resource list.

Indicate whether the resource is a work or material resource.

	ⓘ	Resource Name	Type	Material Label	Initials	Group	Max. Units	Std. Rate
1		Sean Davis (Owner)	Work		SD		100%	$0.00/hr
2		Jean Aaronson (Architect)	Work		JA		100%	$0.00/hr
3		Richard Brooks (General Contractor)	Work		RB		100%	$0.00/hr
4		Mortgage lender	Work				100%	$0.00/hr
5		Concrete contractor	Work				100%	$0.00/hr
6		Concrete	Material	ton				$0.00
7		Finish carpentry contractor	Work				100%	$0.00/hr
8		Lumber	Material	linear foot				$0.00
9		Fencing contractor	Work				100%	$0.00/hr
10		Fencing	Material	linear foot				$0.00

Completing the cost fields can help you track costs throughout the project.

You can build your resource list from resources in your *resource pool*, thereby making it possible for you to use the same resources in different projects. For more information about setting up and using a resource pool, see "Sharing Resources Among Projects" in chapter 17.

Set Resource Availability

In contrast with max units, assignment units designate the amount of time a resource has to devote to a specific assignment, based on the resource's working time calendar.

You can specify how much time work resources have to devote to your project in relation to what is considered full-time for the resource. This amount of time is called *max units*. You can also specify the exact dates when work resources are available to your project. This is referred to as *resource availability*.

If you're entering information for a work resource, use the Max. Units field in the Resource Sheet to enter the percentage of time that this resource is available.

By default, Microsoft Project enters 100% into this field, indicating a single full-time resource. For a resource that represents a set of several full-time resources, enter a multiple of 100%. For example, for three full-time units of a particular resource, type 300%.

Likewise, for a part-time resource, enter the part-time percentage. For example, type 75% for a resource that works 30 hours of a 40-hour workweek, or type 50% for a half-time resource. Later, when you assign resources to tasks, this part-time unit percentage is used as the default for assignment units.

100% max units indicates that the resource is available full-time. This is the default.

A max units percentage less than 100% represents a resource available part-time.

		Resource Name	Type	Material Label	Initials	Group	Max. Units
1		Sean Davis (Owner)	Work		SD		100%
2		Jean Aaronson (Architect)	Work		JA		50%
3		Richard Brooks (General Contractor)	Work		RB		100%
4		Carpenters	Work		C		400%
5		Roofers	Work		R		300%

A max units percentage greater than 100% indicates multiple resources grouped into a set.

To adjust max units for a work resource

1. On the **View Bar**, click **Resource Sheet**.
2. On the **View** menu, point to **Table**, and then click **Entry**.
3. Select the work resource whose max units you want to adjust.
4. In the **Max. Units** field, type the max units for the selected resource.

If a resource is going to start or finish work on the project on dates different from the project start or finish dates, you can specify resource availability dates. You can also indicate changing max units for a resource throughout the life of the project.

For example, suppose you are managing a product development project and you refer to your process engineers as a resource set called "Process Engineers." If you have two engineers starting in January, four engineers starting in April, and just one starting in September, you can set the max units for this resource set as 200%, 400%, and 100% for each of those dates.

Enter the dates for the first level of availability here.

Enter the max unit availability for the indicated dates here.

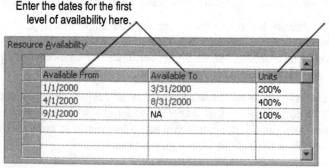

Resource Availability

Available From	Available To	Units
1/1/2000	3/31/2000	200%
4/1/2000	8/31/2000	400%
9/1/2000	NA	100%

You can also change the max units for a single resource if the resource switches between full-time and part-time work on this project. For example, suppose you know that Jean will be available only one day per week until August, when she becomes available to work full-time on your project. You can set her availability as 20% from the project beginning, then as 100% starting in August.

Use the Resource Availability table to indicate when a resource changes the level of availability on the project.

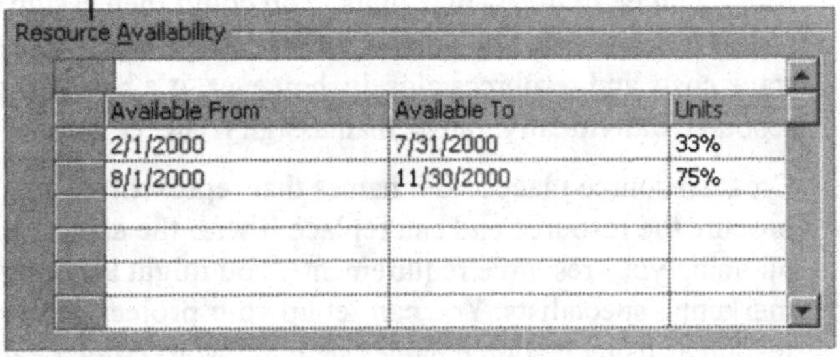

Available From	Available To	Units
2/1/2000	7/31/2000	33%
8/1/2000	11/30/2000	75%

You can also open the Resource Information dialog box by double-clicking the resource in the Resource Sheet.

To set work resource availability

1 On the **View Bar**, click **Resource Sheet**.

2 Select the work resource whose availability you want to adjust.

Resource Information

3 Click **Resource Information**.

4 In the **Available From** field, enter the date the selected resource is to begin at the amount of max units availability indicated in the **Units** field.

For example, if the resource is to start February 1, enter this in the field. Leaving "NA" in the field indicates that the resource is available from the project start date.

You can either type the date or pick it in the dropdown calendar.

5 In the **Available To** field, type the date the selected resource is to finish at the availability indicated in the **Units** field.

For example, if the resource is leaving the project or changing to a different max units availability on July 31, enter this in the **Available To** field. Leaving "NA" in the field indicates that the resource is available at this level until the project finish date.

If you're entering a series of changing max units, you can enter the dates in the Available To fields. Microsoft Project will automatically fill in the dates for the Available From fields.

6 In the **Units** field, type the amount of max units availability for the indicated period of time.

For example, if the resource is working at 33% from February through July, enter the dates and then enter 33% in the **Units** field. If the resource is then working at 75% from August through November, enter 11/30 and 75% in the second row of the **Resource Availability** table.

Organize Resource Categories

Microsoft Project provides three methods for organizing categories of resources. You can:

- Create resource names that refer to the job function rather than specific resource names. You can then assign all or part of this resource set to individual tasks. For example, suppose you create a resource name of "Painters" to represent a set of four painters, or 400% max units. You could then assign 100% of "Painters" to a task if it needs only one painter, or 400% if it needs four, and so on. If you want to track costs and resources closely, however, it's better to name and assign each resource individually, rather than assign resource sets.
- Create resource placeholder names that represent the job function until you hire or procure the resource and can replace it with the actual name. For example, when planning your resource requirements, you might know that you need four marketing specialists. You can set up your project and even start assigning resources using resource names such as "Marketing 1" and "Marketing 2." When you hire the specialists, you can replace "Marketing 1" with "Jean Aaronson" and "Marketing 2" with "Richard Brooks."
- Apply the Entry table to the Resource Sheet, then enter group names in the Group field. This is typically used to provide more information about the resource, such as the resource's department—for example, Marketing or Engineering. The resource group can also be a cost code or skill set. The resource group is typically used to track costs or administrative data for certain categories of resources. You can use names in the Group field for sorting, grouping, or filtering the resources by group name. For more information, see chapter 12. You cannot assign resource group names to tasks.

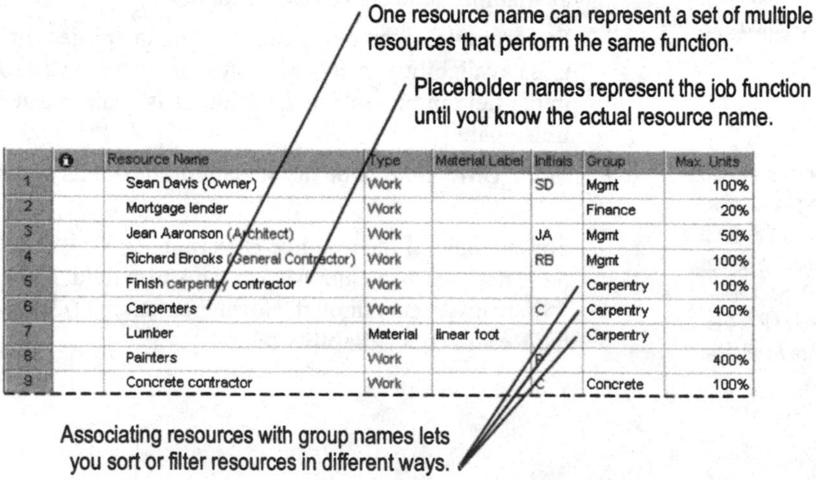
One resource name can represent a set of multiple resources that perform the same function.
Placeholder names represent the job function until you know the actual resource name.
Associating resources with group names lets you sort or filter resources in different ways.

		Resource Name	Type	Material Label	Initials	Group	Max. Units
1		Sean Davis (Owner)	Work		SD	Mgmt	100%
2		Mortgage lender	Work			Finance	20%
3		Jean Aaronson (Architect)	Work		JA	Mgmt	50%
4		Richard Brooks (General Contractor)	Work		RB	Mgmt	100%
5		Finish carpentry contractor	Work			Carpentry	100%
6		Carpenters	Work		C	Carpentry	400%
7		Lumber	Material	linear foot		Carpentry	
8		Painters	Work		P		400%
9		Concrete contractor	Work		C	Concrete	100%

Setting Working Time for Resources

To calculate the schedules of tasks in your project, Microsoft Project needs to know when resources are available for work. If your resources are available Monday through Friday from 8:00 A.M. through 5:00 P.M. only, you wouldn't want Microsoft Project to schedule them for work at 9:00 P.M. on Saturday night. Likewise, if Richard resource doesn't work on Tuesdays, or is taking a two-week vacation in August, you'll probably want to prevent his tasks from being scheduled during those days.

You use *working time calendars* to indicate the working and nonworking days and hours of your project, groups of resources, and individual resources. In the calendars, you specify the workdays, lunch breaks, vacations, holidays, and other days off.

Use working time calendars to set the working time for the project as a whole, for individual resources, or for specialized groups of resources.

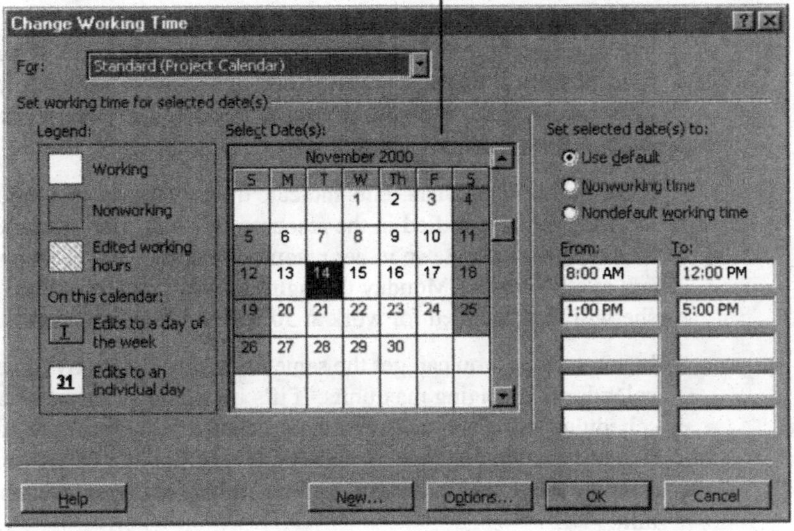

Microsoft Project uses these working time calendars to calculate task schedules. For example, suppose an 8-hour task is scheduled to begin first thing Monday morning. If Joe, a part-timer whose resource calendar indicates he works 4 hours per day, is assigned to the task, the task will span 2 days and finish on Tuesday. But if Mary, scheduled to work 8 hours per day, is given the assignment, the task will span 1 day and finish at the end of Monday.

Because material resources are not affected by working and nonworking time, they are not associated with resource calendars.

There is a third type of calendar: the task calendar, which specifies when a task should be scheduled, if different from the project calendar. For more information, see "Schedule with Task Calendars" in chapter 5.

The *project calendar* initially determines how all tasks are scheduled. The *resource calendar* is the set of working and nonworking time specific to an individual work resource. You can use a resource calendar to specify a resource's vacation, personal days, and so on. The project calendar and resource calendars are based on a calendar template: the *base calendar*.

If you create a task without assigning resources, it will be scheduled according to the working time indicated in the project calendar. If you assign a resource that has different working time in the associated resource calendar, the task schedule will change according to the limitations indicated in that resource calendar.

For example, suppose the project calendar designates February 10 as a workday, but Jean's resource calendar shows that she's taking a vacation day on February 10. If Jean is assigned to a 2-day task that begins on February 9, then Microsoft Project schedules the task to be completed on February 11, not on February 10.

Working Times and Max Units

The resource calendar and max units work hand in hand. If a resource does not work on specific days or times, it's best to edit the resource calendar for that nonworking time. This ensures that the resource is not scheduled for work on days (or hours) that he or she is not available.

On the other hand, max units indicate the percentage of availability based on the working times specified in the resource calendar. For example, if Jean does not work on Fridays, you indicate so in her resource calendar. 100% max units for Jean now means full availability for Monday through Thursday. If you change Jean's max units to 50%, she will be scheduled for work at 50% of the four-day work week.

In some cases, you can get the same or similar results by either changing the resource calendar or changing max units. If it's important to know when exactly work is being scheduled and when tasks will finish, then edit the resource calendar. If you just want to indicate that the resource is working at a percentage of full time, then edit max units. Another advantage to specifying max units is that they become the default assignment unit.

Be sure not to set the resource calendar and max units to do the same thing. For example, suppose Richard works on the project on Wednesdays only, and you edit the resource calendar to designate the other days as nonworking time. If you then also edit Richard's max units to be 20%, you'll inadvertently specify that he is available only for 20% of his working day on Wednesday—that is, 2 hours per week.

Change Your Project's Working Days and Hours

By default, the Standard base calendar is the calendar template on which your project calendar is based. According to the Standard calendar, a full working day is 8 hours long, lasting from 8:00 A.M. to 5:00 P.M., with a 1-hour break from 12:00 noon to 1:00 P.M. Every Monday through Friday are working days, and every Saturday and Sunday are nonworking days.

Although the Standard base calendar is the default project calendar, you can base your project calendar on any base calendar you want. The Night Shift and 24 Hours calendars are provided with Microsoft Project, or you can create your own base calendar to become your project calendar.

The base calendars provided with Microsoft Project do not include holidays. Because of this, it's best to modify your project calendar to show all your company holidays and any other shared time off.

If you use the Standard base calendar as your project calendar, any changes you make can affect all your project resources because, by default, all resource calendars are also based on the Standard calendar. You can modify the resource calendar settings to reflect the actual working time of each resource.

If your resources don't work specific shifts, make sure that the workday's start and finish hours equal the total number of hours they work each day. For instance, if a resource works 10 hours per day, you might specify start and finish times of 7:00 A.M. and 6:00 P.M., with a 1-hour break.

To set the project calendar

1 On the **Project** menu, click **Project Information**.

2 In the **Calendar** box, select the base calendar you want to use as your project calendar.

To change project calendar details

1 On the **Tools** menu, click **Change Working Time**.

2 Select a date on the calendar.

3 To change a day of the week for the entire calendar, select the day heading at the top of the calendar.

4 Click **Use default, Nonworking time**, or **Nondefault working time**.

5 If you clicked **Nondefault working time** in step 3, type the times you want work to start in the **From** boxes and the times you want work to end in the To boxes.

Clicking the Options button in the Change Working Time dialog box opens the Calendar Options dialog box. These options do not affect the project calendar or resource calendars. They affect only how Microsoft Project converts the durations into related time amounts used throughout your project and how constraint times and dates are set.

Create a Base Calendar for a Special Work Schedule

Base calendars are like calendar templates. The project calendar and resource calendars are based on a base calendar that you select, modify, or create. Microsoft Project comes with three base calendars: Standard, Night Shift, and 24 Hours. By default, the project calendar is based on the Standard base calendar. This is the calendar reflecting traditional working days and times: Monday through Friday, 8:00 A.M. through 5:00 P.M., with a one-hour lunch break.

In turn, the project calendar becomes the basis for all resource calendars. However, you can change the base calendar for each resource. You can create your own base calendar and assign it to different groups of resources, or even make it the project calendar. In fact, you can have several base calendars, one for each different set of working time. For example, you can have one base calendar each for a day shift, a swing shift, and a night shift. Or, the electricians might have a different schedule from the painters. When groups of resources have different schedules, you can create a base calendar for each resource group. Then you base each resource calendar on a new base calendar.

When you change a base calendar that's already assigned to resources, that change is transmitted to the resource calendars that are based on it. For example, suppose Richard's and Jean's calendars are based on the Electricians base calendar. If you set March 15 to a nonworking day in the Electricians calendar, then March 15 also becomes a nonworking day in Richard's and Jean's individual resource calendars.

To create a base calendar

1. On the **Tools** menu, click **Change Working Time**.
2. Click **New**.
3. In the **Name** box, type a name for your new base calendar.

   If you want to begin with a default calendar, click **Create new base calendar**.

   If you want to create a new calendar based on an existing calendar, click **Make a copy of**, and then click the calendar name in the calendar box.
4. Click **OK**.
5. On the calendar, select the days you want to change.

   To change a day of the week for the entire calendar, select the day heading at the top of the calendar.
6. Click **Use default, Nonworking time**, or **Nondefault working time**.
7. If you clicked **Nondefault working time** in step 6, type the times you want work to start in the **From** boxes and the times you want work to end in the **To** boxes.

To quickly remove all the changes you've made to a calendar

1 On the **Tools** menu, click **Change Working Time**.

2 In the **For** box, select the base or resource calendar you want to restore to its original state.

3 Select all of the day headings on the calendar.

4 Click **Use default**.

Assign a Base Calendar to a Resource

By default, the calendar for each resource in your plan is based on the Standard base calendar. If you've created a new base calendar to accommodate the working schedules for certain resources, you'll need to assign the new calendar to those resources.

To assign a base calendar to a resource

1 On the **View Bar**, click **Resource Sheet**.

2 In the **Resource Name** field, select the resource to which you want to assign a calendar.

Resource Information

3 Click **Resource Information**, and then click the **Working Time** tab.

4 In the **Base Calendar** box, click the calendar you want to assign to the resource.

Change Working Time for a Resource

Resources on a project often share the same working days, nonworking days, and holidays. So you don't have to specify these shared working and nonworking days for each resource, each resource calendar inherits the same set of working and nonworking days from its base calendar.

However, in many projects, one resource's working days and hours differ from the working time of other resources in the group. For example, people usually take vacations at different times. When resources have different schedules, you can modify the working time in each resource calendar. Whenever you add a resource, Microsoft Project creates a corresponding resource calendar.

To change working time for a resource

1 On the **Tools** menu, click **Change Working Time**.

2 In the **For** box, click the resource whose calendar you want to change.

3 On the calendar, select the days you want to change.

To change a day of the week for the entire calendar, select the day heading at the top of the calendar.

4 Click **Use default, Nonworking time**, or **Nondefault working time**.

5 If you clicked **Nondefault working time** in step 4, type the times you want work to start in the **From** boxes and the times you want work to end in the **To** boxes.

Assigning Resources to Tasks

Now that you've created your resource list and set up the working time calendars, you're ready to assign those resources to tasks. You can assign a single resource to a task, assign several resources to a task, or assign full-time work resources to a task part-time. You can assign both a work resource and material resource to a task. You can also specify whether material resource consumption is to be based on task duration.

Once you make assignments, there's nothing to stop you from making needed changes. You can always replace one resource with another, if necessary, add additional resources, or remove resources from an assignment.

If you need tight controls on when resources work on their assignments, you can control the assignment start and finish dates. You can even specify changing levels of work across the span of an assignment by specifying *work contours*. You can specify a ramp-up contour, for example, for a task in which you expect fewer hours to be worked near the start of a task and increasingly more hours worked as the task progresses.

About Assignment Units

When you assign a work resource or material resource to a task, you need to indicate how much of that resource is to be devoted to this assignment. The mechanism for doing this is the *assignment unit*.

Assignment Units for Work Resources

Learn more about resource overallocation in "Balancing the Workload" in chapter 8.

For work resources, *assignment units* designate the percentage of time a resource has to devote to a specific assignment, based on the resource's working time calendar. This is distinguished from *max units*, which indicate the amount of time a work resource has to devote to your project, also based on the resource calendar. If a resource's max units are less than 100%, the default assignment units is equal to the resource's max units. If you indicate assignment units higher than the resource's max units, the resource will be *overallocated*.

Max units designate the percentage of time a resource is available to the project as a whole.

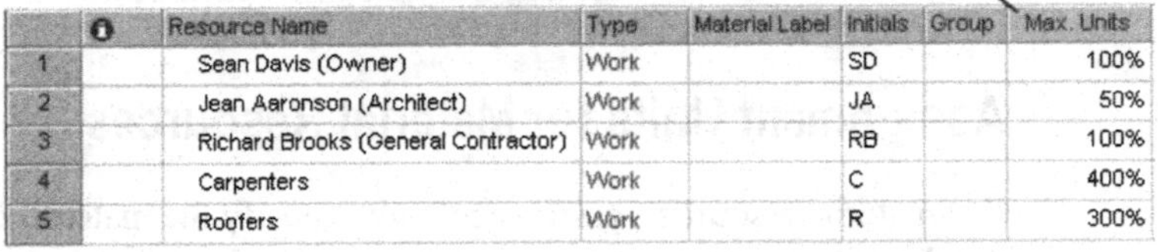

		Resource Name	Type	Material Label	Initials	Group	Max. Units
1		Sean Davis (Owner)	Work		SD		100%
2		Jean Aaronson (Architect)	Work		JA		50%
3		Richard Brooks (General Contractor)	Work		RB		100%
4		Carpenters	Work		C		400%
5		Roofers	Work		R		300%

Assignment units designate the percentage of time a resource is to spend on an assignment.

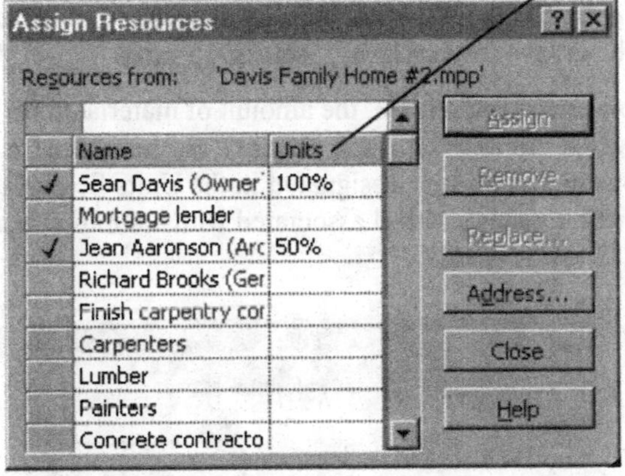

Typically, the Standard base calendar is used for the project and resource calendars. A resource at 100% max units is therefore available 40 hours per week. In this typical case, if you assign the resource at 100% assignment units to a 40-hour task, the resource will be scheduled to work on this task 8 hours per day, and the task will be completed after 5 days.

But you can also assign a full-time resource to work part-time on a task. In this same typical case, if you assign the full-time resource to 50% assignment units on a 40-hour task, the resource will be scheduled to work on this task 4 hours per day, and the task will be completed after 10 days.

This changes if the resource calendar is set for less (or more) working time than the typical 40-hour workweek. For example, if you set the resource's working time calendar to a 20-hour workweek, 100% max units will mean 20 hours a week maximum availability, and 100% assignment units will mean that a 40-hour task will span 10 days rather than 5 days.

Also, suppose you have created a set of multiple resources—for example, Programmers at 400%, meaning four full-time equivalent programmers. If the max units for a resource are 100% or higher, the default assignment units are 100%. When you assign a set of resources to a task, 100% units means you've assigned one full-time equivalent resource from that set to work on the task full-time, 200% means you've assigned two full-time equivalent resources from the set, and so on. This could mean two full-time resources, or one full-time and two half-time resources.

Assignment Units for Material Resources

For material resources, assignment units specify the material consumption rate, or the number or rate of units of material being used for the assignment. There are two types of material assignment units: *fixed consumption rate* and *variable consumption rate.*

With fixed consumption rate, the amount of material to be used for the assigned task remains constant, even if the task duration should change. Fixed consumption rate is designated in the Units field of the Assign Resource dialog box with the amount of material to be used—for example, 5 tons or 15 yards.

With variable consumption rate, the amount of material to be used is based on time. This means if the duration of a task changes, the amount of material used also changes. Variable consumption rate is designated in the Units field of the Assign Resource dialog box with a material label associated with a duration amount—for example, 2 tons/day or 10 yards/week.

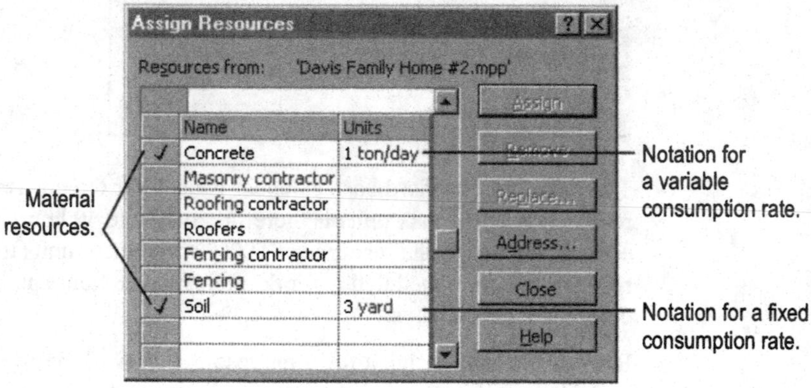

Assign Resources to a Task

When you assign resources to tasks, you allow Microsoft Project to adjust task durations based on the number of resources assigned, keep track of task assignments, calculate task and resource costs, and more. Assigning resources gives you added control over project variables.

You can assign more than one resource to a task and specify whether a resource works full-time or part-time on the task by using assignment units. By default, Microsoft Project assigns each resource at 100% units. If a resource represents a set of resources, then you might want to change the units to reflect the number of resources you're assigning from the set.

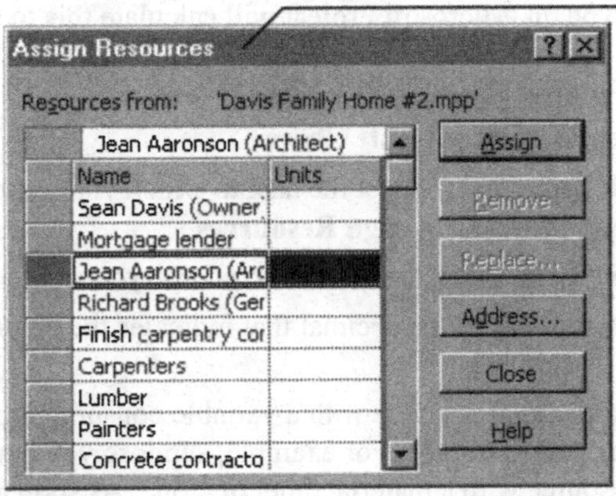

Use the Assign Resources dialog box to assign, add, remove, and replace resources.

The number of resources you assign to a task can affect the task duration. For more information about effort-driven scheduling and task types, see chapter 8, "Fine-Tuning Your Project."

When you assign a resource to a task, the name of the resource appears next to the Gantt bar that represents that task.

To assign a work resource to a task

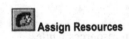

1 On the **View Bar**, click **Gantt Chart**.

Assign Resources

2 In the **Task Name** field, select the task to which you want to assign a resource, and then click **Assign Resources**.

3 In the **Name** field, select the work resource you want to assign to the task or click **Address** to select a work resource from your e-mail address book.

To assign several resources at the same time, select them using either SHIFT for adjacent resources or CTRL for nonadjacent resources.

If a resource has max units of less than 100%, the assignment Units field defaults to the same as the resource's max units.

If a resource has max units of more than 100%, the assignment Units field defaults to 100%.

4 In the **Units** field, type the percentage that indicates the amount of working time you want the resource to spend on the task.

To assign a resource part-time, type a percentage less than 100—for example, 20% for a resource working 8 hours of a 40-hour workweek, or 50% for a resource working half-time.

To assign resources that are part of a multiple resource set, such as "Painters" or "Engineers," indicate the amount of this resource that should be assigned to this task. For example, to assign two full-time engineers from a resource set having 400% max units, enter 200%.

5 Click **Assign**.

A check mark to the left of the Name field indicates that the resource is assigned to the selected task.

If you know that you want to assign a certain amount of time to a task rather than a percentage, first assign the resource at 100%. Then, in the Units field, type the number and the time unit. For example, suppose you want to assign Richard to just 5 hours of a 25-hour task; type 5h. Microsoft Project will calculate this to be 20% assignment units.

To assign a material resource to a task

1 On the **View Bar**, click **Gantt Chart**.

Assign Resources

2 In the **Task Name** field, select the task to which you want to assign a material resource, and then click **Assign Resources**.

3 In the **Name** field, select the material resource you want to assign to the task.

4 In the **Units** field, type the decimal that indicates the amount of material to be consumed on this task.

To assign a material resource with a variable consumption rate, type the quantity of material per period of time. For example, suppose you have designated steel as a material resource with a material label of "ton." As soon as you assign steel to a task, the **Units** field is completed with "1 ton." In the **Units** field, type 2/day to indicate that 2 tons of steel will be consumed for each day of the assigned task duration.

To assign a material resource with a fixed consumption rate, type the total quantity of material to be consumed for this task regardless of its duration.

5 Click **Assign**.

A check mark to the left of the Name field indicates that the resource is assigned to the selected task.

You can keep the Resource Assignment dialog box open and assign resources while you work with the Gantt Chart and other task views.

The Resource Assignment dialog box includes the names of all resources you set up in the Resource Sheet. As you work in the Gantt Chart or other task views, you can add new resource names as you go. As you assign the new resource, it's automatically added to the Resource Sheet. When convenient, you can add necessary resource information details. You can double-click the resource name in the Resource Assignment dialog box to open the Resource Information dialog box. Or, you can return to the Resource Sheet.

To add new work resources while assigning them

1 On the **View Bar**, click **Gantt Chart**.

2 In the **Task Name** field, select the task to which you want to assign a new work resource.

Assign Resources

3 Click **Assign Resources**.
4 In the **Name** field, type a resource name.
  You can also click **Address**, and then select a resource from your e-mail address book.

Assign Part-Time Resources to a Task

Some resources might work on more than one task at the same time, and others might work only part-time on the project. If you assign a resource full-time to concurrent tasks, Microsoft Project will indicate that the resource is overallocated. This means you've scheduled the resource to work more hours than is available in a normal workday. To account for resources who don't work full-time or to avoid overloading resources who work on several tasks concurrently, you can assign resources part-time.

In some cases, you need to have a resource work more than 100% in order to meet deadlines. For information about overtime in Microsoft Project, see "Setting Costs" in chapter 7.

For example, if a resource works on two tasks concurrently, you can assign that resource at 50% units on each task, or at 30% on one task and 70% on the other, and so on, as long as you keep the total at or below 100%. Assigning a resource at more than 100% units for the same time period indicates that you've assigned the resource to work more hours than the resource is normally available.

To assign a resource to a task part-time

Assign Resources

1 On the **View Bar**, click **Gantt Chart**.
2 In the **Task Name** field, select a task, and then click **Assign Resources**.
3 In the **Name** field, select the name of the resource.
4 Type a percentage less than 100 in the **Units** field.
5 Click **Assign**.

Change Resource Assignments

You can assign any resource to any task, but you want to be sure that a resource has the skills required to accomplish the assignment. You also want to be sure you're using your resources in the most efficient manner possible. To make necessary adjustments, you can change your resource assignments at any time. You can replace one resource with another. You can add additional resources and remove unnecessary ones.

Occasionally, a piece of equipment might break down. Maybe you realize you can reduce costs by replacing an expensive resource with a less expensive one. You might want to increase efficiency or quality by replacing a less experienced resource with a more experienced one. In these and other situations, you might need to replace a resource.

With Microsoft Project, you can replace a resource with another resource on your resource list in one step. Rather than removing the assigned resource and assigning another resource in separate actions, you can simply replace one resource with another.

To replace one resource with another

1 On the View Bar, click Gantt Chart.
2 In the **Task Name** field, select a task with a resource you want to replace.
3 Click **Assign Resources**.

 **Assign Resources**

4 Select the resource you want to replace, and then click **Replace**.
5 Click the name of the resource you want, and then click **OK**.
6 If necessary, change the assignment units in the **Units** field.

If work is in progress on this assignment, and if you're tracking actual progress, the old resource remains assigned to the task, credited with the work that's already been completed. The new resource is assigned to the remaining work on the assignment.

To add more resources

1 On the **View Bar**, click **Gantt Chart**.
2 In the **Task Name** field, select a task to which you want to add a resource.
3 Click **Assign Resources**.

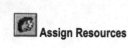

 **Assign Resources**

4 Select the resource you want to add, and then click **Assign**.
   Depending on the scheduling method (effort-driven or not) and the task type (fixed duration, fixed work, or fixed units), the scheduling of the task might change. For more information, see "Effort-Driven Scheduling and Task Types" in chapter 8.

Resources can get sick, leave the project, or be reassigned to more urgent tasks before they've completed their assignments. If a resource is a piece of equipment, it can break down. In such circumstances, you can remove a resource from a task.

Removing assigned resources from tasks can change the durations for those tasks. By default, the work assigned to the removed resources will be redistributed to the remaining assigned resources.

To remove a resource from a task

1 On the **View Bar**, click **Gantt Chart**.

 **Assign Resources**

2 In the **Task Name** field, select the task from which you want to remove a resource, and then click **Assign Resources**.
3 Select the resource you want to remove.
4 Click **Remove**.

Control When a Resource Works on a Task

When several resources are assigned to a task, each resource might not be required to work on the entire task from beginning to end. For example, a supervisor might work at the beginning of a task to help the team get started, then again at the end of the task to close and review the results. To fine-tune exactly when a resource jumps in on a task, you can delay the starting time of one or more resources. You can also apply a *work contour* to an assignment to indicate the "shape" of a resource's work on an assignment.

Control the Dates for an Assignment

When you delay a resource's start on a task, Microsoft Project recalculates the start date and times for the resource's work on the task.

To control the dates when a resource works on a task

1 On the **View Bar**, click **Task Usage**.

The sheet portion of the Task Usage view lists each task, followed by each resource assigned to the task.

2 In the **Task Name** field, select the resource assignment you want to change.

3 Click **Assignment Information**, and then click the **General** tab.

Assignment Information

4 In the **Start** box or the **Finish** box, type the date you want the resource assignment to start or finish.

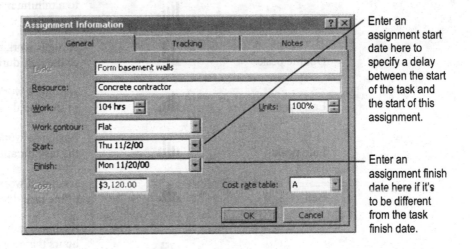

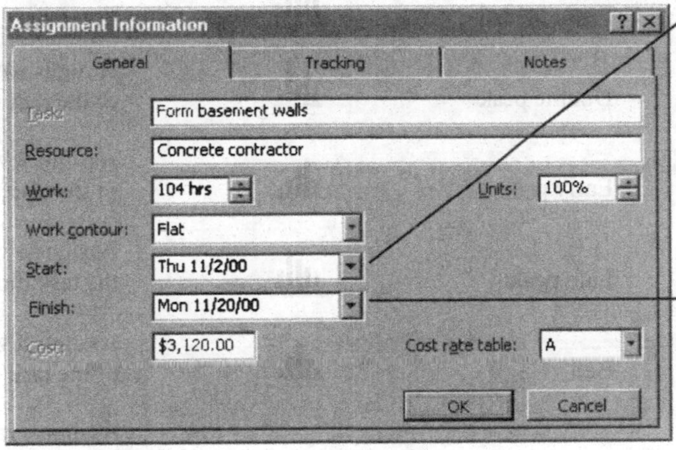

Another method for changing assignment dates is change the Start or Finish fields of the assignment in the Task Usage view.

Control the Amount of Work Throughout an Assignment

When you assign a resource to a task, Microsoft Project assigns the same number of work hours per day to the resource for each day the resource works on the task. For example, if you assign a resource full time (8 hours per day) to a 3-day task, then Microsoft Project assigns the resource to work on the task 8 hours on each day.

But if you know that a resource will not be working a flat amount of hours per day on this task, you can specify a work-hour pattern, or *work contour*, that more closely matches the number of hours per day (week, month, and so on) that the resource will actually work on the task.

For example, a resource might be finishing one task as he or she begins work on another. The resource might step up the work hours gradually before working full-time on the new task, then gradually taper off toward the end of the task. This kind of work contour is called the *bell contour*.

You can apply the following preset work contours:

This work contour...	looks like this...	and has this effect
Flat		Assigns the same number of hours each day throughout the task duration.
Back loaded		Assigns a peak of work at the end of the task duration.
Front loaded		Assigns work peaks at the beginning of the task duration and gradually declines to a minimum at the end of the task duration.
Double peak		Assigns work peaks twice in the middle of the task duration.
Early peak		Assigns a work peak before the middle of the task duration.
Late peak	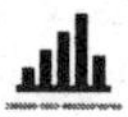	Assigns a work peak after the middle of the task duration.
Bell	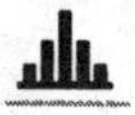	Assigns a work peak once in the middle of the task duration.
Turtle		Assigns gradually increasing work hours that reaches a plateau, gradually declines.

You apply a specific work contour to a specific task. You display work contours on the Resource Usage and Task Usage views. The shape of the contour appears in the Indicators field, and the actual hours scheduled for the assignment in the time period are shown in the timesheet view.

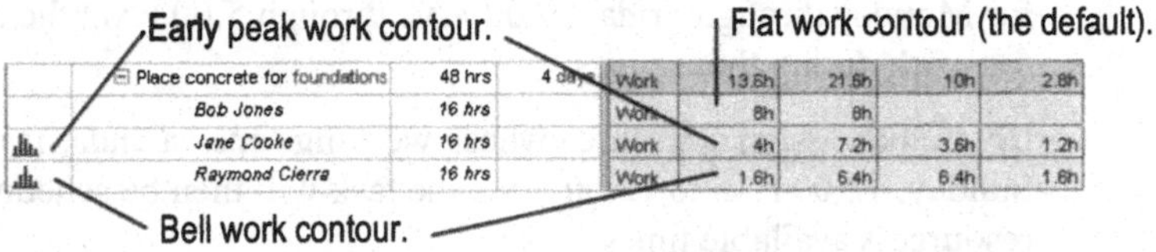

When you apply a work contour to an assignment, note that the contour adheres to certain rules:

- Changing the start date of a task automatically causes the contour to shift and be reapplied to include the new start date. The work values within the task duration change to preserve the pattern of the original contour.
- If you add new total work values to the task, Microsoft Project automatically reapplies the preset work contour pattern, distributes the new task work values across the affected duration, and assigns new work values to the assigned resources.
- If you increase the duration of a task, Microsoft Project stretches the contour to include the added duration.
- When you edit a work value, the contour is removed from the assignment. You can, however, reapply the contour.

To apply a contour to an assignment

You can also review assignments and apply contours in the Resource Usage view.

1. On the **View Bar**, click **Task Usage**.

   Resources are grouped under the tasks to which they are assigned.

2. In the **Task Name** field, select the resource to which you want to apply a preset work contour.

3. Click **Assignment Information**, and then click the **General** tab.

   Assignment Information

4. In the **Work contour** box, click a contour pattern.

   An icon representing the contour pattern appears in the Indicators field. In the timesheet area for the assignment, the work hours change to reflect the pattern of the contour.

Control Assignment Scheduling with Task Calendars

Microsoft Project typically schedules tasks using the working times on the project calendar. When you assign resources to tasks, they're scheduled according to the available resource time. For example, if your project calendar is set with working time for Monday through Friday, 9:00 A.M. through 5:00 P.M., the task is initially scheduled for work during those times.

If you then assign a resource whose working time calendar is set for Friday through Sunday, 12:00 P.M. to 12:00 A.M., the task will then be scheduled for work during the resource's available times.

There's a third method for using calendars to affect task scheduling: creating and applying *task calendars*.

A task calendar is a new base calendar you create, then apply to a task. You then can choose whether the task calendar is to interact with or ignore the resource calendar of any assigned resources.

If the task calendar interacts with the resource calendar, then work is scheduled only during those working times shared by both the resource calendar and task calendar. This is useful, for example, if you have a resource scheduled for work with machinery that has regularly scheduled preventive maintenance downtime during normal working time. You want to make sure that the resource is scheduled for tasks on the machine only when the machine is available.

If the task calendar ignores the resource calendar, the work is scheduled according to the task calendar alone. For example, suppose your human resources typically work Monday through Friday, 3:00 P.M. to 11:00 P.M., but tasks are scheduled for equipment that runs only from 9:00 P.M. until 1:00 A.M. You can create a task calendar for the 4-hour working time, and then assign it to the task. The task, as well its assigned resources, will be scheduled for 9:00 P.M. until 1:00 A.M., as long as you set the task calendar to ignore the resource calendar.

Or, suppose a resource's normal working days are Monday through Friday, but there is a special task that can be done only on the weekend. You can apply a task calendar with weekend working times, then choose to ignore the resource calendar so that the task and resource are scheduled appropriately. You wouldn't want to modify the resource calendar to include the weekend because other tasks might be scheduled for work by this resource during the weekend.

To assign a calendar to a task

1. Create a base calendar for the task as described under "Create a Base Calendar for a Special Work Schedule" above.
2. On the **View Bar**, click **Gantt Chart**.
3. In the **Task Name** field, select the task to which you want to assign the calendar.

Task Information

4 Click **Task Information**, and then click the **Advanced** tab.

5 In the **Calendar** box, click the calendar you want to use for the task.

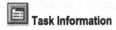

6 Select the **Scheduling ignores resource calendars** check box to have the task calendar ignore the resource calendars of assigned resources.

If you choose to have Microsoft Project ignore resource calendars, the task will be scheduled according to the task calendar, even if it's during nonworking time for the assigned resources.

If you choose not to ignore resource calendars, the task will be scheduled where the task calendar and resource calendar have overlapping working times.

Creating Custom Outline Codes for Resources

You can organize resource information in a specialized way by creating and assigning outline codes for resource categories. Outline codes are custom tags for resources that share common characteristics. You can use outline codes to group resources in various ways, such as job codes or accounting codes. You can create *lookup tables* so you can pick from available codes without having to type them in each time. You can set the codes to have multiple hierarchical levels to provide increasing levels of detail. You can then group the resources according to this hierarchical structure to see your project data summarized in this resource structure. For example, you can identify and assign a hierarchical resource outline code that reflects departmental structure. By grouping on that outline code, you can see your project costs and work values summarized by each resource's department.

For more information, see "Group Resource Information" in chapter 12.

To use outline codes, first you define the format of the code, whether with alphanumeric characters such as "Buyer1" or codes of specific length such as "2044" or "RF19001." If the code is associated with a defined hierarchy, you also define the hierarchical outline levels.

To create custom outline codes for resources

1 On the **View Bar**, click **Resource Sheet**.

2 On the **Tools** menu, point to **Customize**, and then click **Fields**.

3 In the **Type** box, click **Outline Code**.

4 In the box, click the outline code you want to define, for example, **Outline Code1**.

5 Click **Rename**.

6 In the **Rename Field** dialog box, type a name for the custom outline code you want to create—for example, "Job Codes" —and then click **OK**.

7 Click **Define Outline Code**.

8 Click the first row in the **Sequence** column, and then click the character type for the outline code format you want to create.

9 If there is a particular code length or a separator character between the characters of the different outline levels, enter this in the **Length** or **Separator** columns.

10 Click the second row, and then enter the format for the second level of the outline code.

11 Continue in this manner until your outline format is created.

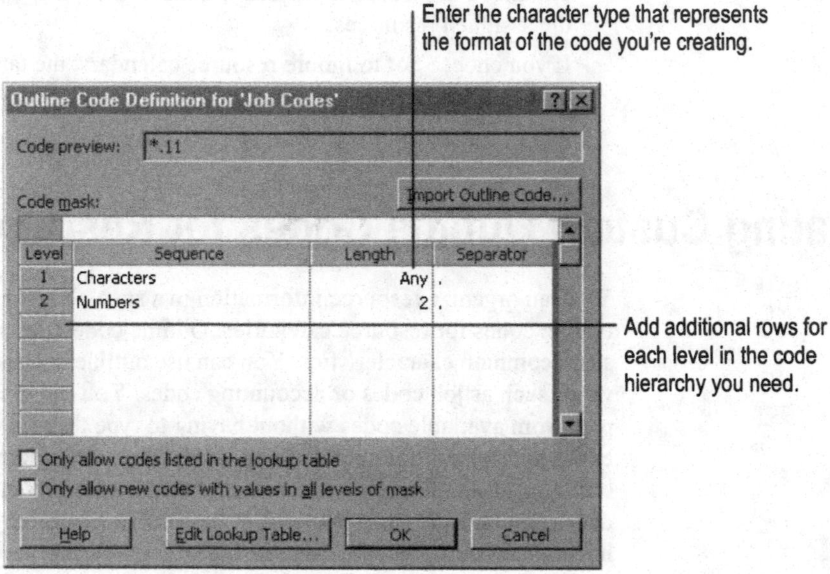

After defining your outline code format, you can create a lookup table for the specific resource outline codes. If you don't want to set up a lookup table ahead of time, you can enter code values in the Resource Sheet itself, thereby creating your lookup table as you work.

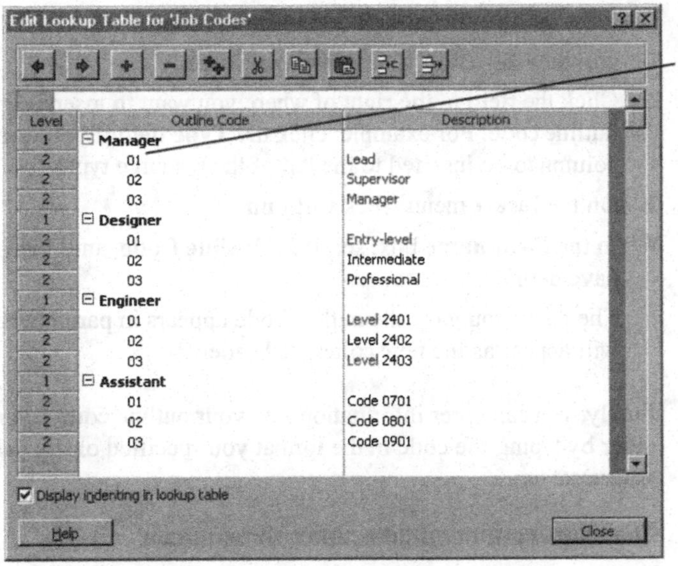

Use the Edit Lookup Table dialog box to enter actual code values you can pick in the Resource Sheet.

To create a lookup table for resource outline codes

1. Create your outline codes as described in the previous procedure.
2. In the **Outline Code Definition** dialog box, click **Edit Lookup Table**.
3. In the first row, under **Outline Code**, type your first outline code, following the format you have established for your outline codes (numbers, characters, and so on).
4. In the **Description** field, type a description for this outline code.
5. Repeat steps 3 and 4 until all your outline codes are entered.
6. To indicate the hierarchy of an outline code, select the code, and then click **Indent**.

Indent

7. When finished entering the outline codes, click **Close**.
8. If you want only the codes you've entered to be used in the Resource Sheet, select the **Only allow codes listed in the lookup table** check box.

   If you want to be able to add outline codes while you work, clear this check box.

The next step is to add the outline code column to your Resource Sheet so you can enter, change, and view outline codes for your resources.

To view custom outline codes for resources

1. On the **View Bar**, click **Resource Sheet**.
2. Click the field to the right of where you want to insert a column for the custom outline code. For example, click the **Type** field if you want the outline codes column to be inserted to the left of the resource types.
3. On the **Insert** menu, click **Column**.
4. In the **Field name** box, scroll to **Outline Code**, and then pick the outline code you have defined.

   The name you gave the outline code appears in parentheses. This is the name that will appear as the new column's header.

Finally, you can enter information into your outline code column in the Resource Sheet, either by typing the code in the format you specified or by picking it from the list you've set up.

To assign custom outline codes to resources

1. Be sure that the outline code column is inserted in the Resource Sheet.
2. Click the outline code field for the task to which you want to assign an outline code.
3. Type an outline code or select it from the list.

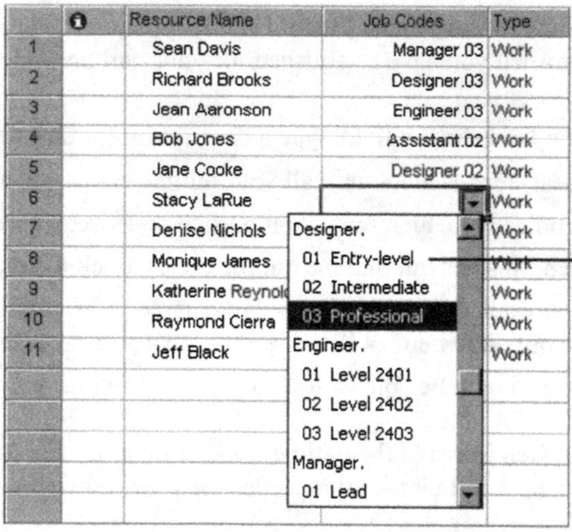

If you create and assign outline codes to resources, you have more information to work with as you manage your resources and your project.

7

Specifying Resource and Task Costs

Examining your costs with the schedule can help set and maintain your priorities. With some projects, the project finish date is the crucial factor in your project management decisions. With other projects, the project budget is the ultimate driver.

Cost management often helps project managers control not only costs but also the schedule. For example, costs can help you decide how quickly tasks should be performed. Should you add more resources now to accomplish tasks sooner (and bring in the schedule) or wait until the budget is approved for the next fiscal year?

If you add cost information to your project, you can use the calculation capabilities of Microsoft Project to help you review detailed and summary cost information and therefore factor costs into your key decisions.

While in the planning phase of your project, setting cost information allows you to:

- Develop a project budget based on estimated task and resource costs so you can know when and where your money is spent.
- Generate more accurate bid proposals by estimating project costs, then reducing those costs to realistic levels.
- View the costs of human, equipment, and material resource for each task.
- Control when task and resource costs are accrued.

While in the managing and tracking phase of your project, you can use the cost information to:

- View the cost to date of tasks or of the project as a whole so you can make the adjustments necessary to stay within your budget.
- Estimate the cost required to complete a task by viewing remaining cost.
- Determine how closely the final project costs match their budget or baseline costs.

Finally, after the project has been completed, you can use the cost information you have planned and tracked to plan budgets for future projects.

Setting Costs

A project budget doesn't just happen. It's the sum of task costs, resource costs, and other project costs. One of the best ways to determine the total project cost, and thus the size of the budget you require, is to associate a cost with each resource and task in your project, and then let Microsoft Project calculate the total cost for you.

The effort required for resources to accomplish tasks is typically the largest project budget item. When you associate costs with resources, then assign those resources to tasks, you will be able to see a realistic estimate of your project costs based on your task duration and material usage estimates. When you also associate fixed costs with tasks, your project budget estimate becomes even more accurate. Once your project begins and you start to track and enter actual durations or costs, Microsoft Project recalculates task and resource costs as well as overall project costs throughout the project.

The key to estimating and monitoring costs effectively is to associate rates with resources. There are three categories of costs you can set in Microsoft Project:

- **Variable costs.** A variable cost depends on the time spent on assigned tasks. For example, suppose a resource is paid hourly (or weekly or monthly). The longer the resource spends on a task, the greater the resource cost will be for that task.
- **Fixed costs.** A fixed cost remains constant regardless of the amount of time required to accomplish a task or the number of hours a resource spends on the task. For example, contractors often bid a fixed price for a job, so the contractor cost stays the same even if the job takes more or less time than planned. The cost of a piece of equipment required to accomplish a task is another example of a fixed cost. While variable costs and per-use costs are typically associated with resources, fixed costs are typically associated with tasks.
- **Per-use costs.** A per-use cost is a flat usage charge you incur each time, and only each time, you use a resource. For example, the fee for renting a tractor might be $100 per use.

When setting costs in Microsoft Project, you can:

- Specify a variable or per-use rate for a resource, to monitor resource costs and let Microsoft Project calculate task costs by multiplying resource rates by task durations or times used.
- Change the standard and overtime default rates, to save time when specifying the rates of new resources.

- Specify different rates for a resource over time, to account for pay increases that go into effect at a particular time.
- Specify a different rate for each kind of task performed by the same resource.
- Specify the cost of a material resource.
- Set fixed costs for a task, to keep track of one-time-only or set costs for accomplishing a specific task.

Establish Resource Rates

When you decide to track costs, probably the most important factor to consider is the cost of resources, as resource costs usually make up the largest portion of task costs, and thus of overall project costs. Mainly, you'll want to monitor how the cost of each task depends on the amount of time its assigned resources spend on it.

You can associate hourly or per-use rates with resources. For hourly rates, you can set a standard rate, which is the rate you pay a resource during normal working hours. To resources you anticipate working longer than the normal working hours, you can also set an overtime rate. To resources who charge a flat amount to do a job, you can set either a cost per use or a fixed cost on the task. You can also set both an hourly rate and a cost-per-use rate for the same resource. For example, you might pay a $100 setup charge for each computer you rent, plus an hourly rate to the personnel who set up the computers.

Even if you don't include resources in your project, you can still track costs. For example, you can associate a fixed cost with each task that includes an estimate for the resource cost. However, you can more accurately track the resource contribution to the cost of your tasks and project if you include resources in your project, associate rates with these resources, and then assign resources to tasks.

To set a resource rate

1. On the **View Bar**, click **Resource Sheet**.
2. Make sure that the Entry table is applied: On the **View** menu, point to **Table**, and then click **Entry**.
3. In the **Std. Rate**, **Ovt. Rate**, and **Cost/Use** fields for the resource, enter the rates that apply.

Setting overtime rates for a resource does not automatically cause Microsoft Project to calculate overtime if a resource is allocated for more than 8 hours a day or 40 hours a week. This is left to your discretion as project manager. To learn how to enter overtime work on an assignment, see "Assign Overtime Work" in chapter 8.

Change the Standard and Overtime Default Rates for New Resources

When you add resources to your project, you often think of and add one group of related resources at a time. For example, you might add all the painters, then all the electricians, and so on. Often, most resources in a related group are paid the same hourly rate.

If each resource you're about to add to your project is paid the same hourly rate, you can save time by specifying the rate as the default rate, then letting Microsoft Project enter this rate automatically. You can specify both standard and overtime default rates.

These default pay rates apply only to the resources you've added after you change the default, not to resources that are already in your project. You can change the default pay rates before you add each new group of resources.

To change the default standard or overtime rate for resources

1. On the **Tools** menu, click **Options**, and then click the **General** tab.
2. In the **Default standard rate** box, enter the new rate.
3. In the **Default overtime rate** box, enter the new rate.

   If you want these rates to be the default for any new projects you create, click **Set as Default.**
4. To change the default currency symbol and number of decimal digits for all cost information in your project, click the **View** tab, and then change the information under **Currency options**.

Specify Different Resource Pay Rates Over Time

The initial pay rate you set for a work or material resource might be applicable for only a portion of the time that the resource works on the project. For instance, a resource's pay rate might change three months into the project due to a scheduled pay increase. You can allow Microsoft Project to apply new resource rates to cost calculations automatically by setting different rate values to be applied at times you specify. In the resource's *cost rate table*, you can specify up to 25 rate levels and specify the date each rate will take effect.

These tabs can be used to set other cost rate tables for different skills and their associated cost rates for this resource.

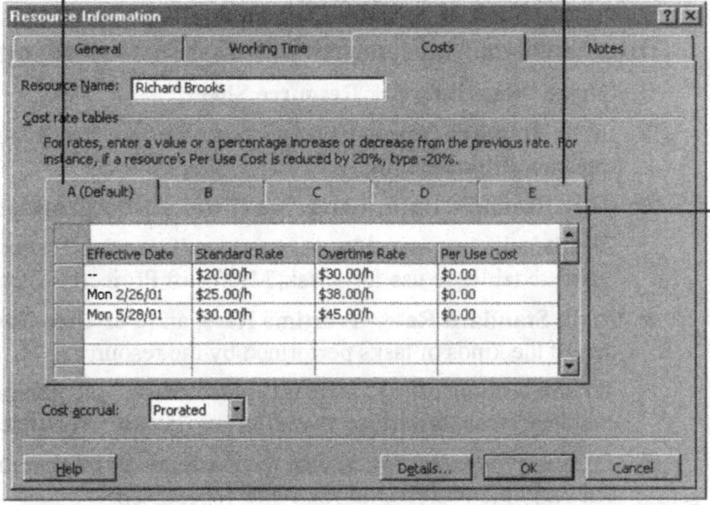

You can enter up to 25 different resource rates in each of the five cost rate tables to support increases or decreases for different initial resource rates.

To specify different resource pay rates over time

1 On the **View Bar**, click **Resource Sheet**.

2 In the **Resource Name** field, select the resource for which you want to enter multiple rates.

3 Click **Resource Information**, and then click the **Costs** tab.

Resource Information

The default cost rate table, A, is on top. If you don't specify which of a resource's cost rate tables to use for a task, Microsoft Project uses cost rate table A by default.

4 In the Cost rate tables, type the effective date and the new standard, overtime, or per-use cost rate in the corresponding fields of the first blank row.

You can enter rate increases or decreases by entering a new rate or a percentage. For example, you can enter +4% or –4%. When you enter a percentage, Microsoft Project will calculate the new rate for you.

Specify Different Rates for Different Skills for the Same Resource

A resource might have several skills, each of which can be applied to a different type of task in your project. For example, an individual resource might be an electrician as well as a painter, skills that usually command different pay rates. If you assign a multitalented resource to tasks that require different pay rates, you can enter different rates into that resource's rate tables.

For each work or material resource, you can specify rates for up to five kinds of skills or grades. When you assign the resource to a task, you can specify which of the five cost rate tables you want to apply.

To set a different rate for each kind of skill performed by a resource

1. On the **View Bar**, click **Resource Sheet**.
2. In the **Resource Name** field, select the resource for which you want to set different rates for different skills.
3. Click **Resource Information**, and then click the **Costs** tab.

   Resource Information

   The default cost rate table, A, is on top. If you don't specify which of a resource's cost rate tables to use for a task, Microsoft Project uses cost rate table A by default.
4. In the **Standard Rate, Overtime Rate,** and **Per Use Cost** fields, type the rates for one of the kinds of tasks performed by the resource.

   To take account of pay increases or decreases, you can specify up to 25 rates for each pay scale or skill set as well as the date on which each rate becomes effective.
5. To specify the rates for another pay scale or skill set performed by the resource, click another cost rate tab, and then repeat step 4.

A good way to identify the designation of each cost rate table is to enter a resource note.

The note icon appears in the Indicators field of the Resource Sheet.

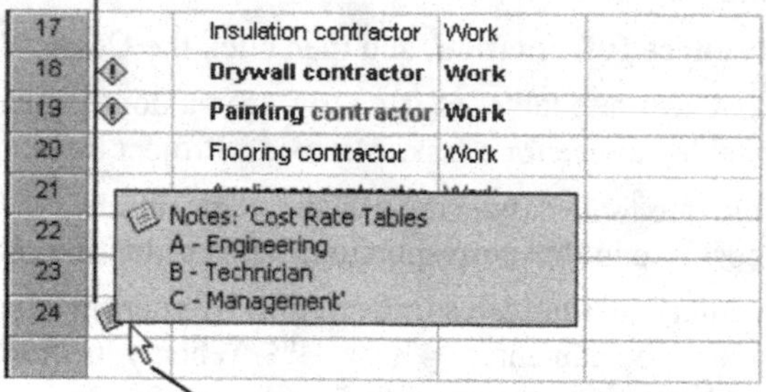

Review a note by resting your mouse over the note icon in the Indicators field, or by double-clicking the icon.

To enter a resource note

1. On the **View Bar**, click **Resource Sheet**.
2. In the **Resource Name** field, select a resource, and then click **Resource Information**.

   Resource Information
3. Click the **Notes** tab.
4. Type information about what each of the cost rate tables represent.

Note

By default, Microsoft Project applies the standard pay rate specified in cost rate table A (which is the same as the Std. Rate column in the Resource Sheet) to each of a resource's task assignments, even if the assignments require different kinds of work. For example, if you enter $20 per hour for Jake in the Std. Rate column of the Resource Sheet, then assign Jake to the tasks "Compact the soil" and "Construct the outer walls," Microsoft Project applies the $20 per hour rate to each task.

But suppose the standard pay rates for compacting soil and constructing walls are $20 per hour and $30 per hour respectively. For the wall construction assignment, you can replace the default $20 per hour rate with the $30 per hour rate. To do so, you specify $30 per hour in one of Jake's other cost rate tables (for example, cost rate table B), and then apply this rate to the wall construction assignment.

To apply a different rate for different skills performed by the same resource

1. On the **View Bar**, click **Task Usage**.

   The sheet portion of the Task Usage view lists each task, followed by each resource assigned to the task.

2. In the **Task Name** field, select the assigned resource whose pay rate you want to change for the associated task assignment.
3. Click **Assignment Information**.
4. Click the **General** tab.
5. In the **Cost rate table** box, click the rate table you want to use for this resource on this task.

Assignment Information

If you're applying different cost rate tables to a number of assignments, it might be more convenient to add the Cost Rate Table column to the Task Usage view. Click the field to the right of where you want to insert the column. On the **Insert** menu, click **Column**. In the **Field name** box, click **Cost Rate Table**.

Specify the Cost of Material Resources

Material resources, which are goods or supplies from silicon to steel, and carpeting to cement, are typically associated with a unit-based price such as $100 per ton, $30 per box, $470 each, and so on. You establish the material's unit price in the Resource Sheet. Then when you assign the material resource to tasks and specify the assignment units—that is, the amount of the material to be used for this task—Microsoft Project calculates the total material cost by multiplying the unit price you enter by the number of assignment units you specified.

You can also specify a per-use cost for a material resource—for example, a $200 delivery charge for the material.

To specify the cost of a material resource

1. On the **View Bar**, click **Resource Sheet**.
2. Make sure that the material resource is entered, designated as a material, and associated with a material label such as tons, yards, or boxes.
3. To enter a unit cost for the material, in the **Std. Rate** field, enter the unit cost for the material. The unit is specified in the **Material Label** field.

   To enter a per-use cost for the material, in the **Cost Per Use** field, enter the cost to be incurred each time the material is assigned to a task.

Now Microsoft Project can calculate costs for those materials that are assigned to tasks, as follows:

- If the material has a unit cost rate and the assignment is fixed, the unit cost is multiplied by the number of assignment units. For example, suppose you have a material resource of "Cement" with a unit cost of $100 per yard. If you assign "Cement" to the "Build foundation" task with assignment units of 20 yards, Microsoft Project will calculate the cement material cost for this task as $2000.
- If the material has a unit cost rate and the assignment is variable, the unit cost is multiplied by the number of assignment units and then by the task duration. For example, suppose you have a material resource of "Gravel" with a unit cost of $10.00 per yard. If you assign "Gravel" to the 3-day "Build access road" task with assignment units of 50 yards/day, Microsoft Project will calculate the gravel material cost for this task at $500/day times 5 days, for a total of $1500.
- If the material has a per-use cost, this cost is incurred each time the material is assigned to a task, without respect to the material assignment units or the task duration.
- If the material has both a unit cost and a per-use cost, the two are figured according to their own rules, then added to form the total material cost for the task.

You can set cost tables for material resources as well as work (human and equipment) resources. This can be useful if you:

- Anticipate the cost of a material to change after a certain date.
- Use different grades of the material for different tasks.
- Benefit from supplier discounts at certain times or within certain payment terms.

Specify a Fixed Cost for a Task

In many projects, the most common type of task cost is a rate-based cost, a cost based on an amount of money spent per unit of time (for example, the hourly rate paid to a resource). But sometimes a fixed cost is associated with a task, such as the cost of equipment used to accomplish the task, or a job bid on a flat rate. Such costs are fixed because they remain constant even if a task takes more or less time than planned.

If you aren't assigning resources to tasks, a fixed cost can represent the total cost of a task, an estimate that includes both resource and materials costs. If you know the cost of materials or if you're not going to assign a resource to a task, you can enter a fixed cost.

If a task is associated with both a fixed cost and rate-based costs, Microsoft Project will add the fixed cost to the rate-based costs to determine the total cost of the task.

To set a fixed cost for a task

1 On the **View Bar**, click **Gantt Chart**.

2 On the **View** menu, point to **Table**, and then click **Cost**.

3 In the **Fixed Cost** field for the task, enter the cost.

In the Cost table, you can also specify when the fixed cost is accrued by selecting an accrual method in the Fixed Cost Accrual field. For more information about cost accrual, see "Plan Your Cash Flow by Setting Cost Accrual" later in this chapter.

Specify Assignment Costs

You might have other costs you want to track that don't fit neatly into any of the existing cost categories: variable resource, per-use resource, or fixed cost for a task. In such a case, you can create a special "resource," assign it to applicable tasks, and enter assignment costs in the Task Usage or Resource Usage view.

For example, suppose you want to track airfare costs associated with the tasks. Using a variable resource rate wouldn't work, as airfares are likely to be different for each trip and don't relate to task duration. Specifying a per-use cost wouldn't work, again because airfares are different for each trip. Using a fixed cost on a task wouldn't work, because you wouldn't be able to get a summary of all airfare costs, and it might get in the way of a task's other fixed costs.

The solution is to create a resource called "Airfare." You can then assign that "Airfare" resource to any tasks that are associated with air travel, and give it an assignment unit of 0. You can then enter costs for specific assignments for "Airfare" in the Task Usage or Resource Usage view.

To enter assignment costs

1 On the **View Bar**, click **Task Usage** or **Resource Usage**.

2 In the sheet side of the view, click the field to the right of where you want to insert the Cost column.

3 On the **Insert** menu, click **Column**.

4 In the **Field name** box, click **Cost**.

5 In the **Cost** field for the applicable assignment, enter the cost.

For more information about task types, see "Task Types" in chapter 8.

Remember to enter assignment units of 0, or you won't be able to enter the costs in the assignment Cost field. Also, if this is the only resource assigned to the task, with assignment units of 0, the duration will probably change to 0. To prevent this, in the Task Information dialog box, click the Advanced tab, and then change the Task type to Fixed Duration.

Viewing Costs

Once you have associated costs with your resources, assigned the resources to their tasks, and set any fixed costs for tasks, you can view cost information for your project. Microsoft Project provides a number of ways to examine costs, both in the planning stage of your project and when the project is underway and you're in the tracking stage. You can:

- View the cost per task, including costs for human, equipment, and material resources.
- View the cost per resource, including information on how much you're spending for regular work, overtime work, and per-use resources.
- View the total project cost, to see if your project is within the proscribed budget.
- View costs per time period, to see how they are distributed across the span of a task.

You can also run cost reports. For more information, see chapter 16.

View the Cost per Task

Because each individual task includes its assigned resources costs as well as any fixed costs for the task, the sum of all the individual tasks represents the total project cost. If the total project cost exceeds your budget, you can view the total cost of each individual task in detail to see where you can pare task costs.

To view the cost per task

1 On the **View Bar**, click **Gantt Chart**.

2 On the **View** menu, click **Table**, and then choose **Cost**.

3 Review the **Total Cost** field for each task.

View the Cost per Resource

Resource costs typically make up the largest portion of task costs, and therefore the overall project cost. Because of this, you'll want to monitor resource costs to help keep costs under control. By viewing a resource cost in detail, you can see exactly the total cost for the resource.

To view the cost per resource

1 On the **View Bar**, click **Resource Sheet**.

2 On the **View** menu, point to **Table**, and then click **Cost**.

3 Review the **Cost** field for each resource.

This represents the total cost of that resource for all the tasks the resource is assigned to.

To view the cost of each resource, broken down by the time period you specify, use the Resource Usage view.

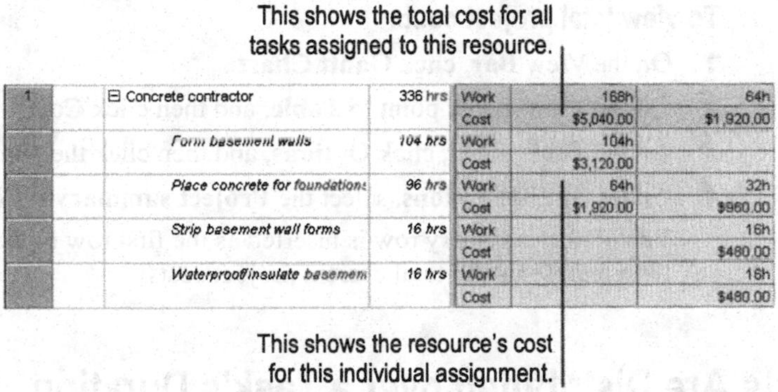

To view a resource cost in greater detail

1 On the **View Bar**, click **Resource Usage**.

2 On the **Format** menu, point to **Details**, and then click **Cost**.

Costs for each resource are shown in the timesheet according to the selected time period.

3 See more or less time period detail by clicking **Zoom In** or **Zoom Out**.

Zoom In

Zoom Out

You can view resource costs graphically in the Resource Graph view.

To view resource cost totals graphically

1. On the **View Bar**, click **Resource Graph**.
2. On the **Format** menu, point to **Details**, and then click **Cost** or **Cumulative Cost**.

   Costs are shown graphically by the time period selected.

View Total Project Costs

When planning your project, you can see the total project cost—that is, the sum of all costs for all tasks in the project. This can help you develop the project budget proposal you'll submit to your clients or upper management. Or, if you've already been given a specific budget to work within, this total project cost will quickly demonstrate whether you're on target, have some cutting to do, or have extra budget to increase scope or add more or better resources.

Later, when tracking the progress of your project, you can review your total project costs to help gauge whether you're staying within budget or not.

To view total project costs

1. On the **View Bar**, click **Gantt Chart**.
2. On the **View** menu, point to **Table**, and then click **Cost**.
3. On the **Tools** menu, click **Options**, and then click the **View** tab.
4. Under **Outline options**, select the **Project summary task** check box.

   The project summary row is inserted as the first row in the project. The Total Cost field represents the total current project costs.

View How Costs Are Distributed over a Task's Duration

Often the cost of a task accumulates over time; it doesn't occur all at once. For example, if a resource assigned to a 2-day (16-hour) task is paid $20 per hour, the task will cost $160 on the first day and $160 on the second day. If the resources assigned to a task are paid an hourly rate or a prorated fixed rate, you can view how the cost of the task breaks down day by day (or week by week, month by month, and so on).

To view how costs are distributed over a task's duration

1. On the **View Bar**, click **Task Usage** or **Resource Usage**.
2. On the **Format** menu, point to **Details**, and then click **Cost**.

When your project begins, you can begin to track *earned value costs*. Earned value, also known as *budgeted cost of work performed* (BCWP), is used by some organizations to analyze and measure project performance. An earned value analysis indicates how much of the budget should have been spent, in view of the amount of work done so far and the *baseline cost* for the task, assignment, or resource. For more information, see "Track Costs Over Time with the Earned Value Table" in chapter 9.

Plan Your Cash Flow by Setting Cost Accrual

You can control when and how you accrue costs for your resources and tasks. Accrual indicates the point when the cost recorded in your project (and possibly, the point at which you are responsible for payment). Controlling cost accrual can help you better plan your cash flow and leverage your budget. With Microsoft Project, you can:

- Control when resource costs are accrued, to incur hourly resource charges all at once or gradually over time.
- Control when fixed costs are accrued.
- Change how actual costs are calculated, either automatically by Microsoft Project or manually.

Control How Resource Costs Are Accrued

You can choose the point at which resource costs are incurred by setting the cost *accrual* for resources. Your accrual choices are:

- The entire cost at the start of an assignment.
- The entire cost at the end of an assignment.
- The prorated cost across the duration of the assignment as it progresses.

When the cash flow in your project is important, you can change how costs are accrued on individual tasks so that the costs of a task occur when you have the cash to pay for them. Except for resource per-use costs, which always accrue at the start of a task, Microsoft Project prorates costs by default. However, you can also accrue the cost of a task when it starts if you must pay a lump-sum amount before work begins. Or, you can accrue the cost of a task when it ends if you hold payment until the work is finished to satisfaction.

To select a method for accruing resource costs

1 On the **View Bar**, click **Resource Sheet**.

2 In the **Resource Name** field, select a resource, and then click **Resource Information**.

Resource Information

3 Click the **Costs** tab.

4 In the **Cost accrual** box, click an accrual method.

You can also use the Accrue At field in the Entry table of the Resource Sheet.

To accrue the cost when the task begins, click **Start**.

To accrue scheduled costs across the span of the task, and actual costs based on the percent complete, click **Prorated**.

To accrue the cost when the task is completed, click **End**.

The cost accrual method you select will be applied to all the rates on each cost rate table.

Control How Fixed Costs Are Accrued

By default, Microsoft Project prorates fixed costs on tasks. Their accrual is distributed across the task duration. However, you can change the default accrual method for fixed costs so that charges are incurred either at the start or finish of the task.

To control how fixed costs are accrued

1 On the **Tools** menu, click **Options**, and then the **Calculation** tab.

2 In the **Default fixed costs accrual** box, click the accrual method you want to apply for all fixed costs on tasks.

This method changes the fixed costs accrual method for any new tasks you enter from this point on. To change the accrual method for existing tasks, apply the Cost table to the Gantt Chart, and change the method in the Fixed Cost Accrual field.

8

Fine-Tuning Your Project

By now, you have built your project plan. You've added, sequenced, and linked tasks, and you probably have resource, assignment, and cost information as well.

Now it's time to look at your project plan as a whole and make sure it reflects the realities of your project, particularly in light of the project finish date, the use of your resources, your budget, and total project scope. Your project plan isn't complete until you analyze it and make the final adjustments needed to create the workable model you need to manage and track progress effectively.

To understand your project plan, you need to understand how Microsoft Project schedules tasks. You also need to know how resources affect task scheduling. You can then make certain adjustments to how Microsoft Project schedules your tasks to make it correspond with your project reality.

There are four major questions to consider as you review and fine-tune your project plan:

- Does the scheduled finish date match any imposed project deadline?
- Are any resources unreasonably overallocated or underutilized?
- Do the projected costs for the project match your budget?
- Do answers to the above questions require that you cut project scope?

Adjusting your plan is something of a juggling act in which you're striving to balance time, money, resources, and scope. To bring in the project finish date, for example, you might need to add resources or overtime and therefore increase cost. To meet your budget, you might need to use less expensive resources or take more time. Or you might find you need to cut scope in order to trim both time and cost.

Review and fine-tune your plan before the project starts. This way, you can pinpoint and resolve problems before they occur. You'll also know that your plan represents your most accurate prediction of what will occur during the project: how long tasks will take, who's working on which tasks, how much tasks will cost, and so on. It will also provide a valid basis for comparing actual data to estimated data. While a deviation from a well-honed plan is significant, a deviation from a rough plan might mean nothing at all.

You'll also want to use the procedures discussed in this chapter to review and adjust your plan periodically after the project begins. If you track progress, the actual data you collect might show that tasks are taking longer than expected, certain resources are working too much overtime, or you're spending money faster than planned. If you occasionally evaluate your plan throughout the project, you can not only see potential problems brewing, but also take corrective measures earlier to ensure your project doesn't stray too far off course.

Checking the Assumptions of Your Project

Now that you have all project information entered into the project plan, check it over to make sure it reflects your expected project reality. Also, look for information that's missing, unessential, or erroneous. For example, a task might be improperly linked, an unnecessary constraint might be applied, or the wrong resource might be assigned to a task.

When you review your plan, you identify aspects that can be made more efficient or that might cause problems during the project. For example, you might find that a Must Start On constraint is making a task start later than it needs to, and it's pushing out the project finish date. You might discover a day when a resource has been assigned to 12 hours of work instead of the usual 8 hours.

Use the following checklist to examine aspects of your plan to make sure your assumptions are correct:

- **Task list.** Are all the tasks, phases, and milestones needed to accomplish your goals included? Should any extraneous tasks be deleted? Are the tasks in a logical order, and outlined with summary tasks and subtasks where appropriate?
- **Task durations.** Are all the task durations entered? Do any still have the default estimate of 1 day that needs to be changed? Should any estimated durations be confirmed?
- **Task dependencies.** Use the Gantt Chart to check all the task linking. Are all the links necessary? Are all the links the correct type (finish-to-start, finish-to-finish, and so on)? Are successors linking to the appropriate predecessor? Should lead time or lag time be added to any links?
- **Task constraints.** Apply the Constraint Dates table to the Gantt Chart to view all the constraints on tasks. (On the **View** menu, point to **Table**, click **More Tables**, then click **Constraint Dates**.) Take a closer look at tasks that have constraints other than As Soon As Possible or As Late As Possible. Wherever possible, make

the constraints more flexible. Change a Must Start On to a Start No Later Than constraint, if appropriate. Or change a Finish No Earlier Than constraint to an As Soon As Possible constraint, and then set a deadline date.

- **Resource list.** Check the resource information in the Resource Sheet to ensure that you have entered all the information you want, and that all the resources you'll be using are listed. Check their resource calendars, max units, and availability dates. Check that the correct standard and overtime rates are entered. Remember to include material resources and equipment resources, if applicable.
- **Resource assignments.** Use the Entry table in the Gantt Chart to make sure that all tasks have at least one resource assigned, if appropriate. Check the resources to ensure that everyone who is supposed to be assigned is indeed assigned. Add, remove, or replace any resources as necessary to make corrections. Also check the assignment units.
- **Costs.** Use the Resource Sheet to check your resource costs. Use the Cost table in the Gantt Chart to check any fixed costs for tasks you've entered.

How Microsoft Project Schedules

Whether your project plan includes tasks only or resources and costs as well, you'll probably want to analyze and adjust the most important part of that plan: the schedule. By adjusting the schedule, you can, for instance, schedule a task to start and finish sooner, reduce task durations, and bring in the project finish date.

Before you adjust your schedule, however, you need to know how Microsoft Project calculates the schedule, so you can predict the effects of the adjustments you make. For example, you need to understand how Microsoft Project calculates the length of your project or how it responds when you add an additional resource to a task.

This section describes:

- The factors that affect scheduling, including duration, *work*, and *assignment units*.
- *Effort-driven scheduling* and its impact when adding or removing resources.
- *Task types* and their impact on task scheduling.

Factors That Affect Scheduling

Many factors contribute to a task's schedule. Certain factors affect the schedule whether or not you have resources assigned to tasks. When you assign resources, additional factors also affect how the schedule is calculated.

For all tasks, with or without resources, the schedule is calculated based on the following:

For more information about setting durations, see "Entering the Time for a Task" in chapter 4.

- **Duration.** The amount of time you estimate a task to take has a great affect on task scheduling. If you assign resources, other factors also affect task duration, but generally, the longer the duration you enter, the later a task finishes. Changing the duration usually changes the task finish date.
- **Task dependencies (or links).** If you link two tasks, you specify when you want the successor task to start in relation to the predecessor task. The type of link you establish between two tasks determines whether the successor task starts after the predecessor task is completed (finish-to-start), starts at the same time the predecessor starts (start-to-start), finishes at the same time the predecessor task finishes (finish-to-finish), or, rarely, finishes when the predecessor task starts (start-to-finish). By replacing one type of link with another, or removing a link altogether, if appropriate, you can change a task's start and finish dates.

For more information about task sequencing, linking, adding lead and lag time, and setting constraints, see chapter 5.

- **Overlap (lead time) and delay (lag time).** The overlap, or lead time, you add between two tasks causes the successor task to begin earlier. The delay, or lag time, you add between two tasks causes the successor task to begin later. If the nature of the task allows it, you can change the successor task start date by changing or removing lead time or lag time on the task link.
- **Constraints.** You can specify when a task should start or finish by specifying a moderate or inflexible constraint. If you need a task to start on a certain date, for example, you can set a Must Start On constraint. If you need a task to finish by a certain date, you can set a Finish No Later Than constraint. Unless you change it, all tasks in a project scheduled from the project start date have the As Soon As Possible constraint applied, which provides for the most flexible scheduling.

Other factors that affect how task are scheduled are the project start date, the working time calendars, and whether a task is interrupted, or split, into multiple portions.

For tasks that have resources assigned, Microsoft Project considers even more information when calculating the schedule. This includes the amount of assigned work, the number of units assigned, and the resource's working time. The following are details of the factors that contribute to the scheduling of a task with resources assigned:

For more information about resources, units, and working time calendars, see chapter 6.

- **Initially assigned resources.** When you first assign resources to a task, all resources are assigned work equivalent to the task duration. For example, if you assign one resource to an 8-hour task, the resource is assigned to 8 hours of work. If you assign two resources to an 8-hour task, both resources are assigned to 8 hours of work, for 16 hours of work altogether.
- **Additionally assigned resources.** By default, after you have assigned resources to a task, if you later decide to assign additional resources, the work will be divided among the new number of resources, and the task duration will change accordingly. For example, if you had initially assigned two full-time resources to a 12-hour task, they would both be assigned to 12 hours of work, for 24 hours of work total. If later you assign a third full-time resource, by default, the 24 hours of work is divided among the three and changes to 8 hours each, and the duration also changes to 8 hours.

- **Units.** When you assign resources to a task, you specify the number of assignment units—that is, the percentage of the resource's available time that the resource is to spend on this task. Typically, you'll leave the default units at 100%, meaning the resource will spend all his or her available time on this task. Sometimes, however, you'll want to specify that a resource only spend 50% or 10%—for example, if the resource should be working half-time on two different tasks, or if the resource is providing intermittent support or supervision on a task that others are working on. Generally, the greater the number of units assigned to a task, the sooner the task will be completed.
- **Work.** Work is the amount of time, or effort, a resource is assigned to spend on a task. For example, if you assign a full-time resource to an 8-hour task, the resource is assigned to 8 hours of work. By changing the amount of work required to accomplish a task, you can change the task duration, and thus its finish date.
- **Working time calendars.** Microsoft Project schedules tasks according to the assigned resources' working time calendars only. If the project working time calendar is set for Monday through Friday, 8:00 A.M. to 5:00 P.M., then Microsoft Project typically schedules tasks during that time. However, if the assigned resource has a working time calendar set for Saturday and Sunday, 12:00 P.M. to 12:00 A.M., the task will be scheduled during those times only. Also, if a task has a task calendar set, this additionally affects the scheduling of the task and any assigned resources.
- **Effort-driven scheduling.** With effort-driven scheduling, the more resources you add to a task, the less time it'll take to complete the task. Conversely, if you remove resources from an effort-driven task, the duration will increase. With non-effort-driven scheduling, task duration is not affected by the number of resources you add. You can turn effort-driven scheduling on or off, either for individual tasks or for all newly entered tasks. Effort-driven scheduling is on by default. You'll learn more in the "Effort-Driven Scheduling" section below.
- **Task type.** The task types are fixed units (the default), fixed work, and fixed duration. The task type governs what happens to a task when you edit one of the three scheduling variables of units, work, or duration. For example, in a fixed-units task, if you change the amount of work, duration is recalculated. In a fixed-duration task, if you change the amount of work, units are recalculated. You can specify the task type for each individual task, or change the default for all newly entered tasks. You'll learn more in the "Task Types" section below.

Effort-Driven Scheduling

Before you assign a resource to a task, the task has the duration you specify but no work associated with it. Only after you assign a resource to the task does Microsoft Project calculate the amount of work required to accomplish it.

By default, the initial calculation of total work required to perform a task stays the same, regardless of the number of additional resources (units) you assign to it. Adding or removing resources can decrease or increase the task duration, but the work remains constant. Duration is calculated according to the following formula:

Duration = Work / Units

The method Microsoft Project uses to calculate a new task duration when resources are added or removed, while holding the amount of work constant, is called *effort-driven scheduling*. This method is on by default for each task. If this method is not appropriate, you can turn effort-driven scheduling off for selected tasks or for all new tasks.

The calculation for the total work on a task is based on the initial assignment of resources made at the same time. It's only after the initial assignment that effort-driven calculations come into play. For example, suppose a task has a duration of 3 days. If you assign 2 resources initially at the same time (that is, you select both at the same time in the Assign Resources dialog box, then click the Assign button), Microsoft Project assumes that there's 24 hours of work for each resource, and so calculates 48 hours of work (with the duration remaining at 3 days). The amount of work is now fixed. If you then assign a third resource, the amount of work remains constant at 48 hours, but Microsoft Project calculates a new duration of 2 days.

Turn Off Effort-Driven Scheduling

By default, with effort-driven scheduling turned on, Microsoft Project decreases or increases the duration of a task as you add or remove resources to or from the task, while the total work on the task remains constant.

For some tasks, however, the total work should actually increase as you assign more resources. To make this happen, you can turn off effort-driven scheduling for a task.

To turn off effort-driven scheduling for an individual task

1 On the **View Bar**, click **Gantt Chart**.

2 In the **Task Name** field, select the tasks for which you want to turn off effort-driven scheduling.

To select multiple adjacent tasks, click the first task, hold down the SHIFT key, and then click the last task.

To select multiple nonadjacent tasks, click the first task, and then hold down the CTRL key as you select the other tasks.

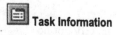

Task Information

3 Click **Task Information**, and then click the **Advanced** tab.

4 Clear the **Effort driven** check box.

To turn off effort-driven scheduling for all new tasks

1 On the **Tools** menu, click **Options**, and then click the **Schedule** tab.

2 Clear the **New tasks are effort driven** check box.

Task Types

The *task type* indicates whether the duration, work, or units should be kept constant in scheduling the task when you edit duration, work, or units. With the task type, you fix one of these values, allowing Microsoft Project to recalculate only one of the two other unfixed quantities. This quantity is calculated according to this formula:

Duration = Work / Units

When one of the three variables is edited, Microsoft Project changes one of the other two variables. Which of the two is changed is determined by its task type.

With effort-driven scheduling turned on, work remains constant regardless of the task type you select for a task. Otherwise, the three task types have the following effect when you assign additional resources:

- **If the task type is fixed units, the default task type, you'll shorten the duration of the task. The assignment units for each resource remain constant.**
- **If the task type is fixed duration, you'll decrease the individual unit values for resources. The task duration remains constant.**
- **If the task type is fixed work, you'll shorten the duration of the task. The total work and the assignment units for each resource remain constant.**

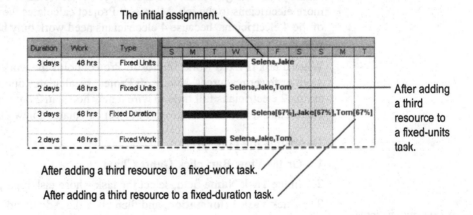

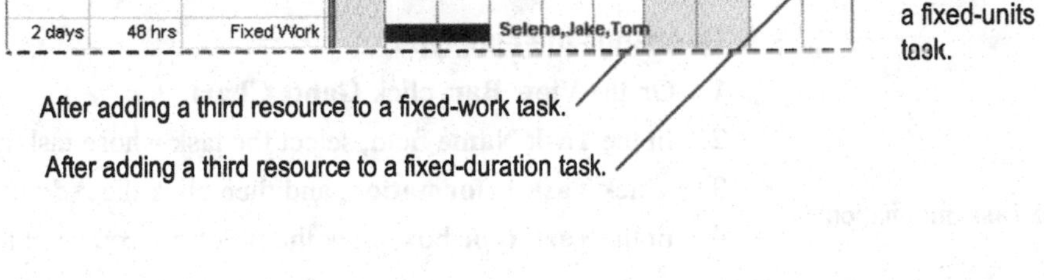

The following table shows the broader view of what happens when you change duration, work, or units for each of the three task types.

If you revise...	...in a fixed-units task, this is recalculated:	...in a fixed-duration task, this is recalculated:	...in a fixed-work task, this is recalculated:
Units	Duration	Work	Duration
Duration	Work	Work	Units
Work	Duration	Units	Duration

Suppose effort-driven scheduling is turned off and the task type is fixed units or fixed duration. If you assign additional resources to a task, the total work increases but the assignment units and duration remain constant. If the task type is fixed work, the calculations occur exactly as they do when effort-driven scheduling is turned on.

Change the Task Type

If you maintain the default of fixed units for a task, Microsoft Project holds work and units constant, and recalculates duration only. For example, suppose the task duration you enter is 2 days and you assign a resource to the task full time at 100% units (where 100% indicates 8 available working hours per day). Microsoft Project calculates the total work to be 16 hours. If you later assign another resource full-time to the task, Microsoft Project calculates a new duration of 1 day. Work remains constant at 16 hours, and for each resource the assignment units remain constant at 100%.

When you set a task as fixed duration, Microsoft Project keeps the duration at the value you entered and recalculates assignment units as you change resource assignments. For example, suppose you want the wiring for a new house to be installed in exactly 2 days. Initially, you assign 2 electricians to the job at 100% units each. Then you assign 2 more electricians to the job. Microsoft Project calculates the units to be 50% for each of the 4 electricians, because 4 electricians need work only half-time to complete the wiring in 2 days.

When a task is fixed work, Microsoft Project holds the work constant. As you assign more or fewer resources, Microsoft Project recalculates duration. For example, if you assign 2 electricians full time to wire a new house in 2 days, and then you assign 2 more electricians to the task, Microsoft Project calculates a new duration of 1 day.

To change the task type

1. On the **View Bar**, click **Gantt Chart**.
2. In the **Task Name** field, select the task whose task type you want to change.
3. Click **Task Information**, and then click the **Advanced** tab.
4. In the **Task type** box, click the task type you want to set.

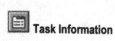

Task Information

To change the task type default for all new tasks

1 On the **Tools** menu, click **Options**, and then click the **Schedule** tab.

2 In the **Default task type** box, select the task type you want for any new tasks.

Shortening the Schedule

After reviewing your project plan, you might find that the finish date is later than is acceptable. The schedule as configured—with the existing task durations, resource assignments, task dependencies, constraints, and so on—just won't meet the required deadline. If this is the case, you can adjust tasks in various ways to shorten the schedule. The key to bringing in the finish date is to analyze the *critical path*, then adjust the tasks along that critical path.

You can bring in the critical path and consequently shorten the schedule by:

- Starting the project sooner or scheduling more working time.
- Shortening the durations of critical tasks.
- Adjusting resources assigned to critical tasks.
- Starting critical tasks sooner.
- Changing critical tasks.
- Reducing the scope of the project.

You can use any of these strategies individually or in combination. While it's best to try the simpler solutions first, the strategies you use depend on whether your project is limited by budget or resources, and how flexible your tasks and schedule are.

Think of the following sections as a checklist of everything that can affect your finish date. Follow the procedures for those strategies that make sense for your project.

The Critical Path and Critical Tasks

In nearly every project, certain tasks can delay the entire project if they're not completed on time. Usually, other tasks can be completed late without affecting the project finish date at all. Tasks that can delay the entire project are *critical tasks*. These are tasks whose early start and late start dates are the same, and whose early finish and late finish dates are the same, because no time is available for any delay. Tasks that can be delayed a day or more before the project finish date without delaying the project finish date are *noncritical tasks*.

Critical tasks make up the task sequence known as the *critical path*. The critical path is that sequence of tasks that ends on the project finish date. The finish date of the last task in the critical path is the project finish date. When you want to shorten your schedule, you begin by shortening the critical path. Most often, the critical path is the longest sequence of linked tasks in your project.

By default, a critical task has zero *total slack* time. Total slack time is the amount of time a task's finish date can slip before it delays the project finish date. If any critical task slips, the project finish date will be delayed.

A noncritical task can be an unlinked task whose finish date is earlier than the project finish date. It can also be a task that's linked in a task sequence that finishes earlier than another task sequence in the same schedule. Noncritical tasks have slack time. Therefore, increasing the duration of a noncritical task to less than its slack time or decreasing its duration has no effect on the project finish date.

Critical tasks can become noncritical tasks and vice versa. Whenever you change data that affects a task's schedule (such as assigning resources, changing links, adding or removing constraints, or changing a duration), Microsoft Project recalculates the critical path.

Before you can adjust critical tasks, you need to identify them. In several views, Microsoft Project graphically distinguishes critical tasks from noncritical ones.

To identify the critical path

1 On the **View Bar**, click **More Views**.

2 In the **Views** list, select **Detail Gantt** or **Tracking Gantt**, and then click **Apply**.

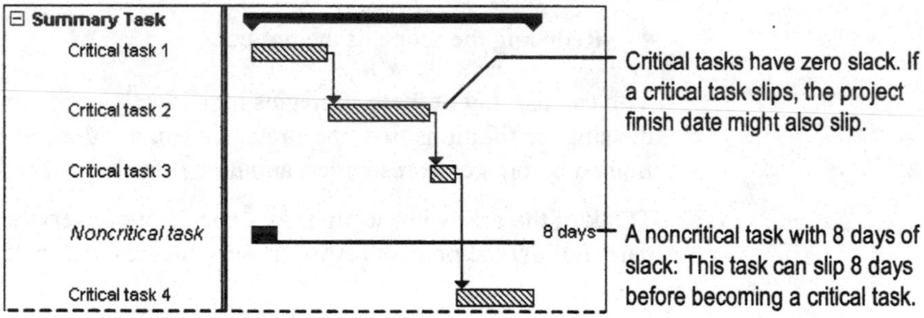

If you just need to see the project finish date, review the Project Information dialog box. On the Project menu, click Project Information. The calculated finish date is shown in the Finish date box.

Adjust the Project

If your finish date isn't acceptable, there are two global strategies you can apply to your project to bring in the finish date: changing the project start date and changing the project calendar.

Change the Project Start Date

If you originally set up your project with a start date in the future, you might be able to bring in the finish date simply by starting the project sooner.

To change the project start date

1 On the **Project** menu, click **Project Information**.

2 In the **Start date** box, change the date to an earlier date.

Change the Project Calendar

For more information about the project calendar, see "Change Your Project's Working Days and Hours" in chapter 6.

Tasks are scheduled according to the working time specified in your project calendar. Some project managers like to set the project calendar for less than 40 hours a week to account for administrative tasks, other projects, and other non-project tasks that take up time during the week. If you've done this and see that your finish date is too late, you can add working time back in to the project calendar.

For more information, see "Create a Base Calendar for a Specific Work Schedule" in chapter 6.

Or, maybe you're using the Standard project calendar, which assumes a 40-hour work week, but your project actually is based on two shifts, a 24-hour day, or weekend work. You can change the project calendar to reflect this. You can also create a new base calendar that reflects your unique working time, then make it the project calendar.

To change to a different project calendar

1 On the **Project** menu, click **Project Information**.

2 In the **Calendar** box, select the name of the base calendar you want to apply to the entire project.

Adjust the Duration of Critical Tasks

The longest critical tasks have the biggest effect on project length. Therefore, one of the most effective methods for bringing in the project finish date is to shorten the critical tasks with the longest duration first. The easiest way to do this is to filter to display critical tasks only, then sort these tasks by duration. You can then review the tasks and determine which might be adjusted to a shorter duration.

First filter for critical tasks.

16		⊟ **Foundation**	**42 days**
18		Form basement walls	13 days
19		Place concrete for foundations & basement wall:	12 days
20		Cure basement walls for 7 days	7 days
17		Excavate for foundations	3 days
21		Strip basement wall forms	2 days
22		Waterproof/insulate basement walls	2 days
24		Backfill foundation	2 days
23		Perform foundation inspection	1 day

Then sort by duration to see if any critical task durations can be shortened.

To sort critical tasks by duration

For more information about filtering and sorting, see chapter 12, "Viewing Your Information."

1 On the **View Bar**, click **Gantt Chart**.
2 On the **Project** menu, point to **Filtered for**, and then click **Critical**.
3 On the **Project** menu, point to **Sort**, and then click **Sort by**.
4 In the **Sort by** box, click **Duration**, and then click **Descending**.
5 Select or clear the **Keep outline structure** check box, depending on how you want to see the tasks.
6 Click **Sort**.

Summary tasks are sorted from the longest to the shortest. The tasks under each summary task are also sorted from the longest to the shortest.

To decrease the duration of a task

1 On the **View Bar**, click **Gantt Chart**.
2 In the **Duration** field, type a new duration for the task.

When finished reviewing critical tasks by duration, restore your view to show all tasks in order again.

To restore all tasks to ID order

1 On the **View Bar**, click **Gantt Chart**.
2 On the **Project** menu, point to **Filtered for**, and then click **All Tasks**.
3 On the **Project** menu, point to **Sort**, and then click **by ID**.

Adjust the Resources Assigned to Critical Tasks

By adjusting resources assigned to critical tasks, you might be able to shorten the critical path and therefore the project finish date. You can:

- Decrease duration by decreasing work.
- Decrease duration by adding or changing resource assignments.
- Assign overtime work.
- Increase the working time in the resource calendar.

Decrease Work on a Critical Task

By default, Microsoft Project calculates a task duration based on the amount of work required to complete the task. For example, if you assign 1 full-time resource to a 2-day task, Microsoft Project calculates the total work to be 16 hours. If you assign a second full-time resource to the task, Microsoft Project holds the work constant and recalculates the task duration to be 1 day.

If you decrease the total work on a task, then Microsoft Project decreases the task duration accordingly.

To decrease total work on a task

1 On the **View Bar**, click **Task Usage**.

2 In the **Work** field of the sheet portion of the view, reduce the total amount of work for the task you want to shorten.

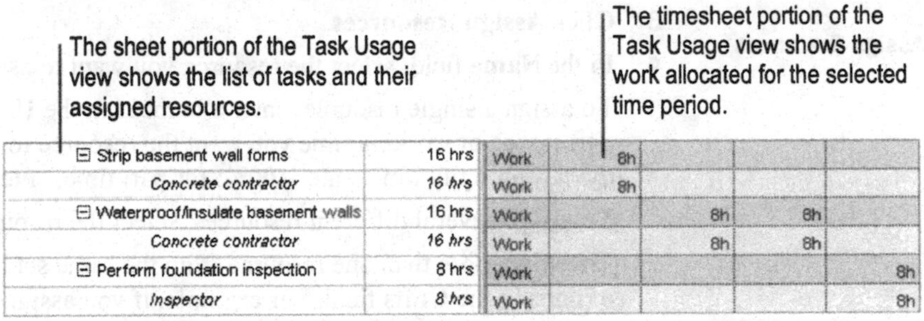
The sheet portion of the Task Usage view shows the list of tasks and their assigned resources.
The timesheet portion of the Task Usage view shows the work allocated for the selected time period.
Strip basement wall forms
16 hrs
Work
8h
Concrete contractor
16 hrs
Work
8h
Waterproof/insulate basement walls
16 hrs
Work
8h
8h
Concrete contractor
16 hrs
Work
8h
8h
Perform foundation inspection
8 hrs
Work
8h
Inspector
8 hrs
Work
8h

Add or Change Resource Assignments

With the default effort-driven scheduling turned on, assigning additional resources to a task decreases its duration. The more resources you assign, the more the duration decreases.

When you assign more resources to a task, use resources that have available working hours on the days you assign them, reassign resources from noncritical tasks to critical tasks so you don't inadvertently lengthen the schedule, or hire new resources. You can also assign additional units of the same resource.

To find resources with available time during certain periods

1. On the **View Bar**, click **Resource Usage View**.

   In the sheet (left) portion of the Resource Usage view, you see a list of resources. Under each resource name is the list of tasks that represent the resource's assignments. Resources that aren't assigned to tasks do not have tasks listed underneath their names. Tasks with no resources assigned are located under Unassigned in the Resource Name field.

   In the timesheet (right) portion of the Resource Usage view, you see the total hours each resource is working, the number of hours the resource is working on each task, and the hours worked for the specified time period.

Zoom Out

Zoom In

2. If necessary, click the **Zoom In** or **Zoom Out** buttons to view the timescale you want.
3. In the timesheet portion of the view, scroll to the time period you want to review for availability.
4. On the **Format** menu, point to **Details**, and then click **Remaining Availability**.
5. Review the resource availability field in the timesheet to see who has time for more assignments.

To assign more resources to a task

1. On the **View Bar**, click **Gantt Chart**.
2. In the **Task Name** field, select the task to which you want to assign more resources.

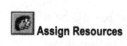

Assign Resources

3. Click **Assign Resources**.
4. In the **Name** field, select the resource you want to assign to the task.

   To assign a single resource, enter a number in the **Units** field to indicate the percentage of working time you want the resource to spend on the task. To assign the resource full time, enter 100%; for part time, enter a smaller number.

   To assign several different resources, select the resources (CTRL+click).

   To assign more than one resource from the same set of resources, enter the number of units in the **Units** field. For example, if you assign 2 painters from the Painters set, choose 200%.

   If necessary, type the name of a new resource in the **Name** field.
5. Click **Assign**.

   A check mark to the left of the Name field indicates that the resource is assigned to the selected task.

Another way to bring in the finish date is to replace a slower resource with a faster one. This could be an equipment resource that has faster throughput, for example, or a more experienced human resource.

To replace a slower resource with a faster resource

1. On the **View Bar**, click **Gantt Chart**.
2. In the **Task Name** field, select the task for which you want to replace a resource.
3. Click **Assign Resources**.

 **Assign Resources**

4. In the **Name** field, select the assigned resource you want replaced on the task.
5. Click **Replace**.
6. In the **Name** field, select the resource you now want to assign to the task, and then click **OK**.

If you don't have other resources available to you, you might be able to increase the units assigned to a critical task. For example, if you find that a critical task has resources assigned at 50% units—that is, half-time effort—you might be able to increase it to 100% and thereby shorten the duration and bring in the finish date.

For more information, see "About Assignment Units" in chapter 6.

To increase the assignment units for a task

1. On the View Bar, click Gantt Chart.
2. In the **Task Name** field, select the task for which you want to increase assignment units.
3. Click **Assign Resources**.

 **Assign Resources**

4. In the **Units** field for the assigned resource, enter the number of units you want, and then click **Assign**.

Assign Overtime Work

Maybe you've done everything you can already do; you've decreased the total work in tasks as much as possible, all your resources are working to their maximum availability, and you can't hire any more new resources. As long as you have budget for it, you can assign overtime work to resources to decrease task durations and shorten the schedule.

For information about entering overtime rates, see "Setting Costs" in chapter 7.

When you assign a resource to work overtime, in many cases, you'll have to pay that resource an overtime rate, which can be costly. Microsoft Project calculates task costs based on the overtime rate you specified for that resource.

To assign overtime work for a task

1. On the **View Bar**, click **Gantt Chart**.
2. On the **Window** menu, click **Split**.
3. Click anywhere in the bottom pane.

4 On the **Format** menu, point to **Details**, and then click **Resource Work**.

5 In the Gantt Chart in the top pane, select the task for which you want to assign overtime work in the **Task Name** field.

6 In the Resource Work form in the bottom pane, type the number of hours in the **Ovt. Work** field for each resource.

7 Click **OK**.

8 When finished working with the Resource Work form, on the **Window** menu, click **Remove Split**.

The task selected in the Gantt Chart in the top pane...

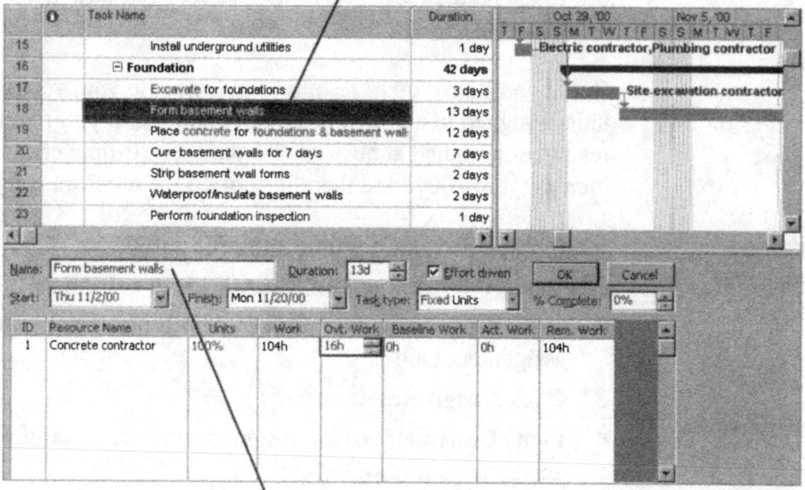

...is detailed in the Resource Work form in the bottom pane.

Another way to assign overtime work is to use the Resource Usage view and apply the Work table. Enter the overtime hours in the Overtime field for each assignment.

The number of overtime work hours is a part of the total work hours, not additional hours of work on the task. If you see that there are 48 hours of work for one resource to do in one week, be sure that the Work field contains 48 hours and the Ovt. Work field contains 8 hours. This indicates that there is 48 hours of work to do, and 8 of them are to be overtime.

Setting overtime work on an assignment reduces the time span of the assignment. It might also reduce the task duration, depending on the nature of other assignments on the task.

Increase Working Time for a Resource

For more information, see "Setting Working Time for Resources" in chapter 6.

In many projects, the normal working day for a resource is 8 hours long, which is the default length of a working day in the Standard project calendar. If you can't get additional resources for a project but need to shorten task durations, you can increase the number of working hours of already assigned resources. You increase a resource's working hours on his or her resource calendar.

A task duration is based partly on the number of working hours of assigned resources. For example, if a resource with an 8-hour working day is assigned to a 24-hour task, the task will take the resource 3 days to complete. If you increase the resource's workday to 12 hours, then the resource will complete the task in 2 days.

To increase working time for a resource

1. On the **Tools** menu, click **Change Working Time**.
2. In the **For** box, click the resource whose calendar you want to change.
3. On the calendar, select the days you want to change.

   To change a day of the week for the entire calendar, select the day heading at the top of the calendar. For example, to make all Saturdays working days, click the S column heading.
4. Type the new working times in the **From** and **To** boxes.

Start Critical Tasks Sooner

If you scrutinize your project plan, you might find that you can start certain critical tasks sooner. This way, without shortening durations or adding more resources, you'll be able to shorten the schedule. Methods for starting critical tasks sooner are:

- Changing a task dependency.
- Adding lead time.
- Changing a constraint.

Change a Task Dependency

For more information, see "Building Your Schedule Using Task Dependencies" in chapter 5.

Tasks linked with start-to-start (SS) and finish-to-finish (FF) links automatically overlap predecessor and successor tasks, which tends to bring in the project finish date. One way to shorten your schedule, then, is to replace finish-to-start (FS) links with either SS or FF links. Look for FS-linked critical tasks in your project whose dependency is better represented by an SS or FF link.

In addition, remember that tasks don't necessarily need to be linked consecutively or with just a single link. Sometimes one task launches a number of other tasks that can start at the same time. One predecessor can have several successors, for example. Look for FS-linked critical tasks that really could start when an earlier task finishes, and not just the task immediately preceding it. You might find that it makes more sense for it to be linked to a task five rows above it.

Also, some tasks don't need to be linked to anything at all, in which case they would be scheduled to start at their summary task or the project start date.

To change a task dependency type

1. On the **View Bar**, click **Gantt Chart**.
2. Double-click the link line you want to view or change.
3. In the **Type** box, check the task dependency.
4. To change the task dependency, click the task link type you want.
   To delete the task dependency, click **Delete**.

You can also delete all links to and from a task by selecting the task and then clicking Unlink Tasks.

To change a task's predecessor

Unlink Tasks

Task Information

1. On the **View Bar**, click **Gantt Chart**.
2. In the **Task Name** field, click the task whose predecessor you want to change.
3. Click **Task Information**.
4. Click the **Predecessors** tab.
5. In the **Task Name** field, select the task name you want to replace the existing predecessor.

Add Lead Time to a Critical Task

In many projects, the most common link between dependent tasks is the finish-to-start (FS) link, the link that gives Microsoft Project the greatest flexibility when scheduling tasks. But by not allowing a successor task to start until its predecessor is completed, the FS link can make your schedule longer than it needs to be.

For more information, see "Overlap and Delay Tasks" in chapter 5.

If the FS link represents the true dependency between tasks, you shouldn't change it to another dependency type. Instead, you can determine if the successor task can start before the predecessor task is completed. If it can, add lead time to the successor task so that it begins on an earlier date and overlaps the predecessor task, thus allowing the project to end on an earlier date.

If the tasks can overlap so much that they can begin on the same start date, you might want to replace the FS link with a start-to-start (SS) link instead of adding lead time.

To add lead time

1 On the **View Bar**, click **Gantt Chart**.

 **Task Information**

2 In the **Task Name** field, select the successor task you want, and then click **Task Information**.

3 Click the **Predecessors** tab.

4 In the **Lag** field, type the lead time you want as a duration (type a negative number) or as a percentage of the predecessor task duration (type the negative percentage complete).

For example, if the predecessor task has a duration of 2 days and you want the successor to begin 1 day before the predecessor task is completed, type either –1d or –50% in the Lag field.

Lead time units are minute, hour, day, week, and month. To specify elapsed duration, precede the time unit with the letter e (for example, edays for elapsed days). Elapsed days include weekends and other nonworking days.

Change the Constraint Type

For more information, see "Scheduling Tasks for Specific Dates" in chapter 5.

Inflexible and moderate constraints set on tasks can limit the ability of Microsoft Project to recalculate and flexibly reschedule tasks. For example, suppose two critical tasks are linked with a finish-to-start (FS) link, and the successor task has a Must Start On constraint. If you decrease the duration of the predecessor task, the start date of the successor task remains unchanged. Neither the successor task nor any task that depends on it starts any earlier. As a result, decreasing the duration of the critical task doesn't shorten the schedule.

One way to avoid such a situation is to replace an inflexible constraint with a flexible constraint: As Soon As Possible or As Late As Possible. Of course, always apply the constraint that best represents the scheduling reality for a task.

To examine and change constraints on tasks

1 On the **View Bar**, click **Gantt Chart**.

2 On the **View** menu, point to **Table**, and then click **More Tables**.

To return to the Entry table, on the View menu, point to Table, and then click Entry.

3 In the **Tables** list, click **Constraint Dates**, and then click **Apply**.

4 Scroll to the right to display the **Constraint Type** and **Constraint Date** fields.

For each task with a constraint other than As Soon As Possible, look at the predecessor tasks and successor tasks on the Gantt Chart to determine if the constraint is necessary.

5 To change a constraint type, click the field and pick the constraint type you want from the dropdown list.

6 To change a constraint date, click the field and pick the date from the calendar. If you don't type or select a date, Microsoft Project uses the task's existing start or finish date as the constraint date.

Review the constraint types to make sure they're as flexible as possible for the task.

⊟ Initial New Product Screening Stage	**9 days**	**\s Soon As Possible**	**NA**
New product opportunity identified	0 days	As Soon As Possible	NA
Describe new product idea (1-page written disclos	2 days	Start No Later Than	Mon 11/13/00
Gather information required for go/no-go decision	6 days	As Soon As Possible	NA
Convene opportunity of screening committee (decis	1 day	Finish No Later Than	Thu 11/23/00
Decision point - go/no-go to preliminary investigatio	0 days	As Soon As Possible	NA
⊟ Preliminary Investigation Stage	**53 days**	**\s Soon As Possible**	**NA**
Assign resources to preliminary investigation	1 day	Must Start On	Mon 11/27/00
Develop preliminary investigation plan	5 days	As Soon As Possible	NA
Evaluate the market	10 days	As Soon As Possible	NA
Analyze the competition	5 days	As Soon As Possible	NA

Review the constraint dates to make sure they're correct.

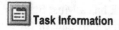

Task Information

You can also review and change constraints on individual tasks. Select the task, click Task Information, select the Advanced tab, and then review the Constraint Type and Date boxes.

If you want to keep important dates visible without setting date constraints, consider setting deadlines. For more information, see "Specify Task Deadlines" in chapter 5.

Change Critical Tasks

Take a good look at your critical tasks. Maybe one or two of them are actually optional or unnecessary and can be deleted. Perhaps a couple of critical tasks can be combined into a single task with a compressed duration. It's possible that a larger critical task can be separated into several noncritical subtasks. Maybe these subtasks could be overlapped, resulting in a shorter overall task duration.

Delete or Combine Critical Tasks

For more information, see "Delete Tasks" in chapter 4.

If you find any critical tasks are actually optional or unnecessary, and your project goals can be satisfactorily met without them, consider deleting them.

Another strategy is to combine two critical tasks into one critical task whose duration is less than the sum of the durations of the separate tasks.

To combine critical tasks

1. On the **View Bar**, click **Gantt Chart**.
2. In the **Task Name** field, select the task you want to keep.
3. Type a new name to represent the combined tasks.
4. In the **Duration** field, enter a new duration to represent the new duration of the combined tasks.

Assign Resources

5. Click **Assign Resources** and assign additional resources to the task, perhaps those who had been assigned to the task to be deleted.
6. In the **Task Name** field, select the task whose information has been combined into the other task.
7. On the **Edit** menu, click **Delete Task**.

When you delete a critical task that's linked to both its predecessor and successor tasks with finish-to-start (FS) links, Microsoft Project relinks its predecessor task to its successor task with an FS link by default. If you delete a task with any other type of link, after you delete the task, you'll need to link its predecessor to its successor manually.

Break a Critical Task into Subtasks

Some of the tasks on the critical path might actually represent a number of smaller tasks. To shorten the schedule, you can break these large critical tasks into subtasks.

Breaking a critical task into subtasks can shorten the schedule in two ways. Perhaps the work on at least some of the subtasks can overlap—for example, with lead time or by being linked with a start-to-start dependency. Perhaps some of the subtasks can be made noncritical tasks, if they don't need to be completed in sequence.

To break a large task into a summary task and subtasks

1. On the **View Bar**, click **More Views**.
2. On the **Views** list, select **Detail Gantt** or **Tracking Gantt**, and then click **Apply**.
3. In the **Task Name** field, select a single task on the critical path that could be completed in several steps.

Unlink Tasks

4. Click **Unlink Tasks**.
5. Remove the resources assigned to this task.
6. Select the task beneath the task you want to change, and then click **New Task** on the **Insert** menu.
7. Repeat step 6 for each subtask you want to add.
   Microsoft Project schedules these new unlinked subtasks to begin on the start date for the summary task.

8 For each new task, type a name in the **Task Name** field and a duration in the **Duration** field.

Indent

9 In the **Task Name** field, select all the new tasks, and then click **Indent** to make them subtasks of the original task.

The original task becomes a summary task. The subtasks are on the critical path.

Link Tasks

10 Click **Link Tasks**.

To shorten the schedule, consider linking the subtasks with start-to-start or finish-to-finish dependencies. Add lead time to subtasks linked with finish-to-start dependencies. If appropriate, consider removing the link altogether, in which case the subtask would probably become noncritical.

11 If necessary, link the last new task to a successor task.

Apply a Task Calendar to a Critical Task

For more information, see "Schedule with Task Calendars" in chapter 5.

If you have one or more critical tasks that don't need to be scheduled according to the project calendar—for example, a task being performed by a machine that operates 24 hours a day—you can create and apply a task calendar to the task. In such a case, this could help bring in your finish date.

To apply a task calendar to a critical task

1 Make sure that the calendar you want to use is created. You can use an existing base calendar, such as 24 Hours or Night Shift, or you can create your own.

For information on creating a new base calendar, see "Setting Working Time for Resources" in chapter 6.

2 On the **View Bar**, click **Gantt Chart**.

3 In the **Task Name** field, select the critical task to which you want to assign a task calendar.

Task Information

4 Click **Task Information**, and then click the **Advanced** tab.

5 In the **Calendar** box, click the calendar you want to use for the task.

6 Select the **Scheduling ignores resource calendars** check box to have the task calendar ignore the resource calendars of any assigned resources.

If you choose to have Microsoft Project ignore resource calendars, the task and any assigned resources will be scheduled according to the task calendar, even if it's during nonworking time for the assigned resources.

If you choose not to ignore resource calendars, the task will be scheduled where the task calendar and resource calendar have overlapping working time.

Task Calendar indicator

Any task with a task calendar applied is shown with the task calendar icon in the Indicators column.

Find Slack in Your Schedule

Suppose you need to shorten a task duration and the only way to do it is to borrow a resource from another task. Or imagine you need to replace an overworked resource with another resource. A good place to look for such a resource is in tasks that have *slack time.*

Only noncritical tasks have slack time. There are two types of slack: total slack and free slack. *Total slack* is the amount of time a task can be delayed without delaying the project finish date. *Free slack* is the amount of time a task can be delayed without delaying the finish date of another task. A noncritical task can have either or both types of slack.

Why would you want to remove slack time from a noncritical task? Primarily, when you want to shorten critical tasks to bring in the project finish date. You can take a resource assigned to a task with slack, and assign him or her to a critical task that can be shortened with additional resources.

For example, to shorten a critical task, you might decide it's best to remove Jean from a noncritical task and assign her to the critical task. When you remove Jean from the noncritical task, the duration of the noncritical task might increase. If the duration increases by an amount that is less than the initial total slack time, the task remains a noncritical task. By reassigning Jean to the critical task, you shorten that task's duration. In effect, you shift time from tasks that have an excess of time (noncritical tasks) to tasks that have a time deficit (critical tasks that are too long).

You can also add a constraint to make a task with slack occur later, and thereby free up a resource to work on critical tasks.

For more information, see "Use Microsoft Project Resource Leveling" later in this chapter.

Another reason for removing slack is to resolve resource overallocations. You can replace overallocated resources with those assigned to tasks with slack. But keep in mind that the Microsoft Project leveling feature automatically uses slack to help resolve overallocations.

You probably wouldn't want a schedule in which every task has close to 0 slack, as this would mean that almost every task is critical or almost critical, and that any delay at all would cause the finish date to be delayed. Because of this, many project managers look at slack in their schedule as a built-in buffer.

To find slack in your schedule

1. On the **View Bar**, click **More Views**.
2. In the **Views** list, click **Detail Gantt**, and then click **Apply**.
   Slack on a task appears graphically as thin slack bars adjoining the regular Gantt bars.
3. On the **View** menu, point to **Table**, and then click **Schedule**.
4. Drag the divider bar to the right to view the **Free Slack** and **Total Slack** fields.

By default, a zero duration in the Total Slack field indicates a critical task. A negative value in the Total Slack field indicates a scheduling conflict. In many cases, the conflict results from a predecessor task that has an FS link with a successor task that has a Must Start On constraint date that's earlier than the finish date of the predecessor task. This situation could occur if the predecessor task start and finish dates are pushed out by schedule changes. If the FS link is true, it must be impossible for the successor task to start before the predecessor task is completed.

It's often helpful to know which tasks have a small amount of slack, as this means they're almost critical and any delay might cause them to become critical. You can change the amount of slack time that defines a critical task. For example, if you specify the default to be 2 days (rather than 0 days), then all tasks with 2 days of slack time or less will be displayed as critical tasks.

To change the default slack time for critical tasks

1 On the **Tools** menu, click **Options**, and then click the **Calculation** tab.

2 In the **Tasks are critical if slack is less than or equal to** box, enter the amount of slack time you want to determine a critical task.

Cut Scope to Shorten the Schedule

Sometimes the best strategy for shortening the schedule is simply to do less. If you can still accomplish the goals of your project, consider cutting scope. Methods for cutting scope to shorten the schedule include:

- **Removing critical tasks.** This might involve removing extra or optional steps from certain processes, combining tasks, or decreasing the number of deliverables.
- **Shorten the durations of critical tasks.** You can shorten durations by removing optional steps or lowering the acceptable level of quality.

For more information on cutting scope, see "Adjusting Project Scope" later in this chapter.

Balancing the Workload

As you now know, Microsoft Project schedules tasks according to factors such as task duration, predecessors, and constraints. When you assign resources to tasks, Microsoft Project further takes into consideration the amount of work assigned, the units, and the working time calendars of assigned resources.

However, Microsoft Project does not consider whether a resource is scheduled for more time than available. For example, it's possible for a resource to be scheduled for two 8-hour tasks on the same day.

As you review your project for potential problems, you can check for any such resource *overallocations* and adjust the assignments to better balance your workload. In any resource view, Microsoft Project highlights resources that are scheduled for more tasks than they have available time for.

For example, Richard is available to work 8 hours per day, as defined in his resource calendar. When defining roofing tasks, you assign Richard to shingle the roof on Monday and Tuesday, full time. Later, when defining wall construction tasks, you assign him to construct the outer walls on Tuesday and Wednesday, also full time. On Monday and Wednesday, Richard is assigned to work 8 hours, exactly what he has available on those days. But on Tuesday, you've assigned him to 2 tasks full time, for a total of 16 hours of work—twice the number of hours he's available to work on that day. Microsoft Project indicates that Richard is overallocated on Tuesday by a total of 8 hours.

For more information about max units, see "Set Resource Availability" in chapter 6.

While resources are scheduled according to their working time in their resource calendar, whether they're overallocated or not is determined by the resource calendar as well as their max units and resource availability.

It's also a good idea to check for any *underallocations*—that is, resources that are not being used to their maximum availability. Suppose you hired Jean to work full time on your project, in which you're tracking costs because you have a strict budget. Although you're paying Jean a full-time salary, you'll probably see only the costs for work assigned to Jean, even if she is being used at 50% of her available time. Because of this, not only are you not using Jean's full potential for your project, your cost data are inaccurate.

When you resolve resource overallocations and underallocations, your goal is to distribute the workload as evenly as possible among resources. Each resource should be working at just about maximum capacity—each available work hour is filled by a task—but no more.

There are a number of ways you can use Microsoft Project to resolve resource overallocations. You can:

- **Change resource availability.** Adjust the resource calendar of the overallocated resource to increase working time, lengthen the resource availability dates, or increase the max units.
- **Assign overtime.** While this approach might or might not resolve the overallocation, it will account for the overallocation as an accepted reality of the project. If you're tracking costs, assigning overtime will also help you track how much you're spending in overtime.

- **Change the assigned resources.** Add additional resources, replace the overallocated resource with an underallocated resource, or remove an overallocated resource from tasks.
- **Adjust the time and effort on assignments with overallocation.** You can adjust assignment dates, decrease an overallocated resource's work or units on tasks, and apply work contours to tasks.
- **Change tasks to resolve overallocations.** Consider delaying or interrupting (splitting) work on tasks until when the overallocated resource has time to finish them. You can also change task durations by changing assignment units or work.
- **Level resources.** Resource leveling *splits* and *delays* tasks assigned to overallocated resources until all the overallocations are resolved. You can do this with the Microsoft Project resource leveling feature, or you can manually add splits and delays yourself.
- **Cut scope.** If possible, reduce task durations or eliminate optional tasks to resolve resource overallocations. See "Adjusting Project Scope" later in this chapter.

You can invert many of these strategies to resolve underallocations.

Remember that no matter what you do, some amount of overwork and underwork might be unavoidable and acceptable in your project plan.

Also, be aware that there are trade-offs when you resolve resource overallocations. For example, when you resolve an overallocation, you might increase a task duration or push out the project finish date.

Think of the following sections as a checklist of all possible strategies for balancing your resource workload. Many of the suggestions are procedures you've learned in previous chapters, and those are cross-referenced for you. New procedures are delineated in this section.

Check the Resource Workload

Before you can resolve resource overallocations, you need to find out which resources are overallocated, when they're overallocated, and what tasks they're assigned to during the time periods they're overallocated. You'll also want to know which resources are underallocated or unassigned and which tasks have no work assigned to them. You can do all of this by checking the resource workload in the Resource Usage view.

To check resource workload

1. On the **View Bar**, click **Resource Usage**.
2. If necessary, click the **Zoom In** or **Zoom Out** buttons to view the timescale you want.

Zoom Out

Zoom In

3 Review the amount of work for the time period you've chosen in the timesheet portion of the view to determine whether a resource is overallocated or underallocated.

The sheet portion of the Resource Usage view shows the list of resources and their assignments.

The timesheet portion of the Resource Usage view shows the work allocated for the selected time period.

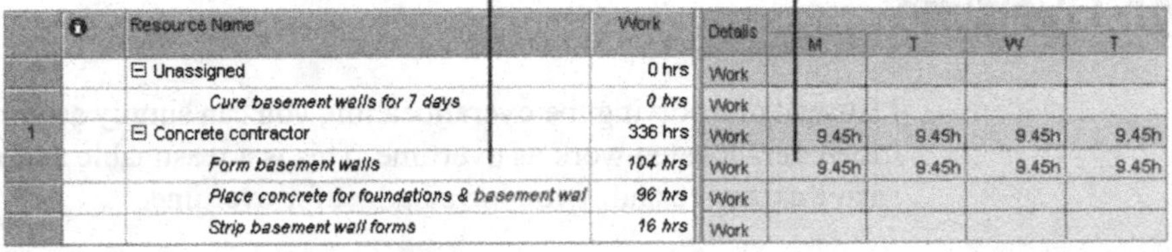

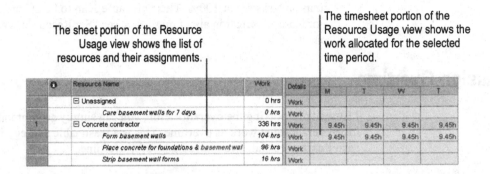

	Resource Name	Work	Details	M	T	W	T
	⊟ Unassigned	0 hrs	Work				
	Cure basement walls for 7 days	*0 hrs*	Work				
1	⊟ Concrete contractor	336 hrs	Work	9.45h	9.45h	9.45h	9.45h
	Form basement walls	*104 hrs*	Work	9.45h	9.45h	9.45h	9.45h
	Place concrete for foundations & basement wal	*96 hrs*	Work				
	Strip basement wall forms	*16 hrs*	Work				

Leveling indicator

The names of overallocated resources are in red. The leveling indicator appears in the Indicators column for overallocated resource. You can also add the Overallocated field to the timesheet portion of the view. This will show the amount of overallocation for each time period.

Go To Next Overallocation

Use the Resource Management toolbar to help find overallocated resources. On the View menu, point to Toolbars, and then click Resource Management. While working in the Resource Usage view, or any other resource view, click Go To Next Overallocation.

To see a graphical representation of overallocated resources, display the Resource Graph view.

Check and Adjust Resource Availability

Before changing resource assignments or tasks to resolve resource overallocations, check the assumptions you've made about the overallocated resource's availability.

- **Check the resource calendar.** Check the overallocated resource's working time calendar and make sure it's correct. The resource calendar determines when the task is scheduled. If the resource actually works more than is reflected in the working time calendar, make the adjustment. For more information about how to review and change the resource calendar, see "Setting Working Time for Resources" in chapter 6.
- **Check the resource availability dates.** Check the overallocated resource's start and end dates on the project. If a resource is scheduled for a task before the resource's start date or after the end date, the resource will be overallocated. For more information about resource start and end dates, see "Set Resource Availability" in chapter 6.

- **Check the resource's max unit availability.** Check the overallocated resource's max units for the time period when the overallocation occurs. If a resource is scheduled for more effort than is specified by the max units, the resource will be overallocated. For example, suppose Jean's max units are 75% but her assignment units on tasks are at 100%. This will cause Jean to be at least 25% overallocated. For more information about max units, see "Set Resource Availability" in chapter 6.

Assign Overtime

Instead of resolving the overallocation, you can simply accommodate it by assigning the overallocated work as overtime. This is a reasonable strategy if the overallocation isn't excessive and if you have budget for overtime.

You can review the amount of overallocation in the Resource Usage view in the timesheet ...

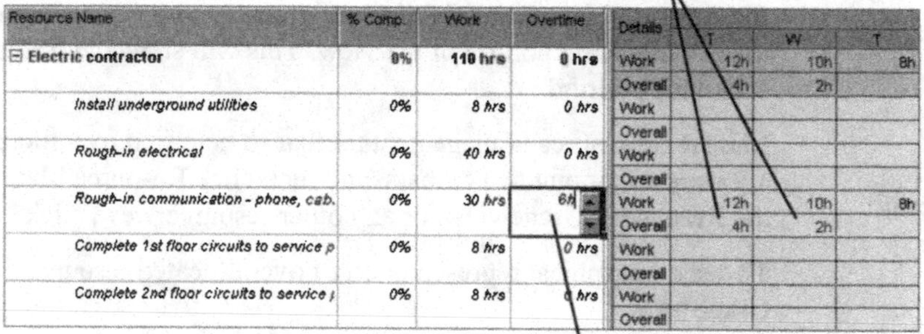

...and enter an amount of Overtime in the Work table.

To assign overtime work to account for overallocations

1. On the **View Bar**, click **Resource Usage**.
2. Under **Resource Name**, select the overallocated resource.
3. Scroll the timesheet to the time period in which the resource is overallocated.
4. On the **Format** menu, point to **Details**, and then click **Overallocation**.
5. Review the overallocation field in the timesheet to help determine the time and amount of overtime needed.
6. On the **View** menu, point to **Tables**, and then click **Work**.
7. In the **Overtime** field for the assignment, enter the number of overtime hours you want to assign.

   Remember that the number of overtime work hours is a part of, rather than in addition to, the total work hours. If the overallocated resource is assigned to 10

If you're tracking costs, make sure that the resource overtime rates are entered correctly. See "Setting Costs" in chapter 7.

hours of work in one day, for example, you leave the 10 hours in Work field, and add 2 hours in the Overtime field.

Change the Assigned Resources

If your resource availability assumptions are correct and if you've added all the overtime you can but still have overallocated resources, you can change the assigned resources to resolve the overallocations.

- **Add more resources.** When you add more resources to tasks to which the overallocated resource is assigned, the work will be divided among all the assigned resources (assuming the default effort-driven scheduling and fixed-unit tasks). This reduces the number of hours the overallocated resource must work for this task.
- **Replace an overallocated resource with an underallocated resource.** You can take an overallocated resource off an assignment or two, replacing the resource with an underallocated resource.
- **Remove the overallocated resource from assignments.** If you remove the overallocated resource from an assignment that is also still assigned to other resources, the work will be divided among the remaining resources. Again, this works for fixed-unit effort-driven tasks.

For more information about any of these three procedures, see "Change Resource Assignments" in chapter 6.

Adjust the Time and Effort on Assignments

You can adjust how much time and effort an overallocated resource is spending on assignments in a number of ways. For example, if you reduce the number of hours the resource is spending on tasks, or change the resource from a full-time to part-time effort for the overallocated time period, you can alleviate the overallocation.

- **Adjust the dates that the resource works on the assignment.** By default, the resource is assigned to the full time span of the task. You can adjust those dates if necessary. If the resource is overallocated during the first two days of a 10-day task, you can have the resource not start on this assignment until the third day.
- **Adjust the level of effort, or units, that the resource works on the assignment.** Resources are typically assigned to 100% units on a task, or 100% of the availability designated in the resource's working time calendar. You can resolve overallocations by reducing the units to a part-time effort during the time period of the overallocation. This will typically increase duration.
- **Decrease the resource's work on the assignment.** You might be able to decrease the number of hours an overallocated resource is assigned to a task. However, with

the default effort-driven fixed-units tasks, decreasing work will also decrease duration. If you want to decrease work without decreasing duration, apply fixed duration as the task type. This will change units instead.

- **Apply work contours to assignments.** You can specify changing levels of work across the span of an assignment with work contours. For example, a ramp-up contour assigns fewer hours near the start of the assignment and increasingly more hours as the task progresses. Several shapes can accommodate your need to resolve overallocations. You can create your own contour by editing individual timephased work values in the timesheet portion of the Resource Usage or Task Usage view. For details on using and applying work contours, see "Control the Amount of Work Throughout an Assignment" in chapter 6.

Adjust the Dates on Assignments

You can resolve overallocations by changing the assignment dates for the overallocated resource. Instead of being assigned to the task from the beginning to the end of the task, you can specify when the resource can start and finish work on this assignment, independent of the task start and finish dates. Remember, however, that this might increase the task duration.

When you delay a resource's start on a task, Microsoft Project recalculates the start date and times for the resource's assignment. Changing the start date for an assignment is also referred to as *assignment delay*.

To control the dates for an assignment

1 On the **View Bar**, click **Resource Usage**.

2 In the **Resource Name** field, select the task assignment whose dates you want to change.

Assignment Information

3 Click **Assignment Information**, and then click the **General** tab.

4 In the **Start** box or the **Finish** box, type the date you want the resource to start or finish.

Reassign a Resource to Work Part Time on Assignments

Suppose Richard's full working day is 8 hours long, and he's assigned full time to 2 tasks on the same day. Microsoft Project indicates that he's assigned to 16 hours of work on that day, an overallocation of 8 hours. This is a 200% allocation, or a 100% overallocation. One way to reduce this overallocation is by assigning Richard part time to each task, so that the sum of his allocations on the 2 tasks is no more than 100% assignment units.

For example, if you assign Richard at 25% assignment units (which is equal to 2 hours of work) to one task and at 75% assignment units (which is equal to 6 hours of work) on the other task, Richard will no longer be overallocated.

To reassign a resource to work part time on a task

1 On the **View Bar**, click **Gantt Chart**.

2 In the **Task Name** field, select a task.

3 Click **Assign Resources**.

Assign Resources

4 In the **Name** field, select the resource.

5 In the **Units** field, enter the percentage of time the resource is assigned to work on the task.

For example, if you want the resource to work 25% of the time on the task, type 25.

6 Press ENTER.

See "Change the Task Type" earlier in this chapter.

When you decrease the number of assignment units on an effort-driven fixed-unit task, Microsoft Project increases the task duration. If you need the duration to remain constant, because it's the type of task that has a fixed duration regardless of the number of resources assigned, you can change the task type to fixed duration. On a fixed-duration task, decreasing the units will increase the amount of work.

Decrease a Resource's Work on Assignments

To resolve overallocations, you might be able to decrease the amount of work required of an overallocated resource on a task that's contributing to the overallocation.

To decrease the amount of work assigned to a resource

1 On the **View Bar**, click **Resource Usage**.

Under each resource are the tasks to which they are assigned. Overallocated resources are highlighted in red and have an icon in the Indicators field.

2 In the **Work** fields for the tasks to which the overallocated resource is assigned, type a lesser value until the overallocation is removed (the resource name is no longer red). You can adjust the assignment work amounts in the **Work** field either in the sheet portion or the timesheet portion of the view.

See "Change the Task Type" earlier in this chapter.

When you decrease a resource's total work on an effort-driven fixed-unit task, Microsoft Project decreases the task duration. You can instead edit individual timephased work values in the timesheet portion of the Resource Usage or Task Usage view. With this method of decreasing work, duration is not affected.

Change Tasks to Resolve Overallocations

Another way to resolve overallocations is to change tasks to which overallocated resources are assigned.

- **Change task durations.** Changing task durations directly won't resolve overallocations. However, on an effort-driven fixed-units task (the default), if you decrease the overallocated resource's work on the task, the duration will also be decreased. If you decrease the overallocated resource's units on the task, the duration will be increased. For more information, see "Adjust the Time and Effort on Assignments" earlier in this chapter.
- **Add lag time to a task.** If a successor task is assigned to an overallocated resource, you can delay the successor until a point when the assigned overallocated resource has time for it, and thus relieving some of the overallocation.
- **Add delay to a task.** Whether a task is linked to a predecessor or not, you can add an amount of delay from when the task is scheduled to start to when it actually does start. This is called leveling delay; it is used specifically to resolve overallocations. You can add leveling delay manually or with the Microsoft Project resource leveling feature.
- **Interrupt work on a task.** If an overallocated resource is assigned to two full-time tasks at the same time, you can resolve the overallocation by splitting one of the tasks, allowing work to complete on the other task, then resuming work on the first task. You can split tasks manually or with the Microsoft Project resource leveling feature.

Add Lag Time to a Task

Many resource overallocations occur because a resource is assigned to work on two or more tasks at the same time—that is, the assignments overlap. One easy way to resolve such an overallocation is to delay one of the tasks until the resource can work on it without being overallocated. Frequently, this means adding enough delay to a task so that it no longer overlaps another task. One way to delay a task is to add lag time. You add some lag time, check to see if the overallocation is resolved, then add more lag time, if necessary.

When you add lag time to a task, you'll delay the task as well as its successor tasks. You could even delay the project finish date. Therefore, it's best to delay noncritical tasks first, and then only by an amount less than or equal to their total slack.

For information about delaying tasks by adding lag time, see "Overlap or Delay Tasks" in chapter 5.

Add Delay to a Task

See "Use Microsoft Project Resource Leveling" below.

Another method for adding delay to a task to resolve overallocations is to add *leveling delay*. With leveling delay, you can add an amount of time between the scheduled start of a task and the time when work should actually begin on the task.

While leveling delay is added automatically by the Microsoft Project resource leveling feature, you can also add leveling delay yourself. This might be more effective if you have only one or two overallocated resources. Plus, you have more control, as you can choose the tasks to which you want to add delay.

When you add a delay to a task yourself, first delay tasks that won't delay the project finish date—that is, noncritical tasks with total slack. If you add delay time only up to the amount of total slack time for each task, you won't delay the project finish date. If you need to, you can add delay to critical tasks, but by doing so you'll push out the project finish date.

Task delay is always expressed as elapsed time—that is, nonworking time is included in the delay time. Total slack, on the other hand, is a regular duration value. For example, suppose you have a task with a 1-day slack, and you want to delay it from Friday to Monday. You enter 3ed. While this is a higher number, it's still within the 1 day slack on the task.

To delay a task

1 On the **View Bar**, click **More Views**.

2 In the **Views** list, click **Resource Allocation**, and then click **Apply**.

In the Resource Usage view in the top pane, overallocated resources are highlighted in red.

The Resource Usage view appears in the top pane of the Resource Allocation view.

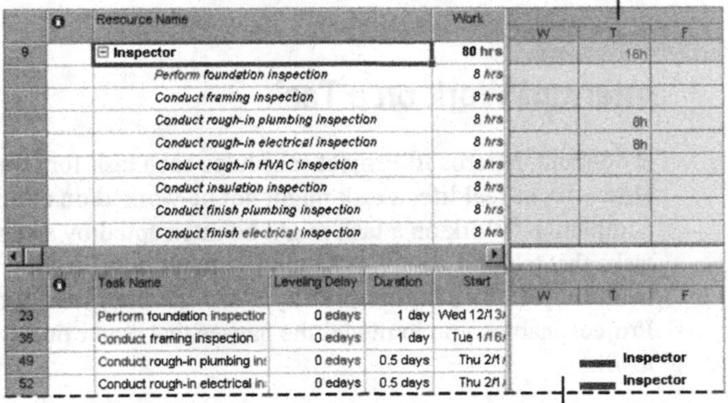
Resource Name
Work
W
T
F
9
Inspector
80 hrs
16h
Perform foundation inspection
8 hrs
Conduct framing inspection
8 hrs
Conduct rough-in plumbing inspection
8 hrs
8h
Conduct rough-in electrical inspection
8 hrs
8h
Conduct rough-in HVAC inspection
8 hrs
Conduct insulation inspection
8 hrs
Conduct finish plumbing inspection
8 hrs
Conduct finish electrical inspection
8 hrs
Task Name
Leveling Delay
Duration
Start
23
Perform foundation inspectior
0 edays
1 day
Wed 12/13/
35
Conduct framing inspection
0 edays
1 day
Tue 1/16/
49
Conduct rough-in plumbing in
0 edays
0.5 days
Thu 2/1/
52
Conduct rough-in electrical in
0 edays
0.5 days
Thu 2/1/
Inspector
Inspector

The Leveling Gantt view appears in the lower pane.

3 In the top pane, select an overallocated resource in the **Resource Name** field.
4 In the bottom pane, select a task in the **Task Name** field that is assigned to the resource during the time the resource is overallocated.
5 In the **Leveling Delay** field, enter the amount of time (in elapsed duration) you want to delay a task that occurs during the time of overallocation.

   You can see the total slack for a task (in regular duration) by inserting the Total Slack column into the Leveling Gantt view in the bottom pane.
6 Press ENTER.

   A task's slack is displayed as a bar to help you decide how much you can move a task before successor tasks or the end date of the project is affected.
7 If the resource is still overallocated, increase the delay value.
8 When finished working with this split view, in the **Window** menu, click **Remove Split**.

You can add leveling delay to an individual assignment rather than to the entire task. Enter assignment leveling delays as regular (not elapsed) duration values.

To delay an individual assignment on a task

1 On the **View Bar**, click **More Views**.
2 In the **Views** list, click **Resource Allocation**, and then click **Apply**.
3 In the top pane, click the column to the right of where you want to insert the **Leveling Delay** column.
4 On the **Insert** menu, click **Column**.
5 In the **Field Name** box, click **Leveling Delay**.
6 Select the assignment to which you want to add leveling delay.
7 In the **Leveling Delay** field in the top pane, type the amount of time you want to delay the task.

Interrupt Work on a Task

By default, Microsoft Project schedules each task for consecutive time periods. However, in real life, a task might not be worked on continuously from its start to its completion. Work on a task might be interrupted by sickness, vacation, or unplanned tasks that take priority. For example, suppose the 16-day "Complete exterior brick" task is interrupted by a higher-priority 3-day masonry task during the same time. Microsoft Project enables you to model the pauses that occur during a task's lifetime by *splitting tasks*.

When you split tasks, you show not only the overall start and finish dates for a task, but also the dates when work stops and resumes. On the Gantt Chart, you also see the time gap representing the interruptions between portions of a Gantt bar.

If you know of a task interruption ahead of time, you can plan for it. If an interruption has already happened, you can reflect it in your project plan and reschedule accordingly.

Splitting tasks is also a good method for resolving overallocations. You can split a less important task during a period when a resource is overallocated and have the task resume later when the resource has the time for it. Just like leveling delay, splits can be done automatically by the Microsoft Project resource leveling feature.You can also split tasks yourself to better control how your overallocations are resolved.

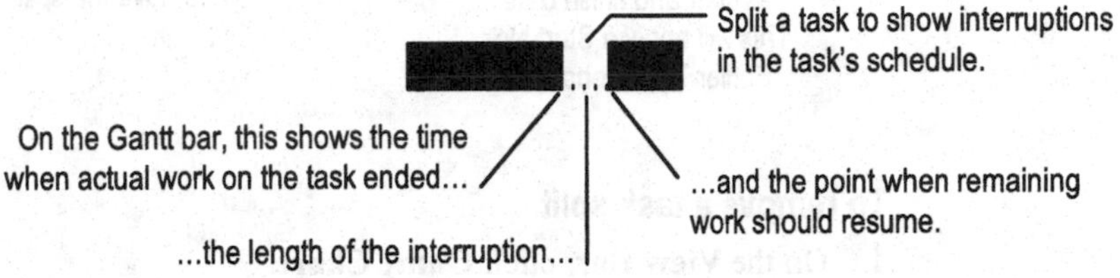

Split a task to show interruptions in the task's schedule.
On the Gantt bar, this shows the time when actual work on the task ended…
…the length of the interruption…
…and the point when remaining work should resume.

To split a task

1 On the **View Bar**, click **Gantt Chart**.

Split Task

2 Click **Split Task**.

3 Move the pointer over the Gantt bar you want to split, and then click the Gantt bar where you want the split to occur.

To create a longer split, drag the Gantt bar to the right.

To move the entire Gantt bar to another date, drag the left portion of the Gantt bar to the new date. The duration and splits are maintained as you drag.

Split Task

You can create as many splits on a single task as you want. Double-click **Split Task**, make the splits, then single-click **Split Task**.

To change how a task is split

1 On the **View Bar**, click **Gantt Chart**.

2 Drag a portion of the split Gantt bar to reflect the change you want. Depending on where and how you drag, you can change the amount of the split, change the duration of time before the split, change the duration of time after the split, or change when the task starts and finishes.

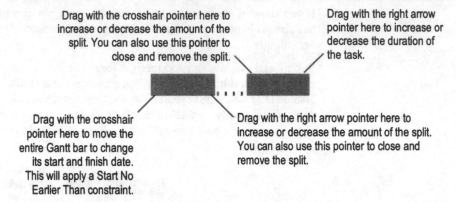

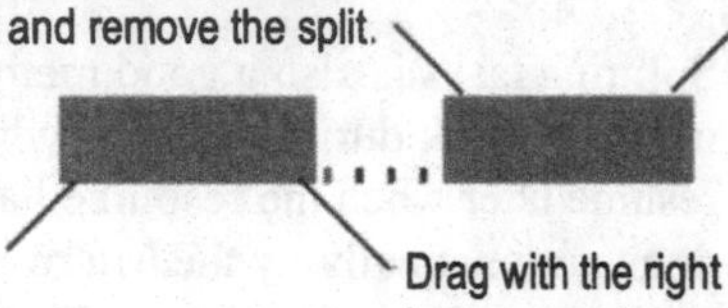

To remove a task split

1 On the **View Bar**, click **Gantt Chart**.

2 Drag a portion of a split task so that it touches another portion of the Gantt bar.

If you drag the right side of a split task toward the left to remove the split, the duration and start date remain the same and the task finish date is changed.

If you drag the left side of a split task toward the right to remove the split, the task start and finish date remain the same and the duration is increased.

Use Microsoft Project Resource Leveling

When you have a large project that contains many resource overallocations, you can resolve them all at once by having Microsoft Project *level* them. Microsoft Project levels overallocations by delaying or splitting tasks until the resources assigned to them are no longer overallocated. Even if you need to adjust tasks afterward, using automatic leveling is much more efficient than adding delay and splits to one task at a time for one resource at a time.

Before you level overallocations automatically, refine your schedule yourself as much as possible. The results of automatic leveling can improve if your schedule is as clean and lean as possible.

The process for leveling includes:

- Setting leveling priorities, if necessary.
- Selecting whether you want some or all resources to be leveled.
- Specifying the leveling options you want.
- Leveling.

Set Leveling Priorities

You can set priorities on specific tasks to control how they are leveled in relation to one another. Priorities range from 0 to 1000, with the highest priority being 1000. Tasks with a priority level of 1000 are not leveled. This means Microsoft Project never delays or splits these tasks when leveling. Tasks with lower priorities are leveled (delayed or split) before tasks with higher priorities.

To set leveling priorities for tasks

1 On the **View Bar**, click **Gantt Chart**.

Task Information

2 In the **Task Name** field, click the task whose priority you want to change, and then click **Task Information**.

3 Click the **General** tab, and then enter a priority in the **Priority** box.

The default priority setting is 500.

4 Repeat steps 2 and 3 for all other tasks whose priorities you want to set for leveling.

To review priority settings

For more information about adding and removing columns, see "Create or Modify a Table" in chapter 12.

1 On the **View Bar**, click **Gantt Chart**.

2 Click the column to the right of where you want to insert the **Priority** column.

3 On the **Insert** menu, click **Column**.

4 In the **Field Name** box, click **Priority**.

You can sort or group by priority to review current priority settings. For more information, see chapter 12.

Level Overallocated Resources

You have a number of choices when leveling your project. If you're unsure of which choices to make, it's safest to use the default settings. You can review the results of the leveling afterwards and see if it met your needs. If it didn't, you can undo the leveling, fine-tune your choices, and level again.

You can level tasks for any resources or for selected resources only. To level specific resources only, select them in the Resource Sheet. If there is a resource that you never want leveled, add the Can Level field to a resource sheet and set the value to No for the resource.

The Microsoft Project leveling process never changes who is assigned to tasks, and never changes the amount of assignment units. Also, work resources only (people and equipment) are leveled. Leveling does not apply to material resources.

To level overallocated resources

1 On the **Tools** menu, click **Resource Leveling**.

The Resource Leveling dialog box provides numerous choices for resolving resource overallocations.

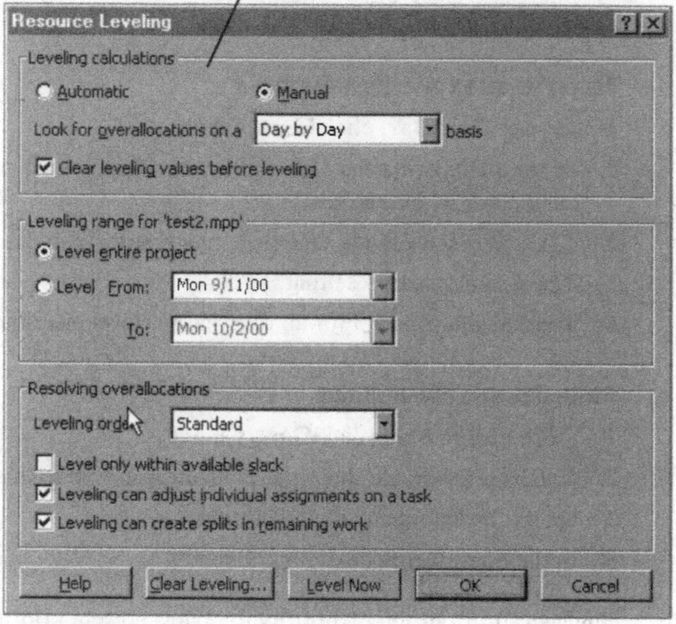

2 Click **Level Now**.

Click **OK** only if you've selected automatic leveling, or if you've selected manual leveling and you're not ready to level right now.

The following table summarizes all your leveling options.

Use this leveling option	To
Manual option.	Level resources only when you click the **Level Now** button.
Automatic option.	Level resources whenever you change a task or resource. This can significantly slow your work in your project plan, as Microsoft Project delays, splits, and recalculates the schedule whenever you make a change.
Look for overallocations on a basis box. Select the time period you want.	Determine the sensitivity, or time period, with which leveling will recognize overallocations. In this case, leveling will occur only if a resource is scheduled to do more work than it has the capacity for in the specified period.

Use this leveling option	To
Clear leveling values before leveling check box.	Specify whether you want to clear any leveling delays present from previous leveling or from leveling delays you've added yourself. If you have Automatic leveling on, turn this setting off. This way automatic leveling will not be leveling from scratch every time you make an edit to your schedule.
Leveling range for.	Select whether you want the entire project leveled or only those tasks falling within a specific time range.
Leveling order box.	Select the order in which tasks are to be leveled: Click ID Only to have Microsoft Project only check those tasks in the ascending order of their ID numbers to determine which tasks to level. Click Standard to have Microsoft Project check tasks in the order of their predecessor dependencies, slack, dates, priority, and then task constraints. This is the default. Click Priority, Standard to have Microsoft Project check tasks priorities before considering predecessor dependencies, slack, dates, and then task constraints. Regardless of the leveling order type you choose, Microsoft Project skips any task with a priority of 1000.
Level only within available slack check box.	Prevent the finish date of your project from being moved out.
Leveling can adjust individual assignments on a task check box.	Have leveling adjust when a resource works on a task independent of other resources working on the same task. If there is a task whose assignments you never want adjusted by leveling, add the Level Assignments field to the sheet portion of the Task Usage or Resource Usage view, and set the value to No for the assignment.
Leveling can create splits in remaining work check box.	Interrupt tasks by creating splits in the remaining work on tasks or resource assignments. If there is an individual task that you never want to be split by leveling, add the Leveling Can Split field to a task sheet, and set the value to No for the task.

Immediately after leveling, you can undo all of the changes if you don't like the results. You can also adjust or remove individual changes yourself at any time.

To immediately undo the effects of leveling

- Before doing any other operation, on the **Edit** menu, click **Undo Level**.

You can also remove all leveling values, including any leveling delay you've manually added to tasks or assignments.

To clear leveling

1. On the **Tools** menu, click **Resource Leveling**.
2. Click **Clear Leveling**.

   This button is available only if there is any delay on any tasks or assignments due to previous leveling or leveling delay changes.

Review the Results of Leveling

Because Microsoft Project resource leveling follows a specific set of rules, it's a good idea to check the changes in the Leveling Gantt view.

To review the results of leveling

1. On the **View** menu, click **More Views**.
2. Click **Leveling Gantt**, and then click **Apply**.
3. Review your tasks in the Leveling Gantt view to see the effect of leveling and how much delay leveling has added to tasks.

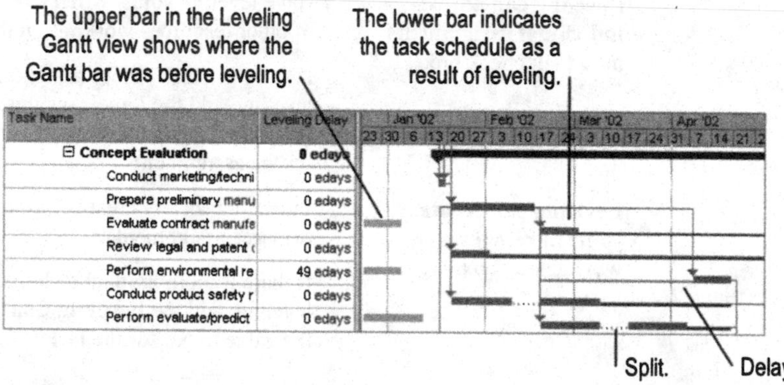

When you automatically level overallocations in a project scheduled from the finish date, Microsoft Project applies a negative delay value to the affected tasks. This causes a task or assignment's finish date to occur earlier because the delay is applied from the finish date of the task or assignment.

Meeting Your Budget

Some projects are driven by the finish date; other projects are driven by the budget. Many projects balance the two forces, striving for the ideal of completing the project ahead of schedule and under budget.

For more information about project costs, see chapter 7.

If you have decided to plan and track costs, and if you have entered all costs associated with hourly resources, per-use resources, equipment and material costs, and fixed costs for tasks, Microsoft Project can provide a forecast of how much it will cost to complete your project.

If this forecast indicates that your costs are greater than your budget allows, you can make adjustments to reduce costs and bring your project in line.

In many projects, resources contribute to costs more than any other single factor. If this is the case in your project, minimizing resource costs should be your main goal. But the size of a project can play a role, too. Often, the bigger the project, the more it costs.

Methods for reducing costs include:

- **Adjust the costs themselves.** Check your assumptions and make sure the costs are entered properly. Check the variable costs of resources, including standard and overtime rates, per-use costs, and the fixed costs on tasks.
- **Adjust resources to reduce costs.** Replace expensive resources with less costly ones or remove extra resources.
- **Adjust the time a resource spends on an assignment.** Reduce the amount of work assigned, the number of units assigned, or the overtime hours. Fine-tune the assignment start or finish dates, or contour the work assignments.
- **Cut scope to meet your budget.** Shorten the schedule, remove extra steps from processes, combine tasks, remove optional tasks, decrease task duration, decrease the number of deliverables, or decrease the level of quality.

If you find that your project plan is coming in ahead of budget, you can either accept the cost savings or expand your project to use the money. For example, you might to add optional processes that will improve quality, or hire more resources to finish the project sooner.

Display and Review Cost Information

A good strategy for cutting costs is to focus on reducing the cost of the factors that are the most expensive. You can determine which factors cost the most by displaying the cost of each factor in your project. For example, you can display:

- Total project cost, which is the cost of all the tasks, resources, assignments, and materials in your project.
- Total cost of an individual task, which is the cost of the resources and materials used to accomplish the task.
- Total cost of a resource, which is based on hourly and fixed costs.
- Costs distributed over a task's duration, which can be a baseline cost, cumulative cost, or actual cost that's apportioned over time.

For information about displaying costs, see "Viewing Costs" in chapter 7.

Check and Adjust the Cost Settings

Before changing resources, assignments, or tasks to meet your budget, check the assumptions you've made about the costs of the project.

- **Check the costs of resources.** This includes the standard and overtime rates, and per-use costs. This also includes the cost rate tables. For more information about variable costs and cost rate tables, see "Setting Costs" in chapter 7.
- **Check how resources with per-use costs are assigned.** If you combine assignments, you might be able to reduce the frequency of per-use costs. For more information, see "Assigning Resources to Tasks" in chapter 6.
- **Check the fixed costs on tasks.** Make sure the fixed costs are accurately represented in your plan, and not inflated or added multiple times. For more information, see "Specify a Fixed Cost for a Task" in chapter 7.
- **Check the costs of materials resources.** Check the unit costs for the materials and make sure they're accurate. Also check how the material resources are assigned, either with a *fixed consumption rate* or *variable consumption rate* in their assignment units. The type of consumption rate affects how material usage and therefore costs are calculated. For more information, see "About Assignment Units" in chapter 6 and "Specify the Cost of Material Resources" in chapter 7.

Adjust Resources to Reduce Costs

Although you might have several resources of the same type, they might differ widely with regard to quality and cost. Some resources produce better results than others, and some resources cost more than others, even though they perform the same job. If a less expensive resource can achieve the same level of quality as a more expensive one, you might consider replacing the more expensive resource.

The less expensive resource needs to be qualified, available, and able to accomplish the task without increasing the task duration. If you're strapped for resources, you can consider assigning the more expensive resource to fewer tasks.

Keep in mind that a more expensive resource might end up actually being more cost-effective. For example, suppose you have two team members who are billed at different hourly rates for your project. If the more expensive resource is more experienced and faster than the less expensive one, the assignment might actually be finished in less time, costing you less overall.

To compare resource costs, display the Resource Sheet view. For more information about replacing a resource, see "Change Resource Assignments" in chapter 6.

Adjust the Time a Resource Spends on an Assignment

You can meet your budget by adjusting how much time and effort your resources are spending on assignments. Start by focusing on the more expensive resources and make adjustments to their assignments. Be aware that, in many cases, decreasing the amount of time and effort resources spend on tasks can increase task duration and result in a later project finish date.

- **Adjust the dates that the resource works on the assignment.** By default, the resource is assigned to the full time span of the task. You can adjust those dates, if necessary. You might be able to save money by having a more expensive resource start on a longer task a little later than the other resources. For example, suppose you have three resources assigned to a 21-day task. Delay the start of the more expensive resource on the task until the second week. See "Adjust the Dates on Assignments" earlier in this chapter.
- **Adjust the level of effort, or units, that the resource works on the assignment.** Resources are typically assigned to 100% units on a task, or 100% of the availability designated in the resource's working time calendar. You can reduce your costs by reducing the units to a part-time effort. See "Reassign a Resource to Work Part Time on Assignments" earlier in this chapter.
- **Decrease the resource's work on the assignment.** You might be able to decrease the number of hours an expensive resource is assigned to a task. However, with the default effort-driven fixed-units tasks, decreasing work will also decrease duration. See "Decrease a Resource's Work on Assignments" earlier in this chapter.
- **Add or remove overtime.** Look at any assigned overtime to make sure it's necessary and properly calculated. Reassign overtime work to be standard work for a resource who has more standard time available. On the other hand, if you're considering hiring more resources to handle extra work, consider which is more cost-effective, hiring more resources or assigning more overtime. See "Assign Overtime" earlier in this chapter.

Cut Scope to Meet Your Budget

If you're able to cut any tasks, or the duration of any tasks, and still accomplish the goals of your project, consider doing so to cut the scope and therefore the costs of your project. By deleting tasks, you cut the resource and fixed costs associated with those tasks. By reducing the duration of tasks, you might be able to reduce the length of the project and, therefore, many of the variable resource costs associated with time.

Adjusting Project Scope

Scope refers to the size, depth, or quality of work you're proposing to undertake in your project. If your project has a larger scope, you're probably committing to a greater number of tasks. For example, suppose you have two home construction projects, one on Belfair Lane and the other on Spring Street. The home on Belfair Lane is to be 3500 square feet, two stories, with three fireplaces, professional landscaping, and a wrought-iron gate. The home on Spring Street is to be 1800 square feet, one story, one fireplace, and no landscaping. Both projects have the same outcome—a finished home—but they have a very different scope. Because the Belfair Lane home has a much larger scope, it will have a longer schedule, require more work and material resources, and cost more to build.

Being tied to the number of tasks in your project, scope can be reduced when you need to shorten the schedule, balance the workload, or meet the budget.

To cut scope, you can:

- Remove extra steps from processes.
- Combine tasks.
- Remove optional tasks.
- Decrease task duration.
- Decrease the number of deliverables.
- Decrease the level of quality.
- Change goals to where certain tasks become unnecessary.

All of these measures serve to cut tasks or reduce duration. Either of these results can shorten the schedule.

For information on deleting tasks and changing task durations, see chapter 4.

Part 3

Tracking and Updating Your Project

The power of your project plan is that it can not only help predict your project but also keep it on course. Your original, refined plan represents your best estimate of how the project will proceed. It includes estimates of project length, task durations, work amounts, costs, and more. You're finally ready to say "Go!" and have the project begin.

As soon as you begin your project, you leave the planning phase and enter the tracking phase. Once a project starts, reality sets in. A task starts later than planned. A flu epidemic among your team members threatens to blow the project deadline. An unexpected rise in the price of an essential material strains your budget. By using your project plan to track actual project progress, you improve your ability to make the changes that keep your project on schedule and within budget. Methods for tracking progress that fit your team's working preferences are covered in chapter 9.

To track project progress, you need to collect project data. One of the best ways to collect and incorporate actual project data is to use the predefined Microsoft Project *workgroup* messages. Workgroup messages are used to request and confirm task assignments, send updated task assignment information to the workgroup manager, and incorporate updated information into the project plan. They can be exchanged across an e-mail system, an intranet, or the World Wide Web. Chapter 10 explains the workgroup concept in general, as well as the details of communicating and collecting data with e-mail. Chapter 11 discusses the powerful workgroup capabilities of Microsoft Project Central, with which you can use your intranet or the Web to keep current with your team.

9

Keeping Your Project on Track

Your project plan is your blueprint for achieving your project goals. But how do you know if your project is proceeding according to plan? You can identify deviations from your plan by tracking the progress of your project.

When you track progress, you compare how your project is really going with how your plan says it should be going. To track progress, you first need to save the *baseline* against which you will compare actual progress. The baseline is like a snapshot of key information in your scheduled and fine-tuned project, taken just before you set the project's wheels in motion.

The second aspect of tracking progress is to periodically collect and enter *actual data* (or *actuals*) into your project. This information indicates what has actually been done with scheduled tasks.

Finally, you compare this actual data against your baseline data, and see if there are any differences between them. If the variances are large or tend in the wrong direction, such as finishing later, taking more time than planned, or costing more than planned, you can take corrective action early enough to bring your project back on track.

You can compare as many or as few details as you want. For example, you might decide to track only percent complete and finish dates. Or, you might also track start dates, duration, work, and costs.

By tracking progress, you can:

- Monitor the status of your project, which can include monitoring task completion dates, remaining work on tasks, costs, and the project finish date.
- Identify the sources of problems, such as the project finish date being pushed out or costs exceeding the budget.
- Determine solutions to any problems you discover and resolve them before they affect the desired project outcome.

- Develop a project history you can use to improve future project planning. For example, you can use the actual duration of a task in the next project that requires that task.

For some projects, you might want to know only whether your project is proceeding well enough. To know that, you can compare actual data to baseline data and take no further action. But because projects are often limited by time, money, or resource availability, deviations from the project plan, even small ones, can require compensatory action on your part. For example, suppose a task that's taking longer than estimated pushes out a non-negotiable project deadline. If you track your project, you'll be able to identify this problem readily. Then, going one step further, you can use the Microsoft Project scheduling tools to analyze the problem and determine the best way to get back on track.

As you analyze the variations between your baseline and actual data, you identify scheduling problems. You can resolve or account for these problems by adjusting the project to shorten the schedule, resolve resource overallocations, and reduce costs. These techniques are found in chapter 8.

The value you receive from tracking progress depends, to some extent, on how diligently you track. Your project plan will give you the most control over the project outcome if you update the plan at a set interval—say, every two weeks. If you need to provide regular status reports, that might be the most convenient and logical time to update your project.

Setting the Baseline

As your project progresses, some tasks might take longer or shorter than planned. Resources might cost more or less than you estimated. And some resources, who in the original, refined project plan were assigned the same number of work hours per day as they had available, might find themselves overworked or underworked. If you're tracking, you record some measure of progress, such as actual dates or percent complete. But to know whether all the actuals mean you're ahead of schedule or behind, within your budget or exceeding it, you need to be able to compare your actual schedule to some reference point. That reference point is the *baseline*.

The baseline consists of key information, including dates and costs, that represent your best estimates of how your project will progress. Typically, you arrive at these best estimates after you fine-tune your project plan. Then you set or freeze these estimates by saving baseline data before the project begins. After you save baseline information, it won't be overwritten as you adjust your project plan. The baseline information is always available for you to compare with actual data.

When you freeze the baseline, Microsoft Project saves the baseline data as part of the project file. The baseline is not a separate file, nor is it a copy of all the data in your project. The baseline consists of key progress-indicating data that Microsoft Project displays in baseline fields so that you can later compare baseline data to actual data. The following table lists the progress-indicating data saved for tasks, resources, and assignments when you set the baseline:

This baseline information is saved	For
Duration	tasks
Start	tasks and assignments
Finish	tasks and assignments
Total Cost	tasks, resources, and assignments
Total Work	tasks, resources, and assignments
Timephased Cost	tasks, resources, and assignments
Timephased Work	tasks, resources, and assignments

A project of any size and duration can benefit from a baseline. However, the longer a project is, or the more constrained it is by time, resource availability, or cost, the more valuable a baseline becomes in terms of tracking variances.

At certain key points of your project, you might want to save an *interim plan*. While the full set of baseline information is retained, the interim plan saves the current task start and finish dates. Saving interim plans in addition to the baseline plan gives you a solid basis for comparison.

If you add new tasks after you've begun tracking, you can incorporate them into the baseline or interim plan. In extreme cases in which there have been significant changes to the project, you can even change the baseline itself for one, several, or all tasks.

Set and Save a Baseline

When you set a baseline, Microsoft Project saves baseline data and stores them in baseline fields. This information includes task start and finish dates, work, and costs, which you can display in the Baseline Start, Baseline Finish, Baseline Work, and Baseline Cost fields, respectively.

If the Planning Wizard appears when you save your project file, you can have it save a baseline for you. If not, you can use the following procedure.

To set a baseline

1. On the **Tools** menu, point to **Tracking**, and then click **Save Baseline**.
2. Click **Save baseline**, and then click **Entire project**.

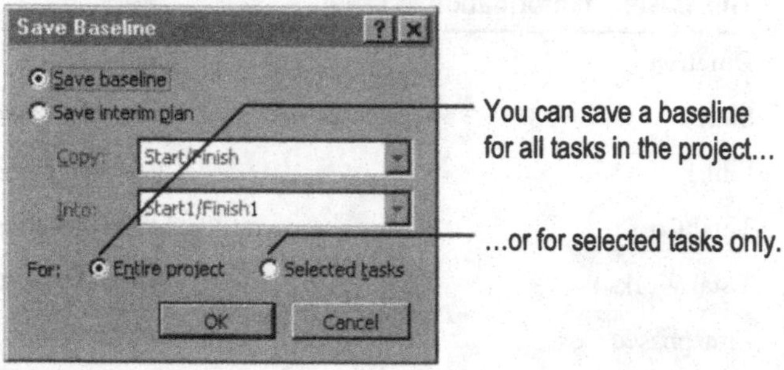

Setting a baseline does not create a separate baseline file; it only saves certain fields of information such as the start and finish dates, durations, work, costs, and so on. However, you can create a backup copy of your entire project file for later comparison. Give the project a name that distinguishes it from your working project file.

To save a backup of the project file

1. On the **File** menu, click **Save As**.
2. In the **File name** box, type a name that reminds you that this file is a backup of your file.

   For example, you might type *<project name>* **backup** *<today's date>*
3. Click **Save**.

Save an Interim Plan

As you begin updating your schedule, you might want to know how accurate your original scheduling estimates are. A good way to do this is to save an *interim plan*, which includes task start and finish dates only. By comparing the information in an interim plan with baseline information, you can determine the accuracy of your scheduling estimates. You can also determine when your project began to deviate from the original project plan.

For more information about columns and fields, see "Create or Modify a Table" in chapter 12.

Like the baseline plan, an interim plan is not a separate project file but rather a set of task start and finish dates that are stored in columns. When you save an interim plan, you specify which start and finish dates you want to save and into which columns (or fields) you want to save them. For example, for the first interim plan, you might specify that you want to copy the dates from the Start and Finish columns into the Start1 and Finish1 columns.

One way to use an interim plan is to save the current start and finish dates from a particular pair of start/finish columns before you overwrite those dates with new dates. For example, if changes in your project require you to change the dates in the Start and Finish columns, you can keep a record of those dates by copying them into the custom Start1 and Finish1 columns. Then you can type the new dates over the old dates in the Start and Finish columns. Later, if you again need to overwrite the dates in the Start and Finish columns, you can copy those dates into the Start2 and Finish2 columns.

When you save an interim plan, you can copy the dates from any pair of start/finish columns into any other pair. For example, if you want to save the dates in the Start2 and Finish2 columns, you might copy those dates into the Start5 and Finish5 columns.

When you want to see the information stored in an interim plan, you can insert the appropriate columns into the Gantt Chart or the Task Sheet. For example, if your sixth interim plan is stored in the Start6 and Finish6 columns, you can insert those columns. You can save up to ten interim plans for each schedule at any time during the project.

To save an interim plan

1. On the **Tools** menu, point to **Tracking**, and then click **Save Baseline**.
2. Click **Save interim plan**.
3. In the **Copy** box, click the pair of start and finish dates you want to save.

   The predefined pairs of columns range from Start/Finish to Start10/Finish10. You can copy from any pair into any other pair.
4. In the **Into** box, click the names of the start and finish fields into which you want to save the interim plan start and finish dates.
5. Click **Entire project** or **Selected tasks** to save the portion of the schedule you want.

To show interim plan columns

1. On the **View Bar**, click **Gantt Chart**.
2. On the **View** menu, point to **Table**, and then click **Variance**.

   This table shows columns for baseline and scheduled start and finish dates.
3. Scroll to the right and click the **Start Var.** column header.
4. On the **Insert** menu, click **Column**.
5. In the **Field name** box, click the name of the Start field that contains your interim start date, for example, Start1.
6. Repeat steps 3 and 4 to add a second column for the Finish field.
7. In the **Field name** box, click the name of the Finish field that contains your interim finish date, for example, Finish1.

Add a Task to a Baseline or Interim Plan

As your project progresses, you might find that you occasionally need to add new tasks to your plan that were initially overlooked or that are a result of increased scope. Depending on the standard practices governing your project, you might want the information from these new tasks to be considered a variance from the original baseline. Or, you might need approval to change baseline information. But if appropriate, you can add new tasks to your baseline and any interim plan you might have saved.

To add a task to a baseline or interim plan

1. On the **View Bar**, click **Gantt Chart**.
2. In the **Task Name** field, select the task you want to add to the baseline or interim plan.
3. On the **Tools** menu, point to **Tracking**, and then click **Save Baseline**.
4. To add the task to the baseline plan, click **Save baseline**.

   To add the task to the interim plan, click **Save interim plan**, and then select the fields you want in the **Copy** and **Into** boxes.
5. Click **Selected tasks**.

Change Baseline Information for One or More Tasks

Large and unanticipated changes to your project can render your baseline information less than useful at best, and obsolete at worst. Using baseline data as a reference point is most effective when the baseline reflects project realities fairly accurately. If comparing actual data with baseline data has become meaningless because the baseline data is so far off reality, you might have good reason to change your baseline.

Suppose that, after the project has begun, upper management abruptly decides to cut project goals by half (and thus also cut the project duration and costs by about half). In this case, it is no longer useful to compare actual data to the original baseline data. For meaningful tracking, you'd need to revise the project and then change the baseline information. You can also clear baseline or interim plan information for selected tasks or the entire project. You can then set the baseline again.

To change baseline information for one or more tasks

1. On the **View Bar**, click **Gantt Chart** or any other task view.
2. In the **Task Name** field, select the tasks whose baseline information you want to change.
3. On the **Tools** menu, point to **Tracking**, and then click **Save Baseline**.

4 Click **Save baseline**, and then click **Selected tasks**.

When you click **Selected tasks**, Microsoft Project updates the baseline data for the tasks you selected.

To clear baseline information

Use SHIFT+click to select multiple adjacent tasks. Use CTRL+click to select multiple nonadjacent tasks.

1 If you want to clear baseline information for certain tasks only, select those tasks.
2 On the **Tools** menu, point to **Tracking**, and then click **Clear Baseline**.
3 Click **Clear baseline plan**.
4 Click **Selected tasks** if you want to clear the baseline information for selected tasks only. Otherwise, the baseline will be cleared for the entire project.

After clearing the obsolete baseline, be sure to set baseline again for your revised project information.

To clear an interim plan

1 If you want to clear interim plan information for certain tasks only, select those tasks.
2 On the **Tools** menu, point to **Tracking**, and then click **Clear Baseline**.
3 Click **Clear interim plan**, and then select the fields that contain the interim plan dates you want to clear—for example Start1/Finish1.
4 Click **Selected tasks** if you want to clear the interim start/finish dates for selected tasks only. Otherwise, the interim start/finish dates will be cleared for the entire project.

Review Baseline Information

The progress-indicating information in your project includes start and finish dates, work, duration, percent complete, costs, and more. As you move along the road in tracking your project, you'll start to see that there are three versions of the progress-indicating information:

- **Scheduled.** When you first set up and fine-tune your project plan, the progress-indicating information is as scheduled—that is, the way that you have entered and Microsoft Project has calculated your dates, work, costs, and so on. As you track and adjust your plan, this information is likely to change, because the scheduled information is recalculated to include actual information and remaining values. But these values are always considered the current calculated values for your project.
- **Baseline.** As soon as you choose the command to set the baseline, the scheduled information is saved as it stands at that moment. This snapshot becomes the set of baseline information.
- **Actual.** As you enter and update actual information in your project, reflecting when tasks really began and ended, how long they really took, and how much they really cost, you have your set of actual information.

For example, suppose you set up a task with a 5-day duration, and then you save a baseline. At this point:

- Actual duration is 0 days.
- Scheduled duration is 5 days.
- Baseline duration is 5 days.

Then suppose you enter 3 days of actual duration and 4 days of remaining duration, based on the latest status report from the assigned resource. At this point:

- Actual duration is 3 days.
- Scheduled duration changes to 7 days.
- Baseline duration is still 5 days.

You can analyze differences between your baseline and scheduled information, between baseline and actual, and other combinations. As you start to make these comparisons, you need to show the columns that include the baseline fields.

To view baseline fields

1. On the **View Bar**, click **Tracking Gantt**.
2. On the **View** menu, point to **Table**, and then click **More Tables**.
3. In the **Tables** list, click **Baseline**, and then click **Apply**.

   Microsoft Project displays the baseline dates in the Tracking Gantt view.

Collecting and Entering Actual Project Information

Now that you have fine-tuned your plan and set your baseline, your project can officially begin. If you have decided to track progress, you need to determine which actual information you're going to track, and how you're going to gather and enter this information into your project.

You can track and update:

- **Task start and finish dates.** It's a good idea to at least track task start and finish dates. Even if you don't track any other information, these will help you discern whether your project will finish on time.
- **Percentage of each task that is complete.** Team members often find it easiest to report how far along they are on a task in terms of percent complete.
- **Task duration.** Another method for tracking actuals is to note how long a task took from beginning to end.

- **Work.** You can track how much time, or work, each team member spends on an assignment.
- **Task cost.** Although Microsoft Project typically calculates all costs associated with tasks, including variable and per-use resource costs and fixed costs for tasks, you can track additional or unexpected costs that came up when doing the task.

You can collect information in task, resource, and assignment notes. For example, if a resource wasn't available for a task as expected, you can explain the reason in a resource or assignment note. If some problem occurred in carrying out a task, you can describe the problem in a task note.

Where Do You Get Actual Information?

Before you start the project, discuss with your team how you will measure progress, and how often. There are several sources for data on task progress:

- You can collect all the data yourself. This might be feasible in a small project where you can track everything.
- Have the supervisor or manager report on the tasks in their area.
- Have team members provide status reports for their assigned tasks.
- Verify progress through inspection, quality control, or test data.

One method of collecting actual data is by exchanging Microsoft Project *workgroup* messages, which are electronic messages used to assign tasks, send updated task status information, and incorporate updated information into the project plan, without the workgroup manager (or project manager) needing to enter the information manually. For more information about using workgroup messages, see chapters 10 and 11.

The data collected should be based on some measurable physical progress, not just the time that has passed since that task started. Time from the start date to the present might not necessarily reflect the actual working time spent on the task nor progress made on the task; resources might not be working on the task as scheduled, or progress might be faster or slower than planned.

Try to use objective data wherever possible. Use sources such as timesheets, bills for materials and services from vendors, purchase orders, and other direct charges to projects. If a task involves material resources, such as laying pipe or stringing wire, you can base progress on the quantity used to date versus expected total use, such as feet of pipe used so far compared with the quantity needed for the completed task.

By using information from all your sources, you should be able to come up with data in which you have some confidence. Here, the judgment or experience of those responsible for the tasks will help when deciding just how far along a task is.

Enter Actual Start and Finish Dates for Tasks

The project finish date is most affected by the schedules of the individual tasks, especially critical tasks. If tasks start and finish on time, it's likely the project as a whole will finish on time. If tasks start and finish late, it's likely the project will finish late. Therefore, if meeting the planned project deadline is important, you'll want to track and update task start and finish dates.

To enter actual start and finish dates for a task

1. On the **View Bar**, click **Gantt Chart**.
2. In the **Task Name** field, select the task you want to update.
3. On the **Tools** menu, point to **Tracking**, and then click **Update Tasks**.
4. Under **Actual**, type the dates in the **Start** and **Finish** boxes.

   The dates you type will appear in the Actual Start and Actual Finish fields of the selected task.

You can view actual dates by inserting the Actual Start and Actual Finish columns into any task table or by applying the Tracking table to a task sheet view.

Enter actual start and finish dates here.

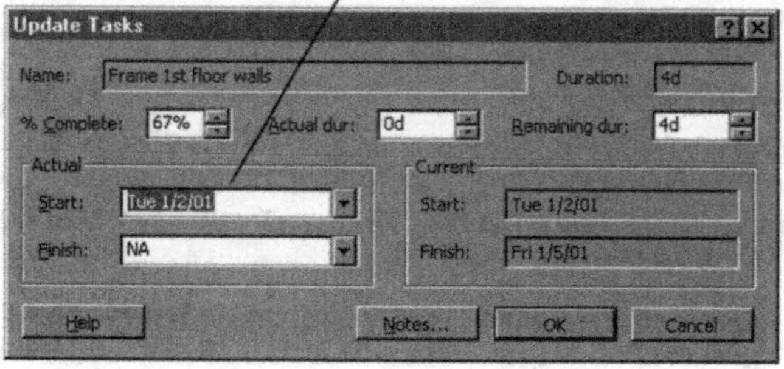

If several tasks started and finished on time—that is, their actual start and finish dates are the same as the planned dates that appear in the Start and Finish fields—you can set the actual start and actual finish information for all of those tasks at once. With this procedure, Microsoft Project copies the dates from the Start and Finish fields to the Actual Start and Actual Finish fields of the selected tasks.

Select adjacent tasks by holding down SHIFT while you select. Select nonadjacent tasks by holding down CTRL while you select.

To enter actual start and finish dates for several on-time tasks at once

1. On the **View Bar**, click **Gantt Chart**.
2. In the **Task Name** field, select the tasks that started and finished on time.
3. On the **Tools** menu, point to **Tracking**, and then click **Update Project**.
4. Click **Update work as complete through**.
5. Click **Set 0% or 100% complete only**.

6 Enter the date.

7 Click **Selected tasks.**

Tasks whose scheduled finish dates are before the status date are set to 100% complete. Their scheduled start and finish dates are set as their actual start and finish dates.

Enter Percent Complete on a Task

When a task is in progress, you can indicate how much progress has been made by entering the percentage of the total task duration that has been completed. A task is 0% complete when it has not yet begun, and it is 100% complete when it is finished. For example, if 8 hours of work have been completed on a 16-hour task, then you'd enter 50% complete. For a summary task, Microsoft Project calculates a percent complete that's based on the progress of its subtasks.

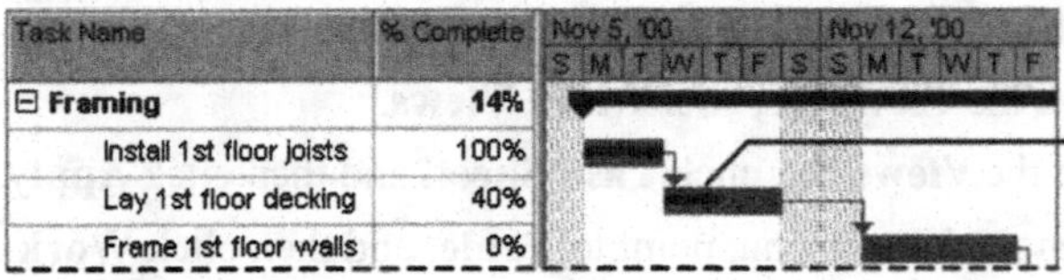

Microsoft Project displays percent complete as a thin black line within Gantt bars.

When you enter the percent complete for a task that's currently 0 percent complete, Microsoft Project sets the actual start date to be the scheduled start date and calculates the actual duration and remaining duration. When you enter 100% complete for a task, Microsoft Project sets the actual finish date to be the scheduled finish date and changes the actual duration to match the scheduled duration. If the task was critical, Microsoft Project changes it to noncritical.

Entering percent complete is equivalent to entering actual duration.

To indicate progress on a task as a percentage

1 On the **View Bar**, click **Gantt Chart.**

2 In the **Task Name** field, select the task you want to update.

Task Information

3 Click **Task Information**, and then click the **General** tab.

4 In the **Percent complete** box, type a whole number between 0 and 100.

If several tasks have the same percent complete, update their progress at the same time. Select the tasks (using the SHIFT or CTRL key), and then click Task Information.

To enter percent complete with the Tracking toolbar

1 On the **View Bar**, click **Gantt Chart**.

2 On the **View** menu, point to **Toolbars**, and then click **Tracking**.

3 In the **Task Name** field, select the task you want to update.
You can select and update percent complete for multiple tasks.

25% Complete

4 Click the button that represents the percent complete for the selected task. For example, click **25%** to indicate that the task is 25% completed.

Enter Percent Work Complete

If you assigned resources to tasks and you are tracking work, you can indicate the percentage of work that has been completed on a task. By specifying a percentage of work complete between 0% and 100%, you can compare actual completed work against planned work.

To enter percent work complete on a task

1 On the **View Bar**, click **More Views**.

2 In the **Views** list, click **Task Sheet**, and then click **Apply**.

3 On the **View** menu, point to **Table**, and then click **Work**.

4 In the **% W. Comp** field, type the percentage of work that's been completed for the tasks you want to update.
Recalculated values for actual work and remaining work appear in the Actual and Remaining fields.

If you have assigned resources, and especially if there are many resources working on the same tasks, you might prefer to update the percentage of work completed on an assignment rather than a task. It might be easier for multiple resources to report, and easier for you to track.

To enter progress on an assignment

1 On the **View Bar**, click **Task Usage**.

2 In the **Task Name** field, select the assignment (the resource name under the task) you want to update.

Assignment Information

3 Click **Assignment Information**, and then click the **Tracking** tab.

4 In the **% Work complete** box, type a whole number between 0 and 100.

You can update percent work complete on assignments in the Resource Usage view as well. Which view you use depends on whether you want to update work by task or by resource.

Enter the Actual Duration of a Task

If you know how long a task has been worked on and it's progressing as planned, you can enter the actual duration for the task. For example, if a 5-day task has been worked on for 2 days (and it's likely to be completed in 3 more days), you can enter an actual duration of 2 days.

When you enter the actual duration for a task, Microsoft Project calculates percent complete according to this formula:

Percent Complete = Actual Duration / Duration

When you enter actual duration, Microsoft Project also calculates remaining duration according to this formula:

Remaining Duration = Duration – Actual Duration

If you enter an actual duration that's greater than the scheduled duration before the task is complete, Microsoft Project updates the scheduled duration to equal the actual duration, changes the remaining duration to 0, and marks the task as 100% complete. This might not be accurate, especially if you've added resources to tasks and use effort-driven scheduling, which causes the duration to decrease when you add resources. To prevent this side effect, enter actual work rather than actual duration.

Entering actual duration is the same as entering percent complete.

To enter the actual duration of a task

1. On the **View Bar**, click **Gantt Chart**.
2. Select the task for which you want to enter the actual duration.
3. On the **Tools** menu, point to **Tracking**, and then click **Update Tasks**.
4. In the **Actual dur** box, enter the actual duration of the task.

If you think the task is going to be finished sooner or later than originally scheduled, you can enter a new value in the Remaining dur box.

Enter the Work Completed on a Task

If the availability of resources is crucial to your project and you want to track the work that each resource is performing, you can track task progress by updating the work completed on the task by each resource. For example, suppose that the scheduled work for a task assigned to 2 resources is 20 hours. At the end of a day, a total of 10 hours of work has been completed, 7 hours by one resource and 3 hours by the other. You can enter the amount of hours each resource has worked on his or her respective assignments on the task for that day.

After you update the actual number of hours a resource has worked on a task, Microsoft Project automatically calculates the remaining work. Entering actual work is equivalent to entering percent work complete.

To enter the work completed on a task

1. On the **View Bar**, click **Task Usage.**
2. On the **View** menu, point to **Table,** and then click **Tracking.**
3. Drag the divider bar or scroll to the right to view the **Act. Work** field.
4. In the **Act. Work** field, type the updated work value and the duration abbreviation for the assigned resource under the appropriate task.

Drag the divider bar to the right to see the Actual Work field.

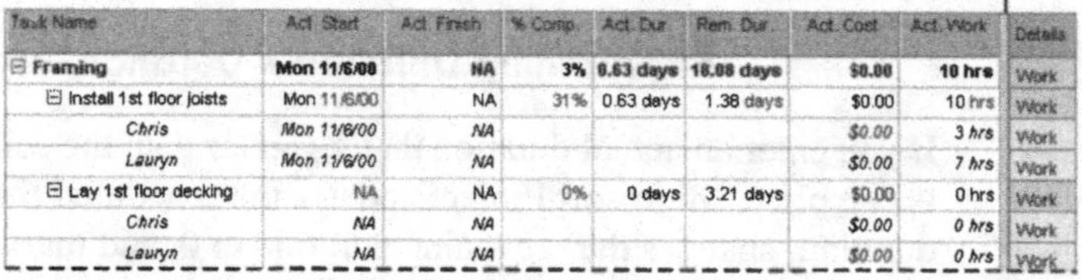

Task Name	Act. Start	Act. Finish	% Comp.	Act. Dur.	Rem. Dur.	Act. Cost	Act. Work	Details
Framing	Mon 11/6/00	NA	3%	0.63 days	18.08 days	$0.00	10 hrs	Work
Install 1st floor joists	Mon 11/6/00	NA	31%	0.63 days	1.38 days	$0.00	10 hrs	Work
Chris	Mon 11/6/00	NA				$0.00	3 hrs	Work
Lauryn	Mon 11/6/00	NA				$0.00	7 hrs	Work
Lay 1st floor decking	NA	NA	0%	0 days	3.21 days	$0.00	0 hrs	Work
Chris	NA	NA				$0.00	0 hrs	Work
Lauryn	NA	NA				$0.00	0 hrs	Work

If you would rather track the amount of work on the task as a whole, rather than on the individual assignments, simply type a value for the combined work done on the task by all the resources in the Act. Work field for the task itself. Microsoft Project divides the actual and remaining work among the resources.

If your schedule is tight and you need to closely track and control the project, you can enter the actual work done by each resource on a periodic, even daily, basis. Use the timephased fields in the Resource Usage or Task Usage view. Because the timephased fields break the project duration into days, weeks, or months, you can enter actual work on a daily, weekly, or monthly basis.

To update actual work on a periodic basis

1. On the **View Bar**, click **Task Usage.**
2. On the **View** menu, point to **Table,** and then click **Work.**
3. On the **Format** menu, point to **Details,** and then click **Actual Work.**
4. Choose the time period for which you want to update actual work.

   Use the **Zoom In** or **Zoom Out** buttons to switch the view to daily, weekly, or monthly periods.

Zoom In

Zoom Out

5. To enter actual values for a task, select the timesheet column for the period you want to track and type a value into the **Act. Work** field of the task.
6. To enter actual values for an assignment, select the timesheet column for the period you want to track and type a value into the **Act. Work** field of the assignment.

You can update actual work for assignments in the Resource Usage view as well.

Adjust the Remaining Work on a Task

Microsoft Project calculates the remaining work on a task by subtracting the actual work from the scheduled work. However, sometimes you find out that there's more work remaining than Microsoft Project has calculated. In those cases, you can update the remaining work on a task yourself.

To manually update the remaining work on a task

1 On the **View Bar**, click **Gantt Chart**.

2 On the **View** menu, point to **Table,** and then click **Work**.

Drag the divider bar or scroll to the right to see the **Remaining** field.

3 In the **Remaining** field of the task you want to update, enter the remaining work value you want.

Insert a Time Gap Between Actual Work and Remaining Work

A resource might not always work on a task continuously from beginning to end. For instance, a resource might complete part of a task, get interrupted to go work on a more urgent task, then resume work on the first task. If the interruption is short and doesn't significantly affect the finish date of the interrupted task, you might not need to track the interruption. But if the length of the interruption is significant or you simply want to track as precisely as possible, you can display a gap between the actual work and the remaining work on a task. The gap, or split, spans the stop and resume dates.

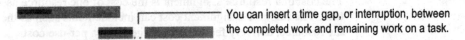

You can insert a time gap, or interruption, between the completed work and remaining work on a task.

To insert a split between actual work and remaining work

1 On the **View Bar**, click **Gantt Chart**.

2 With your pointer on the remaining work portion of the Gantt bar, drag the Gantt bar to the right to when you want the remaining work to resume.

The task splits at the end of the actual work completed.

Reschedule Uncompleted Work to Start on the Current Date

If your project falls behind schedule and you and your team are scrambling to catch up, it can be all too easy to forget about tasks that should have been completed by the current date but were not. You can account for all tasks that should have been completed by the current date by rescheduling uncompleted work to start on the current date.

You can reschedule uncompleted work for all tasks or for selected tasks. If a task has no work done on it, Microsoft Project calculates its new start date to be the current date or later, depending on any task dependencies. If a task is partially complete, Microsoft Project inserts a split between the completed work and the remaining work portions of the task. If a task has an inflexible constraint, such as Must Start On or Must Finish On, Microsoft Project might replace the inflexible constraint with a more flexible constraint, such as Start No Earlier Than. If you want to keep a constraint, it's best to reschedule the remaining work for a task manually.

To reschedule uncompleted work to start on the current date

Use SHIFT+click to select multiple adjacent tasks. Use CTRL+click to select multiple nonadjacent tasks.

1 On the **View Bar**, click **Gantt Chart**.

2 If you want to reschedule certain tasks only, select the tasks you want to reschedule.

If you want to reschedule all remaining work in the project, you do not need to select any tasks.

3 On the **Tools** menu, point to **Tracking**, and then click **Update Project**.

4 Click **Reschedule uncompleted work to start**, and then type the date from which you want to reschedule all remaining work.

5 To reschedule the entire project, click **Entire project**.

To reschedule the selected tasks only, click **Selected tasks**.

Manually Enter Actual Costs

The cost of a resource assignment is the cost of one resource assigned to a particular task. The resource assignment cost can include items such as the standard rate paid to the resource, delivery fees, setup charges, and a per-use cost.

By default, Microsoft Project calculates the actual cost of a resource assignment as the task progresses, according to the accrual method you choose. If you want to enter the actual cost of a resource assignment yourself, you can do so as soon as remaining work on the task is zero.

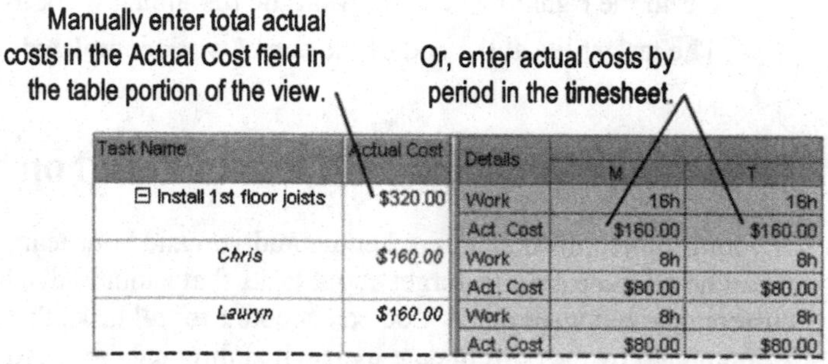

To manually enter actual costs for an assignment

1. On the **View Bar**, click **Task Usage**.
2. On the **View** menu, point to **Table,** and then click **Tracking**.
3. Drag the divider bar or scroll to the right to view the **Act. Cost** field.
4. In the **Act. Cost** field, type the actual cost for the completed assignment or task for which you want to update costs.

Just as you can track actual work on a periodic basis, you can also manually enter actual costs on a daily, weekly, or monthly basis. You can track the actual costs of tasks as well as resource assignments. You might need to do this if costs are an overriding concern in your project, perhaps because of a limited budget.

To do this, add the Actual Cost to the timesheet portion of the Task Usage view. On the **Format** menu, point to **Details**, and then click **Actual Cost**.

Prevent Resource Information from Changing When Updating Tasks

By default, when you update information for a task that has resources assigned to it, Microsoft Project automatically updates the tracking information for the assigned resources. As Microsoft Project updates the resource information, it distributes the actuals information based on the remaining work values and the resources' assignment allocation across the period of time.

You can specify the tracking information for each resource independent of the task information by turning off the automatic updating of resource tracking information. This way, you can enter percent complete on tasks without affecting actual work values on the task or assignments while the task is in progress. However, as soon as the task is 100% complete, its resource work values are set to be completed as well.

To prevent resource information from being updated

1. On the **Tools** menu, click **Options**, and then click the **Calculation** tab.
2. Under **Calculation options**, clear the **Updating task status updates resource status** check box.

Enter Notes

As you enter tasks, resources, and assignments, fine-tune your plan, and track and enter actual information, you might want to document or explain various conditions. You can enter notes and associate them with an individual task, resource, or assignment. These notes stay with the item and can be viewed and updated at any time.

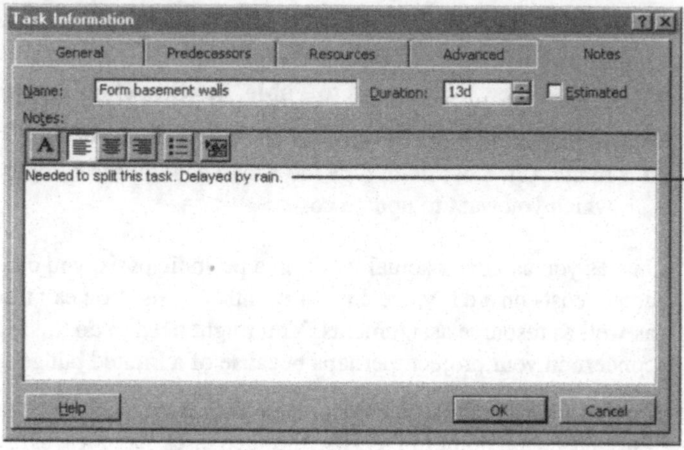

Enter a note to explain a special issue.

To add a note to a task

1. On the **View Bar**, click **Gantt Chart**.
2. Select the task to which you want to add a note.
3. Click **Task Information**, and then click the **Notes** tab.
4. Type the note.

   You can format the note using the buttons on the note toolbar.

Task Information

Note

When a task includes a note, the note icon appears in the Indicators column of any task sheet. When you rest the mouse pointer over the icon, the first few lines of the note appear. If you double-click the note icon, the entire note appears.

To add a note to a resource

1. On the **View Bar**, click **Resource Sheet**.
2. Select the resource to which you want to add a note.
3. Click **Resource Information**, and then click the **Notes** tab.
4. Type the note.

Resource Information

Note

When a resource includes a note, the note icon appears in the Indicators column of any resource sheet.

To add a note to an assignment

1. On the **View Bar**, click **Task Usage** or **Resource Usage**.
2. Select the assignment to which you want to add a note.
3. Click **Assignment Information**, and then click the **Notes** tab.
4. Type the note.

Assignment Information

Note When an assignment includes a note, the note icon appears in the Indicators column of the Task Usage or Resource Usage view.

To update an existing note

1. Double-click the note indicator for the note you want to update.
2. Make any text or formatting changes to the note you want. You can also delete the entire note, if necessary.

Analyzing Variances from Your Baseline Data

A *variance* is any difference between baseline data and scheduled data. For example, if the baseline start date for a task is February 12 and its scheduled start date (based on actual and remaining information entered so far) is February 14, there's a variance of 2 days. Variances alert you to potential problems in your schedule that might need corrective action. But variances can be good, as when a task starts 2 days earlier than planned. You can analyze a variance to determine the exact effect it has on your schedule. Microsoft Project can display variances only when you've first set a baseline before beginning to track and collect actual progress data.

Among the most important variances you should look for when comparing your updated schedule to the baseline plan are:

- Tasks that are starting or finishing late.
- Tasks that require more or less work than scheduled.
- Tasks that are progressing more slowly than planned.
- Tasks that are costing more than planned for actual work that's completed.
- Resources that aren't working hours as scheduled.

After you find variances, you need to determine what corrective action, if any, you need to take.

Display Progress Lines to Determine Project Status

Looking at the variance for each task start and finish date can show that some tasks are early, some late, and others on time. You might not get a good impression of whether your project is, overall, ahead or behind schedule. One way to see quickly whether your project is ahead or behind schedule is to display *progress lines* on the Gantt Chart.

A progress line is a vertical line that represents either the current date or a status date that you specify. Jutting out from a progress line are horizontal peaks connected to Gantt bars representing tasks that are either in progress or should have started prior to the current date or *status date*. A peak pointing leftward indicates a task that's behind schedule. A peak pointing rightward indicates a task that's ahead of schedule. A progress line does not connect to completed tasks or tasks that start after the date of the progress line.

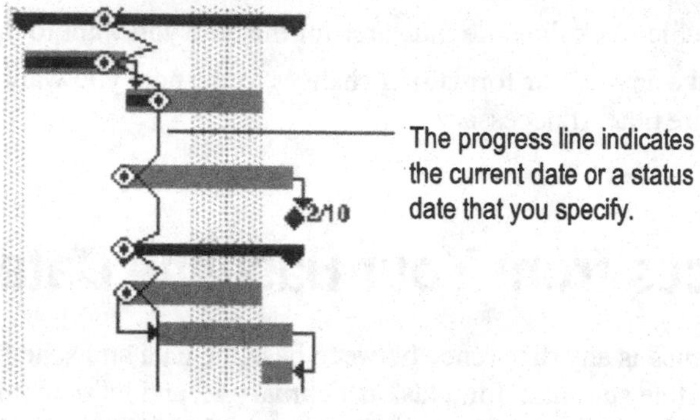
2/10
The progress line indicates the current date or a status date that you specify.

You can view more than one progress line at a time, either by specifying each one individually or at set intervals.

To display progress lines in your project

1. On the **View Bar**, click **Gantt Chart**.
2. On the **Tools** menu, click **Options**, and then click the **Calculation** tab.
3. Select the **Edits to total task % complete will be spread to the status date** check box, and then click **OK**.
4. On the **Tools** menu, point to **Tracking**, and then click **Progress Lines**.
5. Click the **Dates and Intervals** tab.
6. Select the **Always display current progress line** check box.
7. To show progress for the project status date, click **At project status date.**

   To show progress for today's date, click **At current date**.

   To show progress for another date, or a series of dates, click the **Display selected progress lines** check box, and then enter the dates in the rows.
8. To show your progress relative to baseline data, under **Display progress lines in relation to**, click **Baseline plan**.

You set the project status date in the Project Information dialog box. On the Project menu, click Information.

View a Summary of Project Variances and Totals

You can review overall project start and finish dates, and duration, work, and cost statistics in terms of the current schedule, the baseline, any actuals recorded so far, the remaining values, and variances. To see this bottom-line summary, review the Project Statistics.

The Statistics dialog box shows the current big-picture status on all your progress indicators.

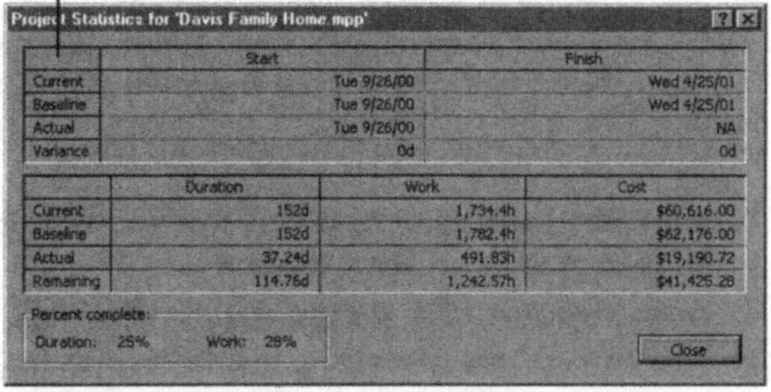
Project Statistics for 'Davis Family Home.mpp'
Start
Finish
Current
Tue 9/26/00
Wed 4/25/01
Baseline
Tue 9/26/00
Wed 4/25/01
Actual
Tue 9/26/00
NA
Variance
0d
0d
Duration
Work
Cost
Current
152d
1,734.4h
$60,616.00
Baseline
152d
1,782.4h
$62,176.00
Actual
37.24d
491.83h
$19,190.72
Remaining
114.76d
1,242.57h
$41,425.28
Percent complete:
Duration: 25%
Work: 28%
Close

To view total project statistics

1 On the **Project** menu, click **Project Information**.

2 Click **Statistics**.

Determine if Tasks Are Starting and Finishing on Time

Progress can be measured only against some reference point. In Microsoft Project, that reference point is the baseline start and finish dates. To determine how your project is progressing, you need to compare the scheduled start and finish dates with the baseline start and finish dates. The Tracking Gantt view enables you to view both sets of dates at the same time. Based on your analysis of any variances you identify, you can adjust your schedule as necessary to keep your project on track.

Variance fields display the difference between baseline values and scheduled values. For example, if the baseline start date for a task is February 2 and the scheduled start date is February 5, the variance is 3 days.

To determine if tasks are starting and finishing on time

1 On the **View Bar**, click **Tracking Gantt**.

2 On the **View** menu, point to **Table**, and then click **Variance**.

Microsoft Project displays the scheduled and baseline dates for each task.

3 Drag the divider bar or scroll to the right to view the **Variance** fields.

A negative variance indicates that the task started or finished ahead of schedule.

Determine if Tasks Are Using More or Less Work Than Planned

The amount of work required to complete a task affects the task duration as well as the workload of the resources assigned to a task. If your original work estimate for a task is inaccurate, the task could end up taking longer than planned or requiring additional resources to complete on time. If there's a difference between estimated and scheduled work, you might very well need to take corrective action.

To determine if tasks are using more or less work than planned

1. On the **View Bar**, click **Gantt Chart**.
2. On the **View** menu, point to **Table**, and then click **Work**.
3. Drag the divider bar to the right to view the **Baseline** field.
4. Compare the values in the **Work** and **Baseline** fields.

   The values in the **Variance** column indicate the difference between baseline work and scheduled work.

Respond to Variances by Adjusting the Project

After you find variances, you need to determine what corrective action, if any, you need to take. For example, some things you can do to speed critical tasks are:

- Adjust task dependencies.
- Assign overtime work.
- Hire or assign additional resources
- Add shifts.
- Decrease the amount of work required to complete a task.

To resolve resource overallocations, you can:

- Reassign resources.
- Delay tasks.
- Change working hours.

For details about these and other methods for adjusting your project to account for variances, see chapter 8, "Fine-Tuning Your Project."

Tracking Project Costs and Variances

In some projects, the success of a project is determined by whether the project goals are accomplished within the budget. If staying within a budget is important to you, you can view your project's total scheduled, baseline, actual, and remaining costs. You can then compare the project costs in your plan with your budget to determine whether you'll meet your budget and whether any corrective action is needed. There are a number of methods for looking at your project cost status:

- Compare total baseline costs with total scheduled costs.
- Compare baseline costs with scheduled costs on a periodic basis.
- Review costs in terms of earned value.
- Review a summary of total project costs to date.

Determine if Tasks Cost More or Less Than Planned

When you're working with a budget and tracking costs, you'll want to know if your tasks are running over budget before your project progresses too far. This way, you can either adjust your budget or reduce costs so you don't go over budget before the project finish date.

In Microsoft Project, you can compare the total cost of a task—which consists of fixed costs for tasks plus resource costs—to the baseline cost and actual cost. This can be especially useful if your baseline costs are the basis of your project budget. Microsoft Project also calculates the remaining cost of a task that's in progress.

The Cost table helps you compare your current total costs...

...with your baseline costs.

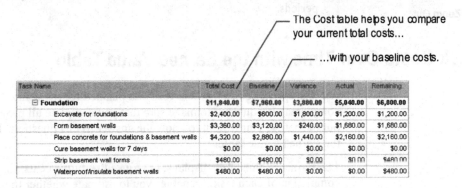

Task Name	Total Cost	Baseline	Variance	Actual	Remaining
Foundation	**$11,840.00**	**$7,960.00**	**$3,880.00**	**$5,040.00**	**$6,800.00**
Excavate for foundations	$2,400.00	$600.00	$1,800.00	$1,200.00	$1,200.00
Form basement walls	$3,360.00	$3,120.00	$240.00	$1,680.00	$1,680.00
Place concrete for foundations & basement walls	$4,320.00	$2,880.00	$1,440.00	$2,160.00	$2,160.00
Cure basement walls for 7 days	$0.00	$0.00	$0.00	$0.00	$0.00
Strip basement wall forms	$480.00	$480.00	$0.00	$0.00	$480.00
Waterproof/insulate basement walls	$480.00	$480.00	$0.00	$0.00	$480.00

To determine if tasks cost more or less than budgeted

1. On the **View Bar**, click **Gantt Chart**.
2. On the **View** menu, point to **Table**, and then click **Cost**.
3. Drag the divider bar to the right to view the **Total Cost** and **Baseline** fields.

4 Compare the values in the **Total Cost** and **Baseline** fields.

The Total Cost field includes the costs of any actual work recorded so far, added to the costs of any scheduled work yet to be done, plus any fixed costs for tasks.

5 For the cost variance, look at the value in the **Variance** field.

View Baseline Costs and Scheduled Costs on a Periodic Basis

When costs matter, you probably want to track them closely, perhaps daily or weekly. You can do that by comparing baseline costs with scheduled costs in the Task Usage view, which breaks down costs (as well as work and other values) on a periodic basis: day by day, week by-week, or month by month. In the Task Usage view, you can display both baseline costs and scheduled costs in detail.

To view baseline costs and scheduled costs on a periodic basis

1 On the **View Bar**, click **Task Usage**.

2 On the **View** menu, point to **Table**, and then click **Cost**.

3 On the **Format** menu, click **Detail Styles,** and then click the **Usage Details** tab.

4 In the **Available fields** list, hold down CTRL, and then click **Actual Cost**, **Baseline Cost**, and **Cost**.

The Cost field represents scheduled costs—that is, any actual costs recorded so far added to costs for remaining work, plus any fixed costs for tasks.

5 Click **Show**.

Zoom In

Zoom Out

6 Choose the time period for which you want to view costs.

7 Click **Zoom In** or **Zoom Out** to switch the view to daily, weekly, or monthly periods.

Track Costs Over Time with the Earned Value Table

Are you spending more or less than you planned for the actual task work that's been completed? If you want to make sure that you complete all project tasks before you run out of money, you'll want to know the answer to this question. The answer lies in using the Earned Value table.

The Earned Value table displays, in terms of resource costs, the actual percentage of completion of each task. It enables you to estimate whether the task will finish under budget or over budget based on the cost incurred while the task is in progress. For example, if a task is 50% complete but has already cost 75% of the budget allotted to it, the task will probably cost more than planned when it's completed. You can use the Earned Value table to analyze the cost of each task in this way.

The following table lists the earned value fields available in Microsoft Project.

This earned value field...	Means...	And contains...
BCWS	Budgeted Cost of Work Scheduled	Cumulative *timephased* baseline costs up to the status date or today's date. The timephased calculation assumes an even distribution of costs over the task duration, and indicates how much of the baseline should have been spent on a task by the status date.
BCWP	Budgeted Cost of Work Performed	Cumulative value of the task's timephased percent complete multiplied by the task's timephased baseline cost. BCWP is calculated up to the status date or today's date. This information is also known as *earned value*.
ACWP	Actual Cost of Work Performed	Costs incurred for work already done, up to the project status date or today's date.
SV	Schedule Variance	Difference in cost terms between current progress and the baseline plan of the task up to the status date or today's date.
CV	Cost Variance	Difference between how much it should have cost to achieve the current level of completion on the task (BCWP), and how much it has actually cost (ACWP) up to the status date or today's date.
EAC	Estimate at Completion	Total scheduled, or projected, cost for a task, based on costs already incurred for work performed, in addition to the costs planned for the remaining work. Same as the Cost or Total Cost field.
BAC	Budget at Completion	Total planned cost for a task. Same as the Baseline Cost field.
VAC	Variance at Completion	Difference between the BAC (Budgeted at Completion) or baseline cost and EAC (Estimated at Completion) or total cost for a task.

To analyze costs over time with the Earned Value table

1. On the **View Bar**, click **Gantt Chart**.
2. On the **View** menu, point to **Table**, and then click **More Tables**.
3. In the **Tables** list, click **Earned Value,** and then click **Apply**.
4. Drag the divider bar to the right to display all of the **Earned Value** table fields.

You can also view earned value data on a periodic basis.

To view earned value data on a periodic basis

1. On the **View Bar**, click **Task Usage**.
2. On the **Format** menu, click **Detail Styles**, and then click the **Usage Details** tab.
3. In the **Available fields** list, hold down CTRL, click the fields you want to display, such as ACWP, BCWP, and BCWS, and then click **Show**.
4. Choose the time period for which you want to review earned value fields.

Zoom In

Zoom Out

Use the **Zoom In** or **Zoom Out** buttons to switch the view to daily, weekly, or monthly periods.

Respond to Cost Variances by Adjusting the Project

If you find cost variances, you need to determine what corrective actions you should take to bring your project back into budget compliance. For example, you can:

- Adjust the budget.
- Replace expensive resources with inexpensive ones.
- Delete tasks.

For details about these and other methods for adjusting your project to account for cost variances, see "Meeting Your Budget" in chapter 8.

10

Updating Task Information Using E-Mail

Effective communication is vital for successful project management. You need to advise managers, clients, and other stakeholders of progress on the project. Resources need to know which tasks they're assigned to and when they're due. Resources need to inform you of their progress, which might include task start dates, overtime, how far along a task is, and whether or not a task will finish on time.

Microsoft Project facilitates several means of communicating information. With your existing e-mail system, you can use Microsoft Project to send or route project files to resources or stakeholders. You can also send a note about one or more tasks to resources or other interested parties. If your e-mail system is Microsoft Outlook, you can send reminders to yourself regarding the start or finish of a task.

With the Microsoft Project workgroup communication capabilities, you can use your e-mail system to exchange messages with the resources working on your project. You can also use Microsoft Project Central, the Web-based companion product to Microsoft Project, to exchange messages and provide unique and secure views into the product for resources and other individuals over your organization's intranet or the World Wide Web.

With workgroup communication using either e-mail or Microsoft Project Central, you can:

- Assign tasks to resources.
- Inform resources of changes to assigned tasks.
- Request and receive actual status information from resources.
- Enter actual progress information automatically into your project.

This chapter details how you can exchange files and notes using your e-mail system. It also gives an overview of workgroup communication involving your tasks and resources. This chapter also covers procedures for using your existing e-mail system to exchange task messages with your workgroup. Procedures for using Microsoft Project Central to exchange task messages with your workgroup, are covered in chapter 11.

Sending Project Files, Notes, and Reminders

Whether you use e-mail or Microsoft Project Central for workgroup communication, or even if you don't use electronic workgroup communication for your project at all, you can still use your e-mail system to send or route a project file or schedule notes to others in your organization.

Route your project file to your team leads, for example, when you want to gather feedback on a draft of your project. Send your project to key stakeholders when you achieve major milestones so they can see your progress on the schedule and budget. Send schedule notes to resources when you have questions about certain tasks.

Your recipients must have Microsoft Project installed on their computers to view a project file you send or route. Certain types of schedule notes, on the other hand, can be viewed from e-mail by recipients who might or might not have Microsoft Project.

If your e-mail program is Microsoft Outlook, you can set task reminders for the start or finish of one, several, or all tasks in your schedule. Use Outlook reminders for important tasks or milestones whose dates you want to monitor closely.

You might find the Workgroup toolbar convenient, especially if you use workgroup functions regularly. Throughout this chapter, shortcuts with the Workgroup toolbar are noted in the margin next to the related procedures.

To show the Workgroup toolbar

1. On the **View** menu, point to **Toolbars**.
2. Click **Workgroup**.

Send a Project File

When you want others in your group to review a new or revised project, you can attach the project file to an e-mail message and send it. You can send it to as many individuals on your e-mail system as you need. To view the project, your recipients must have Microsoft Project installed on their computers.

To send an entire project file

1 Open the project file.

On the Workgroup toolbar, click  **Send to Mail Recipient.**

2 On the **File** menu, point to **Send To**, and then click **Mail Recipient**.

A mail message form appears, with the project file already attached.

3 In the **To** box, enter the e-mail names of the recipients.

If the resource is outside your organization, be sure to include the entire address. For example, if the resource's e-mail name is richardb and he can be reached through an Internet service provider called provider.com, enter the address as *richardb@provider.com.*

4 In the message area, type your message.

5 Click **Send**.

Send Schedule Notes

You can also send a project file and other schedule information to resources and other contacts in your workgroup by sending a schedule note. With a schedule note, you can communicate with selected or all resources in your project. You can send a note alone, attach a picture of selected tasks in the current view, or attach the entire project file.

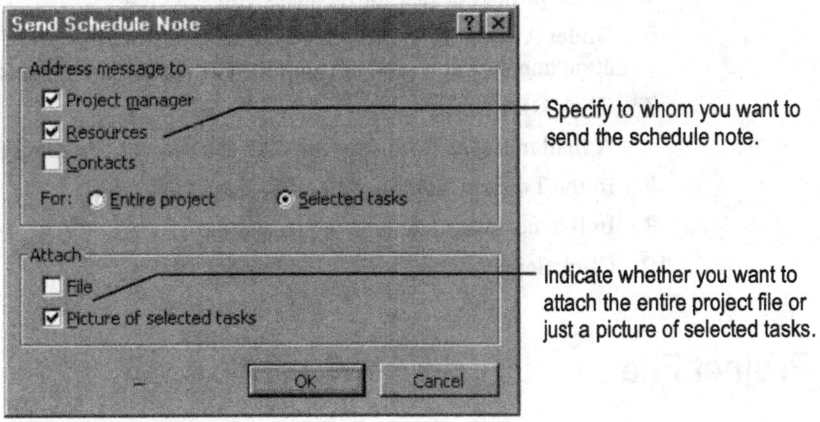

To send a schedule note

1 Open the project file.

Use the SHIFT key to select multiple adjacent tasks. Use the CTRL key to select multiple nonadjacent tasks.

2 If you are sending a schedule note to certain resources regarding specific tasks, go to the view and select the tasks.

For example, if you want to send a portion of the Gantt Chart, on the **View Bar**, click **Gantt Chart**, and then click the tasks you want to include in the note.

3 On the **Tools** menu, point to **Workgroup**, and then click **Send Schedule Note**.

If you have not set up resource e-mail addresses yet, you can pick them from your e-mail system address book. Or, add resource names in the Resource Information dialog box.

4 Under **Address Message To**, select the check boxes for the categories of individuals to whom you want the schedule note to be sent.

   If you choose **Project Manager** or **Contacts**, a mail message form appears, ready for you to enter the e-mail names from your e-mail system's address book.

   If you choose **Resources**, a mail message form appears, showing the e-mail names of the resources assigned to the selected tasks.

5 Next to **For**, select whether you want to send the message to the resources for the entire project or just for the tasks you selected.

To send a schedule note with an attachment

1 Open the project file.

2 If you are sending a schedule note regarding specific tasks, go to the view and set it up the way you want it to show in your attachment. Select the tasks.

   For example, if you want to send a portion of the Task Usage view, on the **View Bar**, click **Task Usage**, and then click the tasks you want to attach to the note.

3 On the **Tools** menu, point to **Workgroup**, and then click **Send Schedule Note**.

4 Under **Address Message To**, select the check boxes for the categories of individuals to whom you want the schedule note to be sent.

5 Next to **For**, select whether you want to send the message to the resources for the entire project or just for the tasks you selected.

6 Under **Attach**, select whether you want to send the entire project file as an attachment or as a picture (bmp file) of the tasks you selected.

7 Click **OK**.

   A mail message form appears, with the project file or picture file already attached.

8 In the **To** field, enter e-mail addresses if necessary.

9 In the message area, type your message.

10 Click **Send**.

Route a Project File

If your workgroup shares an e-mail system, and if everyone has Microsoft Project installed on their computers, you can *route* a project file. Routing a project file enables all resources to review a project before it becomes final, or to review a major change to the schedule. You can also route a project file to upper management or other key stakeholders to get their feedback and approval.

Routing a project file usually means that the file is attached to an e-mail message and sent to one or more persons on a routing list, then eventually returned to the original sender. With Microsoft Project, a file can be routed so that one person at a time receives it, reviews it, perhaps enters changes or notes, then sends it to the next person. Or the file can be routed to each person on the routing list at the same time.

To route a project file

1 Open the profile file you want to route.

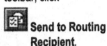

On the Workgroup toolbar, click  **Send to Routing Recipient.**

2 On the **File** menu, point to **Send To**, and then click **Routing Recipient**.

3 Click **Address**, hold down CTRL, click the names of the recipients, click **To**, and then click **OK**.

4 To change the order of the recipients, click a name in the **To** box, and then click a **Move** button.

5 Type a subject in the **Subject** box.

6 In the **Message Text** box, type instructions or other information.

7 Under **Route to Recipients**, click the delivery option you want.

8 If you don't want the file returned to you after the last recipient on the routing list receives the project, clear the **Return When Done** check box.

When you're ready to route the file, on the File menu, point to Send To, click Next Routing Recipient, and then click OK.

9 If you don't want to be notified each time the file is routed to the next recipient on the routing list, clear the **Track Status** check box.

10 If you aren't ready to route the file just yet, click **Add Slip** to save the routing slip with the project file.

11 To route the project file to the recipients, click **Route**.

View and Forward a Routed Project File

When you receive a routed project file, you review it according to the instructions from the originator. You then forward the project file to the next person on the list. If you're the last person on the routing list, you can send the project file to the person who originated the routing message.

To forward a routed project file

1 In your e-mail program, open the routed message.

2 To open the project, double-click the Microsoft Project icon in the e-mail message.

 **Save**

3 Review and modify the project, and then click **Save**.

4 On the **File** menu, point to **Send To**, and then click **Next Routing Recipient**.

Set E-Mail Reminders for Selected Tasks

If Microsoft Outlook is your e-mail program, you add Outlook reminders for your project tasks. You can have Outlook remind you when a certain task is due to start or finish. This is particularly useful for important tasks you want to keep a close eye on.

Use reminders with Microsoft Outlook to be alerted to the start or finish of important tasks.

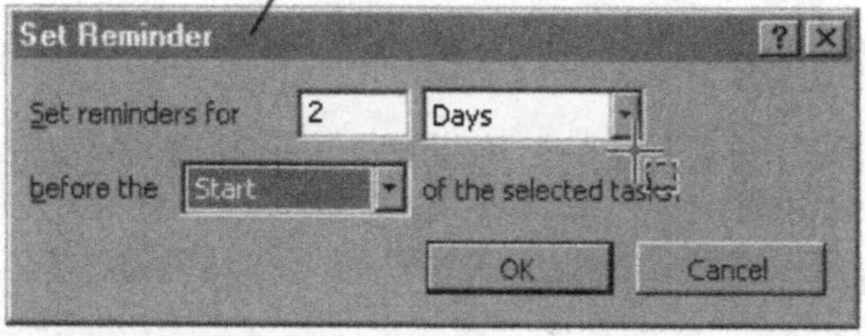

You can set multiple reminders at once. Use the SHIFT key to select multiple adjacent tasks. Use the CTRL key to select multiple nonadjacent tasks.

On the Workgroup toolbar, click **Set Reminder**.

To set an e-mail reminder for a task

1. On the **View Bar**, click **Gantt Chart**.
2. Select the task for which you want a reminder.
3. On the **Tools** menu, point to **Workgroup**, and then click **Set Reminder**.
4. In the **Set Reminders For** boxes, indicate how far in advance you want to be notified. For example, enter **2** in the first box and **Days** in the second box if you want to be notified two days before the task date.
5. In the **Before The** box, indicate whether you want to be notified in advance of the start date or finish date of the task.

Communicating Information with Resources

Collecting up-to-date project information and incorporating it into your project plan is an essential activity if you want to track progress, but it can also be time-consuming. Periodically, you need to collect information from each resource assigned to a task that should have started by the current date. Then you need to enter this information into your project, one task at a time. A faster and more convenient way to update your project is to use the Microsoft Project workgroup feature.

A *workgroup* is a set of resources and their manager who work on the same project and are connected to an electronic communication system. Across this communication system, resources who perform the tasks in your project exchange information with the project manager, who is responsible for tracking the project.

Because the workgroup feature distributes responsibility for updating the project plan among the entire team, the project manager doesn't have to do it all. After accepting a task assignment, each resource periodically sends updated task information to the project manager. The project manager then incorporates this information into the project plan.

The project manager and resources exchange task information by using Microsoft Project *workgroup messages*. The project manager uses these messages to make task assignments, inform resources of proposed schedule changes, and request actual task information. The resources use these messages to accept or decline task assignments, provide feedback on proposed schedule changes, and send actual task information to the project manager. The project manager can incorporate all the actual task information from a workgroup message directly into the project plan without having to enter each piece of information separately and manually.

You can exchange project workgroup messages with either an e-mail system or with Microsoft Project Central, the Web-based workgroup communication system for Microsoft Project. Microsoft Project Central uses the World Wide Web, which is a part of the Internet, or a network internal to an organization called an *intranet*, which looks and works like the World Wide Web. You can use any one of these systems or all at the same time for different resources. You can exchange e-mail or Microsoft Project Central workgroup messages with resources working outside your organization as well.

The Flow of Project Information in Workgroup Communication

In a project workgroup, task information is exchanged between the project manager and the resources in the project. This information is collected into special workgroup messages. The three types of Microsoft Project workgroup messages are *TeamAssign*, *TeamUpdate*, and *TeamStatus*.

At the hub of the communication system, the project manager can send workgroup messages to one, several, or all resources at a time. Workgroup messages are received in an electronic inbox. In an e-mail system, the resources and project manager receive their workgroup messages in their respective e-mail inboxes. With Microsoft Project Central, resources and the project manager receive workgroup messages when they log on to Microsoft Project Central.

The project manager and resources exchange task information by sending, receiving, and replying to workgroup messages. Whether you use e-mail or Microsoft Project Central, the cycle typically works like this:

1. The project manager sends a TeamAssign request, which is a workgroup message assigning or requesting a task assignment, to a resource.
2. The resource sends the project manager a reply to the TeamAssign request that indicates his or her acceptance or rejection of the task assignment. Once the TeamAssign message is acknowledged by the resource, the assignment is confirmed in the project plan.
3. If there's a change to the schedule of a task, the project manager can notify each assigned resource with a TeamUpdate message.

4 A resource who receives a TeamUpdate message can send a TeamUpdate message to the project manager, if necessary, to explain how the changes affect him or her.

5 To gather up-to-date progress information about each task, the project manager periodically sends each resource a TeamStatus message requesting actual information about tasks.

This information might be actual start date, actual finish date, actual work, actual duration, percent complete, and so on. The information requested in a TeamStatus message can be customized by the project manager.

6 Each resource responds to a TeamStatus message by replying with the requested task status information. The project manager can then automatically incorporate the actuals into the project, adding all the necessary tracking data without having to manually enter them.

Choose Your Workgroup Communication System

Which communication system you use, e-mail or Microsoft Project Central, depends on the systems you already have and how your group operates. It can also depend on where your resources are located: internal or external to your organization. To use an e-mail-based communication system, your workgroup needs access to a MAPI-compliant, 32-bit e-mail system. Examples of such e-mail systems include Microsoft Outlook, Microsoft Exchange, LotusNotes 4.5 and later, and cc:Mail 7.0. You can exchange workgroup messages with resources outside your organization using a different e-mail system, as long as theirs is also a MAPI-compliant, 32-bit e-mail system.

To use Microsoft Project Central, each of your resources needs a license for the Microsoft Project Central client and access to a Web server. You can exchange workgroup messages with resources outside your organization as long as they have access to your Internet or intranet site.

When making your choice, keep in mind that while the e-mail workgroup system offers all the basic communication capabilities described in the previous section, you gain additional functionality when you use the Web-based Microsoft Project Central. The following table summarizes these capabilities.

Basic functionality of e-mail workgroup communication	Additional capabilities with Microsoft Project Central
Resources receive and respond to TeamAssign, TeamUpdate, and TeamStatus messages regarding their assigned tasks.	Resources also get a personalized Gantt Chart that includes all their own tasks. They can group and filter their tasks to view and organize them as necessary.
Resources see their own assigned tasks when they receive workgroup messages.	Resources can review continually updated information for the entire project. The project manager and the Microsoft Project Central administrator can determine which information is viewable for whom, and can apply security privileges to filter out sensitive information.
Project managers can create new tasks and send them to the resources for acknowledgment.	Resources can also create new tasks and send them to the project manager for approval and incorporation into the project.
Project managers can request and receive actual information with TeamStatus messages.	Project managers can also request and receive narrative status reports from resources and consolidate them into a single project status report. Project managers can set up their status reports to include the headings and information they want.
Project managers can specify whether or not actuals are automatically incorporated into the project.	Project managers can also set up message rules as to how updates from resources are accepted and incorporated. They can specify that updates from certain members only be automatically accepted. They can also specify that certain conditions require the project manager's review.
Project managers can delegate tasks to resources.	If the project manager allows it, workgroup resources can also delegate tasks to other workgroup members. Project managers can then send tasks to a lead, for example, who in turn can assign the tasks to individual resources.

Your choice of workgroup communication system does not have to be exclusive. That is, you can communicate with some of your resources with e-mail and with other resources with Microsoft Project Central.

The rest of this chapter focuses on the setup and use of the e-mail workgroup communication system. If you have decided to use Microsoft Project Central only for your workgroup communication, skip to chapter 11.

Using E-Mail Workgroup Communication

If your workgroup is to use e-mail as the means for communicating project information, the detailed requirements are described in the following table:

Requirement	Resource	Project manager
Connected to a network, such as a local area network (LAN).	Required	Required
Use a MAPI-compliant, 32-bit e-mail system, such as Microsoft Outlook.	Required	Required
Microsoft Project installed on computer.	Optional	Required
WGsetup.exe installed on computer.	Required	Not applicable, because Microsoft Project must be installed.

The e-mail program you use must comply with the Messaging Application Programming Interface (MAPI). MAPI is the standard programming interface proposed and supported by Microsoft for accessing electronic messaging. Examples of MAPI-compliant e-mail programs are Microsoft Outlook, Microsoft Outlook Express, Microsoft Exchange, Microsoft Mail, LotusNotes 4.5 and later, and cc:Mail 7.0 and later. In addition, the e-mail program you use must be a 32-bit program.

The WGSetup.exe program is provided on the Microsoft Project installation CD and can be easily copied onto each resource's computer. This program enables workgroup communication with e-mail.

The rest of this chapter describes activities done by the project manager or system administrator. However, certain procedures presented toward the end of the chapter can help resources in the workgroup learn how to use the Microsoft Project e-mail workgroup communication capabilities. Those are marked with *Resources* in their titles.

Setting Up E-Mail Workgroup Communication

To establish the e-mail workgroup communication system for your project, you need to:

- Set up Microsoft Project for e-mail workgroup communication.
- Set up the resources in your project for e-mail workgroup communication.
- Specify the information you want to be included in your workgroup messages.

Set Up Microsoft Project for E-Mail Workgroup Communication

The first step toward setting up e-mail workgroup communication for your project is to select the default communication system. This sets the default for all your resources. You can still change the communication method for individual resources.

Selecting a communication system doesn't make that system operational. You're simply enabling Microsoft Project to communicate with the system you select.

To select e-mail as the default method for workgroup communication

1. On the **Tools** menu, click **Options**, and then click the **Workgroup** tab.
2. In the **Default Workgroup Messages** box, click **Email**. This specifies e-mail as the workgroup communication default you want to use for most of your resources. You can change the message option for individual resources.
   If you don't want to specify a default workgroup system, perhaps because most of your resources do not have access to an e-mail system or Microsoft Project Central, click **None**. You can also specify the workgroup system for individual resources.
3. To apply your workgroup selections to all new projects, click **Set as Default**.
4. Click the **General** tab.
5. In the **User Name** box, type the name by which you want to be identified in the workgroup messages you send.

To change the message option for individual resources, see "Change the Workgroup System a Resource Will Use" later in this section.

Set Up Resources for E-Mail Workgroup Communication

The second step to setting up the e-mail workgroup communication system for your project is to set up your resources. This involves:

- Adding and running the workgroup setup program on each resource's computer.
- Ensuring that all resources are added to your project.
- Adding the resources' e-mail names to your project.
- If necessary, changing the messaging system for an individual resource for whom the default system is not available.

Material resources are automatically excluded from workgroup communication setup requirements.

Set Up Workgroup Capabilities on Resources' Computers

To enable your resources to exchange Microsoft Project workgroup messages over e-mail, the workgroup setup program needs to be installed on each resource's computer. The workgroup setup program, WGSetup.exe, on the Microsoft Project setup CD.

To set up resources for e-mail workgroup communication using the network

1. Copy the entire WGSetup folder, found on the Microsoft Project CD, to a network drive that can be accessed by all your resources.
2. Using Windows Explorer on the resource's computer, access the network drive, and then copy the WGSetup folder onto the resource's computer disk drive.
3. Open the WGSetup folder.
4. Double-click WGSetup.exe, and then follow the instructions.
5. Repeat steps 2–4 on the computers of all resources who will be using e-mail for workgroup communication.

To set up resources for e-mail workgroup communication using diskettes

1. Using Windows Explorer, copy the contents of the WGSetup folder from the Microsoft Project CD onto two diskettes. On disk 2, copy Prj2k_2.cab. On disk 1, copy all the other files.
2. On the resource's computer, insert disk 1 into the disk drive.
3. Click the **Start** button, and then click **Run**.
4. In the **Open** box, type:

   ***a*:\WGsetup.exe**
5. Click **OK**, and then follow the instructions.
6. Repeat steps 2-5 on the computers of all resources who will be using e-mail for workgroup communication.

Add Resource E-Mail Addresses to Your Project

Review your resource list and make sure that all resources are properly added to your project. For information about entering a resource list into your project, see "Create a Resource List for Your Project" in chapter 6.

Now you can add your resources' e-mail names to their resource information. This ensures that Microsoft Project knows where to send your workgroup messages.

You can save a step if you initially enter resource names as their e-mail addresses. If the resource's Email Address field is blank, Microsoft Project uses the entry in the Resource Name field as the e-mail address.

To add e-mail addresses to the resources in your project

1 On the **View Bar**, click **Resource Sheet**.

2 Click the field to the right of where you want to insert the Email Address column. For example, if you want the new column to be between the **Resource Name** and **Type** columns, click in the **Type** column.

3 On the **Insert** menu, click **Column**.

4 In the **Field Name** box, select **Email Address**, and then click **OK**.

5 Enter the e-mail address for each resource in the **Email Address** field.

If the resource is outside your organization, be sure to include the entire address. For example, if the resource's e-mail name is Jodie and that resource can be reached through an Internet service provider called provider.com, enter the address as *jodie@provider.com*.

Resource Information

If you need to add or change just a few e-mail addresses, you can do so with the Resource Information dialog box. In the Resource Sheet, select the resource. Click Resource Information, then click the General tab. In the Email box, type the e-mail address for that resource.

Change the Workgroup System a Resource Will Use

When you select a workgroup messaging system (Email, Web, or None) on the Workgroup tab of the Options dialog box, that system becomes the default for all resources. If a resource doesn't have access to the default system, however, you can change the communication system used by that resource.

For example, suppose the majority of your resources use Microsoft Project Central on your company's intranet as their workgroup communications system. But suppose you also have another resource, an outside consultant, who doesn't have access to your intranet but does have a MAPI-compliant 32-bit e-mail system. You can set this resource up for e-mail workgroup communications.

To change the workgroup messaging system for a resource

1 On the **View Bar**, click **Resource Sheet**.

2 Select the resource or resources (CTRL + click) whose workgroup messaging option you want to change.

Resource Information

3 Click **Resource Information**, and then click the **General** tab.

4 In the **Workgroup** box, click the method of workgroup messaging you'll be using with the resource.

To use the settings on the **Workgroup** tab of the **Options** dialog box, click **Default**.

If you choose an option other than Default, that option will be applied to the selected resource or resources.

If you don't want Microsoft Project to try to send messages to this resource, click **None**.

Specify the Assignment Information to Be Exchanged

By default, the three workgroup messages contain the Task Name, Work, Start, Finish, and Comments fields. Other fields are added to the TeamStatus message. You can change the fields that are included in the workgroup message. You can also change which fields can be updated by the resource and which fields should be included in the TeamStatus message

Along with adding and removing fields, you can customize your workgroup messages by changing the report period and tracking overtime work. This is also where you specify whether or not you will allow resources to decline assigned tasks.

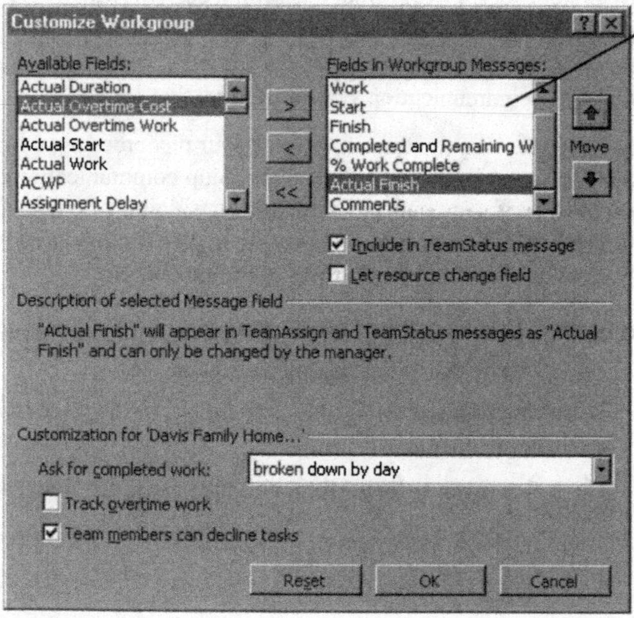

Select the information you want to include in your workgroup messages.

To specify assignment information in workgroup messages

1 On the **Tools** menu, point to **Customize**, and then click **Workgroup**.

Add

2 To add a field, in the **Available Fields** box, click the field you want, and then click the **Add** button.

If you add a field, use the check boxes to indicate whether or not you want the field to be included in the TeamStatus message and whether or not resources can modify the field.

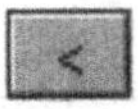
Remove

3 To remove a field, click the field you want to remove in the **Fields in Workgroup Messages** box, and then click the **Remove** button.

Move Up

Move Down

4 To change the order of fields, click the field you want to move in the **Fields in Workgroup Messages** box, and then click **Move Up** or **Move Down**.

5 Specify how you want resources to report completed work with the **Ask for completed work** box.

To report the number of hours per day that a resource has worked on a task, click **broken down by day**.

To report the number of hours per week that a resource has worked on a task, click **broken down by week**.

To report the total number of hours a resource has worked on a task during the entire reporting period, click **as a total for the entire period**.

6 To track overtime work, click **Track overtime work**.

7 To specify whether resources can decline tasks, select or clear the **Team members can decline tasks** check box.

8 To return workgroup messages to their default settings, click **Reset**.

Exchanging Information with Resources Using E-Mail

Now that you've set up Microsoft Project to communicate project information via your e-mail system, updating and tracking tasks assigned to resources can be fast and efficient. You won't have to constantly meet with resources to collect up-to-date task information.

From your computer, you use Microsoft Project and e-mail to simply send task assignments, task update information, and status requests to resources. They receive these messages in their e-mail inboxes. Their responses return to your e-mail inbox as confirmations and task actuals that you can automatically and instantly incorporate into the project.

Send Assignments to Resources

The process of using the Microsoft Project workgroup feature to track task progress and incorporate updated task information into the project starts as soon as the project manager sends a resource a TeamAssign message. The TeamAssign message requests that the resource work on one or more specified tasks. At the project manager's discretion, the resource can accept or decline the task assignments.

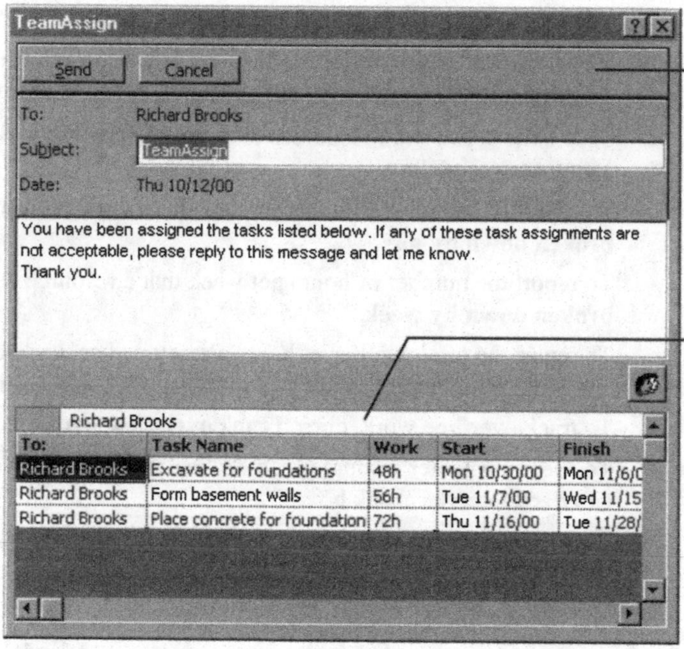

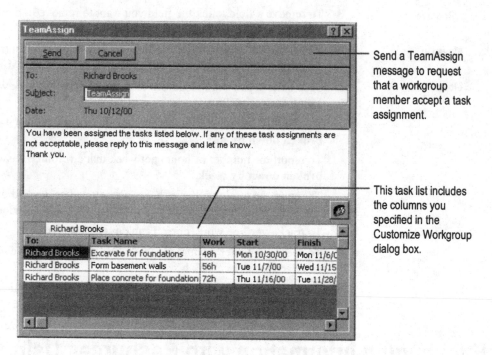

Send a TeamAssign message to request that a workgroup member accept a task assignment.

This task list includes the columns you specified in the Customize Workgroup dialog box.

The workgroup feature can be used to track only those tasks that have a resource assigned to them through workgroup communication, because actual task information must be sent by a person working on the task. For example, TeamUpdate and TeamStatus messages can be sent only to a resource assigned to a task.

To send an assignment to a resource

1. On the **View Bar**, click **Gantt Chart**.
2. If you want to send assignments only for selected tasks, select the tasks.
3. On the **Tools** menu, point to **Workgroup**, and then click **TeamAssign**.

On the Workgroup toolbar, click  **TeamAssign**.

4 To assign the selected task only, click **Selected Task**, and then click **OK**. This will result in a TeamAssign message being sent only to the resources assigned to the selected task.

To send a request about all the tasks in your project, click **All Tasks**, and then click **OK**. In this case, a TeamAssign message will be sent to all resources assigned to all tasks in the project.

5 In the **Subject** box, change the subject, if necessary.

6 In the message area, change the default message, if necessary.

7 If a resource hasn't already been assigned to the task:

Assign Resources

If you add a new resource here, remember to go to the Resource Sheet later and complete the resource information such as the calendar, rates, and units.

Select the **To** field for a task, and then click **Assign Resources**.

In the **Resources From** field, select the resources you want, and then click **Assign**. Or, in the **To** field for a task, type the e-mail name of the resource you want to assign to the task, and then press ENTER. Resources already assigned to the task who haven't confirmed their assignment are listed automatically in the **To** field. If a resource is new, it's added to the resource list when you send the message.

8 Click **Send**.

TeamAssign pending

In the **Indicators** field of those tasks for which you've requested a resource, the TeamAssign pending icon appears, signifying that you've sent an assignment request and are awaiting a response from the resource.

Receive Assignment Acknowledgments from Resources

After you send your first workgroup messages, you can start expecting messages back from the resources. Responses from the resources come to your e-mail inbox in a special format. You can use special buttons in this format to reply to the resource or to update your project with information from the resource.

A TeamAssign message received from a resource contains the resource's acceptance or rejection of a task assignment. You can then automatically update the project with this information.

For more information, see "Change Resource Assignments" in chapter 6.

When you open the message and update the project, the TeamAssign icon is removed from the task Indicator field. If the resource rejected the assignment, replace the assignment with another resource, and send another TeamAssign message.

To view and act on a TeamAssign message response

1 In your e-mail inbox, double-click the resource's reply to your TeamAssign message.

2 If you need to reply to the workgroup message, click **Reply**, type your response, and then click **Send**.

TeamAssign pending

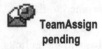

3 If you don't want to update your project, click **Close**.

If you close a message without updating your project, you can update it later. The TeamAssign pending icon is displayed until you update the project.

4 To update your project, click **Update Project**.

The TeamAssign pending icon will disappear from the Indicators field.

Send Updates for Changed Assignments

Whenever there's a change in the schedule, you can send a TeamUpdate message to all those resources whose tasks are affected by the change. For example, if the project deadline is shortened by two weeks, you might inform assigned resources that they need to complete their tasks sooner than planned.

Whenever you make such a schedule change, a TeamUpdate alert icon appears in the Indicators column of any task or resource sheet, reminding you to send a TeamUpdate to notify the resources of the change.

You cannot send a TeamUpdate message for a task that has not changed.

Using a TeamUpdate message to notify resources about a schedule change gives those resources a chance to inform you about how the change affects their work. This feedback can be invaluable in helping you avoid schedule problems.

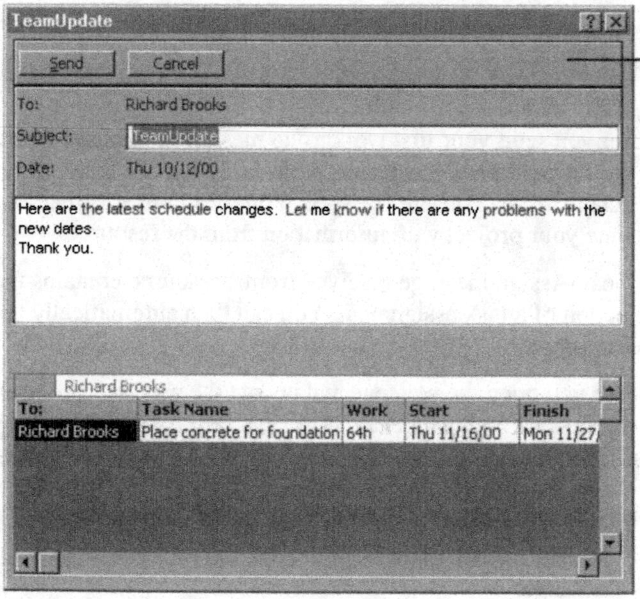

Send a TeamUpdate message to notify team members of schedule changes that affect them.

To send a TeamUpdate message

1 On the **View Bar**, click **Gantt Chart**.

2 On the **Tools** menu, point to **Workgroup**, and then click **TeamUpdate**.

The TeamUpdate message lists all tasks that have changed.

On the Workgroup toolbar, click  **TeamUpdate.**

3 In the **Subject** box, change the subject, if necessary.

4 In the message area, change the default message, if necessary.

5 Click **Send**.

 **TeamUpdate alert**

As soon as you send a TeamUpdate message, the TeamUpdate alert icon is cleared from the Indicator fields for the task or resource.

Receive Assignment Change Acknowledgments from Resources

A TeamUpdate message you receive from a resource contains no data that can be automatically incorporated into the project plan. Typically, a TeamUpdate message sent to you by a resource contains comments about how a schedule change affects his or her tasks. You can read these comments without replying to them. There's also no way to automatically update the project plan so that it includes comments from a TeamUpdate message. However, you can adjust the schedule, or the assignment, or add a note that reflects the resource's concerns.

To view a TeamUpdate message response

1 In your e-mail inbox, double-click the resource's reply to your TeamUpdate message to view it.

2 To reply to the workgroup message, click **Reply**, type your response, and then click **Send**.

3 To return to the inbox without replying to the message, click **Close**.

Request Assignment Status from Resources

The TeamStatus message is the cornerstone of Microsoft Project workgroup communication. It replaces considerable legwork, automates an important but potentially time-consuming process, and involves all resources—not just the project manager—in the process of collecting actual project data.

As the project manager, you send a TeamStatus message to a resource to obtain actual data on one or more of the resource's tasks—for example, percent complete or finish date. The resource replies to the message by including the actuals you've requested. You can automatically insert the actuals from this TeamStatus reply directly into the project.

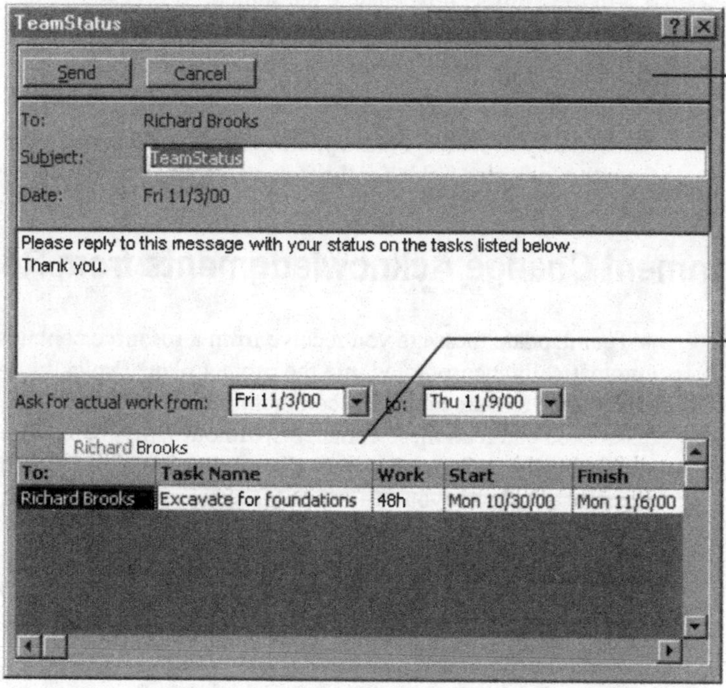

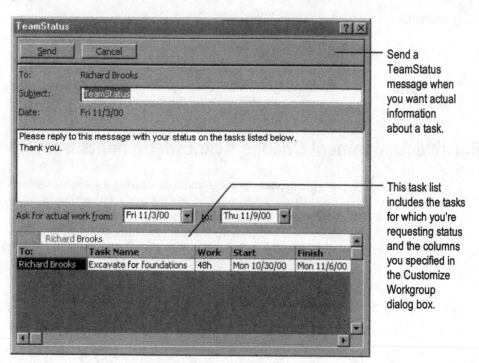

Send a TeamStatus message when you want actual information about a task.

This task list includes the tasks for which you're requesting status and the columns you specified in the Customize Workgroup dialog box.

To request task status from resources

1 On the **View Bar**, click **Gantt Chart**.

2 If you want status on certain tasks only, select them.

3 On the **Tools** menu, point to **Workgroup**, and then click **TeamStatus**.

On the Workgroup toolbar, click  **TeamStatus**.

4 To send a request about the selected tasks only, click **Selected Task**, and then click **OK**.

To send a request about all the tasks in your project, click **All Tasks**, and then click **OK**.

5 In the **Subject** box, change the subject, if necessary.

6 In the message area, change the default message, if necessary.

7 Click **Send**.

TeamStatus pending

In the **Indicators** field of those tasks for which you've requested status, a TeamStatus pending indicator appears, signifying that you've sent a status request and are still awaiting a response from the resources.

Incorporate Assignment Status into Your Project

A TeamStatus message received from a resource contains actual information about a task, information that indicates a task's progress. To track task progress and keep the schedule up to date, incorporate the information from a TeamStatus message into the project.

To view and act on a TeamStatus message response

1 In your e-mail inbox, double-click the resource's reply to your TeamStatus message to view it.

2 To reply to the workgroup message, click **Reply**, type your response, and then click **Send**.

3 If you don't want to update your project, click **Close**.

TeamStatus pending

If you close a message without updating your project, you can update it later. The TeamStatus pending icon is displayed until you update the project.

4 To incorporate the status updates into your project, click **Update Project**.

The TeamStatus pending icon disappears from the **Indicators** field.

Any actual information is added to the project. Any comments are added to the task notes.

Updating Task Information Using E-Mail (Resources)

This section is especially for project resources using e-mail to communicate and update information about the tasks you're responsible for. By quickly sending and receiving special project messages through e-mail, you can keep the project manager informed of your progress without taking valuable time away from the project tasks themselves.

The project manager will send you task assignments that you can accept or decline. The project manager will also send task updates, informing you of changes to task schedules, such as an earlier start date, increased duration, or additional assigned resources, that affect tasks you're assigned to.

Finally, the project manager will send status requests, which you can answer with reports of your progress on your tasks. Depending on how the project manager needs the information, you might respond with the actual number of hours you've worked on a task, your percent complete on tasks, or the actual start and finish dates.

Accept or Decline a New Assignment (Resources)

As soon as your computer is set up for workgroup communication, you need to start checking for workgroup messages from the project manager in your e-mail inbox.

After you receive a TeamAssign request from the project manager, you can send a reply to the project manager to accept or decline the request. If you accept the assignment, the project manager can begin to use the Microsoft Project workgroup feature to track the task and incorporate actual information about that task into the project plan.

Some project managers might not allow task requests to be declined.

If you decline a task assignment request, the project manager might need to send another, perhaps revised, request to you or to another resource until the request is accepted. You might have to decline a task request, for example, if you are unavailable during the time the task must be accomplished, if you want to revise the assignment, or if you feel you're not the right person for the assignment. If you need to decline a task, include a note in the mail message stating your reason.

Send a TeamAssign reply to acknowledge an assignment.

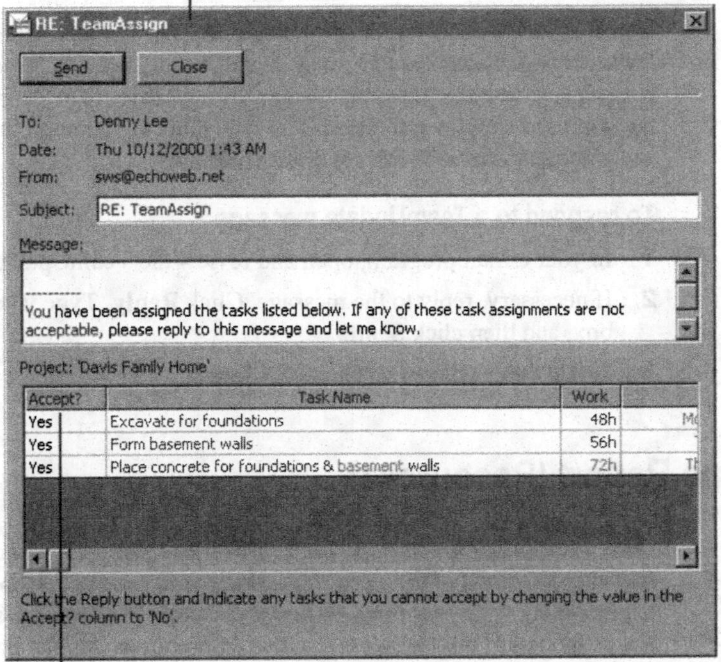

Use this Accept? field to indicate whether you accept or decline an assignment.

To accept or decline an assignment

1. In your e-mail program, open and review the TeamAssign message.
2. Click **Reply**.
3. In the message area, type a reply.
4. In the **Accept?** field, accept or decline the task assignment request:

   To accept the request, type **Yes**.

   To decline the request, type **No**.
5. Click **Send**.
6. If you want to add a note about this task for the project manager, enter it in the **Comment** field.

Acknowledge an Assignment Update (Resources)

When schedule details of a task change, such as the start date or duration, the project manager will probably send you a TeamUpdate message. If you receive a TeamUpdate message, review the schedule changes. If necessary, you can reply to the TeamUpdate message and explain any impact this schedule change might have on your other assignments, your schedule, or your workload.

To respond to a TeamUpdate message

1. In your e-mail program, open and review the TeamUpdate message.
2. If necessary, reply to the message. Click **Reply**. Type your reply in the **Message** box, and then click **Send**.
3. If you don't need to reply, click **Close**.

Submit a Status Report (Resources)

The project manager customizes the TeamStatus message with the types of actual information he or she wants to receive from you.

With communication through the TeamStatus messages, you can keep the project manager informed of your progress, along with potential problems you might be experiencing with your tasks. When you receive a TeamStatus message, you summarize the progress of your tasks, enter actual information into the provided fields, such as actual start date and actual work, and then send it back to the project manager. The project manager can then automatically insert your information from the message into the project plan.

To send task status to the project manager

1. In your e-mail program, open and review the TeamStatus message.
2. Click **Reply**.
3. If necessary, type a message in the message area.
4. In the appropriate fields, enter information about the task's actual status for each period.

   For example, type the actual start date in the **Start** field and remaining work in the **Remaining Work** field.
5. Click **Send**.

11

Updating Task Information Using the Web

Microsoft Project Central is the Web-based companion product to Microsoft Project, designed for exchanging messages and providing unique and secure views into the project for resources and other individuals. You set up and use Microsoft Project Central with your organization's intranet or the World Wide Web.

You can use Microsoft Project Central as your primary means for workgroup communication, or you can use your existing e-mail system.

If you'll be communicating workgroup information with e-mail, see chapter 10. Chapter 10 also covers workgroup communication systems in general, how to determine whether to use e-mail or the Web, and procedures for sending project files, notes, and reminders through e-mail.

Procedures for sending and receiving workgroup messages with Microsoft Project Central are detailed in this chapter. As the project manager or system administrator, you'll also learn the basics for setting up Microsoft Project Central and your working preferences. Sections toward the end of this chapter are designed for the resources in your workgroup, and explain how they respond to the workgroup messages and how they can most effectively use Microsoft Project Central. These sections are marked with *Resources* in their titles.

Overview of Microsoft Project Central

With Microsoft Project Central, the project manager creates and maintains the project plan in Microsoft Project 2000. The project manager makes schedule information available to resources, upper management, and other stakeholders by publishing it to Microsoft Project Central. This database is stored and maintained independently of the project.

Microsoft Project Central users look at and act on this project data, which is made available through the Microsoft Project Central Web server, and accessed from an intranet or Internet Web site. Any updates and proposed changes are sent between the resources and the project manager in the form of workgroup messages, namely the TeamAssign, TeamUpdate, and TeamStatus messages.

The project manager reviews these messages before approving the change and integrating their content into the project.

While Microsoft Project Central contains the same functionality as the workgroup messaging through e-mail (as described in chapter 10, "Updating Task Information Using E-Mail"), it provides the following additional features:

- Resources get a personalized Gantt Chart that includes all their tasks. They can group and filter their tasks to view and organize them as necessary.
- Resources can create new tasks and send them to the project manager for approval and incorporation into the project.
- If the project manager allows it, resources can delegate tasks to other resources in the workgroup. For example, project managers can send tasks to a lead, who in turn can assign the tasks to individual resources.
- Project managers can request and receive narrative status reports from resources and consolidate them into a single report. Project managers can set up their status reports to include the headings and information they want.
- Project managers can set up message rules to govern how updates from resources are accepted and incorporated. They can specify that updates from only certain members be automatically accepted. They can also specify that certain conditions require the project manager's review.
- Resources can review continually updated information for the entire project. The project manager can determine which information is viewable for whom, and can apply security privileges to filter out sensitive information.

Setting Up Web Workgroup Communication

To establish Microsoft Project Central as the workgroup communication system for your project, you need to:

- Set up the Microsoft Project Central Web server.
- Set up Microsoft Project to work with Microsoft Project Central.
- Set up your resources to use Microsoft Project Central.

You can exchange workgroup messages with resources outside your organization, as long as they have access to your Internet or intranet site.

For information on Microsoft Project Central system requirements, see svrsetup.htm on the Microsoft Project 2000 CD, in the pjcntrl\help\1033 folder.

Set Up the Microsoft Project Central Web Server

The first step to setting up Microsoft Project Central is to set up a Web server. To do this, you need either:

- Windows NT Server 4.0 with the Microsoft Internet Information Server version 4.0 and Microsoft Internet Service Manager, or
- Windows 2000 with Microsoft Internet Information Server version 5.0.

Set up the Microsoft Project Central Web server

1. Insert the Microsoft Project 2000 CD into the CD-ROM drive of the computer that is to be the server.
2. Click **Install Microsoft Project Central Server**.
3. Enter your user name and organization, and then click **Next**.
4. Read and accept the license agreement, and then click **Next**.
5. In **the Install Microsoft Project Central Server** here box, specify where you want to install the server. The default location will be the drive that has the most disk space. If this is the c drive, then the default location will be c:\ProjectCentral. The location you specify will become the name of the new virtual directory that is created on the Web server.
6. Select **Install now** if you want to install an MSDE database with the Microsoft Project Central server. This is appropriate if there will be no more than 10–15 concurrent users of Microsoft Project Central, and if you're not going to use a SQL Server or Oracle database.

   Select **Customize** to specify the database you want to use as the Microsoft Project Central store. You can specify a SQL Server, MSDE, or Oracle database. If there will be more than 10-15 concurrent users of Microsoft Project Central, you'll need to set up either a SQL Server or Oracle database.

For additional detailed information on Microsoft Project Central setup and the database store, see svrsetup.htm on the Microsoft Project 2000 installation CD, in the pjcntrl\help\1033 folder.

After you have installed the Microsoft Project Central server and associated database, users will be able to connect to it using the URL (uniform resource locator):

http://*servername*/ProjectCentral

where *servername* is the name of the Web server where you have installed the Microsoft Project Central server.

Set Up Microsoft Project for Web Communication

The second step in setting up Microsoft Project Central for your project's workgroup communication is to select the default communication system. This sets the default for all your resources. You can still change the communication method for individual resources.

Selecting a communication system doesn't make that system operational. You're simply enabling Microsoft Project to communicate with the system you select.

To select the Web as the default method for workgroup communication

To change the message option for individual resources, see "Change the Workgroup System a Resource Will Use" later in this section.

1. On the **Tools** menu, click **Options**, and then click the **Workgroup** tab.
2. In the **Default workgroup messages** box, click **Web**. This specifies the Web, with Microsoft Project Central, as the workgroup communication default you want to use for most of your resources.

   If you don't want to specify a default workgroup system, perhaps because most of your resources do not have access to an e-mail system or Microsoft Project Central, click **None**. You can still specify the workgroup system for individual resources.
3. In the **Microsoft Project Central Server URL** box, enter the Internet address (URL) for the Microsoft Project Central Web server.

   For example, if the server name is Davis, the URL would be:

   http://Davis/ProjectCentral
4. To apply your workgroup selections to all new projects, click **Set as Default**.
5. Click the **General** tab.
6. In the **User name** box, type the name by which you want to be identified in the workgroup messages you send.

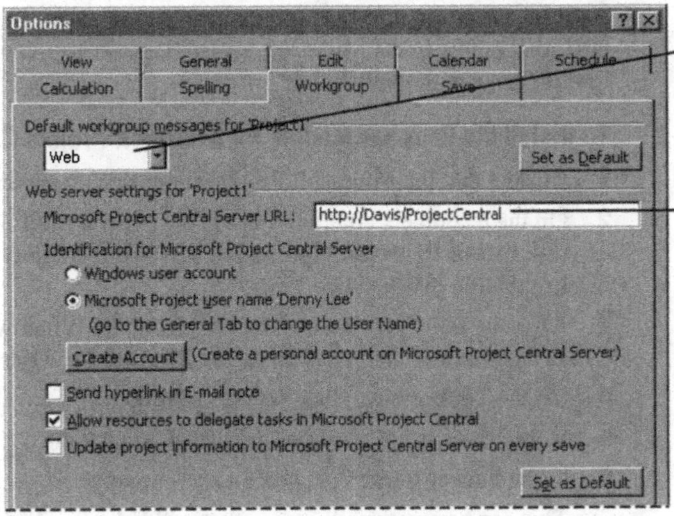

Set Up Resources for Web Communication

The third and final step to setting up the e-mail workgroup communication system for your project is to set up your resources. This involves:

- Making sure that each resource has the appropriate Web browser installed.
- Ensuring that all resources are added to your project.
- Adding the resources' e-mail names or other unique identifiers to your project.
- If necessary, changing the messaging system for an individual resource for whom the default system is not available.

Material resources are automatically excluded from any workgroup communication setup requirements.

Set Up Web Browsers for Resources

To enable your resources to exchange Microsoft Project workgroup messages with Microsoft Project Central, each resource must have a *Web browser*. The Web browser is the window in which workgroup members can display and respond to their Microsoft Project Central workgroup messages, as well as view aspects of the entire project.

Microsoft Project Central works with the Web browser Microsoft Internet Explorer 4.01 or later. If your resources don't use Internet Explorer, they can install and use the Browser Module for Microsoft Project Central, which comes with Microsoft Project Central. While this Browser Module is similar to Internet Explorer, it does not register itself on the computer as a browser and can only view a Microsoft Project Central site.

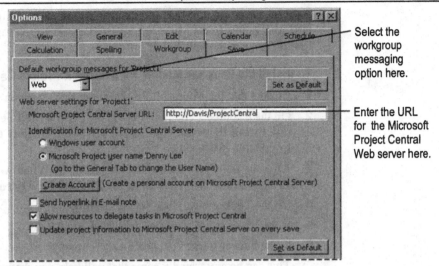

As soon as you set up Microsoft Project Central, send your workgroup members the URL that points to the Microsoft Project Central Home page. They will need this to find the page with their Web browser.

To install the Browser Module for Microsoft Project Central

1 Be sure that the Microsoft Project Central Web server is set up.

2 On the resource's computer, insert the Microsoft Project 2000 CD and click the link **Install Browser Module for Microsoft Project Central**, and then follow the installation instructions.

3 After the setup process is complete, from the Windows **Start** menu, point to **Programs** and then click **Browser Module for Microsoft Project Central**.

4 On the **Tools** menu, click **Server Settings**.

5 If the server is not already established, click **Add**.

6 In the **Server name** box, enter a server name.

This can be any friendly name that will help you distinguish one Microsoft Project Central Web server from another.

7 In the **Server address** box, enter the server address as:

http://*servername*/ProjectCentral

For example, http://Davis/ProjectCentral.

8 Click **OK** twice.

Add a Resource's Identifier to Your Project

For information about entering a resource list into your project, see "Create a Resource List for Your Project" in chapter 6.

Review your resource list and make sure that all resources are properly added to your project.

Now you can add a unique identifying name for each resource to ensure that Microsoft Project knows exactly where to send your workgroup messages. This name could be the resource's name as it appears in your project's resource list, or it could be the resource's e-mail name.

You can save a step if you initially enter resource names as their e-mail addresses. If the resource's Email Address field is blank, Microsoft Project uses the entry in the Resource Name field as the e-mail address.

If you use the resource name as the unique identifier, be sure that each resource name is indeed unique.

User accounts for these resources will be created automatically as soon as you send the resources their first TeamAssign messages.

To add e-mail addresses to the resources in your project

1 On the **View Bar**, click **Resource Sheet**.

2 Click the field to the right of where you want to insert the **Email Address** column. For example, if you want the new column to be between the Resource Name and Type columns, click the **Type** column.

3 On the **Insert** menu, click **Column**.

4 In the **Field name** box, select **Email Address**, and then click **OK**.

5 Enter the e-mail address for each resource in the **Email Address** field.

If the resource is outside your organization, be sure to include the entire address. For example, if the resource's e-mail name is Jodie and that resource can be reached through an Internet service provider called provider.com, enter the address as *jodie@provider.com*.

Resource Information

If you need to add or change just a few e-mail addresses, you can do so with the Resource Information dialog box. In the Resource Sheet, select the resource. Click Resource Information, and then click the General tab. In the Email box, type the e-mail address for that resource.

Change the Workgroup System a Resource Will Use

When you select a workgroup messaging system (Email, Web, or None) on the Workgroup tab of the Options dialog box, that system becomes the default for all resources. If a resource doesn't have access to the default system, however, you can change the workgroup messaging system used by that resource.

For example, suppose the majority of your resources use Microsoft Project Central on your company's intranet as their workgroup communication system. But suppose you also have another resource, an outside consultant, who doesn't have access to your intranet, but does have a MAPI-compliant 32-bit e-mail system. You can set this resource up for e-mail workgroup communication.

Use SHIFT+click to select multiple adjacent resource names. Use CTRL+click to select multiple nonadjacent resources.

To change the workgroup messaging system for a resource

1 On the **View Bar**, click **Resource Sheet**.

2 Select the resource or resources whose workgroup messaging option you want to change.

3 Click **Resource Information**, and then click the **General** tab.

Resource Information

4 In the **Workgroup** box, click the method of workgroup messaging you'll be using with the resource.

If you don't want Microsoft Project to send messages to this resource, click **None**.

Convert from E-Mail to Microsoft Project Central Communication

If you have been communicating with your workgroup using your e-mail system, and you now want to use Microsoft Project Central, set up the Microsoft Project Central Web server, set up Microsoft Project, and set up your resources as described in the previous sections. To get all the task assignment information to date into Microsoft Project Central, you'll need to resend the workgroup messages.

To convert from e-mail to Microsoft Project Central communication

1. On the **View Bar**, click **Gantt Chart**.
2. On the **Tools** menu, point to **Workgroup**, and then click **Resend All Messages**.
3. Click **All tasks**, and then click **OK**.
4. In the **Subject** box, change the subject if necessary.
5. In the message area, change the message if necessary.
6. In the **Comments** column, enter any comments you want about the assignment.
7. Click **Send**.

   Current actual information for each task is sent to the assigned resources, including percent complete and actual hours.

If a resource ever loses some or all task information, you can also use the **Resend All Messages** command to restore this information.

Setting Preferences for Microsoft Project Central

You can set up Microsoft Project Central to reflect the way you and your workgroup prefer to operate. You can:

- Specify the types of assignment information you're going to exchange.
- Notify resources when they receive new workgroup messages.
- Allow or prohibit tasks to be delegated among resources.
- Specify how you want the server updated with your project changes.
- Define the content and frequency of narrative status reports.
- Designate which messages can be automatically incorporated into the project.

Specify the Assignment Information to Be Exchanged

By default, the TeamAssign, TeamUpdate, and TeamStatus workgroup messages contain the Task Name, Work, Start, Finish, and Comments fields. Other fields are also added to the TeamStatus message. You can change the fields that are included in a workgroup message. You can also change which fields can be updated by the resource, and which fields should be included in the TeamStatus message

Along with adding or removing fields, you can also customize your workgroup messages by changing the report period and tracking overtime work. This is also where you specify whether you will allow resources to decline assigned tasks.

To specify assignment information in workgroup messages

1 On the **Tools** menu, point to **Customize**, and then click **Workgroup**.

Add

2 To add a field, in the **Available Fields** box, click the field you want, and then click the **Add** button.

If you add a field, use the check boxes to indicate whether you want the field to be included in the TeamStatus message, and whether resources can modify the field.

Remove

3 To remove a field, click the field you want to remove in the **Fields in Workgroup Messages** box, and then click the **Remove** button.

Move Up

Move Down

4 To change the order of fields, click the field you want to move in the **Fields in Workgroup Messages** box, and then click **Move Up** or **Move Down**.

5 Specify how you want resources to report completed work with the **Ask for completed work** box.

To report the number of hours per day that a resource has worked on a task, click **broken down by day**.

To report the number of hours per week that a resource has worked on a task, click **broken down by week**.

To report the total number of hours a resource has worked on a task during the entire reporting period, click **as a total for the entire period**.

6 To track overtime, click **Track overtime work**.

7 To specify whether resources can decline tasks, select or clear the **Team members can decline tasks** check box.

Set Up New Workgroup Message Notification

You can specify whether you want resources to be notified in e-mail of any new workgroup messages you have sent them.

To set up new workgroup message notification

1 In Microsoft Project, on the **Tools** menu, click **Options**, and then click the **Workgroup** tab.

If you need to set up e-mail addresses, see "Add a Resource's Identifier to Your Project" earlier in this chapter.

2 Select the **Send hyperlink in E-mail note** check box.

This e-mail message will include a hyperlink to Microsoft Project Central. When a resource opens the e-mail message, and clicks the hyperlink, Microsoft Project Central opens so he or she can review the new workgroup message.

This works as long as the resources' e-mail addresses are included in the Resource Information dialog box.

Set Up Task Delegation Options

You can allow or prohibit the resources to whom you assign tasks to delegate tasks to other resources in the workgroup. This is especially useful if you have different functional teams with supervisors or leads. You can assign the leads to the tasks appropriate to their function. In turn, the leads can delegate the tasks to the appropriate resources. You are always notified of delegations, and you can have the resource assignment information updated in your project.

To set up task delegation options

1. In Microsoft Project, on the **Tools** menu, click **Options**, and then click the **Workgroup** tab.
2. If you want resources to be able to delegate their assigned tasks to other resources in your workgroup, select the **Allow resources to delegate tasks in Microsoft Project Central** check box.

Set Up Server Update Options

You can indicate when you want information to be updated to the Microsoft Project Central server—whenever you save your project, or only when you give a specific update command.

This ensures that your workgroup and other stakeholders who might be reviewing project information from Microsoft Project Central always see the most up-to-date information.

To set up Microsoft Project Central server update options

1. In Microsoft Project, on the **Tools** menu, click **Options**, and then click the **Workgroup** tab.
2. If you want to update the server whenever you save new information in your project, select the **Update project information to Microsoft Project Central Server on every save** check box.

   If you want to manually update the server at your discretion, clear this check box.

To manually update project information to the Microsoft Project Central server

1 On the **Tools** menu, point to **Workgroup**.

2 Click **Update Project to Web Server**.

The Microsoft Project Central server is updated with the latest information from your project file.

Define and Request Narrative Status Reports

With the TeamStatus message, your resources periodically complete and send the form in which they indicate percent complete, actual hours worked, and a brief comment. You can incorporate such actuals into your project to help with tracking progress.

With Microsoft Project Central, you can add another level of status reporting. You can design a template with which resources submit a text-based status report. You set up the report sections, such as "Major Accomplishments," "Goals for Next Period," and "Issues." If you want, you can even add text prompts to help resources fill in the report.

You can set up automatic requests—to be sent every Friday morning, for example—or you can send requests manually. When you receive the individual status reports, you can compile them into a single narrative status report that can form your project or group status for a given reporting period. The report can be reviewed and edited in Microsoft Project Central. Once the group status report is compiled, you can:

- Print the report.
- Save the report as an HTML file.
- Send the HTML file to others.
- Publish the HTML file to a Web server.

To set up and request narrative status reporting

1 In Microsoft Project, on the **Tools** menu, point to **Workgroup**, and then click **TeamInbox**.

2 On the **Status Reports** menu, click **Request a Status Report**.

3 Click **Set up a new status report for your team to respond to**, and then click **OK**.

4 Work through the **Request a Status Report** wizard, answering the questions and clicking **Next** after each page.

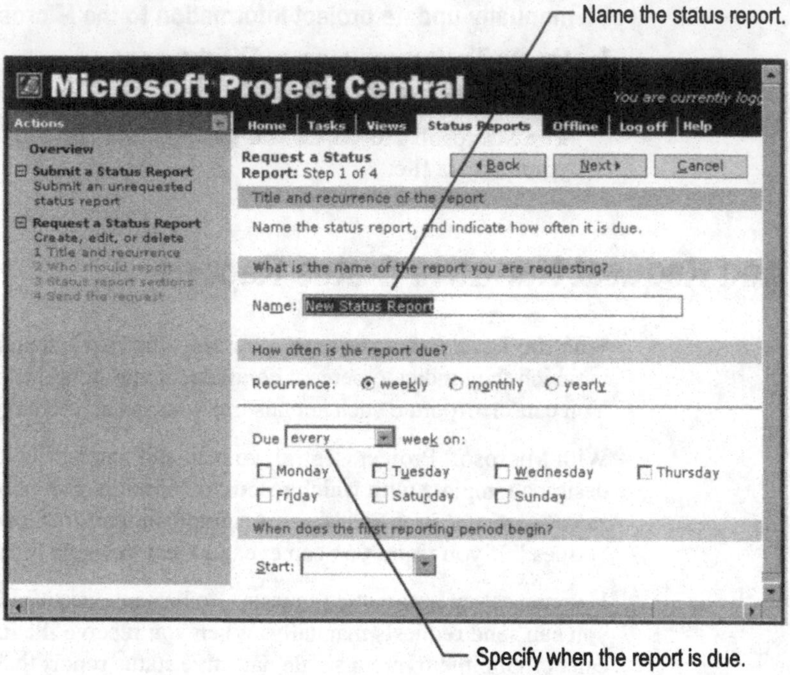

In this wizard, you define the name of the status report, the frequency (weekly, monthly, and so on), the resources from whom you're requesting this status report, and the topics or sections of the status report.

5 On the last page, click **Send** to send the status report request to the resources you identified.

If you want to send the request later, click **Save**.

Set Up Message Rules

Especially if you have a large team, you're likely to receive many workgroup messages to review and process. To save time, you can automatically process the more routine messages by setting up message rules.

You can set up rules having to do with the task assignments, task updates, status reports, and delegations. You can apply rules to individual resources, to groups of resources, to specific actions, or only to actions with a specified impact on the budget or schedule.

Specify which messages you want to automatically incorporate into the project.

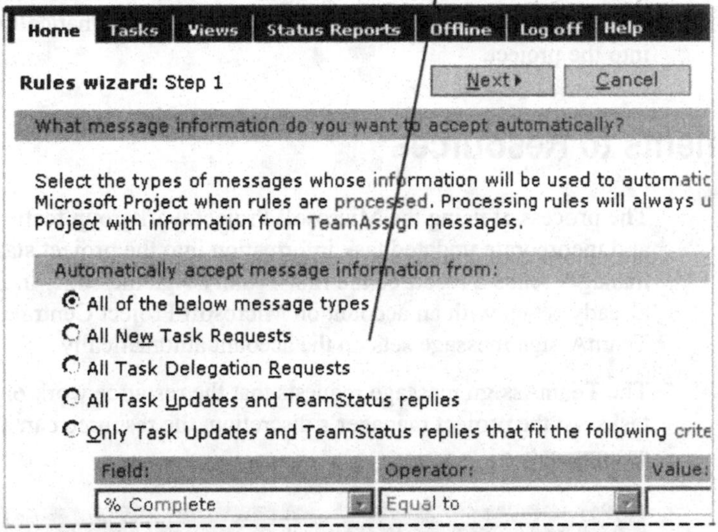

To set up message rules

1. In Microsoft Project, on the **Tools** menu, point to **Workgroup**, and then click **TeamInbox**.
2. On the **Home** menu, click **Rules**.
3. Click **New Rule**.
4. Follow the instructions in the wizard to set up your rules.

Exchanging Information with Resources Using the Web

Now that you've set up Microsoft Project to communicate project information with Microsoft Project Central, updating and tracking tasks assigned to resources can be fast and efficient. You won't have to meet with resources constantly to collect up-to-date task information.

From your computer, you use Microsoft Project and Microsoft Project Central to send task assignments, task update information, and status requests to resources. Resources receive these messages in Microsoft Project Central, which they log on to from their Web browser. Their responses return to you, also in Microsoft Project Central, as confirmations and actual task data that you can automatically and instantly incorporate into the project.

Send Assignments to Resources

The process of using the Microsoft Project workgroup feature to track task progress and incorporate updated task information into the project starts as soon as the project manager sends a resource the first TeamAssign message. In fact, if the resource isn't already set up with an account on Microsoft Project Central, sending the first TeamAssign message sets up the account automatically.

The TeamAssign message requests that the resource work on one or more specified tasks. At the project manager's discretion, the resource can accept or decline the task assignments.

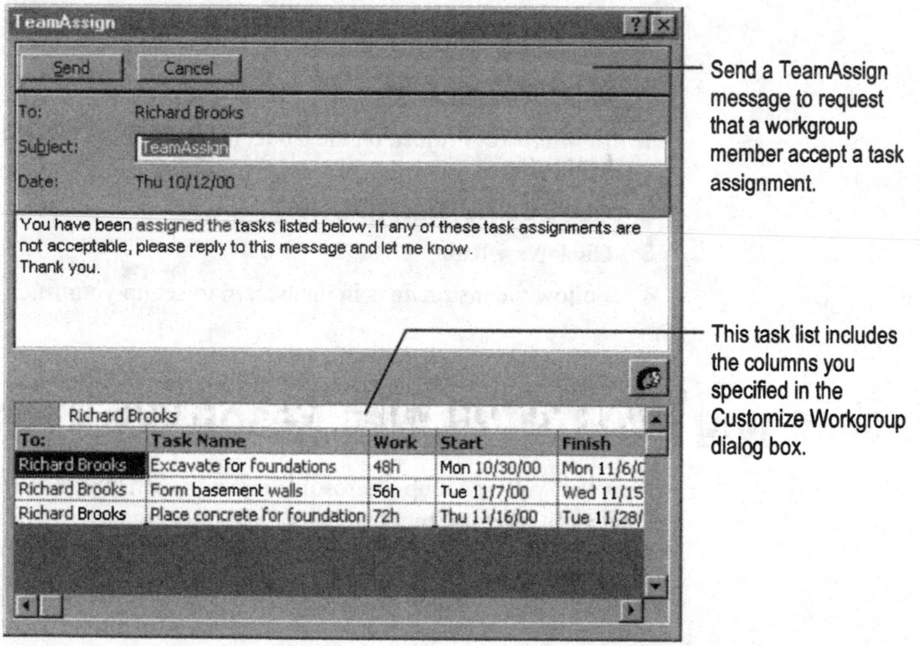

The workgroup feature can be used to track only those tasks that have a resource assigned to them through workgroup communication, because actual task information must be sent by a person working on the task. For example, TeamUpdate and TeamStatus messages can be sent only to a resource assigned to a task.

To send an assignment to a resource

1 On the **View Bar**, click **Gantt Chart**.

2 If you want to send assignments for selected tasks only, select the tasks.

On the Workgroup toolbar, click  **TeamAssign.**

3 On the **Tools** menu, point to **Workgroup**, and then click **TeamAssign**.

4 To assign the selected tasks only, click **Selected task**, and then click **OK**. This will result in a TeamAssign message being sent only to the resources assigned to the selected tasks.

To send a request about all the tasks in your project, click **All tasks**, and then click **OK**. In this case, a TeamAssign message will be sent to all resources assigned to all tasks in the project.

5 In the **Subject** box, change the subject if necessary.

6 In the message area, change the message if necessary.

7 If a resource hasn't already been assigned to the task:

 **Assign Resources**

If you add a new resource here, remember to go to the Resource Sheet later and complete the resource information such as the calendar, rates, and units.

Select the **To** field for a task, and then click **Assign Resources**.

In the **Resources from** field, select the resources you want, and then click **Assign**.

Or, in the **To** field for a task, type the name of the resource you want to assign to the task, and then press ENTER. Resources already assigned to the task who haven't confirmed their assignment are listed automatically in the **To** field. If a resource is new, he or she is added to the resource list when you send the message.

8 Click **Send**.

 **TeamAssign pending**

In the Indicators field of those tasks for which you've sent an assignment to a resource, the TeamAssign pending icon appears, signifying that you've sent the assignment and are awaiting a response.

Check for Workgroup Messages

Workgroup messages are exchanged between you and your resources in Microsoft Project Central. You access Microsoft Project Central from within Microsoft Project.

When you open Microsoft Project Central, you first see the Home page. The Home page provides a summary of current Microsoft Project Central activities. You can then click a link to follow up on the selected activity. The activities summarized on the Home page are Messages, Tasks, and Status Reports. Click a link within the section to work on that activity.

You can open most Microsoft Project Central pages and activities using the Actions pane on the left. You can also click any of the tabs across the top of the page to give a command or go to another page.

To go to Microsoft Project Central

1. On the **Tools** menu, point to **Workgroup**, and then click **TeamInbox**.
2. If you've set up a password for Microsoft Project Central, you'll be prompted for it.

   The Microsoft Project Central Home page appears.

To check for workgroup messages

1. Log on to Microsoft Project Central.
2. In the **Messages** section of the Home page, check to see whether you have any messages.
3. If you have messages, click **Microsoft Project Central Inbox** to review and act on the messages.

   Or, in the **Action** pane on the left, click **Messages**.

See "Set Up Message Rules" earlier in this chapter for more information.

Task delegation message rules are run as soon as you log on to Microsoft Project Central. All other rules are not automatically applied to new messages. If you have set up message rules and want to run them on the current messages, click **Run Rules Now** on the Messages page.

Receive Assignment Acknowledgments from Resources

After you send your first workgroup messages, you can start expecting responses from the resources. Responses come to your messages area in Microsoft Project Central in a special message format. You can use buttons in these messages to reply to the resource or to update your project with information from the resource.

A TeamAssign message received from a resource contains the resource's acceptance or rejection of a task assignment. You might also receive a task delegation message, indicating who the task was delegated to and how it will be tracked in the workgroup. You can automatically update the project with this information.

For more information, see "Change Resource Assignments" in chapter 6.

When you open the message and update the project, the TeamAssign icon is removed from the task Indicator field. If the resource rejected the assignment, replace the assignment with another resource, and send another TeamAssign message.

To view and act on a TeamAssign message response

1. On the **Tools** menu, point to **Workgroup**, and then click **TeamInbox**.
2. Enter your password, if necessary, and then click **OK**.
3. On the Home page, click **Microsoft Project Central Inbox** to see your messages.

   Or, in the **Action** pane on the left, click **Messages**.
4. On the **Messages** page, double-click the resource's response to your TeamAssign message.

5 If you need to reply to the message, click **Reply**, type your response, and then click **Send**.

TeamAssign pending

6 If you don't want to update the project, click **Close**. If you close a message without updating your project, you can update it later. The TeamAssign pending icon is displayed until you update the project.

To update your project, click **Update**. The TeamAssign pending icon disappears from the Indicators field.

If there are multiple messages, you can click **Update All** to update all the tasks at once.

Send Updates for Changed Assignments

Whenever there's a change in the schedule, you can send a TeamUpdate message to all those resources whose tasks are affected by the change. For example, if the project deadline is shortened by 2 weeks, you might inform assigned resources that they need to complete their tasks sooner than planned.

Whenever you make such a schedule change, a TeamUpdate alert icon appears in the Indicators column of any task or resource sheet, reminding you to send a TeamUpdate to notify the resources of the change.

You cannot send a TeamUpdate message for a task that has not changed.

Using a TeamUpdate message to notify resources about a schedule change gives those resources a chance to inform you about how the change affects their work. This feedback can be invaluable in helping you avoid schedule problems.

To send a TeamUpdate message

1 On the **View Bar**, click **Gantt Chart**.

On the Workgroup toolbar, click

TeamUpdate.

2 On the **Tools** menu, point to **Workgroup**, and then click **TeamUpdate**.

The TeamUpdate message lists all tasks that have changed.

3 In the **Subject** box, change the subject if necessary.

4 In the message area, change the message if necessary.

5 Click **Send**.

TeamUpdate alert

As soon as you send a TeamUpdate message, the TeamUpdate alert icon is cleared from the Indicator fields for the task or resource.

Receive Assignment Change Acknowledgments from Resources

A TeamUpdate message you receive from a resource contains no data that can be automatically incorporated into the project plan. Typically, a TeamUpdate message sent to you by a resource contains comments about how a schedule change affects a resource's tasks. You can read these comments without replying to them. There's also no way to automatically update the project plan so that it includes comments from a

TeamUpdate message. However, you can adjust the schedule, the assignment, or add a note that reflects the resource's concerns.

To view a TeamUpdate message response

1. On the **Tools** menu, point to **Workgroup**, and then click **TeamInbox**.
2. Enter your password, if necessary, and then click **OK**.
3. If you have messages, click **Microsoft Project Central Inbox** to review and act on the resource's reply to your TeamUpdate message.

   Or, in the **Action** pane on the left, click **Messages**.
4. To reply to the workgroup message, click **Reply**, type your response, and then click **Send**.

Request Assignment Status from Resources

The TeamStatus message is the cornerstone of Microsoft Project workgroup communication. It replaces considerable legwork, automates an important but potentially time-consuming process, and involves all resources—not just the project manager—in the process of collecting actual project data.

As the project manager, you send a TeamStatus message to a resource to obtain actual data on one or more of the resource's tasks, for example, percent complete or finish date. The resource replies to the message by including the actuals you've requested. You can automatically insert the actuals from this TeamStatus reply directly into the project.

To request assignment status from resources

1. On the **View Bar**, click **Gantt Chart**.
2. If you want status on certain tasks only, select them.

On the Workgroup toolbar, click

TeamStatus

3. On the **Tools** menu, point to **Workgroup**, and then click **TeamStatus**.
4. To send a request about the selected tasks only, click **Selected task**, and then click **OK**.

   To send a request about all the tasks in your project, click **All tasks**, and then click **OK**.
5. In the **Subject** box, change the subject if necessary.
6. In the message area, change the message if necessary.
7. Click **Send**.

TeamStatus pending

   In the Indicators field of those tasks for which you've requested status, a TeamStatus pending indicator appears, signifying that you've sent a status request and are still awaiting a response from the resources.

Incorporate Assignment Status into Your Project

A TeamStatus message received from a resource contains actual information about a task, information that indicates a task's progress. To track task progress and keep the schedule up-to-date, incorporate the information from a TeamStatus message into the project.

To view and act on a TeamStatus message response

1 On the **Tools** menu, point to **Workgroup**, and then click **TeamInbox**.

2 Enter your password, if necessary, and then click **OK**.

3 Double-click the resource's reply to your TeamStatus message to view it.

4 To reply to the workgroup message, click **Reply**, type your response, and then click **Send**.

5 If you don't want to update your project, click **Close**. If you close a message without updating your project, you can update it later. The TeamStatus pending icon is displayed until you update the project.

TeamStatus pending

To incorporate the status updates into your project, click **Update**. The TeamStatus pending icon disappears from the Indicators field. Any actual information is added to the project. Any comments are added to the task notes.

If there are multiple messages, you can click **Update All** to update all tasks at once.

Compile a Narrative Status Report

If you have set up a status report to be automatically requested at regular intervals, your resources will be reminded to complete and send them to you at the designated periods. However, you can also request status reports on an ad-hoc basis. For information about setting up and requesting narrative status reports, see "Define and Request Narrative Status Reports" earlier in this chapter.

When your resources send their narrative status reports, you can merge them into a single status report for the reporting period. This can form the basis of your group status report. You can view and edit it from within Microsoft Project Central.

To compile a narrative status report

1 In Microsoft Project, on the **Tools** menu, point to **Workgroup**, and then click **TeamInbox**.

2 On the **Status Reports** menu, click **Group Status Reports**.

3 Complete the steps to compile the status reports for your group.

When finished, you can print the report for distribution. Or, you can save the report as an HTML file and send it through e-mail or publish the file to a Web server.

Updating Task Information Using Microsoft Project Central (Resources)

The rest of the chapter is for project resources using Microsoft Project Central to communicate and update information about task assignments. By quickly sending and receiving special project messages through the Web, you can keep the project manager informed of your progress without taking valuable time away from the project tasks themselves.

The project manager will send you task assignments that you can in turn accept or decline. In addition, the project manager might request that you create your own task assignments, or provide detailed tasks for summary tasks or phases the project manager has identified. In this case, you can create new tasks and send them to the project manager for incorporation into the overall project plan.

If the project manager has set up your workgroup to allow delegations, you might be able to delegate task assignments to other resources. This is especially useful if you're a team lead, and you need to delegate tasks to others on your team. When you delegate tasks, a message is sent to the project manager to update the project plan with the actual task assignment.

As the project progresses, the project manager will send task updates, informing you of any changes to task schedules, such as an earlier start date, or an increased duration, any of which can affect tasks you're assigned to.

As you become aware of changes to tasks, you can send task updates to the project manager as well.

Finally, the project manager will send status requests, which you can answer with reports of your progress on your tasks. Depending on what kind of information the project manager needs, you might respond with the actual number of hours you've worked on a task, your percent complete on tasks, or the actual start and finish dates. There are two types of status requests: the TeamStatus form-based status report, and the text-based status report.

Starting to Use Microsoft Project Central (Resources)

To get started with Microsoft Project Central, you first log on with your Web browser.

To log on to Microsoft Project Central

1 Start the Web browser you use for Microsoft Project Central, either Microsoft Internet Explorer, or the Browser Module for Microsoft Project Central.

2 In the **Address** box, enter the URL (uniform resource locator) of the Microsoft Project Central Web server. Obtain the URL from the project manager. It will be in the format of:

http://*servername*/ProjectCentral

where *servername* is the name of the Web server where the Microsoft Project Central server is installed.

The Microsoft Project Central logon screen appears.

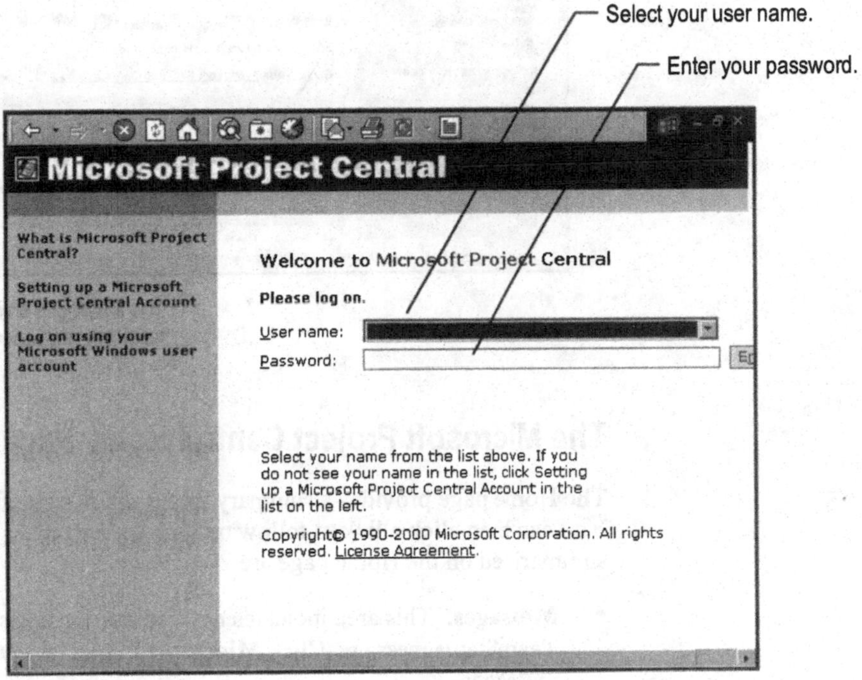

3 In the **User name** box, type or select your name from the list.

You will be able to log on to Microsoft Project Central as soon as the project manager sends you an assignment request or the system administrator adds an account for you.

4 In the **Password** box, enter your password.

5 Click **Enter**.

The Microsoft Project Central Home page appears.

The Actions pane lists the major activities of Microsoft Project Central.

Point at any of the menus in the menu bar for more commands.

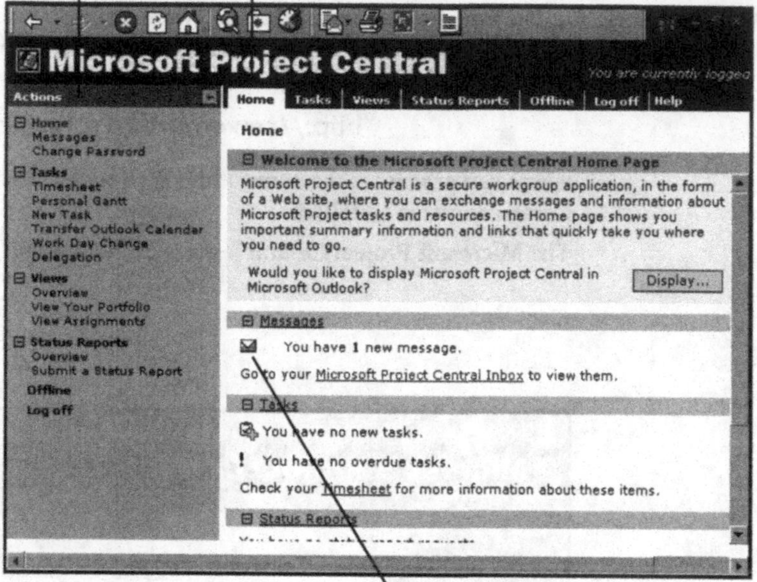

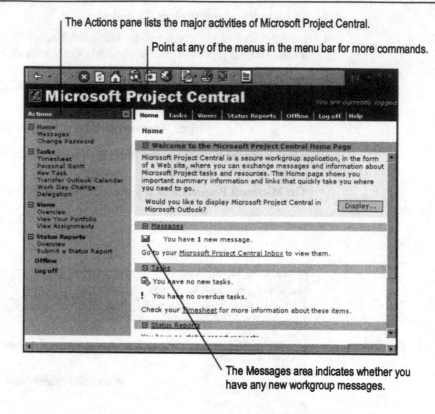

The Messages area indicates whether you have any new workgroup messages.

The Microsoft Project Central Home Page (Resources)

The Home page provides a summary of current Microsoft Project Central activities. You can then click a link to follow up with the selected activity. The activities summarized on the Home page are:

- **Messages.** This area indicates new workgroup messages, such as a TeamAssign or TeamStatus message. Click **Microsoft Project Central Inbox** to view your messages.
- **Tasks.** This area indicates new tasks or overdue tasks. Click **Timesheet** to see the full list of your tasks.
- **Views.** This area lets you review all assignments made through Microsoft Project Central, or even view information in other projects.
- **Status Reports.** If your workgroup uses narrative status reports, this area reminds you of upcoming status reports you need to submit, along with their due dates.

You can open most Microsoft Project Central pages and activities by using the Actions pane on the left. You can also click any of the tabs across the top of the page to give a command or go to another page.

Check for Workgroup Messages on the Web (Resources)

As soon as your computer is set up for workgroup communication, you can start checking for workgroup messages from the project manager (and possibly from other resources) in Microsoft Project Central.

The project manager might send automated e-mail messages to you whenever there's a message waiting for you in Microsoft Project Central. If this is the case, a hyperlink will be included in the message that will take you to Microsoft Project Central.

To check for workgroup messages

1. Log on to Microsoft Project Central.
2. In the **Messages** section of the Home page, check to see whether you have any messages.
3. If you have messages, click **Microsoft Project Central Inbox** to go to Microsoft Project Central to review and act on the messages.

   Or, in the **Action** pane on the left, click **Messages**.

Accept or Decline a New Assignment (Resources)

After you receive a TeamAssign request from the project manager, you can send a reply to the project manager to accept or decline the request. If you accept the assignment, the project manager can begin to use the Microsoft Project workgroup feature to track your task and incorporate actual information about that task into the project plan.

Some project managers might not allow task requests to be declined.

If you decline a task assignment request, the project manager might need to send another, perhaps revised, request to you or to another resource until the request is accepted. You might have to decline a task request, for example, if you are unavailable during the time the task must be accomplished, if you want to revise the assignment, or if you feel you're not the right person for this assignment. If you need to decline a task, include a note in the e-mail message stating your reason.

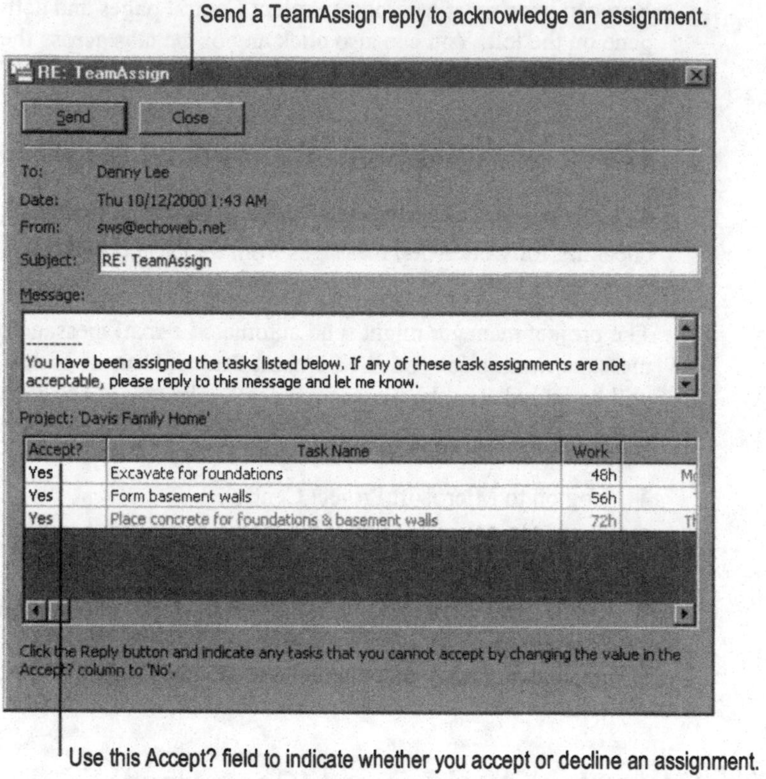

To accept or decline an assignment

1. In the **Messages** section of the Home page, click **Microsoft Project Central Inbox** to review and act on your messages.

   Or, in the **Action** pane on the left, click **Messages**.
2. On the **Messages** page, double-click the TeamAssign message.
3. Click **Reply**.
4. In the message area, type a reply.
5. In the **Accept?** field, accept or decline the task assignment request.
6. Click **Send**.
7. If you want to add a note about this task for the project manager, enter it in the **Comment** field.

Work with Your Task List (Resources)

When you accept a TeamAssign request, the assignments from the message are automatically incorporated into your task list. You can view your task list with either the Personal Gantt view or the Timesheet.

Use the Personal Gantt view to see your task list with a Gantt Chart reflecting your scheduled work. Use the Timesheet to enter and send updated actual information about your tasks.

To view your task list

1. On **Tasks** menu, click **Personal Gantt.**
2. To see a specific task's Gantt bar, select it on the task list, and click **Go to selected task.**
3. To switch to the timesheet, click **Timesheet.**

Create New Tasks (Resources)

If the project manager wants you to create your own task assignments, or to provide detailed tasks for summary tasks or phases already identified, you can do so with Microsoft Project Central. Then you can send the new tasks to the project manager for review and incorporation into the overall project plan.

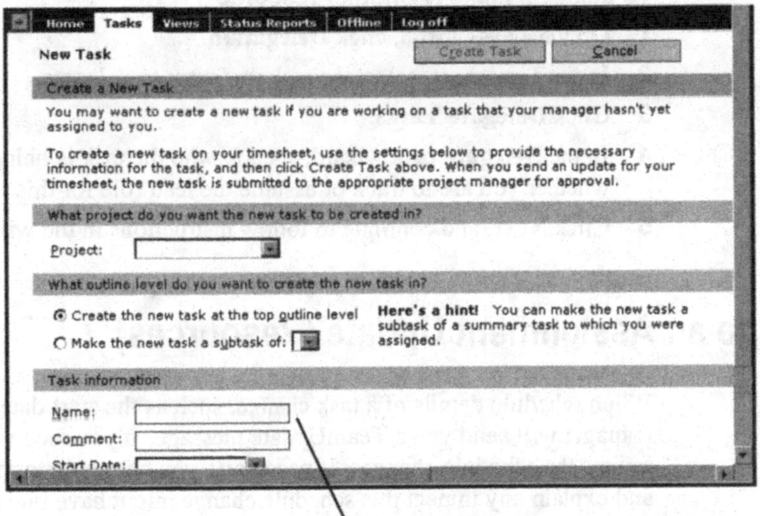

Enter the new task name and details here.

To create new tasks

1. On the **Tasks** tab, click **New Task**.
2. On the **New Task** page, if you are working with multiple projects, select the project this task is for in the **Project** box.
3. Under **What outline level do you want to create the new task in?**, select the option you want.
4. Under **Task information**, complete the task details, including task name, start date, estimated work, and a comment if necessary.
5. Click **Send an Update**.

   This sends the New Task Request message to the project manager.

Delegate Tasks (Resources)

Your project workgroup might be set up for delegating tasks. That is, you might be able to delegate task assignments to other resources, or other resources besides the project manager can delegate assignments to you. This is often the case when resources report to team leads, who in turn report directly to the project manager.

Whenever a task is delegated, a workgroup message is sent to the project manager so that the project plan can be updated with the name of the person who's actually assigned to the task.

To delegate tasks to another resource

1. On the **Tasks** menu, click **Delegation**.
2. In the Timesheet, select the task you want to delegate.
3. Click **Delegate Tasks**.
4. In the **Delegate task** wizard, specify who the task is being delegated to, and whether you are to track or assume the lead role for this task.
5. Click **Next**, and continue to follow instructions in the wizard.

Acknowledge an Assignment Update (Resources)

When schedule details of a task change, such as the start date or duration, the project manager will send you a TeamUpdate message. If you receive a TeamUpdate message, review the schedule changes. If necessary, you can reply to the TeamUpdate message and explain any impact this schedule change might have on your other assignments, your schedule, or your workload.

To respond to a TeamUpdate message

1. In the **Messages** section of the Home page, click **Microsoft Project Central Inbox** to review your messages.

   Or, in the **Action** pane on the left, click **Messages**.
2. On the Messages page, double-click the TeamUpdate message.
3. Review the changed schedule information.
4. If you need to reply, click **Reply**. Type your reply in the Message box, and then click **Send**.

   You don't have to reply to a TeamUpdate message. However, you might want to inform the project manager how the schedule changes affect you, the schedule, or other tasks.
5. Change your record of the tasks to reflect the update, and then click **Update Task List**.
6. If you want to add a note about this task for the project manager, type it in the **Comment** field.
7. Click **Close**.

Delete Tasks in the Task List (Resources)

If a task is cut from a project or if you complete a task and report its completed status to the project manager, you can delete the task from your task list.

To delete a task

1. On the **Tasks** menu, click **Personal Gantt** or **Timesheet**.
2. Select the task you want to delete.
3. Click **Delete**.

Submit Actuals with a Status Report (Resources)

The project manager customizes the TeamStatus message with the types of actual information he or she wants to receive from you.

You can update actual information on your tasks either by responding to a TeamStatus message or by sending your own status update.

With communication through the TeamStatus messages, you can report on your progress with the actual information the project manager has specified. When you receive a TeamStatus message, you summarize the progress of your tasks, enter actual information into the provided fields, such as actual start date and actual work, and then send it back to the project manager. The project manager can then automatically insert your information from the message into the project plan.

If you want to send your own status update, edit the available fields in your task list with your current status, and then send the updated information to the project manager.

To respond to a TeamStatus request

1. In the **Messages** section of the Home page, click **Microsoft Project Central Inbox** to review and act on your messages.

   Or, in the **Action** pane on the left, click **Messages**.
2. On the Messages page, double-click the TeamStatus message.
3. Click **Reply**.
4. If necessary, type a message in the message area.
5. In the appropriate fields, enter information about the task's actual status for each period.

   For example, type the actual start date in the **Start** field and remaining work in the **Remaining Work** field.
6. If you want to add a note about a task for the project manager, enter it in the **Comment** field.
7. Click **Send**.

To initiate your own status update, update your task list and then send the changed tasks to the project manager.

To revise and update assignment status

1. On the **Tasks** menu, click **Timesheet**.
2. In the **Show timescale period from** boxes, enter the dates for the time period you're reporting on.
3. If necessary, in the **Timescale** box, select the timescale you're reporting on, such as days or weeks.
4. Click the task you're updating.
5. In the timescale (right) portion of the Timesheet, enter the actual hours for the time period.
6. If you want, in the table (left) portion of the Timesheet, enter any other updates, for example, for remaining work or percent complete.
7. You can change more than one task at a time. The update will send all the tasks that have changed for the selected time period.
8. Click **Save Changes**.
9. When you are ready to send the TeamUpdate message, click **Send Update**.

Submit a Narrative Status Report (Resources)

The project manager might periodically send a request for a narrative status report. With such a report, you can keep the project manager informed of your progress, along with problems you might be experiencing with your tasks. This goes beyond reporting actual information, as this is a text-based report rather than a form-based one.

If any upcoming status reports are due, it will be listed on the Home page in the Status Reports area.

The project manager can compile everyone's status report to form a group or project status report.

You can also create and send your own unrequested status report.

To send a narrative status report

1 On the **Status Reports** menu, click **Submit a Status Report**.

2 Complete the template for the status report as set up by the project manager.

For example, there might be headings such as "Accomplishments for this week" or "Goals for next week."

3 Click **Send**.

On the Status Reports page, you can also review your archive of previously submitted or saved status reports.

Reviewing Project Information (Resources)

You can review project information for the tasks to which you've been assigned. You can filter and group your tasks by various types of information to help you analyze or work with your tasks more effectively.

If you want to better understand the big picture, or see how your tasks are dependent on other tasks assigned to other resources in your workgroup, you can also review overall project information.

Filter and Group Your Task List (Resources)

In your task list, you already see all tasks in all projects to which you are assigned. You can view your tasks in the Personal Gantt view or in the Timesheet.

In either view, you can filter your tasks, that is, see only the tasks that meet the criteria you specify. For example, you can filter your task list to see only those tasks whose finish date is scheduled for the coming week.

In either view, you can also group your tasks by certain criteria. For example, you can group your tasks by incomplete tasks, tasks in progress, and completed tasks.

By filtering and grouping, you can easily organize your task list the way you want.

Select the category of tasks you want to see.

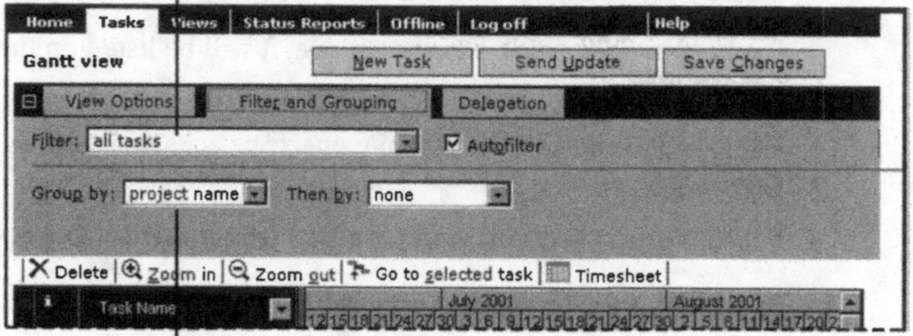

Select how you want tasks grouped.

To filter tasks

1 On the **Tasks** menu, click **Timesheet**.
2 Click the **Filter and Grouping** tab.
3 In the **Filter** box, select the category of tasks you want to see.
4 To see all tasks again, in the **Filter** box, select **all tasks**.

To group tasks

1 On the **Tasks** menu, click **Timesheet**.
2 Click the **Filter and Grouping** tab.
3 In the **Group by** box, select how you want tasks grouped.
  By default, tasks are grouped by project name.
4 If you want a group within a group, select the secondary group in the **Then by** box.

View the Project (Resources)

Periodically, you might find it helpful to review overall project information, or at least elements of the overall project that include tasks to which you're not assigned. For example, you might want to review all the tasks in the phase you're currently working on. You can see who's waiting for a deliverable you're working on or who's assigned to a task you're waiting on.

In Microsoft Project Central, you can see certain aspects of projects, as set up by the project manager and system administrator. You can view:

- Detailed information about projects in your portfolio, which is the collection of all the projects you're working on.
- Assignment information contained within Microsoft Project Central for assignments that you have permission to see.

With these broader views, you can see more than just the tasks you're working on. Plus, the project managers can communicate critical information about the projects throughout your organization.

To view the overall project

1. Click the **Views** menu.
2. Click **View Your Portfolio** to view a collection of projects.
3. Click **View Assignments** to view assignments you have permission to see.

Part 4

Reviewing Project Information

Although Microsoft Project can store thousands of pieces of information, you're probably interested in viewing only a small subset of that information at a time. Today, you might want to see how much certain tasks cost. Tomorrow, you might want to see which resources are overallocated. Any time you use Microsoft Project, you can view only the information you're interested in, and not a piece of data more or less.

When you're viewing project information, you might want that information to look a certain way. For example, you might want the names of critical tasks to stand out. Or, you might need to change the date format to conform with your organization's standards. Microsoft Project provides you with many ways to change the appearance of project information to suit your needs.

Occasionally, you'll want to share a set of particularly useful—and well-formatted—project information with team members, upper management, or clients. In some instances, you might send this information electronically. But in others, it might be more advantageous to share a hardcopy of the information. Microsoft Project enables you to print views as well as a number of predefined reports that meet a wide variety of reporting needs.

Part 4 explains how to view, format, and print project information. Chapter 12 discusses the use of Microsoft Project views, tables, and filters. Chapter 13 explains how to format views to make them look the way you want. Chapter 14 covers the basics of printing, including publishing project information to a Web site. Chapter 15 details options for formatting views, and chapter 16 does the same for reports.

12

Viewing Your Information

Your project plan can contain thousands of separate pieces of information about tasks, resources, and assignments. It stores durations, start dates, finish dates, predecessor tasks, successor tasks, assigned resources, assignment units, pay rates, working days and times, total costs, baseline costs, actual costs, per-use costs, notes, hyperlinks, and much more.

All the information in your project plan couldn't fit on your computer screen at the same time. Nor, most likely, would you want it to. Typically, you're interested in seeing one specific set of information at a time. Perhaps now you want to see the costs of those tasks that begin after a certain date. Later you might want to see which resources have spare time to work on tasks that are taking longer than planned. You can see just the information you're interested in by using views, tables, filters, and details.

A *view* displays a specific set of task, resource, or assignment information. Although there are some views that can only display information, you can use most views to enter and edit information. Each view presents information in a particular format. For example, the Resource Sheet view displays resource information in a table format; the Resource Graph, in a graph format. You can change the view that's displayed on your computer screen, as well as the set of information displayed in each view, most commonly by changing the table, filter, or set of details applied to the view. By default, Microsoft Project displays the Gantt Chart with the Entry table and the All Tasks filter.

A *table* is a set of fields arranged in columns and rows, like a spreadsheet. Each column displays a particular kind of information. For example, the Start column shows on which day a task begins. Each row displays information for a specific task, resource, or assignment. The columns that belong to a particular table display related information—information that you'd likely want to see all at once. For example, the Entry table for tasks consists of the Duration, Start, Finish, Predecessors, and Resource Names columns. You can, however, change the categories of information that appear in a table by adding and removing columns. Tables can be applied only to views that have a table portion, called *sheet views*.

You can arrange the fields in a table by grouping and sorting. With *grouping*, you collect certain tasks or resources together under the group criteria you choose, for example milestones, duration, or complete and incomplete tasks. With *sorting*, you can arrange tasks or resources in a particular order, such as from longest to shortest duration, from highest to lowest priority, by start date, and so on.

A *filter* is a means for displaying only those tasks or resources that meet a certain requirement. For example, you can use one filter to display only those tasks that use a particular resource, another to display only overallocated resources, and another to display only in-progress assignments. *Details* are sets of related information that display detailed task, resource, or assignment information in a special format other than a table. When using a non-table view, such as the Resource Graph, the Network Diagram, or Task Form, you can change the information you're working with. Instead of adding or removing columns or changing tables, though, you're changing the details.

Although views, tables, filters, and details differ in how they affect the project information displayed, they are united by a common principle: they provide sets and subsets of related project information. Your project file is essentially a huge collection of project information. Views present the largest categories of information regarding tasks, resources, or assignments. Tables and details applied to a view narrow the information to a more focused set of task, resource, or assignment information. Filters applied to a view narrow the displayed information still further.

Changing the information in tables, filters, and details is the most common but not the only ways to change the information that appears in a view. For example, you can change the text that appears next to Gantt bars in the Gantt Chart, the Tracking Gantt, and other Gantt Chart views. You can also change the information that appears on the Resource Graph and in the Network Diagram boxes. Because these are closely related to formatting the view, these kinds of changes are covered in chapter 13.

Selecting Views to Display Sets of Information

Views display and organize sets of project information in a logical manner. Think of a view as the first step in a simple winnowing process to display only the information you want. For example, by default, each view shows only task, resource, or assignment information.

But views can help you display even more specific information than that. Consider two views that display task information, the Gantt Chart and the PA_Optimistic Gantt view. By default, the Gantt Chart displays task duration, start and finish dates, predecessor tasks, and resource names. The PA_Optimistic Gantt view, on the other hand, displays your optimistic estimates for task durations and start and finish dates. You can choose a view not only to display task, resource, or assignment information, but also to display a specific set of default information about tasks, resources, or assignments.

Quite often, though, two views can display the same information. For example, the Calendar view can display information that can also be displayed in the Gantt Chart. Which one should you choose? The Calendar view displays task information in a monthly calendar format; the Gantt Chart, in a table and graphical bar format. You can choose the view that enables you to display information in a format that you prefer to work with or suits a particular purpose at a particular time.

As you add, review, and change project information, you'll choose one view for one purpose and a different view for another purpose. As you work with views, keep in mind that you can:

- Quickly switch from one view to another.
- Change the information that appears in a view.
- Customize the appearance of most views to meet your needs.
- Print views or publish them to a Web site.
- Create your own views.

Understand the Different Types of Views

When deciding which view you need for a given purpose, you first need to decide whether you want to display task, resource, or assignment information. Although there is a degree of overlap, the Microsoft Project views are generally categorized as task views, resource views, and assignment views.

Next, you need to decide which format you prefer to work with or that suits your purpose (such as viewing certain types of information or printing project information). You can choose a view that displays the type of information you want, in a specific format.

Microsoft Project comes with 27 predefined views in one of the following six formats:

- Gantt views.
- Usage views.
- Graph and diagram views.
- Sheet views.
- Form views.
- Combination views.

Gantt Views

Gantt views consist of a sheet view on the left and a chart graphically showing timelines, milestones, relationships, and other schedule information. Examples include the default Gantt Chart, the Tracking Gantt, and the Detail Gantt.

The left side of a Gantt Chart is a sheet view.

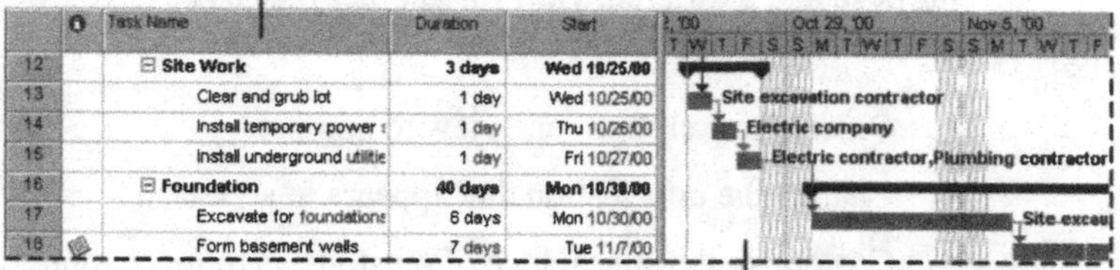
Task Name
Duration
Start
Oct 29, '00
Nov 5, '00
Site Work
3 days
Wed 10/25/00
Clear and grub lot
1 day
Wed 10/25/00
Install temporary power
1 day
Thu 10/26/00
Install underground utilitie
1 day
Fri 10/27/00
Foundation
40 days
Mon 10/30/00
Excavate for foundations
6 days
Mon 10/30/00
Form basement walls
7 days
Tue 11/7/00
Site excavation contractor
Electric company
Electric contractor,Plumbing contractor

The right side of a Gantt Chart graphically shows schedule information.

The following table details the Gantt views available in Microsoft Project.

Gantt View	Type	Description
Bar Rollup	Task	A Gantt Chart that displays each task as a Gantt bar on a summary Gantt bar. When used in conjunction with the Rollup_Formatting *macro*, you can hide subtask Gantt bars, while still seeing the individual tasks represented and named on a summary Gantt bar.
Detail Gantt	Task	A Gantt Chart whose bar chart portion shows *slack* and *slippage*. Use this view to determine how much a task can slip without causing other tasks to slip.
Gantt Chart	Task	A list of tasks and task information in the sheet portion of the view, and Gantt bars showing tasks and durations over time in the bar chart portion. Use this view to enter and edit task information and schedule tasks.
Leveling Gantt	Task	A Gantt Chart that shows task *delay* information in the sheet portion, and the delay added to tasks because of resource leveling in the chart portion. Use this view to see the amount of delay added to tasks by resource leveling.

Gantt View	Type	Description
Milestone Date Rollup	Task	A Gantt Chart that displays the start date for each task as a milestone symbol on a summary Gantt bar. When used in conjunction with the Rollup_Formatting macro, you can hide subtask Gantt bars, while still seeing the individual tasks represented and named on a summary task Gantt bar.
Milestone Rollup	Task	A Gantt Chart that displays each task as a milestone symbol on a summary task Gantt bar. When used in conjunction with the Rollup_Formatting macro, you can hide subtask Gantt bars, while still seeing the individual tasks represented and named on a summary task Gantt bar.
PA_Expected Gantt	Task	A Gantt Chart in which you enter your expected values for task durations, start dates, and finish dates. Use this view in conjunction with PERT analysis tools to evaluate a probable schedule based on an expected-case scenario.
PA_Optimistic Gantt	Task	A Gantt Chart in which you enter your optimistic values for task durations, start dates, and finish dates. Use this view in conjunction with PERT analysis tools to evaluate a probable schedule based on a best-case scenario.
PA_Pessimistic Gantt	Task	A Gantt Chart in which you enter your pessimistic values for task durations, start dates, and finish dates. Use this view in conjunction with PERT analysis to evaluate a probable schedule based on a worst-case scenario.
Tracking Gantt	Task	A Gantt Chart that shows baseline estimates and actual data for each task in the bar chart portion. After you save a baseline and have begun entering actual data, use this view to compare the planned schedule with the actual schedule.

Usage Views

A *usage view* is a special combination view consisting of a sheet view on the left and a timesheet view on the right. In these views, you can see tasks with assignments (Task Usage view) or resources with assignments (Resource Usage view).

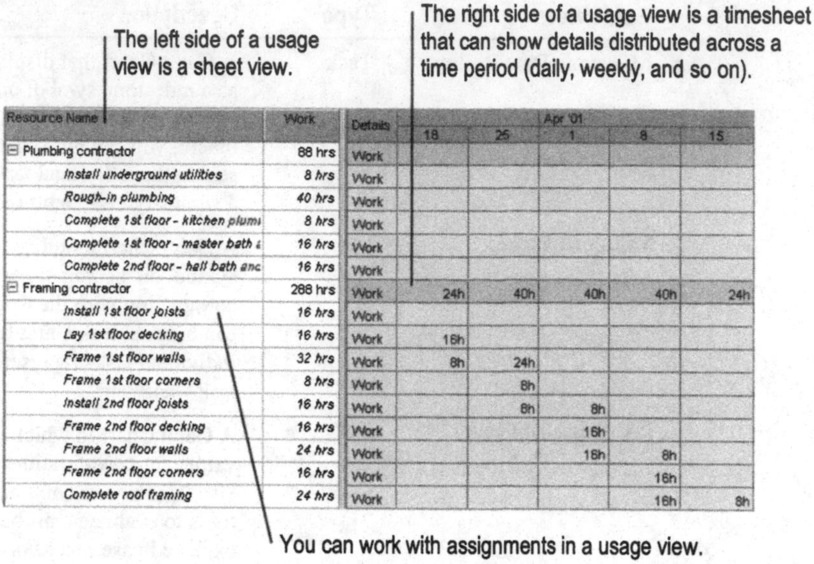
The left side of a usage view is a sheet view.
The right side of a usage view is a timesheet that can show details distributed across a time period (daily, weekly, and so on).
Resource Name
Work
Details
Apr '01
18
25
1
8
15
Plumbing contractor
88 hrs
Install underground utilities
8 hrs
Rough-in plumbing
40 hrs
Complete 1st floor - kitchen plumi
8 hrs
Complete 1st floor - master bath
16 hrs
Complete 2nd floor - hall bath anc
16 hrs
Framing contractor
288 hrs
24h
40h
40h
40h
24h
Install 1st floor joists
16 hrs
Lay 1st floor decking
16 hrs
16h
Frame 1st floor walls
32 hrs
8h
24h
Frame 1st floor corners
8 hrs
8h
Install 2nd floor joists
16 hrs
8h
8h
Frame 2nd floor decking
16 hrs
16h
Frame 2nd floor walls
24 hrs
16h
8h
Frame 2nd floor corners
16 hrs
16h
Complete roof framing
24 hrs
16h
8h
Work
You can work with assignments in a usage view.

The following table details the usage views available in Microsoft Project.

Usage View	Type	Description
Resource Usage	Assignment	A list of resources showing assigned tasks grouped under each resource, a table of resource information, and a set of details about resources and their assigned tasks. Use this view to see the tasks that are assigned to specific resources, set resource contours, and show cost or work allocation information for each resource.
Task Usage	Assignment	A list of tasks showing assigned resources grouped under each task, a table of task information, and a set of details about tasks and their assigned resources. Use this view to see the resources that are assigned to specific tasks and to set resource contours.

Graph and Diagram Views

Graph and *diagram views* display information in a graphical way. For example, the Resource Graph view displays resource information on a set of axes as a curve, line, area, or bars. Network Diagram views show each task in boxes, with specific information in the boxes, with links and colors indicating relationships, critical tasks, milestone tasks, and so on. The Network Diagram is also known as a *PERT Chart*. The Calendar view displays task information in a calendar format.

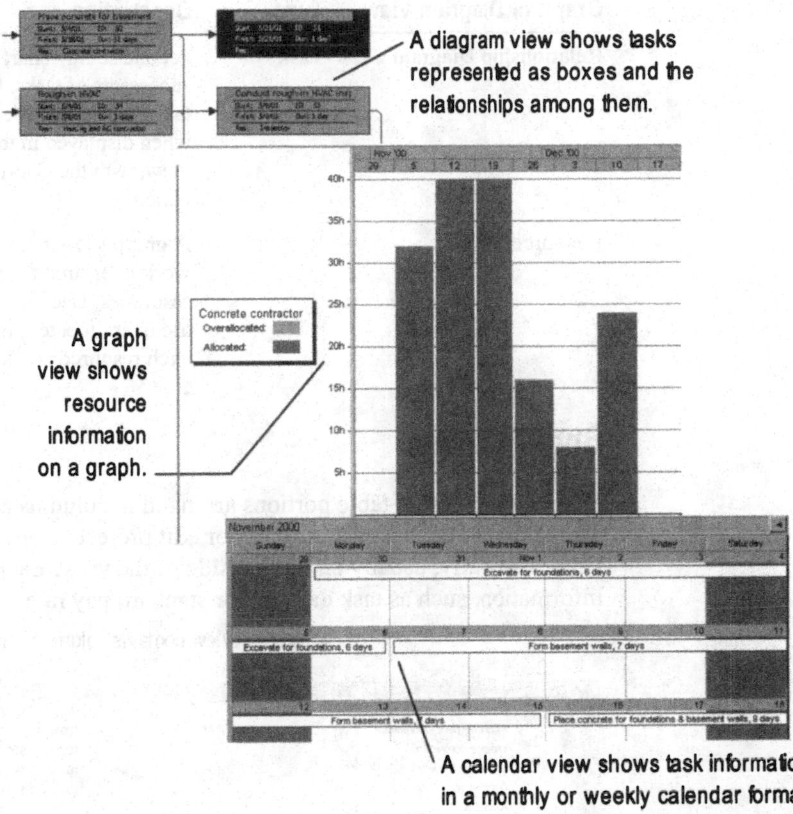
A diagram view shows tasks represented as boxes and the relationships among them.
A graph view shows resource information on a graph.
Concrete contractor
Overallocated
Allocated
November 2000
A calendar view shows task information in a monthly or weekly calendar format

The following table details the graph and diagram views available in Microsoft Project.

Graph or Diagram View	**Type**	**Description**
Calendar	Task	A monthly calendar that displays each task as a bar on a calendar. The length of each bar corresponds to the task's duration. Use this view to see tasks scheduled in a specific day, week, or month.
Descriptive Network Diagram	Task	A flowchart that shows all tasks and their dependencies. This view is identical to the Network Diagram view, except the boxes are larger and contain more fields of information.
Network Diagram	Task	A flowchart that shows all tasks and the dependencies between them. Use this view to get an overview of task sequence or to add, change, or remove task dependencies. You can also use it to create a schedule or add tasks.

Graph or Diagram View	Type	Description
Relationship Diagram	Task	A concise flowchart that shows the predecessors and successors of tasks. Use this view to display all the tasks linked to a specific task. This view is most useful when displayed in the bottom pane of a combination view, with the Gantt Chart or the Task Sheet in the top pane.
Resource Graph	Resource	A graph showing resource allocations, costs, and work over time for an individual resource or group of resources. Use this view to see how much resources are overallocated, the percentage of total work time each resource is assigned to work, and resource costs.

Sheet Views

Sheet views contain table portions arranged in columns and rows, like a spreadsheet. They provide the best way to enter or edit project information. Tasks or resources are listed vertically, usually on the left side of the view. Each column specifies a type of information, such as task duration or standard pay rate.

A sheetview contains columns containing fields of information.

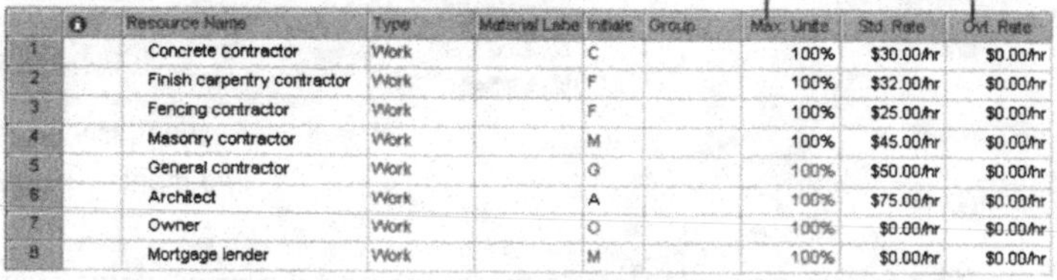

	ⓘ	Resource Name	Type	Material Labe	Initials	Group	Max. Units	Std. Rate	Ovt. Rate
1		Concrete contractor	Work		C		100%	$30.00/hr	$0.00/hr
2		Finish carpentry contractor	Work		F		100%	$32.00/hr	$0.00/hr
3		Fencing contractor	Work		F		100%	$25.00/hr	$0.00/hr
4		Masonry contractor	Work		M		100%	$45.00/hr	$0.00/hr
5		General contractor	Work		G		100%	$50.00/hr	$0.00/hr
6		Architect	Work		A		100%	$75.00/hr	$0.00/hr
7		Owner	Work		O		100%	$0.00/hr	$0.00/hr
8		Mortgage lender	Work		M		100%	$0.00/hr	$0.00/hr

The following table details the sheet views available in Microsoft Project.

Sheet View	Type	Description
PA_PERT Entry Sheet	Task	A set of columns in which you enter your expected, best-case, and worst-case durations for tasks, before you use PERT analysis tools to calculate the most likely durations. Use this view in conjunction with PERT analysis to compare the duration values among the various scenarios.
Resource Sheet	Resource	A list of resources accompanied by columns of frequently used resource information. Use this view to enter and edit resource information.
Task Sheet	Task	A list of tasks accompanied by columns of frequently used task information, such as Duration, Start Date, and Resources. Use this view to review, enter, and edit task information.

Form Views

Form views contain boxes in which you enter, edit, and review fields of project information. Form views are often used effectively in combination with another view to provide details associated with a selected task or resource.

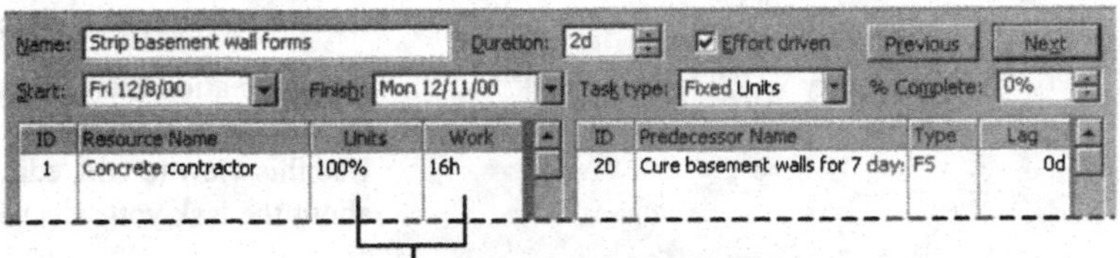

A form view shows detailed information about a selected task or resource.

The following table details the form views available in Microsoft Project.

Form View	Type	Description
Resource Form	Resource	A form for entering, editing, and reviewing information about a specific resource.
Resource Name Form	Resource	A simpler version of the Resource Form. Only the resource name appears at the top, but the same details appear in the Resource Form at the bottom of the view. Use this view for entering and editing the resource name and specific sets of resource details.
Task Details Form	Task	A form for entering, editing, and reviewing detailed information about a specific task. Use this view in the bottom pane of a combination view, with the Gantt Chart in the top pane.
Task Form	Task	A form for entering, editing, and reviewing information about a specific task. Use this view in the bottom pane of a combination view, with the Gantt Chart in the top pane.
Task Name Form	Task	A simpler version of the Task Form. Only the task name appears at the top, but the same details appear in the Task Form at the bottom of the view. Use this view for entering and editing the task name and specific sets of task details.

Combination Views

A *combination view* shows two views in a split screen. You can easily set up your own combination view by splitting your screen. However, two predefined views are combination views: the Task Entry and the Resource Allocation views.

The following table details the predefined combination views in Microsoft Project.

Combination View	Type	Description
Resource Allocation	Resource	A combination view with the Resource Usage view in the top pane and the Leveling Delay Gantt view in the bottom pane. Use this resource view to find and resolve resource overallocations.
Task Entry	Task	A combination view that shows the Gantt Chart in the top pane and the Task Form view in the bottom pane. Use this view to add, edit, and review information about the task you select in the Gantt Chart.

Display a View

Whenever you're working with Microsoft Project, you're looking at a view. By default, the first time you start Microsoft Project, it displays the Gantt Chart. However, each time you open an existing project file, it displays the view that appeared on your screen when you last saved and closed the file. If you want to work with a different kind or set of information or with the same kind of information but in a different format, you can switch to a different view.

When you switch to another view, you don't add information to or remove information from your project. You only change the subset of project information that's displayed.

To display a view

- On the **View Bar**, click the view you want.
  To select a view that doesn't appear on the **View Bar**, click **More Views**, click the view you want in the **Views** list, and then click **Apply**.

Display Two Views at the Same Time

Although you can change the information that appears in a view, each view can display only a limited amount of information at one time. Typically, a single view displays only one type of information: task, resource, or assignment information.

To see a different set of information about a task, resource, or assignment, you can display a second view in the bottom half of the view area at the same time that you display a view in the top half. The result is a *combination view*.

The power of using a combination view is threefold:

- You can see more of the same type of information about a task, resource, or assignment in the top pane. For example, the Gantt Chart in the top pane might display a task's name, duration, and start and finish dates. The Task Sheet in the bottom pane might display fixed cost, total cost, baseline cost, actual cost, and remaining cost for a task.
- You can display a different type of information in each pane. For example, the Gantt Chart in the top pane displays task information. The Resource Graph in the bottom pane displays information about the resources assigned to the tasks in the top pane.
- The bottom view is automatically connected to the top view. For example, when you select a task in the Gantt Chart in the top pane, the Resource Graph in the bottom pane displays information about the resource assigned to the task (if you've assigned a resource to the task). When you select a different task in the Gantt Chart, the Resource Graph displays information about that task's resource.

For a task or resource selected in the top pane in a combination view...

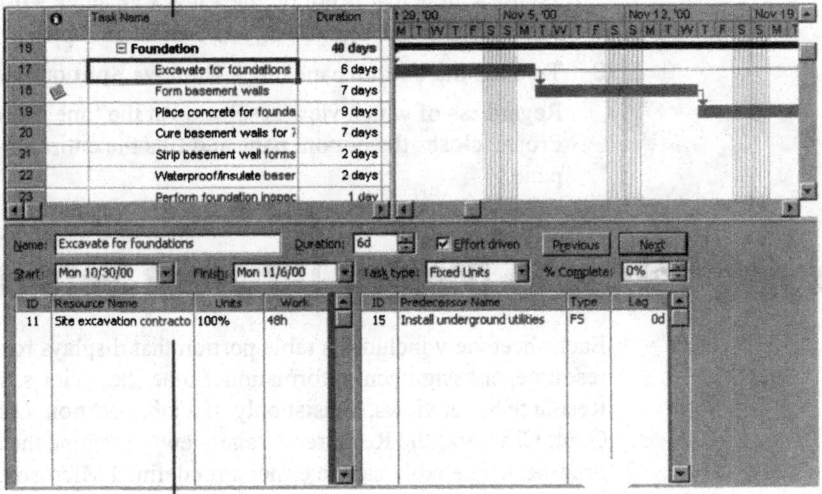

...detailed information is shown in the bottom pane.

The following restrictions apply to combination views:

- You can display at most two views at one time from the same project file. You can't split the view area into three or more view windows.

- In each view, you can choose the information you want to see, but you can't apply a filter or an AutoFilter to the bottom view, only to a sheet in the top view. However, you can still change the information in the bottom view by changing the table or changing details, for example.
- You can't display the Calendar view in the bottom pane.
- You can replace the view in either pane one at a time. But if you choose to display a predefined combination view (such as the Resource Allocation view), the predefined combination view replaces both the top pane and the bottom pane of the currently displayed combination view.

To display and close a second view in the bottom pane

Replace a view in a pane by selecting the view and then choosing another view.

1 On the **Window** menu, click **Split**.

By default, if the view in the top pane is a task view, the Task Form appears in the bottom pane. If the view in the top pane is a resource view, the Resource Form appears in the bottom pane.

1 Click the bottom pane to make the bottom view the active view.

2 On the **View Bar**, click the view you want to appear in the bottom pane.

To use a view that is not on the **View Bar**, click **More Views**, click the view you want to use in the **Views** list, and then click **Apply**.

3 To close the bottom pane, click **Remove Split** on the **Window** menu.

Regardless of which view is selected at the time you click Remove Split, Microsoft Project closes the bottom pane and fills the entire screen with the view in the top pane.

Applying Tables to Display Different Sets of Information

Each sheet view includes a table portion that displays rows and columns of task, resource, or assignment information. Some sheet views, such as the Task Sheet and the Resource Sheet views, consist only of a table portion. Other sheet views, such as the Gantt Chart and the Resource Usage views, combine the table portion with a chart or timesheet. The table can be either a predefined Microsoft Project table or a table you create or modify.

A predefined Microsoft Project table consists of related columns of information. For instance, the Cost table for tasks (there's also a Cost table for resources) includes the Fixed Cost, Fixed Cost Accrual, Total Cost, Baseline Cost, Variance Cost, Actual Cost, and Remaining Cost fields. You can change the type of information displayed in a sheet view by changing the table displayed. By switching to the Work table, for instance, you can view information related to the work required to complete a task, such as the total work and the remaining work.

Understand Types of Tables

Microsoft Project applies a default table to each sheet view. For example, the Entry table is the default table for the Gantt Chart, and the Usage table is the default table for the Resource Usage view. You can change the information displayed in the table portion of a sheet view by applying a different table to the view.

Apply *task tables* to task sheet views, including the Task Usage view. Apply the table that includes the columns of information you want to display.

Entry table for tasks.

	Task Name	Duration	Start	Finish	Predecessors	Resource Na
1	⊟ Lay the Foundation	9 days	Mon 2/2/98	Fri 2/13/98		
2	Dig the foundation	3 days	Mon 2/2/98	Thu 2/5/98		Diggers
3	Compact the soil	2 days	Thu 2/5/98	Mon 2/9/98	2	Jake
4	Set wall molds in place	1 day	Mon 2/9/98	Tue 2/10/98	3	Selena,Tom
5	Let concrete dry	3 days	Tue 2/10/98	Fri 2/13/98	4	
6	Foundation					

Cost table for tasks.

Fixed Cost	Fixed Cost Accrual	Total Cost	Baseline	Variance	Actual	Remaining
$0.00	Prorated	$1,120.00	$0.00	$1,120.00	$0.00	$1,120.00
$0.00	Prorated	$480.00	$0.00	$480.00	$0.00	$480.00
$0.00	Prorated	$320.00	$0.00	$320.00	$0.00	$320.00
$0.00	Prorated	$320.00	$0.00	$320.00	$0.00	$320.00
$0.00	Prorated	$0.00	$0.00	$0.00	$0.00	$0.00
$0.00	Prorated	$0.00	$0.00	$0.00	$0.00	$0.00
$0.00	Prorated	$0.00	$0.00	$0.00	$0.00	$0.00

Tracking table for tasks.

Act. Start	Act. Finish	% Comp.	Act. Dur.	Rem. Dur.	Act. Cost	Act. Work
NA	NA	0%	0 days	9 days	$0.00	0 hrs
NA	NA	0%	0 days	3 days	$0.00	0 hrs
NA	NA	0%	0 days	2 days	$0.00	0 hrs
NA	NA	0%	0 days	1 day	$0.00	0 hrs
NA	NA	0%	0 days	3 days	$0.00	0 hrs
NA	NA	0%	0 days	0 days	$0.00	0 hrs
NA	NA	0%	0 days	3 days	$0.00	0 hrs
NA	NA	0%	0 days	1 day	$0.00	0 hrs
NA	NA	0%	0 days	1 day	$0.00	0 hrs
NA	NA	0%	0 days	1 day	$0.00	0 hrs
NA	NA	0%	0 days	3 days	$0.00	0 hrs
NA	NA	0%	0 days	1 day	$0.00	0 hrs

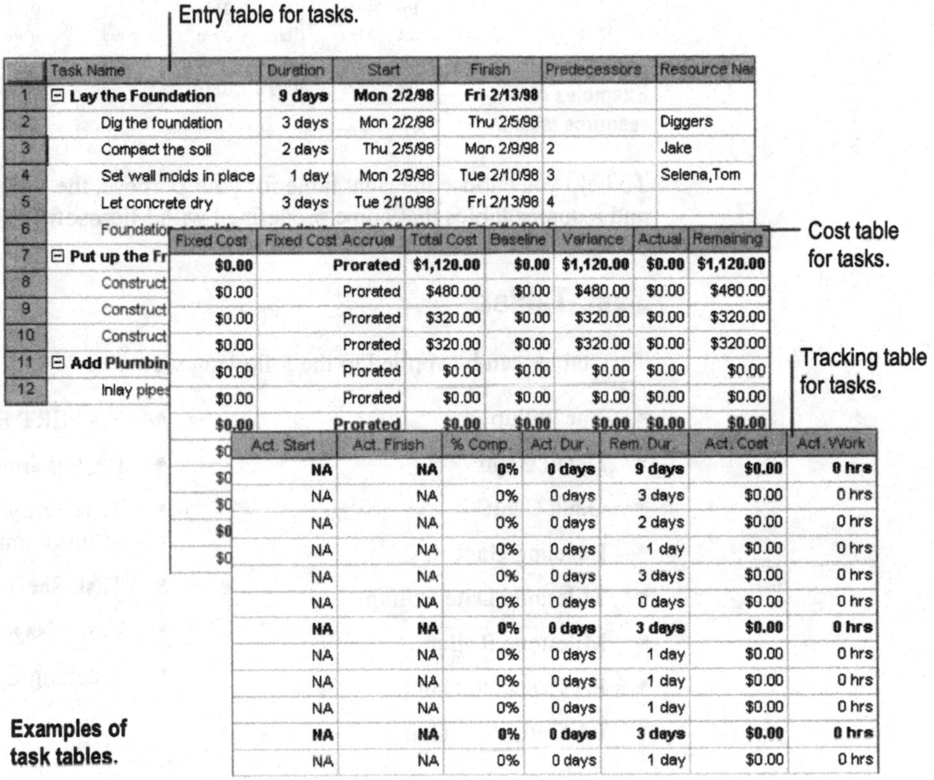

Examples of task tables.

Apply *resource tables* to resource sheet views, including the Resource Usage view. Apply either predefined tables or tables that you create or modify. See "Create or Modify a Table" below for more information.

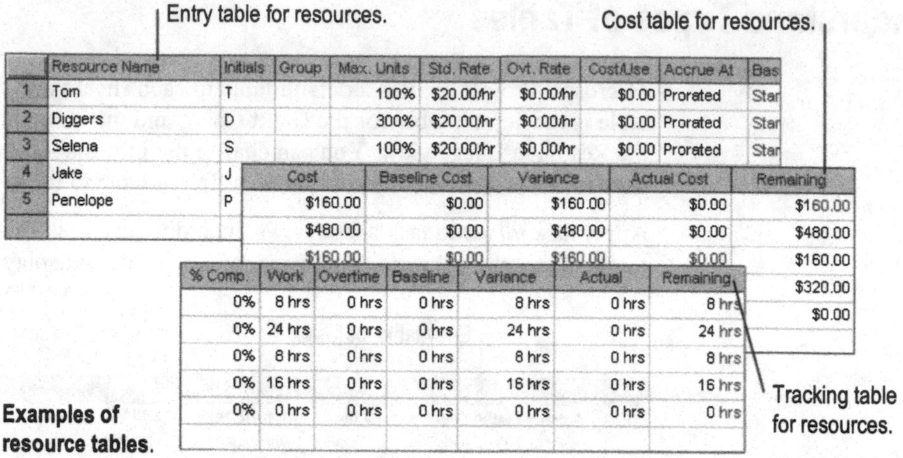

Entry table for resources.

Cost table for resources.

	Resource Name	Initials	Group	Max. Units	Std. Rate	Ovt. Rate	Cost/Use	Accrue At	Bas
1	Tom	T		100%	$20.00/hr	$0.00/hr	$0.00	Prorated	Star
2	Diggers	D		300%	$20.00/hr	$0.00/hr	$0.00	Prorated	Star
3	Selena	S		100%	$20.00/hr	$0.00/hr	$0.00	Prorated	Star
4	Jake	J							
5	Penelope	P							

Cost	Baseline Cost	Variance	Actual Cost	Remaining
$160.00	$0.00	$160.00	$0.00	$160.00
$480.00	$0.00	$480.00	$0.00	$480.00
$160.00	$0.00	$160.00	$0.00	$160.00
				$320.00
				$0.00

% Comp.	Work	Overtime	Baseline	Variance	Actual	Remaining
0%	8 hrs	0 hrs	0 hrs	8 hrs	0 hrs	8 hrs
0%	24 hrs	0 hrs	0 hrs	24 hrs	0 hrs	24 hrs
0%	8 hrs	0 hrs	0 hrs	8 hrs	0 hrs	8 hrs
0%	16 hrs	0 hrs	0 hrs	16 hrs	0 hrs	16 hrs
0%	0 hrs	0 hrs	0 hrs	0 hrs	0 hrs	0 hrs

Tracking table for resources.

Examples of resource tables.

To help you choose the right table for your purpose, the following lists show the task and resource tables that come predefined with Microsoft Project

Task Tables

Task tables can be applied to the following views:

- Bar Rollup
- Detail Gantt
- Gantt Chart
- Leveling Gantt
- Milestone Date Rollup
- Milestone Rollup
- PA Expected Gantt
- PA Optimistic Gantt
- PA PERT Entry Sheet
- PA Pessimistic Gantt
- Task Entry (in the top pane only of this combination view)
- Task Sheet
- Task Usage
- Tracking Gantt

Task table	Description
Baseline	Displays *baseline* durations, start and finish dates, work, and costs.
Constraint Dates	Displays the type of *constraint* applied to each task (such as As Soon As Possible or Must Start On) and the constraint date.
Cost	Displays cost information, such as fixed cost, total cost, baseline cost, cost *variance*, actual cost, and remaining cost.
Delay	Displays resource *leveling* information, including leveling *delay* (in terms of elapsed duration, or *edays*), duration, scheduled start and finish dates, successors, and resource names.

Task table	Description
Earned Value	Shows various *earned value* fields. Compares expected progress on tasks with the actual progress to date. Shows, in terms of resource costs, the actual percentage of completion of each task, to forecast whether a task will finish under budget or over budget. Includes fields such as BCWS (budgeted cost of work scheduled) and SV (schedule variance).
Entry	Displays basic task information for starting to create your project plan. Displays task names, durations, start and finish dates, predecessors, and resources. The default table for the Gantt Chart and Task Sheet views.
Export	Displays the 83 task fields that Microsoft Project can *export* in the *.mpx file format*. Use this table to export a file in the .mpx file format to another program.
Hyperlink	Displays the Web addresses and subaddresses of *hyperlinks* connecting tasks to Web sites and intranet files.
PA_Expected Case	Displays estimates for expected durations, start dates, and finish dates. Use with the Microsoft Project *PERT analysis* features to determine probable task durations and start and finish dates.
PA_Optimistic Case	Displays estimates for optimistic durations, start dates, and finish dates. Use with the Microsoft Project PERT analysis features to determine probable task durations and start and finish dates.
PA_PERT Entry	Compares optimistic, expected, and pessimistic task durations. Use with the Microsoft Project PERT analysis features to determine probable task durations and start and finish dates.
PA_Pessimistic Case	Displays estimates for pessimistic durations, start dates, and finish dates. Use with the Microsoft Project PERT analysis features to determine probable task durations and start and finish dates.
Rollup	Applied after you have run the Rollup_Formatting macro (Tools menu, Macro, Macros, Run), enables you to optimize the display of Gantt bars rolled up and overlaid on top of their respective summary task Gantt bars. It's the default table for the Bar Rollup, Milestone Date Rollup, and Milestone Rollup views.
Schedule	Displays scheduling information, including start and finish dates, late start and finish dates, free *slack*, and total slack. Enables you to see how late a task can start or finish without affecting the dates of successor tasks or the project's finish date.
Summary	Displays a summary of the most important task information, including task duration, start and finish dates, percent complete, cost, and work.
Tracking	Displays *actual* task information (as opposed to *scheduled* information), including actual start dates, actual finish dates, percent complete, actual duration, remaining duration, actual cost, and actual work.
Usage	Displays work, duration, and start and finish dates. It's the default table of the Task Usage view.

Task table	Description
Variance	Displays scheduled start and finish dates, baseline start and finish dates, and the differences, or variances, between the two sets of dates.
Work	Displays work information, including baseline work, work variance, actual work, and remaining work. Enables you to compare scheduled work against baseline work, actual work, or remaining work.

Resource Tables

Resource tables can be applied to the following views:

- Resource Allocation (a table can be applied only in the top pane).
- Resource Sheet.
- Resource Usage.

Resource table	Description
Cost	Displays cost information, such as total cost, baseline cost, cost variance, actual cost, and remaining cost.
Earned Value	Shows various earned value fields. Compares expected resource costs with the actual resource costs to date. Can be used to forecast whether resource costs for tasks will finish under budget or over budget. Includes fields such as BCWS (budgeted cost of work scheduled) and SV (schedule variance).
Entry	Displays basic resource information for creating a resource list for your project plan. Displays *resource groups*, assignment units, standard rates, overtime rates, cost per use, *accrual method*, and resource code. The default table for the Resource Sheet view.
Entry—Material Resources	Displays basic information about *material resources*, including material label, initials, group, standard rate, cost per use, accrue at, and code. Excludes columns that apply only to work resources.
Entry—Work Resources	Displays basic information about *work resources*, including each person's initials, group, maximum units, standard rate, overtime rate, cost per use, accrue at, base calendar, and code. Excludes columns that apply only to material resources.
Export	Displays the 23 resource fields that Microsoft Project can export in the .mpx file format. Use this table to export a file in the .mpx file format to another program.
Hyperlink	Displays the Web addresses and subaddresses of hyperlinks connecting resources to Web sites and intranet files.

Resource table	Description
Summary	Displays a summary of the most important resource information, including resource groups, maximum units, *peak resource usage*, standard rates, overtime rates, cost, and work.
Usage	Displays the amount of work assigned to each resource. It's the default table of the Resource Usage view.
Work	Displays work information, including baseline work, work variance, actual work, overtime work, and remaining work.

Apply a Table

The first time you display a Microsoft Project sheet view, a default table is already attached to it. For example, the Entry table is attached to the default Gantt Chart. However, each time you open an existing project file, each sheet view is displayed with the table that was attached to it when you last saved the file.

To see other columns of information, you can apply a different table to the view. Or, you can add or hide columns in an existing table. When you apply a different table to a sheet view, the new table replaces the old table. You can apply a task table only to a task view and a resource table only to a resource view.

When you replace one table with another, you do not add information to or remove information from your project. You only change the project information displayed at the moment. Also, the list of tasks or resources on the view remains the same. Only the other columns of information change.

To apply a table

1. On the **View Bar**, click the view to which you want to apply a table.

   To select a view that doesn't appear on the **View Bar**, click **More Views**, click the view you want in the **Views** list, and then click **Apply**.
2. On the **View** menu, point to **Table**, and then click the table you want.

   To apply a table that isn't on the **Table** submenu, click **More Tables**, click the task or resource table you want, and then click **Apply**.

You can easily add and remove columns in a table to make it better suit your needs. See "Create or Modify a Table" later in this chapter.

Group Task and Resource Information

You can collect your task or resource information in a table and group it under categories you choose to give you another way to look at your project information. You might want to see your tasks grouped by tasks in progress, tasks not yet started, and then completed tasks. On the resource side, you could view your work resources grouped separately from their material resources.

If you assign outline codes to your tasks or resources, you can group them by outline code to view your data in very specific ways that you design. For more information about outline codes, see "Using Custom Outline Codes" in chapter 4.

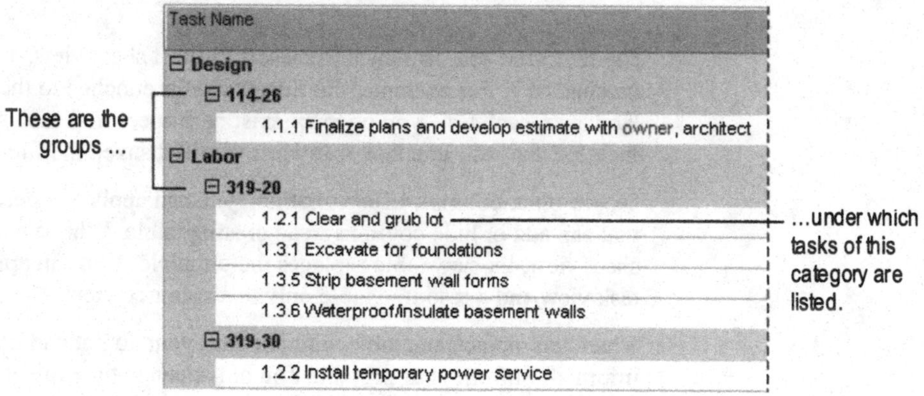

To group task and resource information

1. Display the task or resource sheet view that contains the information you want to group.
2. On the **Project** menu, point to **Group by**, and then click the group you want.

To create a custom group

1. Display the task or resource sheet view that contains the information you want to group.
2. On the **Project** menu, point to **Group by**, and then click **More Groups**.
3. Click **New**.
4. In the **Name** box, type the name you want for the group definition.
5. If this is a grouping you're going to use frequently, select the **Show in menu** check box.
6. In the **Group By** row under **Field Name**, select the field you want to group by, for example **Start**.

   All Microsoft Project task fields are available for grouping on a task table. Likewise, all resource fields are available for grouping on a resource table.

To remove the grouping, on the Project menu, point to Group by, and then click No Group.

7. Under **Order**, specify whether you want the grouping to be alphabetical in ascending or descending order.
8. Click **OK**, and then click **Apply**.

Sort Task and Resource Information

By default, Microsoft Project lists tasks and resources in ascending order by ID number. But you might want to see tasks or resources in a different order. If, for example, you want to decrease the project length, you might want to list tasks from the longest duration to the shortest, to focus on reducing the longest durations first.

The sorting criteria you can choose are the Microsoft Project task and resource fields that are available. For instance, if you want to sort tasks by duration, you specify that the Duration field control the sort order.

The sorting you apply to a view is saved with that view. You can't sort in the Network Diagram.

To sort a view

1. On the **Project** menu, point to **Sort**, and then click the sorting option you want.

   To select a sorting option that doesn't appear on the Sort submenu, point to **Sort**, and then click **Sort by.**
2. In the **Sort by** box, click a field by which to sort your data, and then click **Ascending** or **Descending** to specify the sort order.
3. To sort by an additional field, click the fields in the first **Then by** box, and then click **Ascending** or **Descending** to specify the sort order.
4. To sort tasks within their outline structure so that subtasks remain with their summary tasks, select the **Keep outline structure** check box.
5. To permanently renumber your tasks based on the new sort order, select the **Permanently renumber tasks** check box.

   You can renumber your tasks only if you select **Keep outline structure** first.
6. To return your tasks to their original sequence, click **Reset**.

   If you've permanently renumbered your tasks, you can't return your tasks to their original sequence by clicking **Reset**.

Filtering to Display Only Certain Tasks or Resources

You choose the type of information you want to display—task, resource, or assignment—by choosing a task, resource, or assignment view. You choose the particular set of information that appears in a view by choosing a table or set of details. To display only certain tasks or resources (even in an assignment view), you choose a filter.

By default, each view displays all the tasks or resources in your project (though you might need to scroll to see them all). Often, however, you might want to focus on just those tasks or resources that share certain characteristics. For example, you might want to see only in-progress tasks or only overallocated resources.

For each view, you can determine which tasks or resources Microsoft Project displays or highlights by applying a *filter*. A filter contains instructions, called criteria, that specify the characteristics a task or resource must have in order to appear in a view. You change the filter applied to a view when you want to see information about different tasks or resources in the current format.

If none of the filters provided with Microsoft Project contains the task or resource criteria that you want, you can create a new filter or modify an existing one.

Understand Types of Filters

Microsoft Project displays each view with a default filter applied to it: The All Tasks filter is applied to each task view and the All Resources filter is applied to each resource view. You can display a subset of the tasks or resources that appear in a view by applying a different filter to the view.

There are two major groups of filters: *task filters*, which you apply to task views, and *resource filters*, which you apply to resource views. Each of these groups contains three types of filters: standard, interactive, and AutoFilters. You can apply predefined filters or filters that you create. You apply the filter that contains the criteria for the task or resource information you want to display in a view.

- A *standard* filter identifies tasks and resources based on one or two commonly used criteria. For example, when you apply the Completed Tasks filter, Microsoft Project displays only completed tasks. Most Microsoft Project filters are of this type.

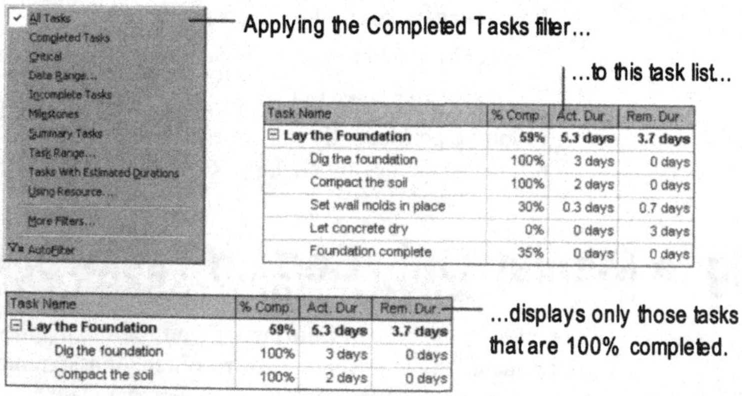

- An *interactive* filter prompts you to enter filtering criteria, such as a single value or a range of values. For example, when you apply the Date Range filter for tasks, you specify two dates that bracket a time period. Microsoft Project then displays only those tasks that start or finish within that time period. In the filter menu, interactive filters are listed with an ellipsis after the name.

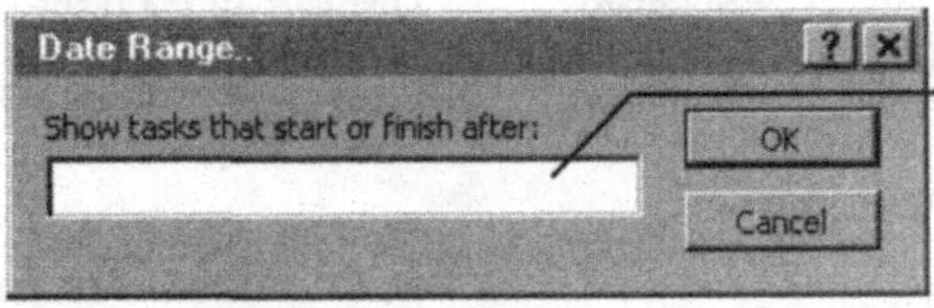

Specify a value or range of values in an interactive filter.

A Microsoft Project AutoFilter works just like a Microsoft Excel AutoFilter.

- An *AutoFilter*, available only in sheet views, displays tasks or resources that share a piece of information contained in a specific column. Each column has one AutoFilter. The criteria in each AutoFilter consist of all the pieces of information listed in the column, plus some predefined criteria.

For example, if one or more tasks listed in the Gantt Chart starts on 10/25/00, the AutoFilter for the Start field lists 10/25/00 among its filtering criteria. If you select 10/25/00 from the AutoFilter criteria list, Microsoft Project displays only those tasks that start on 10/25/00. The Start field AutoFilter also lists predefined criteria such as All, Tomorrow, This Week, and Next Month.

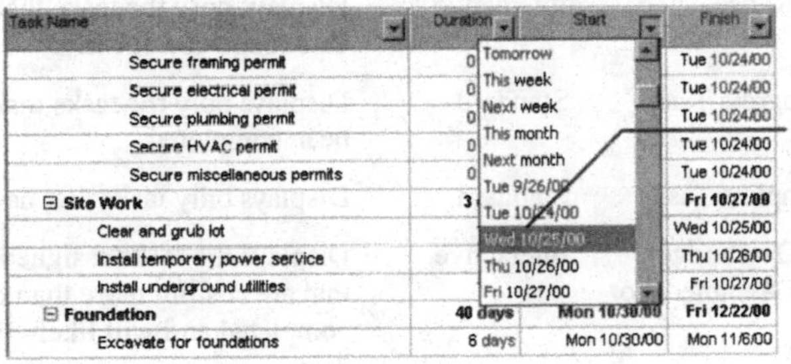

This AutoFilter for the Start field contains the criteria date 10/25/00, among others.

You can use a filter by itself or in combination with other filters. For example, you can use a Start field AutoFilter to display only tasks that start after 10/25/00. Then you can narrow your focus by applying the Critical filter to display only critical tasks that start after 10/25/00. Or, instead of or in addition to the Critical filter, you can select the > 1 day criterion in the Duration field AutoFilter to display only those critical tasks that start after 10/25/00 and have durations greater than 1 day. By using various combinations of filters, you can focus on exactly the tasks or resources you want.

To help you choose the right filter for your purpose, the following lists show the predefined task and resource filters that come with Microsoft Project.

Task Filters

Each task filter can be applied to any task view.

Task filter	Type	Description
All Tasks	Standard	Displays all the tasks in your project plan.
Completed Tasks	Standard	Displays only those tasks that have been marked as 100% completed.
Confirmed	Standard	Displays each task whose resources have agreed to perform the task. (A task is confirmed when each resource requested for the task accepts the task in a workgroup *TeamAssign message* and a Yes appears in the Confirmed field for the task.)
Cost Greater Than	Interactive	Displays whose total cost is greater than the amount that you specify.
Cost Overbudget	Standard	Displays only those tasks whose total cost is greater than the baseline cost.
Created After	Interactive	Displays the tasks you added to your project plan on or after the date you specify.
Critical	Standard	Displays only the tasks that are on the *critical path*.
Date Range	Interactive	Displays only the tasks that start or finish within the date range you specify.
In Progress Tasks	Standard	Displays only the tasks that have started but haven't been completed.
Incomplete Tasks	Standard	Displays only tasks that haven't been completed.
Late/Overbudget Tasks Assigned To	Interactive	Displays the tasks assigned to the resource you specify that are costing more than budgeted or haven't yet been completed and will likely finish after the baseline finish date.
Linked Fields	Standard	Displays tasks to which information from other programs or other projects has been linked.
Milestones	Standard	Displays only milestone tasks.
Resource Group	Interactive	Displays the tasks assigned to the resources who belong to the resource group you specify.
Should Start By	Interactive	Displays only tasks that should have started by the date you specify but haven't.
Should Start/Finish By	Interactive	Displays those tasks that haven't started and finished within the date range you specify.

Task filter	Type	Description
Slipped/Late Progress	Standard	Displays tasks that either haven't finished by their baseline finish date or that haven't been progressing on schedule (by comparing the amount of work scheduled for the task, BCWS, to the amount of work that has been completed, BCWP, in the Earned Value table).
Slipping Tasks	Standard	Displays only tasks that are behind schedule (their actual start or finish dates are later than their baseline start or finish dates).
Summary Tasks	Standard	Displays only tasks that have subtasks indented underneath them.
Task Range	Interactive	Displays only tasks within the ID range you specify.
Tasks With A Task Calendar Assigned	Standard	Displays only tasks that have a *task calendar* assigned.
Tasks With Attachments	Standard	Displays tasks that have *OLE objects* (Object Linking and Embedding) attached or a note in the Notes box of the Task Information dialog box.
Tasks With Deadlines	Standard	Displays only tasks that have a *deadline.*
Tasks With Estimated Durations	Standard	Displays only tasks that have *estimated durations*, rather than confirmed durations. Estimated durations are those that still include a question mark.
Tasks With Fixed Dates	Standard	Displays only tasks that don't have the constraints As Soon As Possible or As Late As Possible or that have an actual start date.
Tasks/Assignments With Overtime	Standard	Displays only tasks or assignments whose assigned resources are working overtime.
Top Level Tasks	Standard	Displays the highest-level summary tasks only.
Unconfirmed	Standard	Displays each task whose resources have not yet agreed to perform the task through workgroup communications and the TeamAssign message.
Unstarted Tasks	Standard	Displays only tasks that have not started.
Update Needed	Standard	Displays tasks whose scheduling information, such as durations, start and finish dates, or resource reassignments, you've changed, and for which you need to send a TeamUpdate message to the affected resources through workgroup communications.
Using Resource In Date Range	Interactive	Displays tasks that have a specified resource assigned during a specified date range.

Task filter	Type	Description
Using Resource	Interactive	Displays the tasks that are assigned to the resource you specify.
Work Overbudget	Standard	Displays only tasks whose actual work is greater than their baseline work.

Resource Filters

Each resource filter can be applied to any resource view.

Resource filter	Type	Description
All Resources	Standard	Displays all the resources in your project plan.
Confirmed Assignments	Standard	Displays each resource who has agreed to perform all the tasks he or she has been asked to perform. (A resource's assignments are confirmed when the resource accepts each task assignment on a workgroup TeamAssign message and a Yes appears in the Confirmed field for the resource.)
Cost Greater Than	Interactive	Displays only those resources whose scheduled cost is greater than the amount you specify.
Cost Overbudget	Standard	Displays only resources whose scheduled cost is greater than the baseline cost.
Date Range	Interactive	Displays only resources whose assignments start or finish within the date range you specify.
Group	Interactive	Displays only resources belonging to the resource group you specify.
In Progress Assignments	Standard	Displays only resources who have started assignments that haven't been completed yet.
Linked Fields	Standard	Displays only resources to whom information from other programs has been linked.
Overallocated Resources	Standard	Displays only resources that are scheduled to do more hours of work than they are allocated to do in a given time period. An example of an overallocated resource is one scheduled to do 10 hours of work in one day but is allocated only 8 hours of work per day.
Resource Range	Interactive	Displays only resources within the ID range you specify.
Resources—Material	Standard	Displays only the material resources in your resource list.
Resources—Work	Standard	Displays only the work resources in your resource list.

Resource filter	Type	Description
Resources With Attachments	Standard	Displays resources that have OLE objects attached or a note in the Notes box of the Resource Information dialog box.
Resources/ Assignments With Overtime	Standard	Displays only those resources that are working overtime, or those assignments on which resources are working overtime.
Should Start By	Interactive	Displays only resources with assignments that should have started by the date you specify but have not.
Should Start/Finish By	Interactive	Displays only those resources with task assignments that should have started or finished within the date range you specify.
Slipped/Late Progress	Standard	Displays resources assigned to tasks that either haven't finished by their baseline finish date or that haven't been progressing on schedule (by comparing the amount of work scheduled for the task, BCWS, to the amount of work that has been completed, BCWP, in the Earned Value table).
Slipping Assignments	Standard	Displays resources whose task assignments are behind schedule (their actual start or finish dates are later than their baseline start or finish dates).
Unconfirmed Assignments	Standard	Displays only resources who haven't yet agreed to perform all the tasks they've been requested to perform (via a workgroup TeamAssign message).
Unstarted Assignments	Standard	Displays only resources who have accepted but haven't yet started their assignments.
Work Complete	Standard	Displays only resources that have completed all of their assigned tasks.
Work Incomplete	Standard	Displays only resources assigned to tasks that are marked as less then 100% complete.
Work Overbudget	Standard	Displays only resources whose scheduled work is greater than baseline work.

Apply a Filter

A filter is always attached to a view. The default filter for each task view is the All Tasks filter. The default filter for each resource view is the All Resources filter. If you want all the tasks or resources in your project to appear in the current view, then you don't need to apply a different filter. If you want to focus on a subset of the tasks or resources in your project, however, then you do need to apply a different filter.

You can apply the filter that displays only those tasks or resources that share certain characteristics. For each filter, you can specify whether the filter displays only those tasks or resources that meet the filter criteria (and hides the tasks or resources that don't) or highlights the tasks or resources of interest in blue (while still displaying the other tasks or resources).

After you apply a filter, you can make all tasks or resources reappear by reapplying the All Tasks or All Resources filter, which removes the filtering effect from the view but leaves the filter itself in your project file.

To apply a filter from the menu

1 On the **View Bar**, click a view.

   To select a view that doesn't appear on the **View Bar**, click **More Views**, click the view you want in the **Views** list, and then click **Apply**.

2 On the **Project** menu, point to **Filtered for**, and then click the filter you want to apply.

To apply a filter not on the menu

1 On the **View Bar**, click a view.

   To select a view that doesn't appear on the **View Bar**, click **More Views**, click the view you want in the **Views** list, and then click **Apply**.

2 On the **Project** menu, point to **Filtered for**, and then click **More Filters.**

3 In the **Filters** list, click the filter you want.

4 Click **Apply**.

5 If you apply an interactive filter, type the requested values, and then click **OK**.

If you want the filter to highlight rather than hide tasks, use this procedure and the More Filters dialog box. Click the filter you want, and then click Highlight.

To add a frequently used filter to the menu

1 On the **View Bar,** click a view.

   To select a view that doesn't appear on the **View Bar**, click **More Views**, click the view you want in the **Views** list, and then click **Apply**.

2 On the **Project** menu, point to **Filtered for**, and then click **More Filters.**

3 In the **Filters** list, click the filter you want to add to the menu.

4 Click **Edit**.

5 Select the **Show in menu** check box.

6 Click **OK**.

7 If you want to apply the filter, click **Apply**

   If you want to close the dialog box without applying the filter, click **Close**.

When you no longer need to see a subset of tasks or resources, you can display all of them again.

To display all tasks or resources

1 On the **Project** menu, point to **Filtered for**.

2 If a task filter is applied, click **All Tasks.**

3 If a resource filter is applied, click **All Resources**.

Filter Your View Quickly Using AutoFilters

Standard and interactive filters typically contain fairly broad sets of criteria that distinguish one category of tasks or resources from another. For example, the Critical filter distinguishes the broad category "critical tasks" from the broad category "noncritical tasks." The Overallocated Resources filter distinguishes the broad category "overallocated resources" from the broad category "not overallocated resources."

Unlike standard and interactive filters, AutoFilters distinguish tasks or resources based on specific criteria; in fact, you typically use an AutoFilter to distinguish a subset of tasks or resources based on one very specific criterion. The reason you can do this is that an AutoFilter takes as its set of criteria the data that currently appear in one column in a sheet view. Change the data, and the set of AutoFilter criteria changes also.

For example, suppose 5 tasks listed in the Gantt Chart have durations of 3 days, 2 days, 4 days, 2 days, and 2 days. Each of these durations appears as a criterion in the AutoFilter for the Duration column. If you select the "2 days" criterion that appears in the AutoFilter's criteria list, then only those 3 tasks with durations of 2 days will be displayed.

AutoFilters not only enable you to distinguish tasks or resources by applying very specific criteria, but also allow you to filter information quickly and easily. After you activate the AutoFilters feature, an AutoFilter button appears in the heading of each column. The high visibility of AutoFilters and the ease with which you can select a particular AutoFilter criterion enable you to filter tasks or resources rapidly.

You can narrow the information displayed by applying more than one AutoFilter at one time. You can also use AutoFilters in conjunction with standard and interactive filters.

The AutoFilter of each field includes the predefined criteria All and Custom in its criteria list. By clicking All, which is the default criterion for all fields, you remove the filter criterion from that field. By clicking Custom, you can create your own filter for that field. In addition to All and Custom, each AutoFilter also includes unique predefined criteria. For example, the AutoFilter for the Duration field includes the predefined criteria <= 1 day, > 1 day, <= 1 week, and > 1 week.

To apply an AutoFilter

 AutoFilter

1. If AutoFilters are not turned on, click **AutoFilter**.

   After you turn on the AutoFilter feature, AutoFilters appear in each sheet view, not just the current sheet view.
2. In the field to which you want to apply an AutoFilter, click the arrow in the column heading, and then click the value for which you want to filter the table.

   The arrow and field name for that column become blue.
3. To filter for an additional condition based on a value in another field, repeat step 2 in the other field.
4. To filter one field for two values or to apply comparison operators other than **Equals**, click the arrow in the column, click **Custom**, and then complete the **Custom AutoFilter** dialog box.
5. If information changes, you can refresh your AutoFilter settings by clicking the column's AutoFilter arrow, and then reselecting the filtering value.
6. To remove the filtering on a specific row, click **All** in the AutoFilter list for that column.

 AutoFilter

7. To turn off all AutoFilters, click **AutoFilter** again.

If you apply a particularly useful custom AutoFilter frequently, it might be faster to save it and then make it available from the **Filtered for** submenu.

To save a custom AutoFilter

 AutoFilter

1. If AutoFilters are not turned on, click **AutoFilter**.
2. Click the AutoFilter arrow in the column heading for the custom AutoFilter you want to save.
3. Click **Custom**, and then click **Save**.
4. In the **Filter Definition** dialog box, make your custom changes to the filter.
5. To display the custom filter on the **Filtered for** submenu (under the **Project** menu), select the **Show in menu** check box, and then click **OK**. Click **OK** again in the **Custom AutoFilter** dialog box.

Creating or Modifying a View, Table, or Filter

The many predefined Microsoft Project views, tables, and filters can be used to display the information you want in most situations. However, suppose you have a unique requirement and none of the predefined views, tables, or filters meet your needs. In this case, you can create a view, table, or filter from scratch, create one based on an existing one, or modify an existing one.

Your new or modified view, table, or filter is saved only with the project file in which you created or modified it, and you can use it only with that project file. You can, however, make it available to other project files by using the Organizer.

Create or Modify a View

The predefined views that come with Microsoft Project are designed to display in useful formats the information you're most likely to want. However, if none of the predefined views meets your information or formatting needs, you can create a new view or modify an existing one.

If the view you want differs significantly from any existing views, create a new view.

If the view you want is similar to a predefined view, modify a copy of the existing view and save the modified version under a different name. The original predefined view remains unchanged.

If the view you want requires only minor changes to a predefined view, you can edit the view. When you edit a view, you change the original view and not a copy of it. After you save the changes you've made to an existing view, you can't automatically reset the view to its original form. If you're not sure you need to edit a view, copy it, and then modify the renamed copy instead.

To create or modify a view

1 On the **View Bar**, click **More Views**.

2 To create a view from scratch, click **New**, click **Single view** or **Combination view**, and then click **OK**.

If you edit an existing view, you can't automatically reset it to its original form.

To create a view based on an existing view, click that view in the **Views** list, and then click **Copy**.

To edit an existing view, click that view in the **Views** list, and then click **Edit**.

3 In the **View Definition** dialog box, enter a name for the view, select a screen type for a view created from scratch, and select a table, group, and filter.

To create a new combination view, click a view name in the **Top** box for the top pane and click a view name in the **Bottom** box for the bottom pane.

4 To specify whether the filter should be a highlighting filter, select or clear the **Highlight filter** checkbox.

5 To display the new view on the **View Bar** and **View** menu, select the **Show in menu** check box.

6 Click **OK**.

7 To display the view, click **Apply**.

Create or Modify a Table

The predefined tables that come with Microsoft Project display many useful sets of task or resource information, most of which should satisfy your information needs most of the time. However, if none of the tables provided with Microsoft Project displays the combination of information you need, you can create a table from scratch, create a table based on an existing table, or edit an existing table.

When you create a table, you start with a blank table to which you add each column and specify details such as the column title, column width, and data alignment within a column. When you create a table based on an existing table, you modify a copy of the existing table to suit your needs, without changing the original table. When you edit an existing table, you change the original table, so you should edit a table only if you're sure you want it changed.

To create or modify a table

1 On the **View** menu, point to **Table**, and then click **More Tables**.

2 To create or modify a task table, click **Task**, and then click a table in the **Tables** list.

To create or modify a resource table, click **Resource**, and then click a table in the **Tables** list.

3 To create a table from scratch, click **New**.

To create a table based on an existing table, click that table in the **Tables** list, and then click **Copy**.

To edit an existing table, click that table in the **Tables** list, and then click **Edit**.

If you edit an existing table, you can't automatically reset it to its original form.

4 In the **Name** box, type a name for the table.

5 If you're creating a table from scratch, then for each field you want to include, select the field name, the field text alignment, and the width of the column.

If you're copying or modifying an existing table, then for each field listed, click the field name, field text alignment, and column width you want.

6 To add a column title other than the field name, type a title in the **Title** field, and then select the text alignment in the **Align Title** field.

7 Repeat steps 5 and 6 for each column you're adding to the table.

8 In the **Date** format box, click a date format for date fields.

9 To display the table on the **Table** submenu, select the **Show in menu** check box.

10 To prevent the first column from scrolling, select the **Lock first column** check box.
11 Click **OK**.
12 To display the table, click **Apply**.

If the table you've created or modified can't be applied to the current view, the Apply button is unavailable. For example, if you've created a table based on Tracking, a task table, and the Resource Sheet is displayed, the Apply button will appear gray.

To delete a table

1 On the **View** menu, point to **Table**, and then click **More Tables**.
2 Click **Organizer**.
3 Make sure the **Tables** tab is active.
4 Select the table you want to delete from the list on the right.
5 Click **Delete**.

If an existing Microsoft Project table displays nearly all the information you need, you can modify it quickly by adding a column to it to display the "missing" information.

To modify a table quickly by adding a column

1 In a sheet view, apply the table to which you want to add a column, and then select the column to the left of where you want to insert the new column.
2 On the **Insert** menu, click **Column**.
3 In the **Column Definition** dialog box, specify the field name, title, title alignment, data alignment and width of the column.
4 To set the column width to the longest item in the column, click **Best Fit**.

If you don't need the field information displayed in a column, you can remove (or hide) that column. When you hide a column, the information that's in the column isn't removed from your project file; it's simply hidden.

To remove a column from a table

1 In a sheet view, click the column heading to select the entire column you want to remove.
2 On the **Edit** menu, click **Hide Column**.

Create or Modify a Filter

The predefined filters that come with Microsoft Project enable you to display many useful subsets of tasks or resources, each subset based on a different set of criteria. However, if none of the filters provided with Microsoft Project displays exactly the subset of tasks or resources you want, you can create a filter from scratch, create a filter based on an existing filter, or edit an existing filter.

When you create a filter, you start with a blank filter to which you add each criterion. When you create a filter based on an existing filter, you modify a copy of the existing filter without changing the original. When you edit an existing filter, you change the original filter.

To create or modify a filter

1. On the **View Bar**, click any view.

   To select a view that doesn't appear on the **View Bar**, click **More Views**, click the view you want in the **Views** list, and then click **Apply**.
2. On the **Project** menu, point to **Filtered for**, and then click **More Filters**.
3. To create or modify a task filter, click **Task**.

   To create or modify a resource filter, click **Resource**.
4. To create a filter from scratch, click **New**.

   To create a filter based on an existing filter, click that filter in the **Filters** list, and then click **Copy**.

   To edit an existing filter, click that filter in the **Filters** list, and then click **Edit**.

   If you edit an existing filter, you can't automatically reset it to its original form.
5. In the **Name** box, type a new name for the filter.
6. Under **Filter**, in the **Field Name** field, click a field name.
7. In the **Test** field, click the test for the filter, such as **equals**, **contains**, or **is less than**.
8. In the **Value(s)** field, click a value to test for. You can select another field name to compare the field with, or you can type in a value.

   If you need to enter a range of values, separated them with a comma (,) For example, if you clicked **is within** in the **Test** field, type **"From"?,"To"?** to create an interactive filter that requests a range of dates to test for.
9. If the filter will contain more than one criterion row, select additional conditions on the row immediately underneath the first row, and then click an operator in the **And/Or** field of the same row. You might need to use the left arrow key to see the **And/Or** field.
10. If you want the filter name to show on the **Filtered for** submenu, select the **Show in menu** check box.
11. Click **OK**.
12. To apply the filter immediately, click **Apply**.

Copy a View, Table, or Filter to Another Project

The views, tables, and filters you create or modify exist only in the current project file. If you want to make them available to another project, you can use the Organizer.

To copy a view, table, or filter to another project

1 On the **Tools** menu, click **Organizer**, and then click the **Views** tab, the **Tables** tab, or the **Filters** tab.

2 If you clicked the **Tables** tab or the **Filters** tab, click **Task** or **Resource**.

3 In the list on the right, click the view, table, or filter you want to copy.

4 Under **Views available in** on the left side, select the project to which you want to copy the view, table or filter.

5 Click **Copy**.

Delete a View, Table, or Filter from Your Project

The global.mpt file contains all standard views, tables, and filters that are available in all project files. It also contains reports, fields, toolbars, calendars, forms, and more.

If you don't need particular views, tables, or filters or you don't want team members to use them, you can delete them. When you delete a view, table, or filter, you delete it from the project file only. A copy of it continues to be stored in the Microsoft Project global file, global.mpt. Deleting a view, table, or filter does not delete information from your project file.

To delete a view, table, or filter from a project

1 On the **Tools** menu, click **Organizer**, and then click the **Views** tab, the **Tables** tab, or the **Filters** tab.

2 If you clicked the **Tables** tab or the **Filters** tab, click **Task** or **Resource** (above the GLOBAL.MPT box on the left).

3 In the list on the right, click the view, table, or filter you want to delete.

4 Click **Delete**.

Modifying Detail Information in Special Views

The majority of Microsoft Project views contain sheet views, such as the Gantt Chart, Resource Usage, and PA_Optimistic Gantt views. To display the information you want in sheet views, you can apply tables and filters.

But other types of views display information in other formats. These special views include:

- Resource Graph.
- Network Diagrams.
- Usage views.
- Forms.

Rather than displaying information in tables as do the sheet views, these special views display information according to their own format. You can change the fields of information shown in these views by changing their *details*. This is done differently for each special view type.

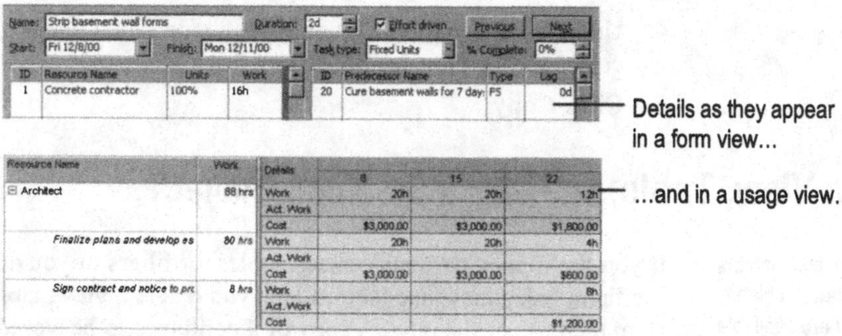

Details as they appear in a form view...
...and in a usage view.

Displaying the information you want in views that don't include table portions or include both table and non-table portions requires that you use one of several methods, depending on the view. One of the most common methods is to change the set of details that appear in a view. You can change the set of details in the Task Usage view, the Resource Usage view, and in all the form views. But both the Network Diagram and the Resource Graph have unique methods for changing the information that appears on them.

Display the Information You Want in the Resource Graph

By default, the Resource Graph displays each resource's peak units in a graph of units across time. In the same graph format, among other details, you can display:

- Work.
- Overallocation.
- Remaining Availability.
- Cost.
- Work Availability.
- Unit Availability.

To display the information you want in the Resource Graph

1 On the **View Bar**, click **Resource Graph**.
2 On the **Format** menu, point to **Details**.
3 Click the type of information you want to display from the list of available details.

Display the Information You Want in Network Diagrams

There are three types of Network Diagram views:

- Network Diagram.
- Descriptive Network Diagram.
- Relationship Diagram.

If the default information that appears in the Network Diagram doesn't meet your information needs, you can display different task information in the Network Diagram boxes. For example, instead of displaying the scheduled start and finish dates, you can display the constraint type and the task type.

You can change the details displayed in the Network Diagram boxes.

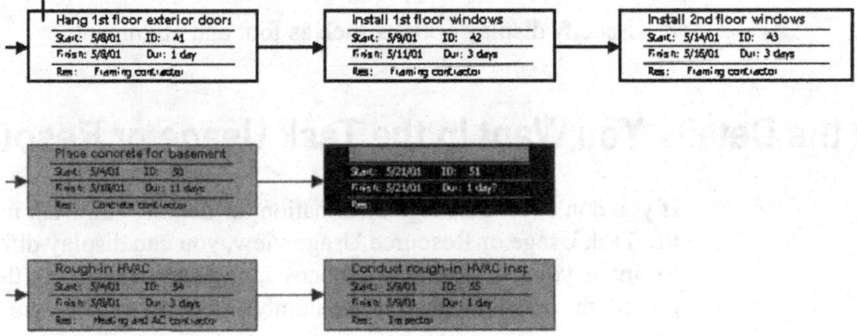

To display the information you want in the Network Diagram

1 On the **View Bar**, click **Network Diagram**.
2 On the **Format** menu, click **Box**.
3 In the **Data template** field of the **Format Box** dialog box, click **More Templates**.
4 Select the type of Network Diagram box whose details you want to change.

   The information and layout of each field in the selected Network Diagram box is shown in the Preview box.

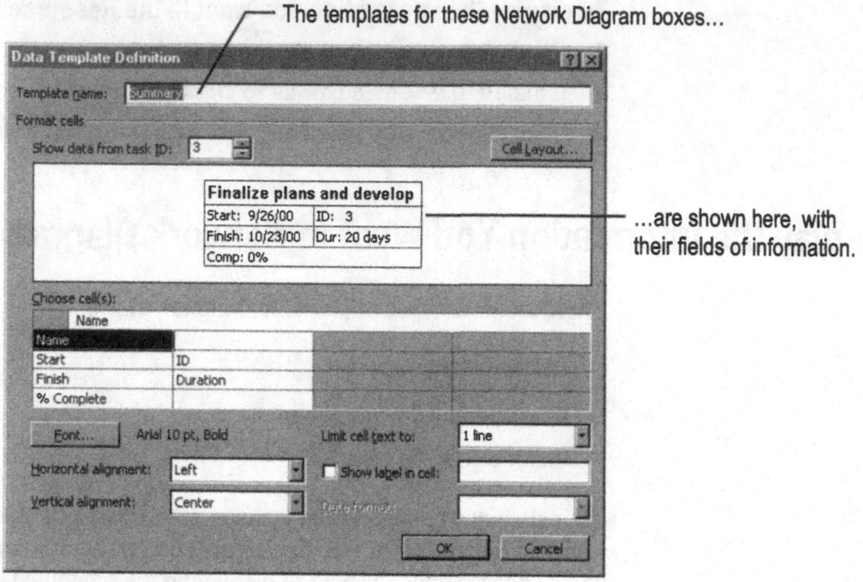

5 Choose **Edit**.

6 Under **Choose cells,** pick the name of the field in the locations of the grid where you want them to appear.

7 Specify display options such as font and alignment.

Display the Details You Want in the Task Usage or Resource Usage View

If you don't see the usage information, or details, you want in the timesheet portion of the Task Usage or Resource Usage view, you can display different information. For example, you can display actual costs, cumulative work, or the cost per resource for a given time period instead of the number of hours each resource is scheduled to work.

To change the details displayed in a Usage view

1 On the **View Bar**, click **Task Usage** or **Resource Usage**.

2 On the **Format** menu, point to **Details**, and then click the type of information you want to display.

Display the Information You Want in a Form View

The bottom portion of each form view displays information as a set of details. If the set of details that appears on a form view doesn't meet your information needs, you can display different information by selecting a different set of details. For example, you can display the resource cost or resource work for a task instead of assigned resources and predecessor tasks on the Task Form.

To display different information in a form view

1. On the **View Bar**, click **More Views**, click the form view you want to use in the **Views** list, and then click **Apply**.
2. If the view is a combination view, like the Task Entry view, click the form.
3. On the **Format** menu, point to **Details**, and then click the type of information you want to display from the list of available details.

13

Making Your Project Look How You Want

After you display the project information in the view you want, with any applied tables, groups, or filters, you can make that information look the way you want. For example, you might decide that certain key information should stand out. To get a project overview, you might want to see more of your schedule at one time. To focus on a few important tasks, you might want to see less of your entire schedule and more of the details.

If the default appearance of a view doesn't meet your needs at first, you can change it. For instance, you can:

- Change the appearance of information. For example, to make key information stand out, you can highlight it by applying bold formatting.
- Display up to four sets of Gantt bars for each task. For example, you might display a normal Gantt bar and one that shows progress on the same task.
- Change the color, pattern, and shape of individual Gantt bars as well as of Gantt bars for specific task categories (such as the Gantt bars for critical tasks).
- Display a longer time period on a timescale to see more tasks and less detail at one time, or a shorter time period to see fewer tasks and more detail at one time.

These are just a few of the ways you can change the appearance of information in views. You can also add information to Gantt bars, change the appearance of Network Diagram boxes, show or hide specific task bars on the Calendar view, change the type of graph displayed on the Resource Graph view, and much more.

General Formatting in Views

This section contains formatting procedures that can be applied to a wide variety of Microsoft Project views. You can:

- Format all the text in a view for a category of tasks or resources.
- Change the timescale in a view to see a different level of detail.
- Format the gridlines in a view.

The types of views in which you can format these items are noted in each section below.

Format the Text of a Task or Resource Category

Suppose yesterday you needed to focus on critical tasks. Today you want to point out overallocated resources to your manager. To visually distinguish a class of tasks or resources—or simply to change its appearance to suit your needs—you can change the appearance of predefined task and resource categories.

Task items whose text can be formatted as a collection include items such as critical tasks, milestone tasks, summary tasks, external tasks, and more.

Resource items whose text can be formatted as a collection include allocated resources and overallocated resources, among others.

When you change the appearance of a category of tasks or resources, you change the appearance of all the information for each task or resource in that category, all at once. For example, if you make a category of tasks on the Gantt Chart view bold, the entire row of text for each task in the category appears bold. If you apply a different table, the appropriate rows in the new table will also appear bold. However, if you switch to the Task Sheet view, the task category that appears bold in the Gantt Chart view will appear as normal, unbolded text in the Task Sheet view. The formatting you apply to text in one view does not transfer to another view.

You change the appearance of task and resource information by changing the font, font style, font size, and color. A *font* is a family of characters—letters, numbers, and symbols—that share a particular look. For example, characters in the Arial font look like this:

Arial characters

Characters in the Rockwell font look like this:

Rockwell characters

There are thousands of fonts for you to choose from for use in displaying and printing your project.

A *font style* consists of any extras you add to text, which can be bold, italic, bold italic, and underlining. You can apply a font style to any font you choose. *Size* refers to the size of the text; it is specified in *points,* such as 10 points or 12 points.

Here are some examples combining fonts, font styles, and font sizes:

Arial bold 10 ***Arial bold italic 12*** *Rockwell italic 10*

You can also add color to the text. The capabilities of your computer and printer determine which fonts, font styles, and font sizes you can display and print.

You can change the text formatting task and resource categories in the following types of views:

- Gantt Charts.
- Usage views.
- Graphs and diagrams except the Relationship Diagram.
- Sheets.

The available categories you can format vary from view to view.

To format the text for a category of tasks or resources

1 On the **View Bar**, click the view you want to reformat.

To select a view that doesn't appear on the **View Bar**, click **More Views**, click the view you want in the **Views** list, and then click **Apply**.

1 On the **Format** menu, click **Text Styles**.

2 In the **Item to Change** box, click the task or resource category whose appearance you want to change, and then select formatting options for that category.

You can change the appearance of text for individual tasks and resources in sheet views. See "Change the Appearance of Individual Text" later in this chapter.

Change the Timescale to See a Different Level of Detail

As a project manager, you probably like to stay on top of time-related information in your project, such as task schedules or the day-by-day breakdown of the hours worked by resources. In Microsoft Project, a number of views display time-related information on a *timescale*:

- Gantt Charts.
- Usage views.

- Resource Graph view.
- Calendar view.

You can display this time-related information in various ways. Sometimes you might want to see as much information as possible within a long time period. Other times you might want to focus on just a few events within a short time period. You can display time-related information within the time period you choose by changing the timescale. When you display a longer time period on a timescale, you can see more events at one time, but in less detail. When you display a shorter time period, you can see fewer events, but in more detail. On views that have both major and minor timescales, such as the Gantt Chart view, you can adjust the scales independently.

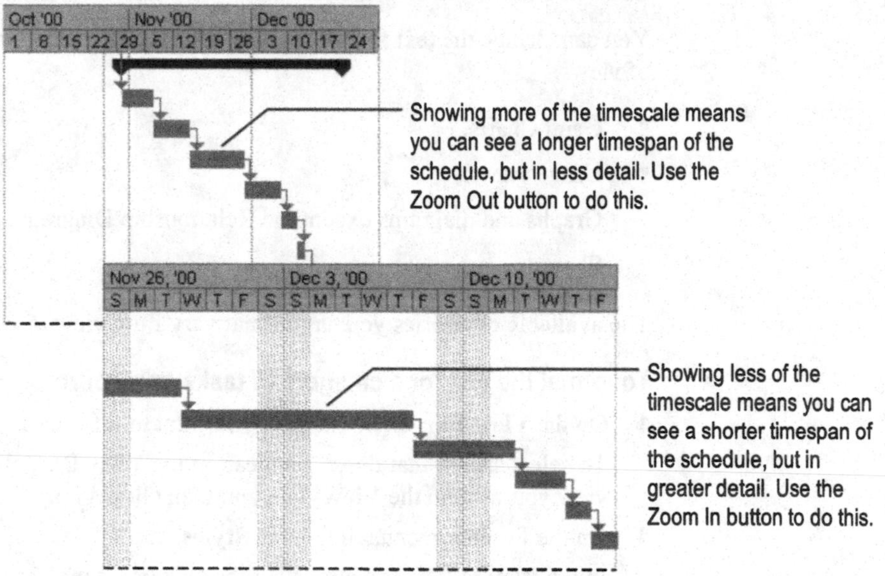

To change the timescale to see a different level of detail

You can quickly zoom in and out of a view by clicking  or .

1. On the **View Bar**, click **Gantt Chart** or another time-related view containing a timescale.

   To select a view that doesn't appear on the **View Bar**, click **More Views**, click the view you want in the **Views** list, and then click **Apply**.
2. On the **Format** menu, click **Timescale**, and then click the **Timescale** tab.
3. In the **Units** boxes under **Major scale** and **Minor scale**, click the units of time you want to use.

The effect of every change you make is shown in the Preview area of the dialog box.

4. To display only the major scale time unit, click **None** in the **Units** box under **Minor scale**.
5. In the **Label** boxes under **Major scale** and **Minor scale**, click the labels you want to use.

6 In the **Align** boxes under **Major scale** and **Minor scale**, click the alignment you want.

7 In the **Count** boxes under **Major scale** and **Minor scale**, type the numbers of intervals you want between the unit labels on the major scale and on the minor scale.

For example, if the major scale unit is months, and you type 1, the scale will be separated into 1-month segments.

8 To display a horizontal line between the major and minor scales, select the **Scale separator** check box.

9 To display vertical lines between unit labels, select the **Tick lines** check boxes.

10 To compress or expand the layout of the timescale so that you can see more or less time in the same space, type a percentage in the **Size** box.

Microsoft Project adjusts major and minor scales by the same amount.

Format Gridlines

Gridlines indicate time intervals, such as on the chart portion of the Gantt Chart. Gridlines separate columns and rows of information in sheet and form views. They separate titles both vertically, as in the columns on a sheet view, and horizontally, as on a timescale. Gridlines make it easier to read and interpret the information in a view.

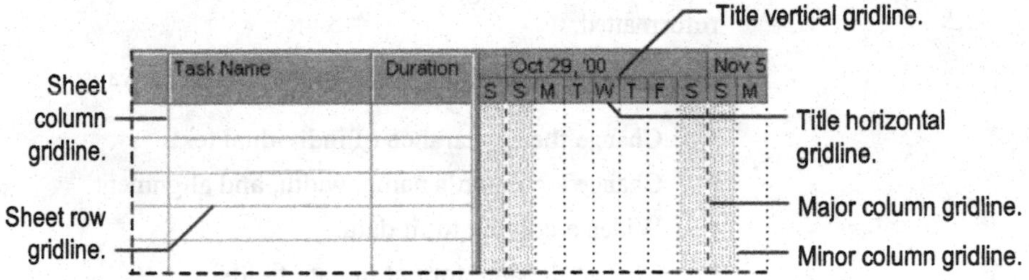

Examples of gridlines you can format on the Gantt Chart view.

You can change the appearance of gridlines in the following types of views:

- Gantt Charts.
- Usage views.
- Resource Graph.
- Sheets.

To format gridlines

1 On the **View Bar**, click the view whose gridlines you want to format.

To select a view that doesn't appear on the **View Bar**, click **More Views**, click the view you want in the **Views** list, and then click **Apply**.

2 On the **Format** menu, click **Gridlines**.

3 In the **Line to change** list, click the type of gridline you want to change.

4 In the **Type** box under **Normal**, click the line pattern you want, for example, a dotted line or a solid line.

5 If you want to hide the selected line type, click the blank option in the **Type** box.

6 In the **Color** box under **Normal**, click the line color you want.

7 If the gridline appears repeatedly and you want contrasting gridlines at specified intervals, click an interval, line type, and line color under **At interval**.

8 To skip a gridline at certain intervals, click the blank option in the **Type** box under **At interval**.

Formatting Sheet Views

Sheet views have some formatting already applied by default. You can take this further and format a variety of sheet view elements yourself. Column headings, individual data, and even entire categories of information can easily be rewritten, realigned, and reformatted.

You can format all sheet views in the following ways:

- Change the appearance of individual text.
- Change a column's name, width, and alignment.
- Widen a column to fit data.
- Change the date format in date fields.

You can apply the formatting procedures in this section to the following sheet views:

- Task Sheet.
- Resource Sheet.
- PA_PERT Entry Sheet.

You can also apply the formatting procedures in this section to the sheet portions of the following types of views:

- Gantt Charts.
- Usage views.
- Combination views.

Change the Appearance of Text

To remain aware of the particular piece of text information, to call someone else's attention to it, or simply to distinguish the text from other text, you can change the appearance of that individual item.

You can change the appearance of text by changing its font, font style, font size, and color.

The capabilities of your computer and printer determine which fonts, font styles, font sizes, and colors you can display and print.

You can change the appearance of individual text only in the table fields of sheet views.

To apply formatting to individual text

1 On the **View Bar**, click the sheet view, such as the Gantt Chart, Resource Sheet, or Task Usage view, whose individual text formatting you want to change.

To select a view that doesn't appear on the **View Bar**, click **More Views**, click the view you want in the **Views** list, and then click **Apply**.

2 In the sheet view, select the text whose appearance you want to change.

To change the text for an entire row, click the row heading.

To change the text for an entire column, click the column heading.

3 On the **Format** menu, click **Font**.

4 Select the formatting options you want.

You can also use the Font, Font Size, Bold, Italic, and Underline buttons on the Formatting toolbar to make individual text changes.

Change a Column's Name, Alignment, and Width

Microsoft Project provides default names for the column headings that appear in tables in sheet views. For example, on the Entry table in the Gantt Chart view, the default name of the column that contains task start dates is Start. If a default column name doesn't tell you what kind of information is contained in the column or the name doesn't conform with your organization's standards, you can change the name that appears in the column heading.

You can also change the default column width to accommodate longer (or shorter) column names and data. You can also specify whether column names and data are centered within the column or aligned left or right.

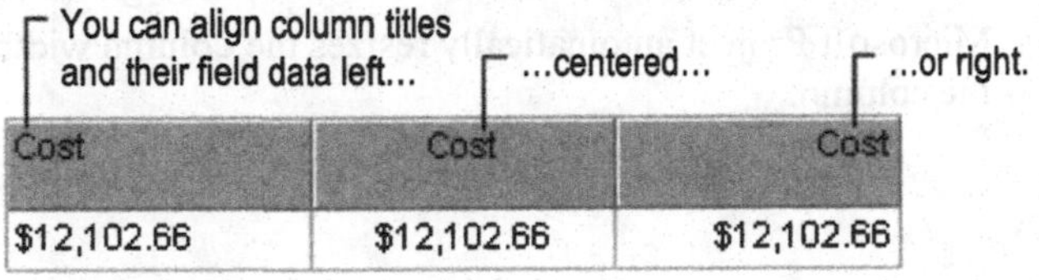
You can align column titles and their field data left...
...centered...
...or right.
Cost
Cost
Cost
$12,102.66
$12,102.66
$12,102.66

The changes you make to a column's name, alignment, or width appear only in the table in which you make the changes. For example, if you change the name of the Start column to Start Date in the Entry table, the Start column in the Schedule table still appears with the name Start unless you explicitly change it there too.

To change a column's name, alignment, or width

1. On the **View Bar**, click the view you want to modify.

   To select a view that doesn't appear on the **View Bar**, click **More Views**, click the view you want in the **Views** list, and then click **Apply**.
2. Double-click the column heading whose name, alignment, or width you want to change.
3. To change the name of the column heading, type a new column heading for the field in the **Title** box.
4. To change the alignment of the column heading, select the alignment you want in the **Align title** box.
5. To change the alignment of the column information, select the alignment you want in the **Align data** box.
6. To change the column width, enter the width you want in the **Width** box.

Widen a Column to Fit Data

A long piece of data in a field of a column is sometimes cut off by the right edge of a column. This means the column isn't wide enough to display the entire piece of data. You can solve that problem by quickly adjusting the width of the column to match the length of the longest piece of data contained in that column.

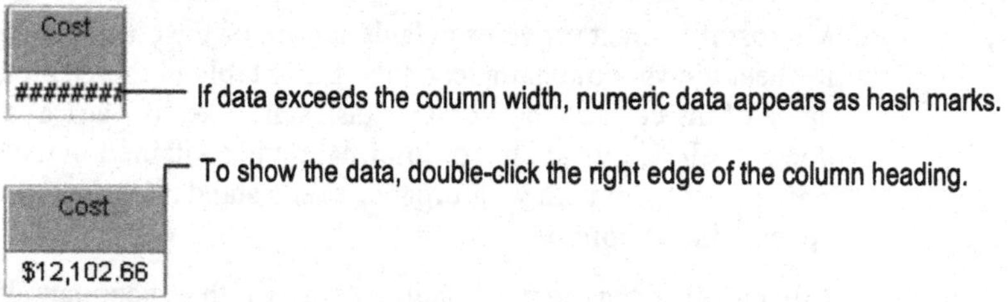

To widen a column to fit all data

- In a sheet view, double-click the border to the right of the column name.

  Microsoft Project automatically resizes the column width to fit the longest entry in the column.

Change the Date Format for Date Fields

Dates appear in several fields, such as the Start and Finish fields, that can be displayed in sheet views. By default, dates in date fields appear in the following format: Fri 10/27/00. If this format doesn't suit your needs, you can change it to any of a number of date formats available in Microsoft Project. Examples of available date formats are:

- 10/27/00
- Fri 10/27/00 4:45 PM
- 10/27
- Oct 27
- Oct 27 '00
- October 27, 2000

Because the date format is a global setting, once you set it, that date format applies in any view that contains date fields.

To globally change the date format for all date fields

1. On the **Tools** menu, click **Options**, and then click the **View** tab.
2. In the **Date format** box, click the format you want to use.

You can also specify which date format you want to display in an individual table without affecting the date format that appears in all other tables.

To change the date format in an individual table

1. On the **View** menu, point to **Table**, and then click **More Tables**.
2. In the **Tables** list, click the table whose date format you want to change, and then click **Edit**.
3. In the **Date format** box, click the date format you want to display.

Formatting the Gantt Chart Views

As the most frequently used of all Microsoft Project views, Gantt Charts can be formatted in more ways than any other view. Although Microsoft Project applies default formatting to Gantt bars, you can change their look to include or highlight certain information, or to conform with organization standards. You can format Gantt bars manually or use the GanttChartWizard.

The procedures in this section explain how to format the chart portion of Gantt Charts in the following ways:

- Change the color, shape, and pattern of Gantt bars.
- Change the height of Gantt bars.
- Add text information to Gantt bars.
- Create a custom Gantt bar for a task category.
- Roll up a Gantt bar to a summary Gantt bar.
- Display multiple Gantt bars for each task.
- Change the appearance of the link lines that connect Gantt bars.
- Change the appearance of nonworking time.
- Format a Gantt Chart automatically with the GanttChartWizard.

The procedures in this section apply to all the Gantt Chart views. They also apply to the Gantt Chart portions of the Resource Allocation and Task Entry views.

For information on formatting other elements of the Gantt Chart view, such as text, timescales, date formats, and gridlines, see the procedures in "General Formatting in Views" and "Formatting Sheet Views" earlier in this chapter.

Change the Color, Shape, and Pattern of Gantt Bars

To help you focus on a particular set of tasks, you can change the appearance of the Gantt bars for all the tasks that belong to a predefined task category. For example, you can change the color, shape, or pattern of all milestone tasks or all summary tasks.

When you change the appearance of Gantt bars for a category of tasks, you change the appearance of all the Gantt bars for all the tasks in that category, all at once.

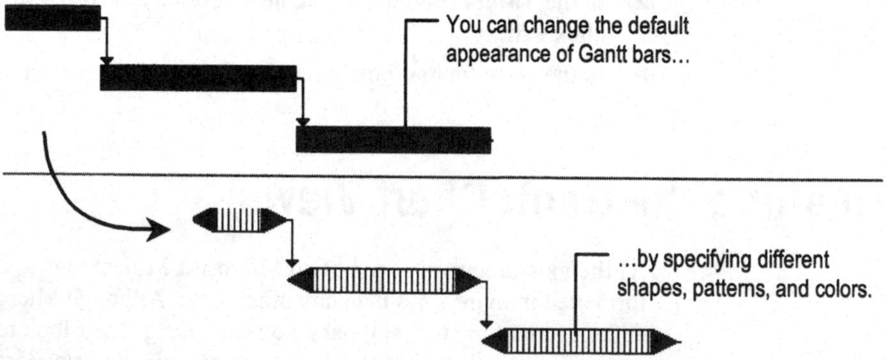
You can change the default appearance of Gantt bars...
...by specifying different shapes, patterns, and colors.

To change the color, shape, or pattern of a Gantt bar category

1 On the **View Bar**, click the view containing the Gantt Chart you want to format.

2 On the **Format** menu, click **Bar Styles**.

3 In the table, under **Name**, select the category (such as Task, Progress, or Summary) you want to change, and then click the **Bars** tab.

4 In the **Shape** boxes under **Start**, **Middle**, and **End**, click the Gantt bar shapes you want for the start, middle, and end of the Gantt bar you're changing.

5 In the **Pattern** box under **Middle**, click a Gantt bar pattern.

6 In the **Color** boxes under **Start**, **Middle**, and **End**, click the bar colors you want for the start, middle, and end shapes of the Gantt bar.

Some categories, such as Milestone and Deadline, have only a start shape. Others, such as Summary, have shapes for the start and end as well as for the middle.

You can draw attention to an individual task by formatting its Gantt bar differently from other bars in that category. When you use the following procedure, you change the appearance of an individual Gantt bar without affecting any other Gantt bars.

To change the color, shape, or pattern of an individual Gantt bar

1 On the **View Bar**, click the view containing the Gantt Chart you want to format.

2 In the **Task Name** field, select the tasks whose Gantt bars you want to reformat.

3 On the **Format** menu, click **Bar**, and then click the **Bar shape** tab.

4 In the **Shape** boxes under **Start**, **Middle**, and **End**, click the Gantt bar shapes you want.

5 In the **Pattern** box under **Middle**, click a Gantt bar pattern.

6 In the **Color** boxes under **Start**, **Middle**, and **End**, click the Gantt bar colors you want.

Change the Height of Gantt Bars

Microsoft Project displays Gantt bars with a standard predefined height that shows up clearly on your screen and in printed Gantt Chart views. However, if the chart portion of the Gantt Chart is dense with information, you might want to make room by reducing the bar height. Conversely, if you want to draw attention to the bars, you can increase bar height. When you adjust the bar height, you change the height of all Gantt bars.

To change the height of Gantt bars

1 On the **View Bar**, click the Gantt Chart view whose Gantt bar heights you want to change.

2 On the **Format** menu, click **Layout**.

3 In the **Bar height** box, enter the height of the Gantt bars in points.

Add Text Information to a Category of Gantt Bars

In the Gantt Chart, the names of assigned resources appear to the right of Gantt bars by default. In the Tracking Gantt, the percent complete appears to the right of the Gantt bars. The Leveling Gantt shows the amount of slack. You can add, change, or remove the text information you want on the Gantt bars. For example, you can add task names, cost, slack, remaining duration, and many other pieces of information. You can specify that the information appear at the top, bottom, left, and right of the Gantt bars, or even inside them.

Adding more text to your Gantt bars is especially useful if you prefer to see your key project information in direct context of the Gantt bars, without having to look back and forth between the table and the Gantt bars.

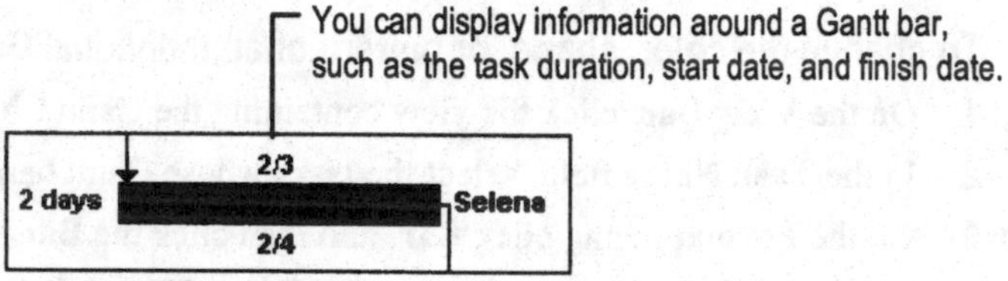

You can display information around a Gantt bar, such as the task duration, start date, and finish date.
2/3
2 days
Selena
2/4

To add text information to a Gantt bar category

1. On the **View Bar**, click the view containing the Gantt Chart you want to format.
2. On the **Format** menu, click **Bar Styles**.
3. In the table, select the type of Gantt bars (such as Task or Milestone) to which you want to add text, and then click the **Text** tab.
4. In the **Left**, **Right**, **Top**, **Bottom**, and **Inside** boxes, click the fields whose data you want to display on the Gantt bar.

If you display dates for a Gantt bar category, such as task start and finish dates, you can change the format for those dates. For example, you can change the date format from 10/25 to Oct 25 '00.

To change the format of dates on Gantt bars

1. On the **Format** menu, click **Layout**.
2. Under **Bars**, in the **Date format** box, click the date format you want.

If you want to call attention to a specific Gantt bar, you can distinguish that Gantt bar from others in the same category by adding information to that Gantt bar only. You can add information to the left, right, top, bottom, and inside of an individual Gantt bar.

To add text information to an individual Gantt Bar

You can also double-click a bar to format it or add information.

1 On the **View Bar**, click the view containing the Gantt Chart you want to format.
2 In the **Task Name** field, select the task whose Gantt bar you want to add information to.
3 On the **Format** menu, click **Bar**, and then click the **Bar Text** tab.
4 In the **Left**, **Right**, **Top**, **Bottom**, and **Inside** boxes, click the fields whose data you want to display on the Gantt bar.

Create a Custom Gantt Bar for a Task Category

Microsoft Project provides a default Gantt bar for each of several predefined task categories. For example, there's a rectangular bar for normal tasks and a diamond shape for milestone tasks. If you want a Gantt bar for a task category that doesn't have its own bar, you can create your own custom Gantt bar for that category. For instance, you can create a custom Gantt bar for critical tasks that are in progress.

To create a custom Gantt bar for a task category

1 On the **View Bar**, click the view containing the Gantt Chart you want to format.
2 On the **Format** menu, click **Bar Styles**.
3 Select the row above which you want to insert a new Gantt bar, and then click **Insert Row**.
4 In the **Name** field of the new row, type a name for the new bar, and then press ENTER.
5 In the **Show For Tasks** field of the new row, click the category that the bar is to represent.

   To combine multiple task categories, for example Critical and In-Progress, click the first category, type a comma, and then click the next category.
6 In the **From** and **To** fields, click the fields you want to use to position the start and finish points of the new Gantt bar. (In most cases, these will be the Start and Finish fields.)

   To create a symbol that represents a single date, such as for a milestone task, click the same field in both the **From** and **To** fields.
7 Click the **Bars** tab.
8 In the **Shape** boxes under **Start**, **Middle**, and **End**, click the Gantt bar shapes you want.
9 In the **Pattern** box under **Middle** and in the **Type** boxes under **Start** and **End**, click a Gantt bar pattern.
10 In the **Color** boxes under **Start**, **Middle**, and **End**, click the Gantt bar colors you want.

Roll Up a Gantt Bar to a Summary Task Bar

The chart portion of the Gantt Chart can become crowded, especially if your project contains many tasks. To make space while still displaying important task information, you can *roll up* selected subtask bars into summary task bars.

When you roll up a subtask bar, it's displayed on the summary task bar, and as a separate bar in its original location. To create space on the Gantt Chart, you can choose to hide the original bar after you've rolled it up. The summary task bar will show you at a glance the start and finish dates of the subtask bars you've rolled up into it.

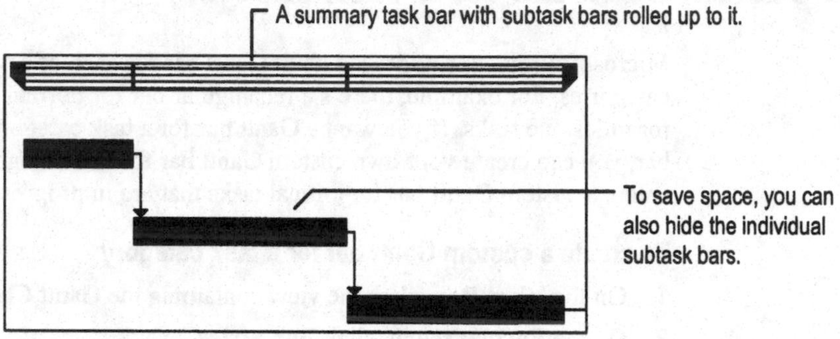

A summary task bar with subtask bars rolled up to it.
To save space, you can also hide the individual subtask bars.

To roll up a Gantt bar to a summary task bar

1 On the **View Bar**, click the view containing the Gantt Chart whose Gantt bars you want to roll up.

2 In the **Task Name** field, click the subtask you want to roll up.

Task Information

3 Click **Task Information**, and then click the **General** tab.

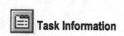

4 Select the **Roll up Gantt bar to summary** check box.
The Gantt bar is displayed as part of the summary task bar.

5 To hide the original subtask Gantt bar, select the **Hide task bar** check box.

Display Multiple Gantt Bars for Each Task

With text, you can show multiple types of information on and around a single Gantt bar. You can also show multiple types of information graphically, using multiple Gantt bars for a single task. You can display up to four Gantt bars per task.

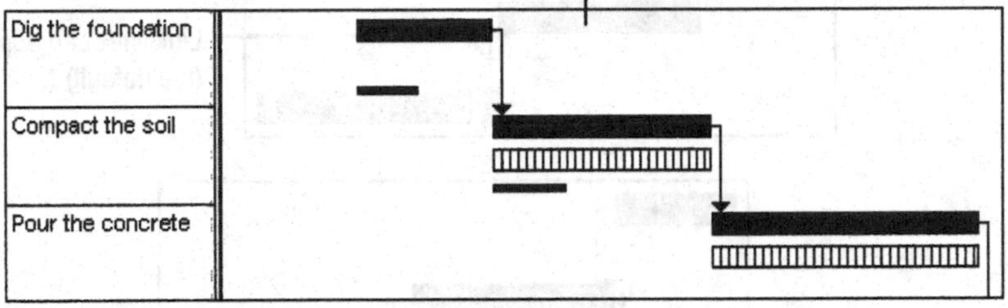

This Gantt Chart shows three Gantt bars per task: normal task, critical task, and percent complete.

To display multiple Gantt bars for each task

1 On the **View Bar**, click the view containing the Gantt Chart for which you want to display multiple Gantt bars.
2 On the **Format** menu, click **Bar Styles**.
3 In the **Row** field of the task category whose Gantt bar you want to be first, type 1.
4 In the **Row** field of the task category whose Gantt bar you want to be second, type 2.
5 If you want to display a third or fourth row of task information, type 3 or 4 in the **Row** field for the category.

The Gantt bar (or Gantt bars) that have a 1 in the Row field will appear in the highest position for each task, and the Gantt bars that have a 4 in the Row field will appear in the lowest position.

Change the Appearance of Link Lines

After you link tasks, Microsoft Project displays link lines between the tasks. By default, an arrow points toward the successor task. If you want, you can change the appearance of these link lines. You can even hide link lines completely.

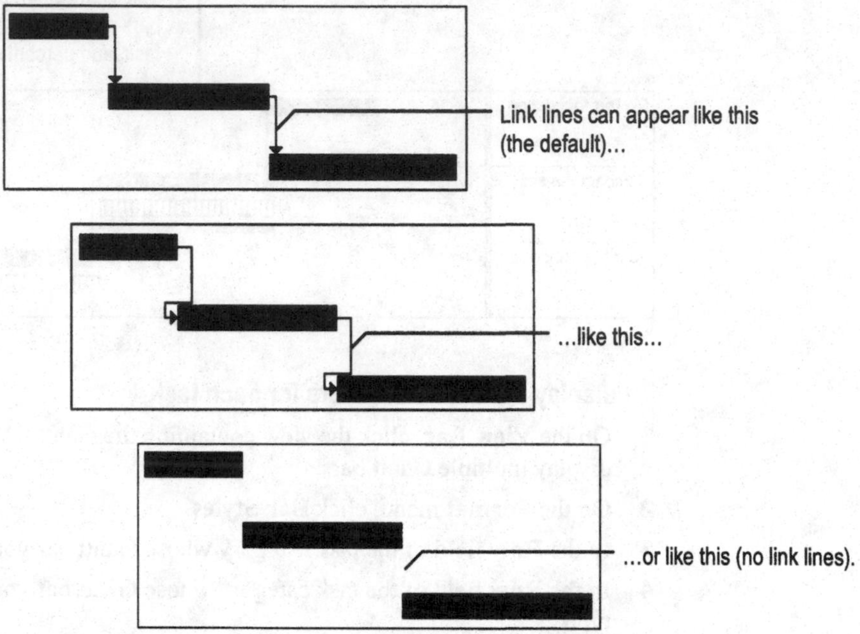
Link lines can appear like this (the default)...
...like this...
...or like this (no link lines).

To change the appearance of link lines

1 On the **View Bar**, click the view containing the Gantt Chart whose link lines you want to change.

2 On the **Format** menu, click **Layout**.

3 Under **Links**, click the link line style you want.

Change the Appearance of Nonworking Time

On the Gantt Chart view, nonworking time appears as a lightly shaded vertical bar in the timescale portion of the view. The shading tells you on which days of the week your resources don't work. You can change the appearance of nonworking time if you want it to stand out more, or if you want its appearance to conform with your organization's standards.

To change the appearance of nonworking time

1 On the **View Bar**, click the view containing the Gantt Chart whose nonworking time you want to format.

2 On the **Format** menu, click **Timescale**, and then click the **Nonworking Time** tab.

3 Under **Draw**, select whether you want the nonworking time bars to appear behind or in front of Gantt bars or not at all.

4 In the **Color** box, select the color of the nonworking time.

5 In the **Pattern** box, select the pattern of the nonworking time.

6 In the **Calendar** box, select the base or resource calendar to which you want to apply the nonworking time format.

Format a Gantt Chart View Automatically

To help you format the Gantt Chart view automatically, Microsoft Project provides the GanttChartWizard. The GanttChartWizard is a series of interactive dialog boxes that present you with options for formatting various aspects of the Gantt Chart view. When you finish selecting the options you want, the GanttChartWizard formats your Gantt Chart view for you.

The GanttChartWizard can help you to format:

- Noncritical tasks.
- Critical tasks.
- Baseline tasks.
- The appearance of information for a category of Gantt bars.
- The color, pattern, and end shapes of Gantt bars for various task categories.
- Link lines.

To format your Gantt Chart view automatically

1 On the **View Bar**, click the view containing the Gantt Chart you want to format.

GanttChartWizard

2 Click **GanttChartWizard.**

3 Follow the instructions, and click **Next** after each step.

4 When finished, click **Exit Wizard.**

Formatting the Task Usage and the Resource Usage Views

The Task Usage and Resource Usage views consist of a sheet view containing a table and a timesheet view containing work, cost, and other details broken down by day, week, month, or other specified time period.

This section discusses changing the appearance of details in a usage view. To format other elements of a usage view, such as text, the timescale, or gridlines, see the procedures in the "General Formatting in Views" and "Formatting Sheet Views" sections earlier in this chapter.

Change the Appearance of Details

To make important information stand out, you can change the appearance of the details in the timesheet portion of the Resource Usage and Task Usage views.

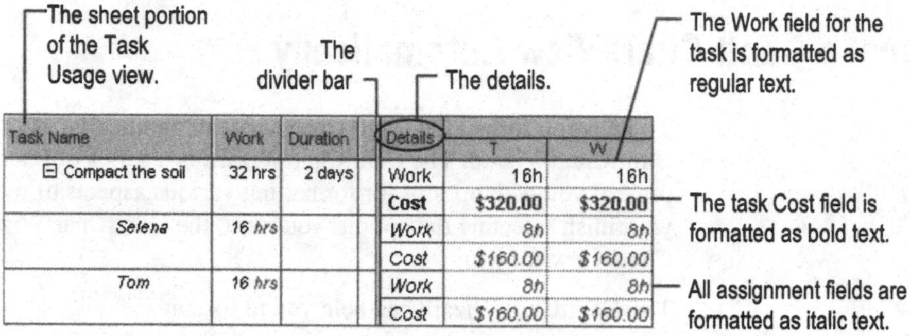

To change the appearance of details

1. On the **View Bar**, click **Task Usage** or **Resource Usage**.
2. On the **Format** menu, click **Detail Styles**, and then click the **Usage Details** tab.
3. In the **Show these fields** list, click the field you want to change.

   If the field you want does not appear in the **Show these fields** list, click the field in the **Available fields** list, and then click **Show**.
4. Under **Field settings**, select a font (click **Change Font**), cell background, and pattern for the field.
5. To hide the details header column, click the **Usage Properties** tab, and then click **No** in the **Display details header column** box.
6. If you don't want to repeat the detail headers on all assignment rows, clear the **Repeat details header on all assignment rows** check box.
7. To display short detail header names, select the **Display short detail header names** check box.

Formatting a Network Diagram

Network Diagram views show each task and associated task information in boxes, with links and colors indicating relationships, critical tasks, milestone tasks, and so on. The Network Diagram is also known as a PERT Chart.

There are three types of Network Diagrams:

- **Network Diagram.** This is a flowchart that shows all tasks and the dependencies between them. Use this view to get an overview of task sequence or to add, change, or remove task dependencies. You can also use it to create a schedule or add tasks.
- **Descriptive Network Diagram.** This view is similar to the Network Diagram view, except the boxes are larger and contain more detailed information. This view has the same formatting choices as the Network Diagram.
- **Relationship Diagram.** This view is also similar to the Network Diagram, but it is very concise. Each box shows just the task name. Its purpose is to quickly show the predecessors and successors of tasks. This view is most useful when displayed in the bottom pane of a combination view, with the Gantt Chart or the Task Sheet in the top pane. This view has no formatting options.

You can format the Network Diagram in the following ways:

- Change the appearance of Network Diagram boxes, including box shape, border, and background.
- Format the text in Network Diagram boxes.
- Display more or less detail with zooming, outlining, and fields.
- Change the layout of the Network Diagram boxes in the view, including link lines, box layout, and progress marks.
- Adjust for page breaks.

Change the Appearance of Network Diagram Boxes

By default, Network Diagram boxes are displayed with a clear and simple format. The top of each box contains a task name. The rest of each box is divided into five fields, each of which contains a piece of task information. If this format doesn't meet your needs, you can change the appearance of Network Diagram boxes. You can change the appearance of:

- All Network Diagram boxes.
- The Network Diagram boxes for a selected task category.
- An individual Network Diagram box.

For instance, each category of task appears with a unique Network Diagram box border. A thin blue line encloses each noncritical task, and a thick red line encloses each critical task. If the default border for a particular category of task doesn't suit your needs, you can change the appearance of that border.

You can show or hide the gridlines between the fields in a Network Diagram box. When a task is in progress, by default, this is indicated by a diagonal line through the box. When a task is completed, by default, this is indicated by crossed diagonal lines through the box.

Another way that Network Diagrams help you graphically distinguish the different task categories is with box shapes. While regular tasks have a rectangular shape, milestones are hexagonal, summary tasks are parallelograms, and so on.

To change the appearance of Network Diagram boxes for a task category

1. On the **View Bar**, click **Network Diagram**.
2. On the **Format** menu, click **Box Styles**.
3. In the **Style settings for** list, click the task category whose box style you want to change.
4. Under **Border**, specify the shape, color, and width you want for the box's border.
5. To show or hide gridlines between the field information, select or clear the **Show horizontal gridlines** and **Show vertical gridlines** check boxes.
6. Under **Background**, specify the color and pattern for the box's background.

To change the appearance of an individual Network Diagram box

1. On the **View Bar**, click **Network Diagram**.
2. Select the Network Diagram box you want to change.
3. On the **Format** menu, click **Box**.
4. Under **Border**, specify the shape, color, and width you want for the box's border.
5. To show or hide gridlines between the field information, select or clear the **Show horizontal gridlines** and **Show vertical gridlines** check boxes.
6. Under **Background**, specify the color and pattern for the box's background.

Format Text in Network Diagram Boxes

You can change the text formatting for all tasks in a selected task category, or for just an individually selected Network Diagram box. You can change the text for all fields in a box, or for just a single or selected fields.

To format text in Network Diagram boxes for a task category

1. On the **View Bar**, click **Network Diagram**.
2. On the **Format** menu, click **Box Styles**.
3. In the **Style settings for** list, click the task category whose font style you want to change.
4. Click **More Templates**.
5. In the **Data Templates** dialog box, click **Edit**.
6. Under **Choose cell(s)**, click the field whose text labels you want to format.
7. Click **Font**.
8. Make the changes you want to the font, style, size, and color, and then click **OK**.
9. To change text alignment in the selected cells, make your choices in the **Horizontal alignment** and **Vertical alignment** boxes.
10. Indicate whether and how you want the field name to be shown in the cell with the **Show label in cell** controls.

You can format text in an individual Network Diagram box in much the same way. Select the Network Diagram box whose text you want to format. On the Format menu, click Box. Follow steps 4–10 above.

Display More or Less Detail

The amount of your project you want to see will vary with the circumstances and the audience. To see a project overview, you'll want to view as many Network Diagram boxes as possible at one time. To focus on details, you'll want to view a few tasks at a time. You can display as much or as little of your project at one time by:

- Zooming in and out.
- Showing or hiding subtasks.
- Adding or removing fields of information.

You can also see more or less detail by viewing a different diagram. By default, the Network Diagram displays 6 fields. The Descriptive Network Diagram displays 8 fields, adding the task category and percent complete to the fields shown in the Network Diagram. The boxes are also larger. The Relationship Diagram displays just the task name field in its boxes, and shows predecessors, successors, and the link name.

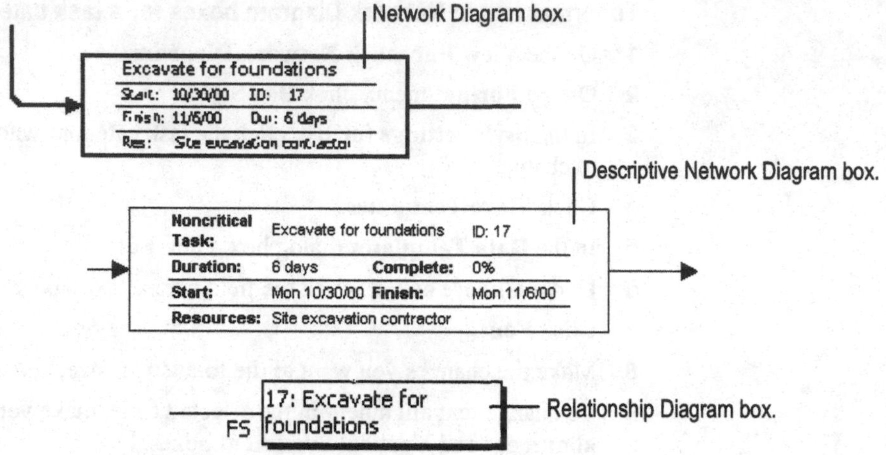

You can add or remove fields of information displayed in the boxes in the Network Diagram or the Descriptive Network Diagram. You can also change the number of rows containing fields in a Network Diagram box. For more information, see "Display the Information You Want in the Network Diagram" in chapter 12.

To zoom the Network Diagram in and out

Zoom In

Zoom Out

1 On the **View Bar**, click **Network Diagram**.
2 To see more detail (and fewer Network Diagram boxes at a time), click **Zoom In**. To see less detail (and more Network Diagram boxes at a time), click **Zoom Out**.

To show and hide subtasks

1 On the **View Bar**, click **Network Diagram**.
2 If a Network Diagram box has a minus sign above its upper left corner, it represents a summary task.

   By default, summary tasks are formatted as blue parallelogram Network Diagram boxes.
3 To hide the subtasks under the summary task, click the minus sign. The minus sign changes to a plus sign.

   You can also click **Hide Subtasks**.

Hide Subtasks

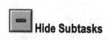

4 To show hidden subtasks, click the plus sign above the summary task's upper left corner.

   You can also click **Show Subtasks**.

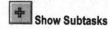

Show Subtasks

To set outlining options for the Network Diagram

1 On the **View Bar**, click **Network Diagram**.
2 On the **Format** menu, click **Layout**.
3 Select or clear the **Show summary tasks** and **Keep tasks with their summaries** check boxes.

Change the Network Diagram Layout

After you link tasks, Microsoft Project displays link lines between the Network Diagram boxes. By default, an arrow points toward the successor task. If you want, you can change the appearance of these link lines. You can even hide link lines completely.

To change the appearance of link lines

1 On the **View Bar**, click **Network Diagram**.
2 On the **Format** menu, click **Layout**.
3 Under **Link Style**, select the type of link lines you want: rectilinear or straight.
4 Select whether you want to show link arrows or labels with the **Show arrows** and **Show link labels** check box.
5 Under **Link color**, specify colors for links to noncritical and critical tasks.

To change Network Diagram box layout options

1 On the **View Bar**, click **Network Diagram**.
2 On the **Format** menu, click **Layout**.
3 Under **Layout Mode**, specify whether you want Network Diagram boxes to be automatically or manually positioned.
4 Under **Box Layout** in the **Arrangement** box, specify the Network Diagram box arrangement you want, such as **Top Down From Left** (the default), or **Centered from Top**, and so on.
5 Specify the row and column alignment, spacing, and size you want for the layout of the Network Diagram boxes in the view.

To set whether progress is marked in the Network Diagram

1 On the **View Bar**, click **Network Diagram**.
2 On the **Format** menu, click **Layout**.
3 Select or clear the **Mark in-progress and completed** check box.

Prevent Network Diagram Boxes from Crossing Page Breaks

If your project has many tasks, there's a good chance that some Network Diagram boxes will straddle page breaks when you print. To give your Network Diagram a more orderly appearance, you can prevent these boxes from crossing page breaks.

To prevent Network Diagram boxes from crossing page breaks

1 On the **View Bar**, click **Network Diagram**.
2 On the **Format** menu, click **Layout**.
3 Select the **Adjust for page breaks** check box.
4 Click **OK**.
5 On the **Format** menu, click **Layout Now**.

To hide page breaks on your screen, click Layout on the Format menu, and then clear the Show page breaks check box.

Formatting the Calendar View

You can format the Calendar view in the following ways:

- Arrange task bars.
- Hide a category of task bars.
- Hide specific task bars.
- Change the bar style for a task category.
- Change the appearance of the headings, date boxes, and rows.

Arrange Task Bars

If you have multiple tasks taking place on a single day, it can be a challenge to see all of them in the Calendar view. Dragging to rearrange Calendar task bars can be painstaking work. You can set up Calendar view layout options to help you see more tasks at a time automatically.

To arrange task bars

1 On the **View Bar**, click **Calendar**.
2 On the **Format** menu, click **Layout**.
3 To display as many tasks as possible in one row without overlapping task bars, click **Attempt to fit as many tasks as possible**.

4 To arrange tasks in the current sort order, click **Use current sort order**.

5 To show task split lines, select the **Show bar splits** check box.

6 To have Microsoft Project automatically arrange task bars when you add or delete tasks, select the **Automatic layout** check box, and then click **OK**.
If you don't select the **Automatic layout** check box, click **Layout Now** on the **Format** menu to rearrange the task bars.

7 If some tasks are not precisely where you want them, drag them to the desired locations.

Hide a Category of Task Bars

When several tasks occur on the same date, Microsoft Project stacks their task bars in a Calendar row. If the Calendar row isn't high enough to fit all the task bars, Microsoft Project displays only some of the task bars. You can make sure that you can see the task bars for the tasks you're interested in by restricting the types of tasks that are displayed on the Calendar.

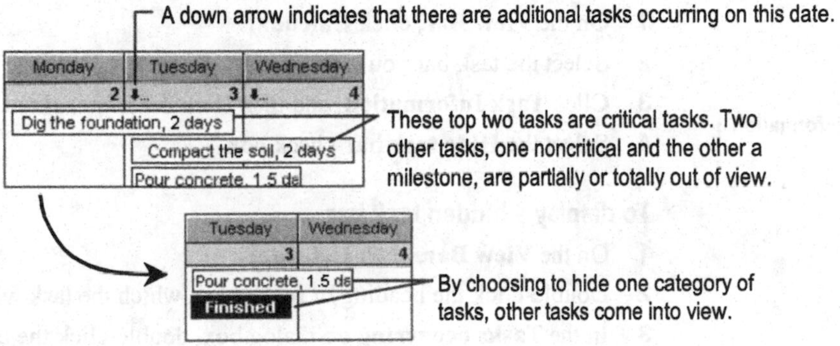
A down arrow indicates that there are additional tasks occurring on this date.
Monday
Tuesday
Wednesday
2
3
4
Dig the foundation, 2 days
Compact the soil, 2 days
Pour concrete, 1.5 da
These top two tasks are critical tasks. Two other tasks, one noncritical and the other a milestone, are partially or totally out of view.
Tuesday
Wednesday
3
4
Pour concrete, 1.5 da
Finished
By choosing to hide one category of tasks, other tasks come into view.

To hide a category of task bars

1 On the **View Bar**, click **Calendar**.

2 On the **Format** menu, click **Bar Styles**.

3 In the **Task type** list, click the task category you don't want to display.

4 In the **Bar type** box, click **None**.

5 Click **OK**.

6 On the **Format** menu, click **Layout**, and then click **Attempt to fit as many tasks as possible**.
The tasks in the remaining categories, including those that are out of view, will fill in the displayable area of the date boxes.

You can also use the following methods to display the task bars you want:

- On the Project menu, point to Filtered for, and then click a filter option.
- Display fewer but larger week rows by dragging the horizontal line between any two week rows up to increase the height of the week row.
- Adjust the height of the week rows to fit the greatest number of tasks scheduled on any date by double-clicking the horizontal line separating one week row from another to get the best fit.

Hide Specific Task Bars

When a Calendar row is too short to display the task bars for all of the tasks that occur on a given date, you can hide the specific task bars of those tasks you're not interested in at the moment. By hiding specific task bars, you might create enough room for the task bars you want to display. If hiding specific task bars doesn't create enough room, you might want to hide the task bars for a category of tasks.

To hide a specific task bar

1. On the **View Bar**, click **Calendar**.
2. Select the task bar you want to hide.
3. Click **Task Information**, and then click the **General** tab.
4. Select the **Hide task bar** check box.

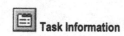

Task Information

To display a hidden task bar

1. On the **View Bar**, click **Calendar**.
2. Double-click the heading of the date on which the task will appear.
3. In the **Tasks occurring on** dialog box, double-click the task you want to display.
4. Click the **General** tab, and then clear the **Hide task bar** check box.

Format the Bar Style for a Category of Calendar Task Bars

To help you focus on a particular set of tasks, you can change the appearance of the task bars for all the tasks that belong to a predefined task category. For example, you can change the color, shape, or pattern of all critical task bars or all milestone task bars. You can also add information, such as the task start date, which appears within each task bar.

When you change the appearance of task bars for a category of tasks, you globally change the appearance of all the task bars for all the tasks in that category.

To change the bar type, pattern, and color of all task bars in a category

1 On the **View Bar**, click **Calendar**.
2 On the **Format** menu, click **Bar Styles**.
3 In the **Task type** list, click the task bar type for which you want to change the formatting.
4 Under **Bar shape**, click a bar type, pattern, color, and split pattern for the task type.
5 To add a shadow behind the bar, select the **Shadow** check box.
6 In the **Field(s)** box, click the information you want to appear within the bar.
   If you want more than one field to appear on the task bar, type a comma (,) after a field name, and then select another field name.
7 In the **Align** box, click the alignment you want to use to position the text within the task bars.

Change the Appearance of Calendar Headings, Date Boxes, and Rows

If the default appearance of the Calendar view doesn't meet your needs, you can change its overall look quickly. For example, you can change the monthly, weekly, and daily titles, such as changing February 2000 to Feb '00 or Monday to Mo or M.

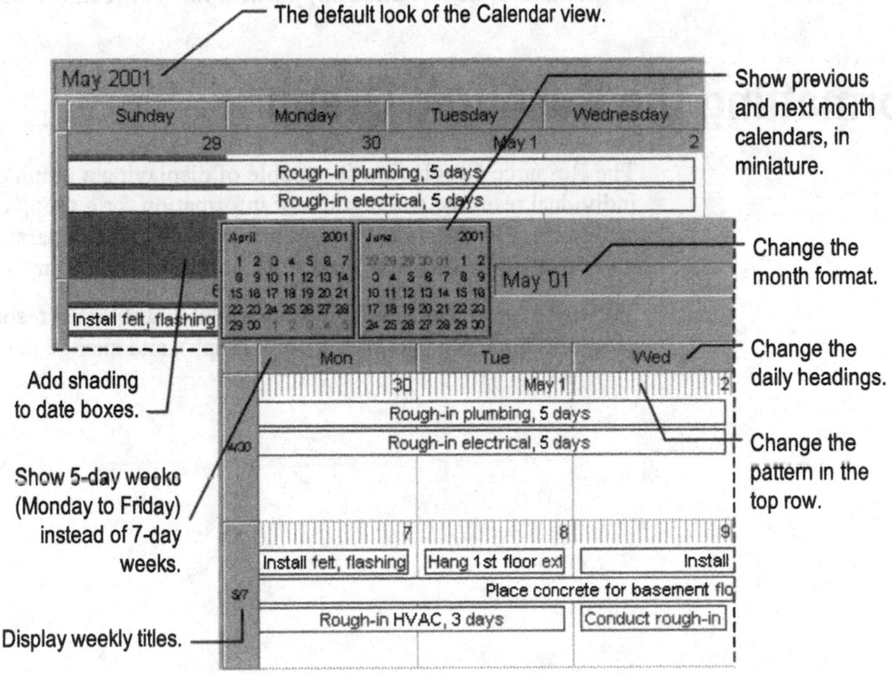
The default look of the Calendar view.
Show previous and next month calendars, in miniature.
Change the month format.
Change the daily headings.
Change the pattern in the top row.
Add shading to date boxes.
Show 5-day weeks (Monday to Friday) instead of 7-day weeks.
Display weekly titles.
May 2001
Sunday
Monday
Tuesday
Wednesday
Rough-in plumbing, 5 days
Rough-in electrical, 5 days
Install felt, flashing
May 01
Mon
Tue
Wed
Hang 1st floor ext
Install
Place concrete for basement flo
Rough-in HVAC, 3 days
Conduct rough-in

To change the appearance of headings, date boxes, and rows

1. On the **View Bar**, click **Calendar**.
2. On the **Format** menu, click **Timescale**, and then click the **Week Headings** tab.
3. In the **Monthly titles, Daily titles**, and **Weekly titles** boxes, click the title formats you want to use.
4. Under **Display**, click **7 days** to display a 7-day week or click **5 days** to display a 5-day week.
5. To add miniature calendars for the next and previous months, select the **Previous/Next month calendars** check box.
6. Click the **Date Boxes** tab.
7. Under **Top row** and **Bottom row**, select the information you want to display in the left and right portion of each row, and then select the pattern and color you want.
8. Click the **Date Shading** tab, and then click the name of the calendar you want to change in the **Show working time for** box.
9. In the **Exception type** list, click the type of date box you want to change, and then select a shade pattern and color.

In the Calendar view, you can change the column width of all date columns by dragging any vertical line between two date boxes to the left to decrease column width or to the right to increase column width. To fit the displayed columns exactly to the width of the calendar area, double-click any vertical line between two date boxes.

Formatting the Resource Graph

The Resource Graph view is capable of displaying a graph of information for an individual resource and a graph of information for a group of selected resources at the same time. For instance, you can format each graph separately, to help you compare an individual resource's allocated work hours with the group's allocated work hours.

You can overlap bar graphs for individual and selected resources, use a different type of graph (such as a bar, area, or line graph), and change the graph color and pattern.

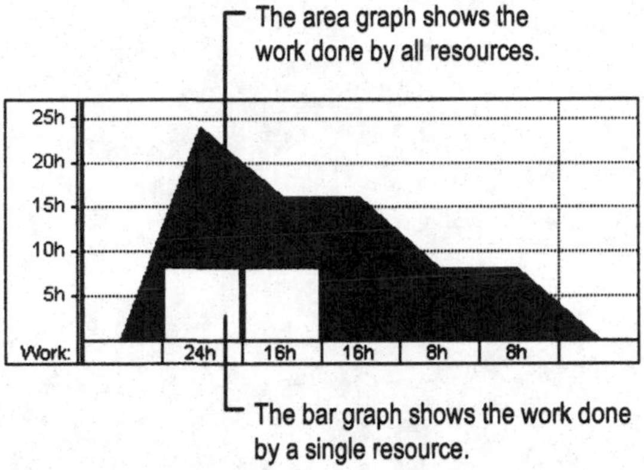
The area graph shows the work done by all resources.
25h
20h
15h
10h
5h
Work:
24h
16h
16h
8h
8h
The bar graph shows the work done by a single resource.

You can also change the appearance of text, gridlines, and the timescale in the Resource Graph. For more information, see "General Formatting in Views" earlier in this chapter.

To change the graph, pattern, and color

1. On the **View Bar**, click **Resource Graph**.
2. On the **Format** menu, click **Bar Styles**.

   The customizing options for the filtered (or selected) resource graph are on the left side of the **Bar Styles** dialog box. The customizing options for the individual resource graph are on the right side.
3. In the **Show as** boxes, click the styles you want to use to represent each graph.

   To remove a graph, click **Don't Show** in the **Show as** box.
4. In the **Color** boxes, click the colors you want to use for the graph.
5. In the **Pattern** boxes, click the patterns you want to use for the graph.
6. If you've chosen to show two bar graphs and you want the bars to overlap, type the overlap percentage in the **Bar overlap** box.
7. If you want to show the numerical value for each graph at the bottom of the graphs, select the **Show values** check box.
8. If you want to show a line to indicate the availability of individual resources, select the **Show availability line** check box.

14

Printing and Publishing Basics

Distributing a completed project schedule for review before the project begins is one of the main reasons for printing project information. During the project, you can also periodically print status information for your managers, clients, and team members.

If the schedule changes significantly, you might want to distribute a printout of the revised schedule to team members. You can also print project overviews for managers, task lists for individual team members, project costs to date, resource usage information, information about in-progress tasks and slipping tasks, and many other kinds of project information.

Views are discussed in detail in "Selecting Views to Display Sets of Information" in chapter 12.

Using Microsoft Project views and reports, you can print exactly the project information required by a particular project participant. A *view* is a collection of task, resource, or assignment information arranged in an orderly manner for viewing on your computer screen, so you can enter, edit, and review information. You can also print views. For example, you can print the Gantt Chart, which is the default view for Microsoft Project.

A *report* is a predefined set of project information in a format that's designed and ready for printing. Information you're likely to want to print is probably in one of the predefined reports. In many cases, all you need to do is select the report that has the information you want and then print it. Examples of reports include Milestones, Tasks In Progress, Overbudget Tasks, and To-Do List. There are 29 predefined reports in Microsoft Project.

Whether you print a view or a report, you can specify exactly the information that appears by using tables and filters. You can also change the appearance of views and reports by making text bold or italic, adding headers and footers, adjusting margins, changing the page orientation, adding borders, specifying how large or how small information should appear on a printed page, and much more.

Even with all the print options available, printing a view or report can still be as easy as clicking a Print button. To this end, this chapter covers the fundamentals of printing views and reports. This includes:

- The differences between views and reports.
- Printing a view.
- Printing a report.
- Publishing project information as an HTML document.
- Examples of project information you can print or publish.
- Setting up a printer or plotter.

Beyond these basics, there are many ways to change the information contained in a view or report, and many ways to format and print them. The following table lists the chapters that provide this information.

For information about	See
Specifying the core information in a view	Chapter 12, "Viewing Your Information"
Specifying the core information in a report	Chapter 16, "Printing Reports"
Changing the appearance of a view	Chapter 13, "Making Your Project Look How You Want"
Specifying print options for views	Chapter 15, "Printing Views"
Specifying print options for reports	Chapter 16, "Printing Reports"
Exchanging project information over e-mail	Chapter 10, "Updating Task Information Using E-Mail"
Exchanging project information with Microsoft Project Central	Chapter 11, "Updating Task Information Using the Web"

Views Versus Reports

One of the main differences between views and reports is that you can enter and edit information directly in a view, but not in a report. However, you can apply different tables and filters to a report, just as you can to views.

An advantage of reports is that they're already designed for displaying information that's most commonly wanted in printed reports. You don't have to set up all the information yourself before printing. You choose the report, and information is collected from various locations in your project and formatted according to the report format. Different types of reports are designed for different audiences: for example, overview reports most suitable for upper management, budget reports for accounting, and resource reports for your team members. You can also create your own report, or modify one of the existing reports.

There are five view formats: Gantt Chart, usage, graph and diagram, sheet, and form views. There's at least one predefined Microsoft Project view of each type. When you create a new view, you base it on one of the predefined views.

There are four report formats of reports: task, resource, crosstab, and monthly calendar reports.

Another difference between views and reports is that you have many choices for changing the appearance of most views. There are tables, filters, details, grouping, sorting, individual text and graphic formatting, and more. While you can change the appearance of reports, for example, with tables and filters, you have fewer options. For example, you can format a category of text but not an individual piece of text.

With both views and reports, you can see a preview of how they will look when printed.

Print a View

The information you see on your screen is contained in a view. If you want to print the information you see on your screen, then print the view. You can print any view except form views and the Relationship Diagram.

To preview a view quickly, click **Print Preview**

Page Right

Zoom

To preview a view before printing

1. Select the view you want and set it up with the information you want to print.
2. On the **File** menu, click **Print Preview**.
3. To move through pages horizontally, click **Page Left** or **Page Right**.

   To move through pages vertically, click **Page Up** or **Page Down**.

   To see more detail, click **Zoom**.

   You cannot change information you see in the Print Preview window, as it's just a picture of the view as it will appear when printed. To change the information or settings, click **Close** in the Print Preview window to return to the view.

To print a view quickly, click **Print.**

To print a view

1. Select the view you want and set it up with the information you want to print.
2. On the **File** menu, click **Print**.
3. Select the printing options you want.

   For more information about view printing options, see chapter 15.

Print a Report

To print a report, you simply select the one you want from the set of predefined reports, review the preview, and then print it.

To print a report

1. On the **View** menu, click **Reports**.
2. In the **Reports** dialog box, click the report type you want, and then click **Select**.
3. Click the report you want to print, and then click **Select**.
4. If a dialog box appears and asks you for specific values, enter the values, and then click **OK**.

   The report is displayed in the preview window.
5. To move through pages horizontally, click **Page Left** or **Page Right**.

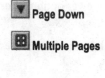

    **Page Down**

   To move through pages vertically, click **Page Up** or **Page Down**.

    **Multiple Pages**

   To see all the pages of the view at one time, click **Multiple Pages**.
6. Click **Print**.
7. Select the printing options you want.

   For more information about printing options, see chapter 16.

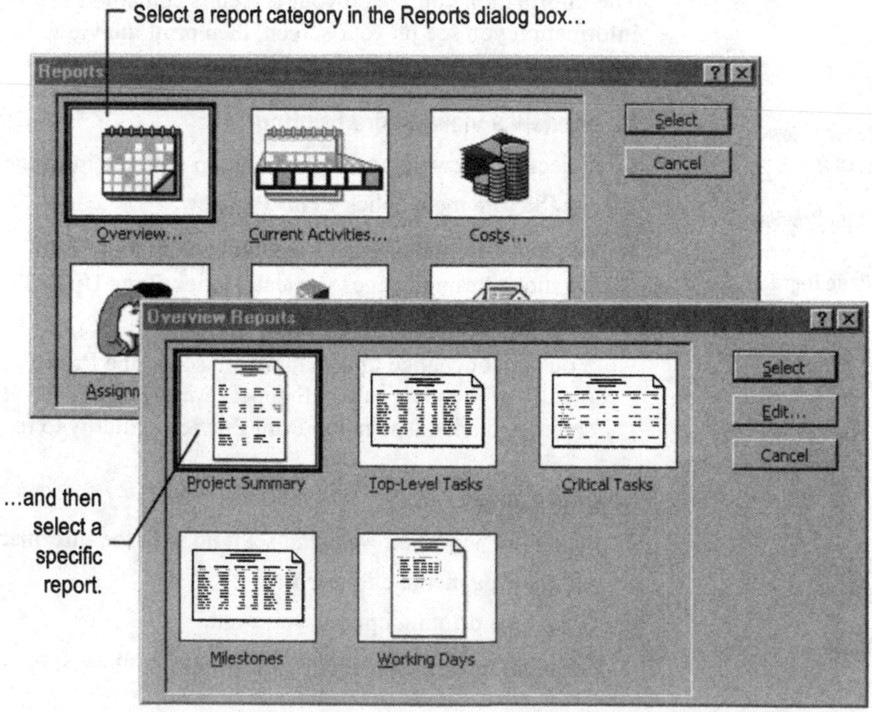

Publish Project Information to a Web Site

You can share project information electronically in one or more of the following ways:

- Sending a project file to an e-mail recipient.
- Routing a project file across an e-mail system.
- Exchanging project information with a workgroup using e-mail.
- Exchanging project information over the Web with Microsoft Project Central.
- Exporting project information with a file in another program.
- Linking project information into a file in another program.

For more information on exporting and linking, see chapter 18.

Sharing project information electronically is especially useful if the clients, managers, or team members work in a different site, city, or country. An especially convenient and effective way to share project information is to save specific information as an HTML document and then publish it to a Web site that your intended audience can access.

Project fields are saved and formatted into an HTML document, which you can then post to your Web site.

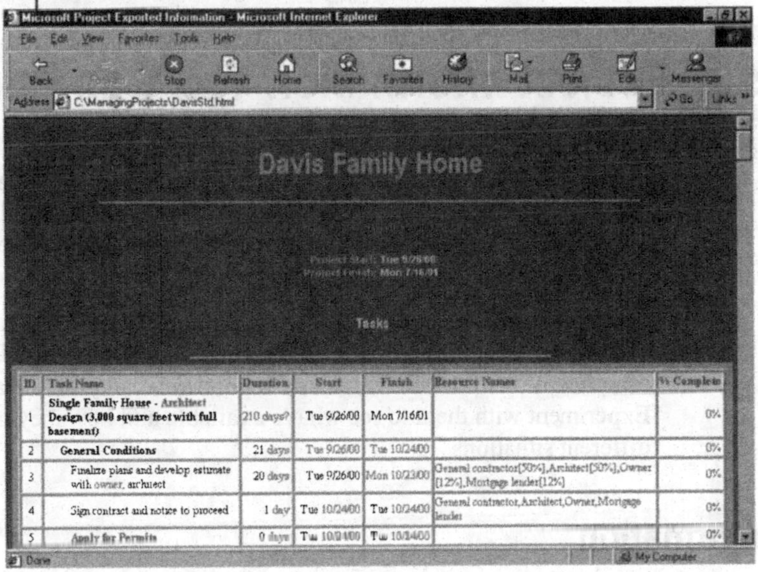

For more information about import/export maps, see "Importing and Exporting Project Information" in chapter 18.

Microsoft Project uses *import/export maps* to determine which Microsoft Project fields are exported to HTML format. You can use one of the predefined export maps for your HTML file, or you can create your own. Of the predefined export maps, the following are especially good for general purposes:

- Export to HTML using standard template.
- Resource "Export Table" map.
- Task "Export Table" map.
- Task list with embedded assignment rows.

To publish project information as an HTML document

1. On the **File** menu, click **Save As Web Page**.
2. Under **Save in**, select the folder in which you want to save the HTML document.
3. In the **File name** box, type the file name for the HTML document. Be sure to keep html as the file extension.
4. Click **Save**.
5. In the **Export Mapping** dialog box, be sure that the **Selective Data** tab is active.
6. In the **Import/export map** list, select the export map you want to use.
7. Click **Save**.

Once you save your project information as an HTML document, post it to your Web site for access and viewing by your intended audience.

Examples of Project Information You Can Print

After you've created your project plan, you can print project information that's tailored to each recipient. For example, you can create summary–level reports for management, projected cost reports for the accounting department, and individual task–level reports for each team lead. Because all reports are based on the same core set of information, it's easy to print exactly the information that's needed.

The following tables show which views and reports you can use when you want to print a particular kind of information. The views and reports listed in each table are only a sampling of the possible views and reports you can print in each information category. Experiment with them to see what's available and how they might meet your needs in different situations.

Summary Information

Views and reports with summary information can show everything from a statistical summary of the project (number of tasks, resources, cost, duration, and so on) to a summary of major phases and milestones in the project. The following table lists several views and reports that show summary information.

To print	Use
A summary of the project, including number of tasks and resources, cost, work, duration, start and finish dates, and project notes	Project Summary report (in Overview reports)
A summary of major phases, with bar chart showing the start and finish dates	Gantt Chart view, with the outline collapsed
A summary of major phases, showing duration, start and finish dates, cost, and percent complete	Top-Level Tasks report (in Overview reports)
Milestones in the project and top-level summary tasks	Milestones report (in Overview reports)
Working and nonworking time	Working Days report (in Overview reports)

Task and Critical Path Information

When you want to get down to more detail about the tasks in the project, you can print information showing details about individual tasks instead of a project overview. The following table lists several ways to report on tasks in your project.

To print	Use
A list of tasks and durations, plus a bar chart of tasks and critical path	Gantt Chart view, with pattern changed for critical task bars
A list of critical tasks and their successors	Critical Tasks report (in Overview reports)
A flowchart that shows all tasks and the dependencies between them	Network Diagram or Descriptive Network Diagram
A task list with durations, start and finish dates, and assigned resources	Task report (in Custom reports)
A list of tasks showing assigned resources grouped under each task, a table of task information, and a set of details about tasks and their assigned resources	Task Usage view or Task Usage report (in Workload reports)
A list of tasks and their work and costs	Task Sheet view, with Summary table applied
A list of tasks scheduled during a particular time period	Task report (in Custom reports) or Tasks Starting Soon report (in Current Activities reports)
A schedule of tasks printed on a calendar	Calendar view

Resource Usage Information

Views and reports that include resource usage information provide information such as the tasks each resource is assigned to, the amount of work allocated to resources, resource costs, and pay rates. The following table lists some of the views and reports you can print with resource usage information.

To print	Use
A list of all resources assigned to work on the project	Resource Sheet view, or Resource report (in Workload reports), or Resource (material) or Resource (work) (in Custom reports)
A list of resources showing assigned tasks grouped under each resource, a table of resource information, and a set of details about resources and their assigned tasks	Resource Usage view, or Resource Usage report (in Workload reports), or Resource Usage (material) report, or Resource Usage (work) report (in Custom reports)
Resource work and cost	Resource Sheet view, with Summary table attached, or Resource Usage view showing work and cost
A list of resources and the tasks to which each is assigned	Who Does What report (in Assignment reports), Resource Usage view, or Resource Usage report (in Workload reports), or Resource Usage (material) report or Resource Usage (work) report (in Custom reports)
A list of resources, the tasks to which each is assigned, and the hours worked on each task during each week	Who Does What When report (in Assignment reports), or Resource Usage view
A list of overallocated resources and task assignments	Overallocated Resources report (in Assignments reports)
A graph showing resource allocations, costs, and work over time for an individual resource, a group of resources, or both	Resource Graph view
A list of tasks an individual resource is assigned to work on	To-do List report (in Assignment reports)
A list of resources scheduled to work on tasks during a specified time period	Resource Usage report (in Workload reports), or Resource Usage (work) report (in Custom reports)

Cost Information

Microsoft Project provides several ways to print cost information. You can print resource costs, task costs, cumulative costs, or a table showing the cash flow over time. Print cost information for team members who need to approve or keep track of project costs, such as your manager or members of the accounting department.

To print	Use
Task costs and totals	Budget report (in Cost reports)
A list of resources whose costs will exceed baseline cost	Overbudget Resources report (in Cost reports)
A list of tasks whose costs will exceed baseline cost	Overbudget Tasks report (in Cost reports)
Expected task costs	Budget report (in Cost reports)
A list of cumulative cost per task	Task Usage view, with Cumulative Cost details displayed in the timescale
A forecast of task costs, such as how much money will be spent on tasks and when	Cash Flow report (in Cost reports)
A forecast of resource costs, such as how much money will be spent on tasks and when	Resource Usage view, with Cost details applied
A summary of resource costs	Resource Sheet view, with Cost table applied
A list of tasks showing whether you're ahead of or behind schedule as compared with the actual costs	Earned Value report (in Cost reports)
Cumulative resource cost over the life of the project	Resource Graph view displaying cumulative cost for all resources

Progress Information

Keeping track of project progress increases your chances of completing your project on time and within budget. The following table lists views and reports that include progress information you'll want to share with managers, task supervisors, and clients.

To print	Use
A list of tasks currently in progress that shows the months in which each task occurs	Tasks In Progress report (in Current Activities reports)
A list of tasks scheduled to start within a time period you specify	Tasks Starting Soon report (in Current Activities reports)

To print	Use
A list of tasks that haven't started yet	Unstarted Tasks report (in Current Activities reports)
A list of tasks that should have started by the date you specify but haven't	Should Have Started Tasks report (in Current Activities reports)
A list of tasks showing actual start and finish dates, percentage of each task completed, and actual and remaining task durations	Gantt Chart view, with Tracking table
A list of tasks that have been rescheduled to occur after their baseline start dates	Slipping Tasks report (in Current Activities reports)
A list of tasks with scheduled start and finish dates, baseline start and finish dates, and the differences between scheduled and baseline dates	Gantt Chart view, with Variance table
A list of completed tasks	Task Sheet view, with Completed Tasks filter
A list of completed tasks showing the time period in which each task occurred	Completed Tasks report (in Current Activities reports)

Set Up a Printer or Plotter for Microsoft Project

If your computer isn't connected to a printer or plotter, consult your printer or plotter reference guide.

After your computer is connected to a printer or plotter and before you can print views and reports, your printer or plotter must be set up for use with Microsoft Project.

If you use Microsoft Windows 95 or later, or Microsoft Windows NT, you set up your printer for use with all your programs; you don't need to set it up just for Microsoft Project. You can, however, switch to a different printer—if you're connected to more than one printer, such as on a network—or change printer settings as you work in Microsoft Project. If your computer is connected to a network that includes several printers, those printers might have different capabilities (speeds, resolutions, colors, and so on). Microsoft Project enables you to specify which of those printers you want to use.

To select a printer or plotter and change its settings in Microsoft Project

1. On the **File** menu, click **Print**.
2. In the **Name** box, click a printer or plotter name, and then click **Properties**.
3. Select the printer options you want to use, and then click **OK**.
4. Click **Close**.

15

Printing Views

You set up core information in a view by selecting the view, then selecting any table, filter, grouping, or details that will display the information you need. Once you're ready to print, you can fine-tune the information as it appears in your printout of the view so it looks exactly the way you want.

For elementary information about printing, see chapter 14.

When setting up the printout of the view, you:

- **Set up view content options.** This includes the date range or columns to be printed. In this step, you're specifying how your content should be printed.
- **Set up the printed page format.** This includes elements such as margins, headers, and footers. In this step, you're specifying the layout and look of the printed page.

Specifying Content Options for Views

You can print all views except form views and the Relationship Diagram.

With print options for views, you can:

- Specify the print range and number of copies.
- Print information relevant only within a specified date range.
- Print specific columns in sheet views.
- Print notes.
- Prevent blank pages from printing.
- Specify the number of weeks or months printed in the Calendar view.
- Print miniature previous and next month calendars in the Calendar view.

The first step to specifying any print options is to select the view you want to print and make sure it contains the right information and is formatted the way you want.

To select a view

1. On the **View Bar**, click a view.
2. To select a view that doesn't appear on the **View Bar**, click **More Views**, click the view you want in the **Views** list, and then click **Apply**.
3. Set up the view by applying tables, filters, grouping, and so on, to show the information you want to print.

For more information about setting up your view, see chapter 12.

If none of the existing views contains the information you want to print or has a suitable appearance, you can edit an existing view, modify a copy of an existing view, or create a view from scratch. For more information, see "Create or Modify a View" in chapter 12.

To change the appearance of a view, see chapter 13.

Specify the Print Range and Number of Copies

You can print only the pages within a certain range, say, just pages 3 to 5. You can also specify the number of copies you'd like of the entire or partial view.

To specify the print range and number of copies for a view

1. Select the view you want and set it up with the information you want to print.
2. On the **File** menu, click **Print**.
3. To print all the pages in the view, under **Print range**, click **All**.

   To print a range of pages, under **Print range**, click **Page(s)**, and then enter the number of the first page in the range in the **From** box and the number of last page you want to print in the **To** box.
4. In the **Number of Copies** box, type the number of copies you want to print.

Specify the Date Range for a View

Several views, like the Gantt Chart and the Calendar view, have *timescales*. By default, when you print a view with a timescale, you print all the information that's available in that view for the entire project duration, from the project start date to the project finish date. Sometimes, however, you might want to print only the information that falls within a certain time period. In this case, you can specify the date range within which you want to print information.

You can specify a date range for printing any view with a timescale. These views are:

- Gantt Charts.
- Usage views.
- Resource Graph view.
- Calendar view.

To specify the date range for a view

1 Select the view you want and set it up with the information you want to print.

2 On the **File** menu, click **Print**.

3 Under **Timescale**, click **Dates**.

4 In the **From** box, click the first date you want included in your printed view. In the **To** box, click the last date you want included in your printed view.

If you specify a **To** date that falls in the middle of a page, Microsoft Project prints the entire page, including information that occurs after the **To** date.

Print All Columns or Repeat Columns in a Sheet View

A sheet view is made up of columns and rows. Examples are the Task Sheet and the Resource Sheet. Sheet views are often part of views, like the Gantt Chart or Resource Usage view.

A printed sheet view includes all portions of the view except for those columns that aren't completely visible on your screen. For example, if the Entry table is applied to the Gantt Chart view and only the Indicator, Task Name, and Duration columns are completely showing, then only those columns will be printed, along with the chart portion of the view. By moving the divider bar to the right, you can show—and print—more columns, but you still might not be able to print all of them, and you might not print the chart portion at all. Instead of moving the divider bar, you can select an option that enables you to print all columns that are part of the view, even those that you'd have to scroll to or move the divider bar to see.

If a printed sheet view is more than one page long, each successive page begins where the previous page leaves off. For example, if a 9-column Gantt Chart is 3 pages long, the first page might contain the first 6 columns, the second page might contain the last 3 columns and the first part of the bar chart, and the third page might contain the remaining part of the bar chart. On the second and third pages, you won't see which task name goes with each Gantt bar, because the task names will appear only on the first page. To alleviate this problem, Microsoft Project enables you to print the first several columns on each page.

To print all columns and repeat certain columns in a sheet view

1 Select the view you want and set it up with the information you want to print.

2 On the **File** menu, click **Page Setup**, and then click the **View** tab.

3 To print all columns, including those that are hidden behind another portion of the view (such as in the Gantt Chart view or the Resource Usage view), select the **Print all sheet columns** check box.

4 To repeat a certain number of columns on each printed page, select the **Print first** check box, and then enter the number of columns in the **columns on all pages** box.

5 Click **Print**.

Print Notes with a View

In task views, such as the Gantt Chart view and the Calendar view, you can add notes to individual tasks. In resource views, such as the Resource Sheet view and the Resource Graph view, you can add notes to resources. In the Task Usage view, you can add notes to both tasks and assignments. In the Resource Usage view, you can add notes to both resources and assignments.

If notes about tasks, resources, or assignments have been added to your project plan, you can print those notes with views. Notes appropriate to the view (task, resource, or assignment) are printed on the last page of a view. If you print the Task Usage view, both task and assignment notes are printed. If you print the Resource Usage view, both resource and assignment notes are printed.

To print notes with a view

1 Select the view you want and set it up with the information you want to print.

2 On the **File** menu, click **Page Setup**, and then click the **View** tab.

3 Select the **Print notes** check box.

Prevent Blank Pages from Printing in a View

A blank page is a page that contains no task, resource, or assignment information. By default, the Gantt Charts, Network Diagrams, and Usage views might be printed with blank pages because of their timescales and graphical layout. To save time and paper, you can prevent blank pages from printing.

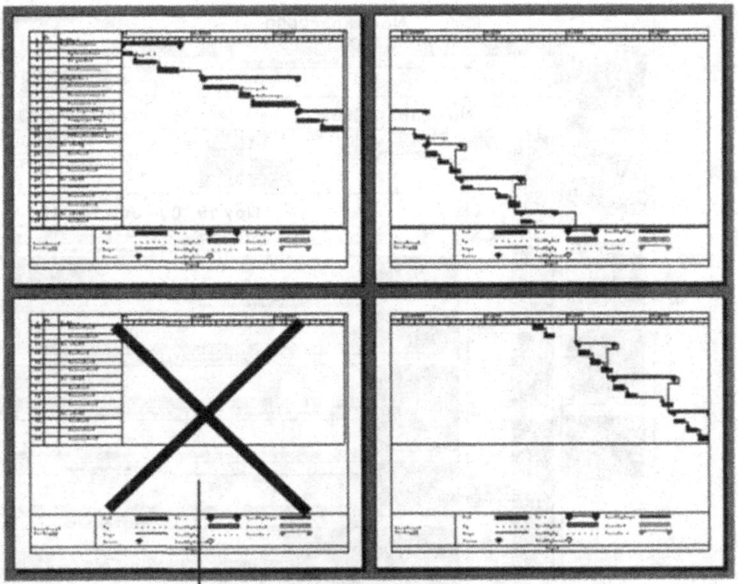

You can prevent the printing of Gantt Chart pages that have no Gantt bars.

To prevent blank pages from printing

1 Select the view you want and set it up with the information you want to print.

2 On the **File** menu, click **Page Setup**, and then click the **View** tab.

3 Clear the **Print blank pages** check box.

When you prevent blank pages from printing, blank pages appear shaded in the Print Preview window.

Specify the Number of Weeks or Months Printed in the Calendar View

The Calendar view displays the project schedule in a monthly calendar format, with rows of weeks. A printed Calendar view can be a useful way for team leads and resources to see which tasks need to be done in a particular week or month. To make a printed Calendar view even more useful, specify how many months or weeks you want to print on each page. You can print up to 2 months or 50 weeks on each page.

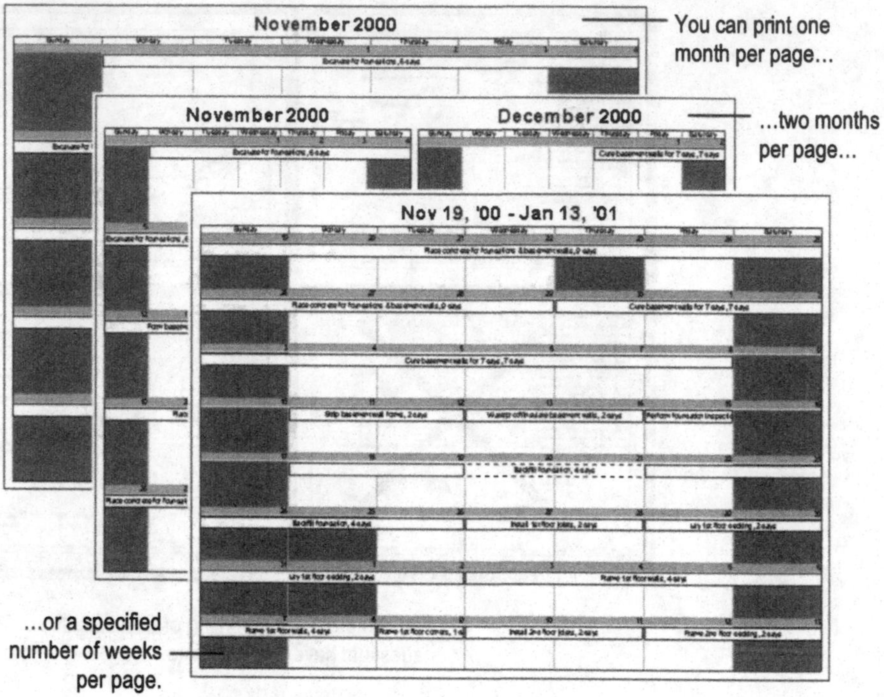

To specify the number of weeks or months printed in the Calendar view

1. On the **View Bar**, click **Calendar**.
2. On the **File** menu, click **Page Setup**, and then click the **View** tab.
3. To specify months, click **Months per page**, and then click **1** or **2**.

   To specify weeks, click **Weeks per page**, and then enter the number of weeks you want to display.

Print the Previous and Next Month in a Calendar View

The calendars that you hang on your wall often show miniature versions of the previous and next month along with the current month. You can quickly see a continuous connection between where you've been, where you are, and where you're going.

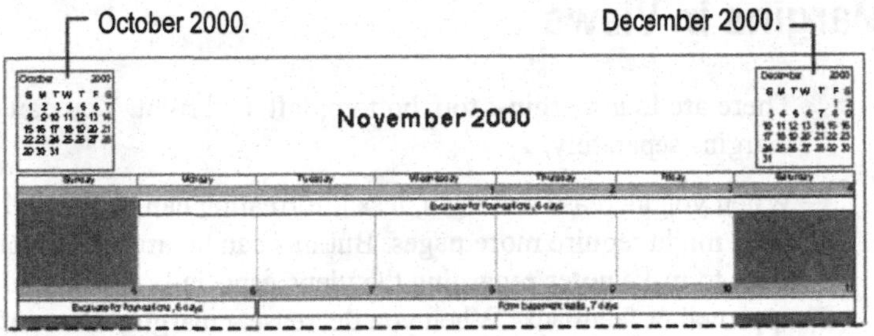

In the same way, you can print insets of the previous and next month with the Calendar view. For example, for November, you can choose to also print miniature calendars of October and December.

To print the previous and next month in the Calendar view

1 On the **View Bar**, click **Calendar**.
2 On the **File** menu, click **Page Setup**, and then click the **View** tab.
3 Select the **Print previous/next month calendars** check box.

Formatting the Page of the Printed View

Setting up the presentation of the printed view make your views look polished and professional. It can clarify aspects of the project or the view, and it can make the view easier to interpret at a glance. Set up the presentation of your pages by doing any of the following:

- Adjust the size of page margins.
- Add and remove page borders.
- Print pages in portrait (vertical) or landscape (horizontal) orientation.
- Add and remove headers, footers, and legends.
- Adjust page fit.
- Adjust the size (scaling) of information that appears on a page.
- Insert and remove page breaks.

Adjust Page Margins in Views

There are four margins: top, bottom, left, and right. You can adjust each of these margins separately.

When you increase a margin, less information can be printed on a page, and a printed view might require more pages. But this can be useful for your recipients who might want to make notes regarding the view, especially if you're distributing the view for approval or feedback. When you decrease a margin, more information can be printed on a page. This can be useful when you're trying to keep the page count to a minimum.

To adjust page margins for a view

1. Select the view you want and set it up with the information you want to print.
2. On the **File** menu, click **Page Setup**, and then click the **Margins** tab.
3. In the **Top**, **Bottom**, **Left**, and **Right** boxes, type the new margin settings.

Add and Remove Page Borders in Views

By default, Microsoft Project adds a thin line border to each printed view. This prints a rectangle drawn around all the information contained in the printed view. The page border is drawn along the edges of the margins.

For the Network Diagram and Descriptive Network Diagram, you can specify that the page border be printed around the outer, or perimeter, pages.

To add page borders to a view

1. Select the view you want and set it up with the information you want to print.
2. On the **File** menu, click **Page Setup**, and then click the **Margins** tab.
3. In the **Borders around** box, click **Every Page**.

   If you're printing a Network Diagram, click **Outer Pages**.

To remove page borders

1. Select the view you want and set it up with the information you want to print.
2. On the **File** menu, click **Page Setup**, and then click the **Margins** tab.
3. In the **Borders around** box, click **None**.

Print Pages Vertically or Horizontally in Views

You can print pages vertically (in portrait orientation) or horizontally (in landscape orientation). For example, if all the columns of a sheet view won't fit on a vertically oriented page, you can try printing the view in landscape orientation.

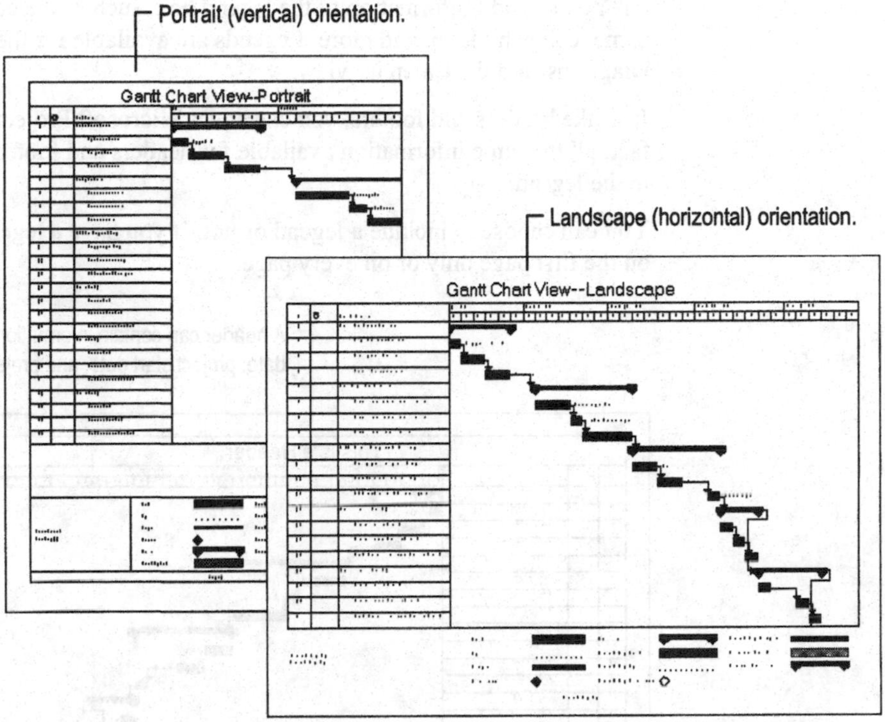

To change the page orientation

1. Select the view you want and set it up with the information you want to print.
2. On the **File** menu, click **Page Setup**, and then click the **Page** tab.
3. Click **Portrait** or **Landscape**.

Add and Remove Headers, Footers, and Legends in Views

A *header* is text printed at the top of every page. A *footer* is text printed at the bottom of every page. Headers and footers add useful information and make your printed views look more professional. Examples of text that you can add to headers and footers are page numbers, the project start date, and your company name.

You can also add a Microsoft Project information field, such as % Complete, Cost, or Actual Work, as a header or footer. The cumulative value of the field for the entire project is shown.

A *legend* is an explanatory list that appears on every page of a printed view. Typically, a legend explains what each symbol in a view means. For example, on the Gantt Chart, the legend explains the symbols for tasks, milestones, summary tasks, deadlines, and so on. You can add information to the legend box, such as the current date, the project file name, company logo, and more. Legends are available for the Gantt Charts, Network Diagrams, and the Calendar view.

Just like headers and footers, you can add a Microsoft Project field to the legend. In fact, all the same information available for headers and footers is available for inclusion in the legend.

You can choose to include a legend or not. If you have a legend, you can have it print on the first page only or on every page.

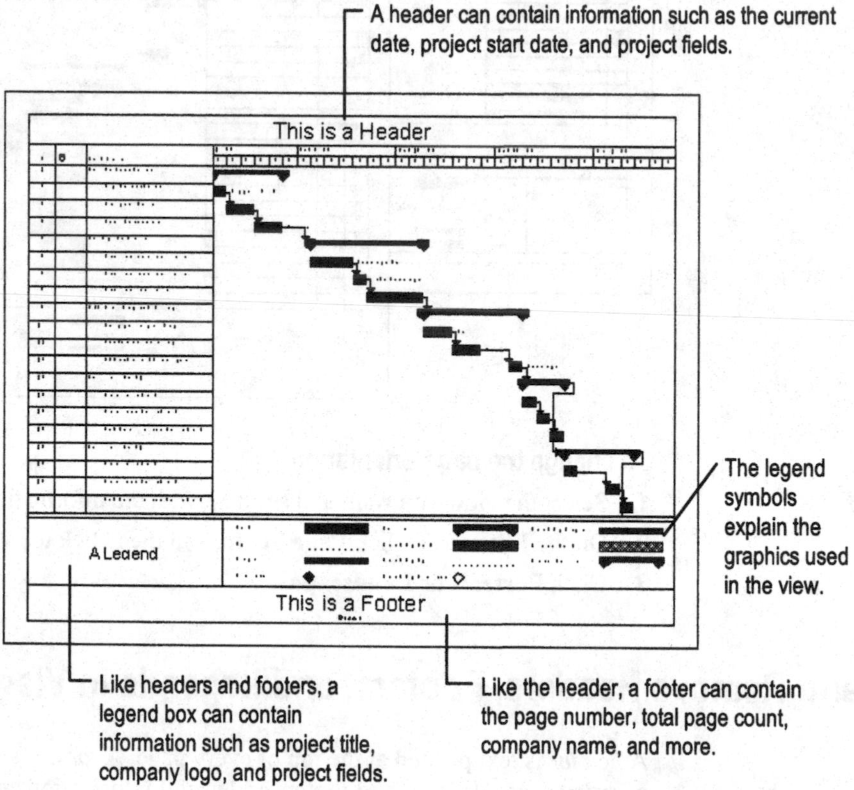
A header can contain information such as the current date, project start date, and project fields.
This is a Header
A Legend
This is a Footer
The legend symbols explain the graphics used in the view.
Like headers and footers, a legend box can contain information such as project title, company logo, and project fields.
Like the header, a footer can contain the page number, total page count, company name, and more.

Add a Header, Footer, or Legend to a View

For information about inserting graphics into a header, footer, or legend, see chapter 18.

Add text or an information field to a header, footer, or legend by typing or selecting it. You can then format the text if you want. You can also insert graphic images, such as a logo.

You can add up to five lines of information to a header and up to three lines to a footer or legend. You can also adjust the width of the legend's text box from 0 to 5 inches.

To add a header, footer, or legend to a view

1 Select the view you want and set it up with the information you want to print.

2 On the **File** menu, click **Page Setup**.

3 Click the **Header**, **Footer**, or **Legend** tab.

4 Under **Alignment**, click the **Left**, **Center**, or **Right** tab.

5 In the text box, type or paste text, or insert or paste a graphic.

Insert Page Number

6 To add common information such as the page number, total page count, date, time, and file name, click the appropriate button below the text box. For example, to add the page number, position the cursor in the text box, and then click **Insert Page Number**.

To add a running page count, type **of** between the Page Number symbol and the Total Page Count symbol:

&[Page] of **&[Pages]**

7 To add general information such as the project title, company name, project start date, and report name, select the information you want from the **General** list, and then click **Add**.

8 To add project information such as % Complete, Actual Work, or Cost, select the field from the **Project fields** list, and then click **Add**.

Format Text Font

9 To change the appearance of text, select the text you want to change in the text box, click **Format Text Font**, choose the font options you want, and then click **OK**.

Remove a Header, Footer, or Legend from a View

A header, footer, or legend appears in a printed view only when you add information to the header, footer, or legend. To remove a header, footer, or legend, you only need to delete the text and/or graphical information that's in it.

When you delete the data in a legend's text box, only the legend's symbol box appears when you print the view. You can, however, prevent the entire legend from being printed by suppressing it when you print. When you suppress a legend, the information remains in the legend; the legend just doesn't get printed. You can also print a legend on a separate page that follows the view.

To remove a header, footer, or legend from a view

1. Select the view you want and set it up with the information you want to print.
2. On the **File** menu, click **Page Setup**.
3. Click the **Header**, **Footer**, or **Legend** tab.
4. Under **Alignment**, click the **Left**, **Center**, or **Right** tab.
5. Select the text or graphic, and then press DELETE.

To print a view without printing its legend

1. Select the view you want and set it up with the information you want to print.
2. On the **File** menu, click **Page Setup**, and then click the **Legend** tab.
3. Under **Legend on**, select **None**.

To print a legend on a separate page

1. Select the view you want and set it up with the information you want to print.
2. On the **File** menu, click **Page Setup**, and then click the **Legend** tab.
3. Under **Legend on**, select **Legend page**.

Adjust Page Fit in a View

When printed, the pages of some views fit together like pieces of a jigsaw puzzle; you have to place the pages correctly in a matrix of rows and columns to see the entire view. An example of a view that gets printed in jigsawlike pages is the Gantt Chart view (especially when it contains many tasks and linked Gantt bars).

A view that prints on several rows and columns of pages can be unwieldy. To make it easier to manage, you can reduce the size of the printed view by specifying how many pages tall and wide the printed view will be. If your printed view is, for example, three pages tall and two pages wide (for a total of 6 pages), you could reduce it by changing the setting to two pages tall. The view will fit on fewer pages, and the information on each page will decrease in size proportionately.

You can only reduce the number of pages tall and wide on which a view prints; you can't increase the number of pages. For example, you can't enlarge a three-page view to five pages. You can, however, enlarge a view by adjusting the size of information that appears on a printed page.

To adjust page fit in a view

1 On the **View Bar**, click any view except the Calendar or Resource Graph.

To select a view that doesn't appear on the **View Bar**, click **More Views**, click the view you want in the **Views** list, and then click **Apply**.

2 On the **File** menu, click **Page Setup**, and then click the **Page** tab.

3 Under **Scaling**, click **Fit to**.

4 In the **pages wide by** box, type the number of pages across that you want the view to fit.

5 In the **tall** box, type the number of pages down that you want the view to fit.

6 Click **Print Preview** to view the result.

To get a better idea of how many pages your view could print on at a reduced size, click Print Preview. In the lower left corner, the Multi-Page Size field indicates the number of rows (pages down) by columns (pages across) that the view would print on in its current size. In the Page Setup dialog box, reduce those numbers by a quarter or a half and look at the preview again to view the results. Microsoft Project will warn you if you're making the information on the pages too small to be legible.

Adjust the Size of Information on a Printed View Page

You can change the size of the information that appears on each page of a view. If the information is difficult to read, you can increase its size. If the view prints on too many pages, you can decrease the size of the information and reduce the number of pages.

The default setting is 100%. If you decrease the setting to, say, 60%, you'll decrease the size of the information by 40%, print more information on each page, and perhaps print fewer pages. If you increase the setting to, say, 150%, you'll increase the size of the information by 50%, print less information on each page, and perhaps print more pages.

To adjust the size of information on a printed page

1 Select the view you want and set it up with the information you want to print.

2 On the **File** menu, click **Page Setup**, and then click the **Page** tab.

3 Under **Scaling**, click **Adjust to**.

4 In the **% normal size** box, type the percentage at which you want information to appear on your printed pages.

5 Click **Print Preview** to view the result.

Insert a Page Break into a View

When a view prints on more than one page, information that should logically be together on the same page might appear on different pages. For example, a summary task might appear at the bottom of one page and its subtasks at the top of the next page. This is because Microsoft Project automatically inserts page breaks after information on a page reaches the bottom margin.

To keep certain information together, you can insert horizontal page breaks exactly where you want them. That might mean that extra white space appears at the bottom of some pages—perhaps causing the view to print on more pages than it otherwise would have—but the convenience of seeing certain pieces of information together on one page might be worth the trade-off.

See "Formatting a Network Diagram" in chapter 13.

You can insert manual page breaks into sheet views only. And you can insert horizontal page breaks between rows, but not vertical page breaks between columns. You can't insert manual page breaks into form views, the Resource Graph view, the Calendar view, or the Network Diagrams. You can, however, adjust page breaks in Network Diagrams so that Network Diagram boxes don't cross page breaks. By default, a page break that you insert appears as a dotted line that you can easily identify.

To insert a page break

1 Select the view you want and set it up with the information you want to print.

2 In the **Task Name** or **Resource Name** field, select the task or resource that you want to appear at the top of a new page.

3 On the **Insert** menu, click **Page Break.**

Remove a Page Break from a View

If you inserted a manual page break in a view and then decided that you don't want it, or you want to break pages in a different place, you can remove the page break. You can remove manual page breaks individually or all at once. By default, manually inserted page breaks appear as dotted lines for easy identification.

You can also leave the manual page breaks in a view, but print the view without the page breaks by suppressing the page breaks when printing.

To remove an individual page break

1 Select the view you want and set it up with the information you want to print.

2 In the **Task Name** or **Resource Name** field, select the task or resource with which the page break is associated. This is the one in the row under the page break.

3 On the **Insert** menu, click **Remove Page Break.**

To remove all manual page breaks at the same time

1 Select the view you want and set it up with the information you want to print.

2 Click any column heading in the view that contains the page break.

3 On the **Insert** menu, click **Remove All Page Breaks**.

To suppress page breaks when printing

1 Select the view you want and set it up with the information you want to print.

2 On the **File** menu, click **Print**.

3 Clear the **Manual Page Breaks** check box.

16

Printing Reports

A *report* is a predefined set of project information in a format that's designed and ready for printing. You choose the report that meets your needs, and information is collected from various locations in your project and formatted according to the report format.

Different types of reports are designed for different audiences: for example, overview reports are most suitable for upper management, budget reports for accounting, and resource reports for your team members. There are 29 predefined reports in Microsoft Project. You can also create your own report or modify an existing report.

For elementary information about printing, see chapter 14.

You set up core information for a report, first by selecting the report, and then selecting any table or filter that will display the information you need. Once you're ready to print, you can fine-tune the information as it appears in the report printout so it looks exactly the way you want.

Task as of Mon 10/30/00
Residential Construction
Sean Thompson

Task Name	Duration	Start	Finish
Finalize plans and develop estimate with owner, ar	20 days	Tue 9/26/00	Mon 10/23/00
Sign contract and notice to proceed	1 day	Tue 10/24/00	Tue 10/24/00
Secure foundation permit	0 days	Tue 10/24/00	Tue 10/24/00
Secure framing permit	0 days	Tue 10/24/00	Tue 10/24/00
Secure electrical permit	0 days	Tue 10/24/00	Tue 10/24/00
Secure plumbing permit	0 days	Tue 10/24/00	Tue 10/24/00
Secure HVAC permit	0 days	Tue 10/24/00	Tue 10/24/00
Secure miscellaneous permits	0 days	Tue 10/24/00	Tue 10/24/00
Clear and grub lot	1 day	Wed 10/25/00	Wed 10/25/00
Install temporary power service	1 day	Thu 10/26/00	Thu 10/26/00
Install underground utilities	1 day	Fri 10/27/00	Fri 10/27/00
Excavate for foundations	6 days	Mon 10/30/00	Mon 11/6/00
Form basement walls	7 days	Tue 11/7/00	Wed 11/15/00

Task report.

When setting up your report, you:

- **Specify report content options.** This includes the date range or columns to be printed. In this step, you're specifying what content should be included and how it should be arranged.
- **Specify the printed page format.** This includes elements such as margins, headers, and footers. In this step, you're specifying the layout and look of the printed page.

If the predefined report does not contain the information or layout you need, you can create your own report, or modify an existing one.

There are four types of reports:

- **Task reports.** A task report is a list or table of information about tasks. Examples include the Project Summary, Critical Tasks, and Slipping Tasks.
- **Resource reports.** A resource report is a list or table of information about resources. Examples include Who Does What, Overbudget Resources, and To-Do List.
- **Crosstab reports.** A *crosstab* report shows information about tasks or resources broken down by time period. It looks similar to the Task Usage and Resource Usage views. Examples of crosstab reports are the Cash Flow, Resource Usage, Task Usage, and Who Does What When reports.
- **Calendar reports.** A calendar report shows the tasks that occur within a given month, much like the Calendar view. Although Microsoft Project doesn't include a predefined calendar report, you can easily create your own.

If you use Microsoft Project Central, you can set up custom reports in Microsoft Project and then use Microsoft Project Central to make these reports available to different audiences. You can set permissions to allow different sets of users to review different reports, even across different projects. For more information about Microsoft Project Central, see chapter 11.

Specifying Content Options for Reports

With print options for reports, you specify how you want the content of the report printed. You can:

- Print supplemental information like notes in task and resource reports.
- Group information by time interval in a task, resource, or crosstab report.
- Change the sort order in a report.
- Print column totals in a task or resource report.

- Print summary tasks in a task or crosstab report.
- Change the rows and columns in a crosstab report.
- Print the first column on every page of a crosstab report.
- Print column and row totals in a crosstab report.
- Specify the date range for a crosstab report.
- Print a monthly calendar for a specific resource.

Print Supplemental Information in Task and Resource Reports

With most reports, you can print not only the core information in the report but also additional information such as notes, objects, and work data. The types of additional information you can print depend on the nature of the report.

With this kind of report	You can print this additional information
Task	• Task notes • Task objects from other programs • Predecessor tasks for each task • Successor tasks for each task • Assignment notes • Assignment schedule fields • Assignment cost fields • Assignment work fields
Resource	• Task notes • Resource objects from other programs • Calendar working and nonworking information • Cost rate information • Assignment notes • Assignment schedule fields • Assignment cost fields • Assignment work fields

The crosstab reports, Base Calendar, and Project Summary reports do not include any additional information. You can see the types of information a report can include by reviewing the report's Details tab.

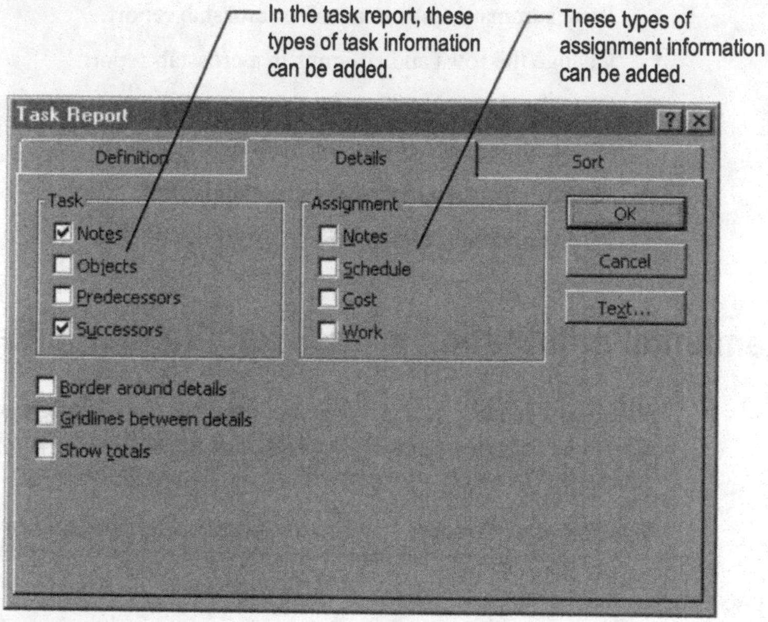

To print supplemental information in a task or resource report

1. On the **View** menu, click **Reports**.
2. Click the report type you want, and then click **Select**.

   If you chose **Custom** as the report type, click a report in the **Reports** list, click **Edit**, and then go to step 4.
3. Click the report you want, and then click **Edit**.
4. Click the **Details** tab.
5. If the report is a task report, then in the **Task** box, select the **Notes**, **Objects**, **Predecessors**, or **Successors** check box.

   If the report is a resource report, then in the **Resource** box, select the **Notes**, **Objects**, **Calendar**, or **Cost Rates** check box.
6. For either a task or resource report, in the **Assignment** box, select the **Notes**, **Schedule**, **Cost**, or **Work** check box.

   If a check box is grayed, the information is not available for this report.

   If no details are listed at all, then no details can be added to this report.

Group Information by Time Interval in Reports

In most reports, information is presented in a continuous list. You see unbroken information for the entire project. When the list is short, you can scan it and easily pick out relevant dates. When the list is long, however, scanning it and picking out important dates can be difficult. To read information in a long report more easily and to focus on information in specific time periods, you can group the information by time periods.

When you group information by time period, a date separates one group of information from another.

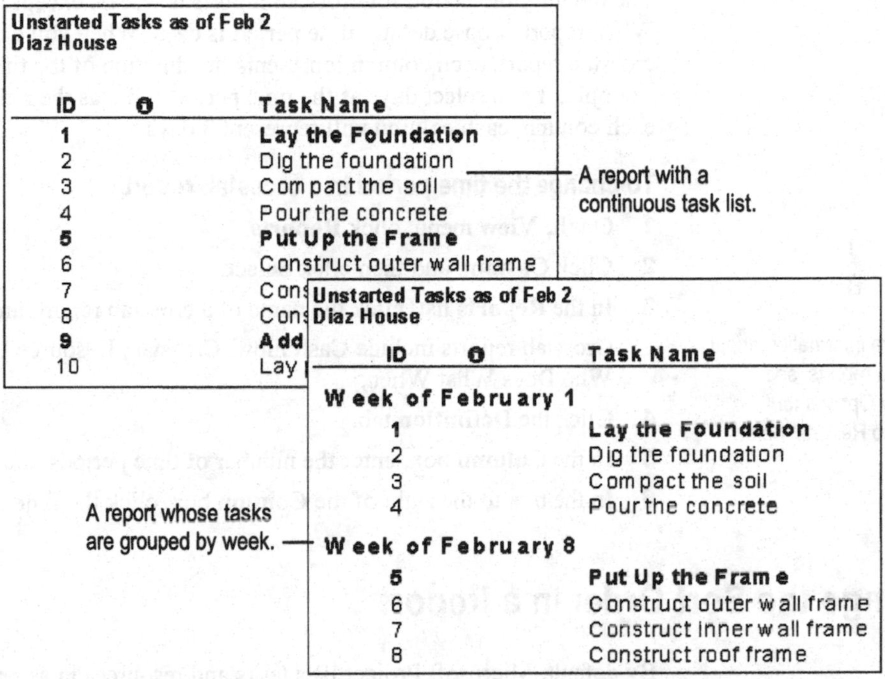

In addition to changing the basic time period unit, such as years, months, weeks, and days, you can also change the count of the time period. For example, in the Unstarted Tasks report, you can group information into one-week periods, two-week periods, three-week periods, and so on.

The default time period for most task and resource reports is the entire project. However, for the Tasks In Progress report and the Completed Tasks report, the default time period is months. Changing the time period might affect the number of pages on which a report is printed.

To change the time period for grouping information in a task or resource report

1 On the **View** menu, click **Reports**.

2 Click the report type you want, and then click **Select**.

If you chose **Custom** as the report type, click a report in the **Reports** list, click **Edit**, and then go to step 4.

3 Click the report you want, and then click **Edit**.
4 Click the **Definition** tab.
5 In the **Period** box, click the time period you want.
6 In the **Count** box, click the number of time periods you want reported as a single unit.

The default time period for crosstab reports is weeks, except for the Who Does What When report, whose default time period is days. When you change the time period in a crosstab report, each column represents the duration of the time period you specify. For example, if you select days as the time period and 3 as the number of time periods in each column, each column will represent 3 days.

To change the time period in a crosstab report

1 On the **View** menu, click **Reports**.
2 Click **Custom**, and then click **Select**.
3 In the **Reports** list, click the name of a crosstab report, and then click **Edit**.
   Crosstab reports include Cash Flow, Crosstab, Resource Usage, Task Usage, and Who Does What When.
4 Click the **Definition** tab.
5 In the **Column** box, enter the number of time periods you want in each column.
6 In the box to the right of the **Column** box, click the time period you want.

For more information about crosstab reports, see "Specify Options for Crosstab Reports" below.

Change the Sort Order in a Report

By default, Microsoft Project lists tasks and resources in ascending order by ID number. But you might want to see tasks or resources in a different order. If, for example, you want to decrease the project length, you might want to list tasks from the longest duration to the shortest, to focus on reducing the longest durations first. Or, you might want to sort resources by how much they're overallocated.

The sorting criteria you can choose are the Microsoft Project task and resource fields that are available. For instance, if you want to sort tasks by duration, you specify that the Duration field control the sort order.

To change the sort order in a report

1 On the **View** menu, click **Reports**.
2 Click the report type you want, and then click **Select**.
   If you chose **Custom** as the report type, click a report in the **Reports** list, click **Edit**, and then go to step 4.
3 Click the report you want, and then click **Edit**.
4 Click the **Sort** tab.

5 In the **Sort by** box, click the field you want to use as your primary sort criterion.
6 Click **Ascending** or **Descending**.
7 If you want to sort by a second and third sort criterion, click the field you want in the appropriate **Then by** box, and then click **Ascending** or **Descending**.

Print Column Totals in a Task or Resource Report

You can only print column totals for those columns in which it makes sense to add the values in the column. For example, there's no total printed for a column that contains start dates.

By default, the total of the values in a column is not printed in a task or resource report. For example, if a resource report includes a Work column, that column will only show the number of hours worked by each resource; it will not show the total number of hours worked by all resources. You can, however, choose to print column totals.

To print column totals in a task or resource report

1 On the **View** menu, click **Reports**.
2 Click the report type you want, and then click **Select**.
If you chose **Custom** as the report type, click a report in the **Reports** list, click **Edit**, and then go to step 4.
3 Click the report you want, and then click **Edit**.
4 Click the **Details** tab.
5 Select the **Show totals** check box.

Print Summary Tasks in a Task or Crosstab Report

Some reports include summary tasks by default, while others do not.

Including summary tasks is a good way to group tasks visually and to see which tasks belong to the same project phase. If you print summary tasks, each summary task is printed above the group of subtasks that belong to the summary task.

To print summary tasks in a task or crosstab report

1 On the **View** menu, click **Reports**.
2 Click the report type you want, and then click **Select**.
If you chose **Custom** as the report type, click a report in the **Reports** list, click **Edit**, and then go to step 4.
3 Click the report you want, and then click **Edit**.
4 To print summary tasks in a task report, click the **Definition** tab.
To print summary tasks in a crosstab report, click the **Details** tab.
5 For a task report, select the **Show summary tasks** check box.
For a crosstab report, select the **Summary tasks** check box.

Specify Options for Crosstab Reports

A crosstab report consists of rows and columns of information. Each row contains information about a single item. Each column represents a period of time. The intersection of a row with a column shows you the total value of the item in the time period represented by the column.

For example, suppose a row contains the number of hours worked by a resource and each column represents a period of 1 day. The intersection of a row with a column shows you the number of hours of work the resource has on a specific day.

The Microsoft Project default crosstab reports are:

- **Cash Flow.** Tasks with assignments by cost.
- **Crosstab.** Tasks with assignments by cost.
- **Resource Usage.** Resource with assignments by work.
- **Resource Usage (Material).** Material resources with assignments by work.
- **Resource Usage (Work).** Work resources with assignments by work.
- **Task Usage.** Tasks with assignments by work.
- **Who Does What When.** Work resources with assignments by work.

Change the Rows and Columns in a Crosstab Report

Each crosstab report comes with default rows and columns. For instance, by default the Resource Usage report shows resource work broken down by 1-week periods. To print different information in the rows, or to break down the information by a different time period, you can change the rows and columns.

The rows in a crosstab report can contain task or resource information, along with assignments. After you decide whether a report's rows will contain information about tasks or resources, you can choose the kind of task or resource information you want. For example, you can select Resources as the row, Work as the row information, and Days as the column to print a report showing the number of hours worked each day by each resource.

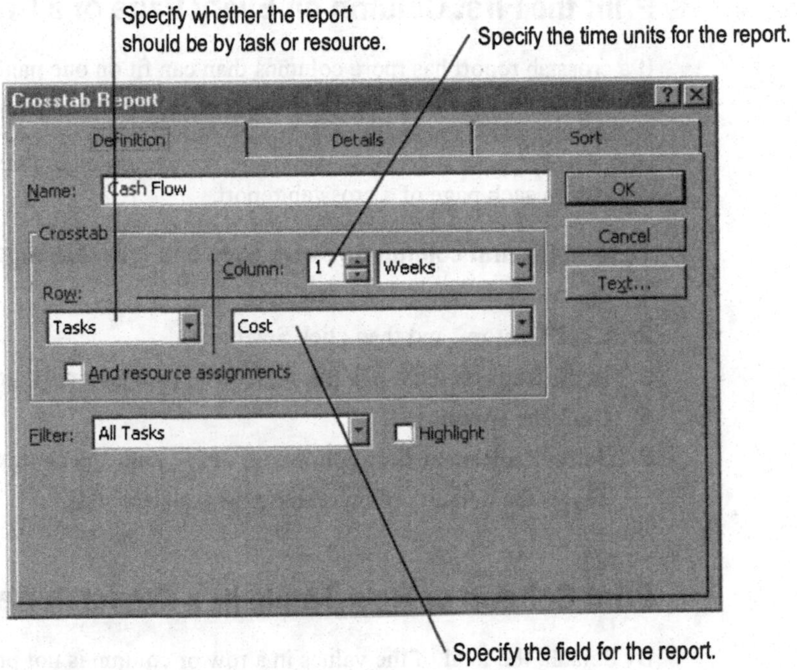

To change the row and column definitions in a crosstab report

1. On the **View** menu, click **Reports.**
2. Click **Custom,** and then click **Select.**
3. In the **Reports** list, click the name of a crosstab report, and then click **Edit.**
4. Click the **Definition** tab.
5. In the **Column** boxes, enter the number of time units each column will represent, and then click the unit of time you want.
6. In the **Row** box, click **Tasks** or **Resources.**
7. In the box to the right of the **Row** box, click the information you want printed for the rows.
8. Select the **And assignments** check box if you want to include the assignments associated with each task or resource.

Print the First Column on Every Page of a Crosstab Report

If a crosstab report has more columns than can fit on one page, the spillover columns will be printed on other pages. On the second and third pages, you won't see which task or resource name goes with each row of information, because the task and resource names will appear only on the first page. To avoid this problem, you can print the first column on each page of a crosstab report.

To print the first column on every page of a crosstab report

1. On the **View** menu, click **Reports**.
2. Click **Custom**, and then click **Select**.
3. In the **Reports** list, click the name of a crosstab report, and then click **Edit**.
4. Click the **Details** tab.
5. Select the **Repeat first column on every page** check box.

   This is the default option on most crosstab reports.

Print Column or Row Totals in a Crosstab Report

By default, the total of the values in a row or column is not printed in a crosstab report. The total for a column shows you the total value of a particular item for all tasks or resources in a particular time period. The total for a row shows you the total value of an item for a particular task or resource over the course of the entire project. If you specify a date range for the report, the total shows you the total value for that date range.

For example, if a crosstab report shows the number of hours worked by each resource each day, then a column total tells you how many hours all resources worked on a particular day, and a row total tells you how many hours a particular resource will work over the course of the entire project or the specified date range.

Resource Usage as of Feb 2
Diaz House

	Jan 26	Feb 9	Feb 23	Total
Tom		16 hrs	40 hrs	56 hrs
Diggers		24 hrs		24 hrs
Selena		16 hrs	16 hrs	32 hrs
Jake			8 hrs	8 hrs
Penelope			32 hrs	40 hrs
Roofers				
Total		56 hrs	96 hrs	160 hrs

Row totals.

Column totals.

To print column or row totals in a crosstab report

1 On the **View** menu, click **Reports**.
2 Click **Custom**, and then click **Select**.
3 In the **Reports** list, click the name of a crosstab report, and then click **Edit**.
4 Click the **Details** tab.
5 Select the **Row totals** check box, the **Column totals** check box, or both.
   In some crosstab reports, these boxes are selected by default.

Specify the Date Range for a Crosstab Report

The time period columns of a crosstab report make up the kind of timescale you find in the Gantt Chart view or the Resource Usage view. Normally when you print a crosstab report, you print all the information that's available in the report, from the project start date to the project finish date. Sometimes, however, you might want to print only the information that falls within a specific time period. In that case, you can specify the date range for the report.

To specify the date range in a crosstab report

1 On the **View** menu, click **Reports**.
2 Click **Custom**, and then click **Select**.
3 In the **Reports** list, click the name of a crosstab report, and then click **Print**.
4 Under **Timescale**, click **Dates**.
5 In the **From** box, click the first date you want included in the report.
   In the **To** box, click the last date you want included in the report.

Create a Monthly Calendar for a Specific Resource

A monthly calendar shows the tasks that occur within a given month. A monthly calendar for a specific resource shows only those tasks assigned to the resource, which can help you and the resource keep track of the tasks that need to be accomplished each month. Although Microsoft Project doesn't include any predefined monthly calendar reports, you can easily create your own monthly calendar reports for specific resources.

A monthly calendar report showing the tasks for one resource.

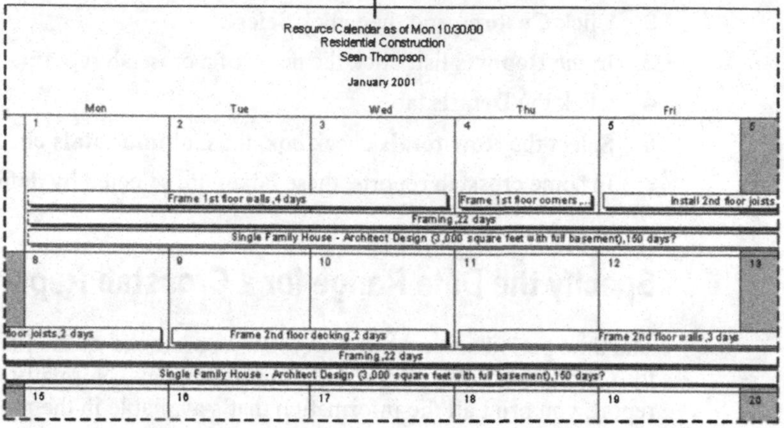

To create a monthly calendar for a specific resource

1. On the **View** menu, click **Reports**.
2. Click **Custom,** and then click **Select**.
3. In the **Reports** list, click **New**, click **Monthly Calendar**, and then click **OK**.
4. In the **Name** box, type a name for the report.
5. In the **Filter** box, click **Using Resource**.
6. In the **Calendar** box, click the *base calendar* you want to use for the resource.

   You can use any calendar defined in your project, including the Standard calendar or the resource's own working time calendar.
7. Specify any formatting and labels you want for the report, and then click **OK**.

   The name of the new monthly calendar is added to the Reports list.
8. Click **Print**, and then click **OK**.
9. In the **Show tasks using** box, click the name of the resource for whom you want to print the monthly calendar.

For information about working time calendars and base calendars, see "Setting Working Time for Resources" in chapter 6.

Formatting the Page of the Printed Report

Reports are preformatted and ready to be printed. But you can fine-tune report page appearance to suit your needs. This section focuses on ways to change the page presentation of reports. It explains how to:

- Adjust the size of page margins.
- Add and remove page borders.

- Print borders around details in a task or resource report.
- Print pages in portrait (vertical) or landscape (horizontal) orientation.
- Add and remove headers and footers.
- Adjust the size of information that appears on a page (scaling).
- Print gridlines.
- Insert page breaks.
- Format report text.
- Specify the print range and number of copies.

Adjust Page Margins in a Report

There are four margins: top, bottom, left, and right. You can adjust each of these margins separately.

When you increase a margin, less information can be printed on a page, and a printed report might require more pages. But this can be useful for your recipients who might want to make notes regarding the report, especially if you're requesting approval or feedback. When you decrease a margin, more information can be printed on a page. This can be useful when you're trying to keep the page count to a minimum.

To adjust page margins for a report

1 On the **View** menu, click **Reports**.

2 Click the report type you want, and then click **Select**.

3 Click the report you want to print, and then click **Select**.

If you chose **Custom** as the report type in step 2, click **Setup**, and then go to step 5.

4 Click **Page Setup**.

5 Click the **Margins** tab.

6 In the **Top, Bottom**, **Left**, and **Right** boxes, type the new margin settings.

Add or Remove Page Borders in a Report

By default, Microsoft Project adds a thin line border to each report. This prints a rectangle drawn around all the information contained in the report. The page border is drawn along the edges of the margins.

To add or remove page borders in a report

1 On the **View** menu, click **Reports**.

2 Click the report type you want, and then click **Select**.

3 Click the report you want, and then click **Select**.

If you chose **Custom** as the report type in step 2, click **Setup**, and then go to step 5.

4 Click **Page Setup**.

5 Click the **Margins** tab.

6 In the **Borders around** box, click **Every Page** or **None**.

Print Borders Around Details in a Task or Resource Report

Details are supplemental information that aren't part of the core information normally included in a report. Examples of details include:

For information on how to define the details you want to include in your report, see "Print Supplemental Information in Task and Resource Reports" earlier in this chapter.

- Notes.
- Graphic objects imported from other programs.
- Cost fields.
- Work fields.
- Successor tasks.
- Predecessor tasks.

When you include details in a report, you can print a border around them.

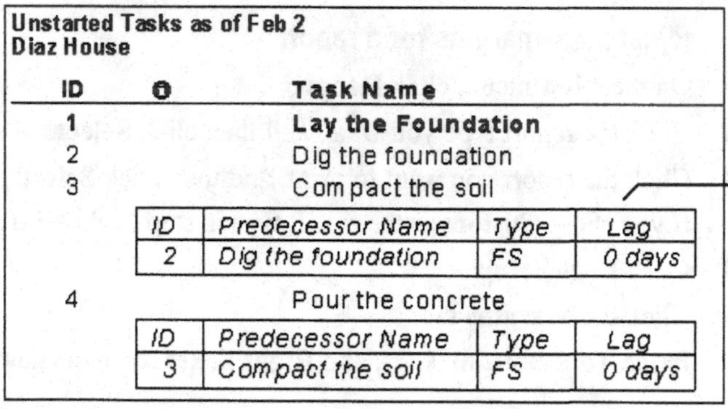
Unstarted Tasks as of Feb 2
Diaz House

ID		Task Name
1		**Lay the Foundation**
2		Dig the foundation
3		Compact the soil

ID	Predecessor Name	Type	Lag
2	Dig the foundation	FS	0 days

ID		Task Name
4		Pour the concrete

ID	Predecessor Name	Type	Lag
3	Compact the soil	FS	0 days

A task report showing borders drawn around details.

You can print borders around details in task and resource reports, but not in crosstab reports.

To print a border around details in a task or resource report

1 On the **View** menu, click **Reports**.

2 Click the report type you want, and then click **Select**.

If you chose **Custom** as the report type, click a report in the **Reports** list, click **Edit**, and then go to step 4.

3 Click the report you want, and then click **Edit**.

4 Click the **Details** tab.

5 Select the **Border around details** check box.

Print Pages Vertically or Horizontally in a Report

You can print pages vertically (in portrait orientation) or horizontally (in landscape orientation). For example, if all the columns of a report won't fit on a vertically oriented page, you can try printing the report in landscape orientation.

To change the page orientation

1 On the **View** menu, click **Reports**.

2 Click the report type you want, and then click **Select**.

3 Click the report you want, and then click **Select**.

If you chose **Custom** as the report type in step 2, click **Setup**, and then go to step 5.

4 Click **Page Setup**.

5 Click the **Page** tab.

6 Click **Portrait** or **Landscape**.

Add and Remove Headers and Footers in a Report

A *header* is text printed at the top of every page. A *footer* is text printed at the bottom of every page. Headers and footers add useful information and make your printed reports look more professional. Examples of text that you can add to headers and footers are page numbers, the project start date, the project file name, and your company logo. You can also add a running page count (such as Page 1 of 3, Page 2 of 3, and Page 3 of 3).

You can also add a Microsoft Project information field, such as % Complete, Cost, or Actual Work as a header or footer. The cumulative value of the field for the entire project is shown.

Add a Header or Footer to a Report

For information about inserting graphics into a header or footer, see chapter 18, "Sharing Project Information with Other Programs."

Add text or an information field to a header or footer by typing or selecting it. You can then format text if you want. You can also insert graphic images, such as a logo. You can add up to five lines of information to a header and up to three lines to a footer.

To add a header or footer to a report

1 On the **View** menu, click **Reports**.

2 Click the report type you want, and then click **Select**.

3 Click the report you want, and then click **Select**.

If you chose **Custom** as the report type in step 2, click **Setup**, and then go to step 5.

4 Click **Page Setup**, and then click the **Header** or **Footer** tab.

5 Under **Alignment**, click the **Left**, **Center**, or **Right** tab.

6 In the text box, type or paste text, add document or project information, or insert or paste a graphic.

Insert Page Number

7 To add common information such as the page number, total page count, date, time, and file name, click the appropriate button below the text box. For example, to add the page number, position the cursor in the text box, and then click **Insert Page Number**.

To add a running page count, type **of** between the Page Number symbol and the Total Page Count symbol:

&[Page] of **&[Pages]**

8 To add general information such as the project title, company name, project start date, and report name, select the information you want from the **General** list, and then click **Add**.

9 To add project information such as % Complete, Actual Work, or Cost, select the field from the **Project fields** list, and then click **Add**.

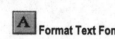

Format Text Font

10 To change the appearance of text, select the text you want to change in the text box, click **Format Text Font**, choose the font options you want, and then click **OK**.

Remove a Header or Footer from a Report

A header or footer appears in a report only when you add information to the header or footer. To remove a header or footer, you only need to delete any text, graphic, or symbol it includes.

To remove a header or footer from a report

1 On the **View** menu, click **Reports**.

2 Click the report type you want, and then click **Select**.

3 Click the report information you want, and then click **Select**.

If you chose **Custom** as the report type in step 2, click **Setup**, and then go to step 5.

4 Click **Page Setup**.

5 Click the **Header** or **Footer** tab.

6 Under **Alignment**, click the **Left**, **Center**, or **Right** tab.

7 Select the text, graphic, or symbol, and then press DELETE.

Adjust the Size of Information on a Report Page

You can change the size of the information that appears on each page of a report. If the information is difficult to read, you can increase its size. If the report prints on too many pages, you can decrease the size of the information and reduce the number of pages.

The default setting is 100%. If you decrease the setting to, say, 60%, you'll decrease the size of the information by 40%, print more information on each page, and perhaps print fewer pages. If you increase the setting to, say, 150%, you'll increase the size of the information by 50%, print less information on each page, and perhaps print more pages.

To adjust the size of information on a report page

1. On the **View** menu, click **Reports**.
2. Click the report type you want, and then click **Select**.
3. Click the report you want, and then click **Select**.

   If you chose **Custom** as the report type in step 2, click **Setup**, and then go to step 5.
4. Click **Page Setup**.
5. Click the **Page** tab.
6. Click **Adjust to**.
7. In the **% normal size** box, type the percentage at which you want information to appear on your printed pages.
8. Click **Print Preview** to review the result.

Print Gridlines Between Details in a Report

Having rows of information without horizontal lines separating one row of details from another can make it difficult to read the information in a report. A simple way to make it easier to read a report is to insert horizontal gridlines between details. You can print gridlines between any details in a task, resource, or crosstab report. In a task or resource report, gridlines separate task, resource, and assignment details, such as notes, cost fields, or work fields. In a crosstab report, gridlines separate resource details, task details, or both.

To print gridlines between details in a task or resource report

1. On the **View** menu, click **Reports**.
2. Click the report type you want, and then click **Select**.

   If you chose **Custom** as the report type, click a report in the **Reports** list, click **Edit**, and then go to step 4.
3. Click the report you want, and then click **Edit**.

4 Click the **Details** tab.
5 Select the **Gridlines between details** check box.

To print gridlines in a crosstab report

1 On the **View** menu, click **Reports**.
2 Click **Custom**, and then click **Select**.
3 In the **Reports** list, click the name of a crosstab report, and then click **Edit**.
4 Click the **Details** tab.
5 In the **Gridlines** box, select the **Between tasks** check box, the **Between resources** check box, or both.

Insert a Page Break in a Report

You can't insert a page break directly into a report. However, page breaks inserted in a view appear in reports that contain the same kind of information as that view. For example, if you select a task and then insert a page break in the Task Sheet view, the page break will occur before that task in the Task Report.

When you filter or sort information in a view or report, each page break remains with the task or resource selected when you inserted the page break. For example, if a task is not displayed when you apply a filter, the page break associated with that task does not appear in the view or report.

Format Text in a Report

On one day you might need to focus on critical tasks. On another day, you might want to point out overallocated resources to your supervisor. To visually distinguish a class of tasks or resources—or simply to change its appearance to suit your needs—you can change the appearance of tasks and resources in predefined categories.

For information about fonts, font styles, and font sizes, see "General Formatting in Views" in chapter 13.

When you change the appearance of a category of tasks or resources, you change the appearance of all the information for each task or resource in that category, all at once. For example, if you make a category of tasks on the Unstarted Tasks report bold, the entire row of text for each task in the category appears bold. The formatting you apply to text in one report does not transfer to another report.

You change the appearance of task and resource information by changing the font, font style, font size, and color.

To format report text

1 On the **View** menu, click **Reports**.

2 Click the report type you want, and then click **Select**.

If you chose **Custom** as the report type, click a report in the **Reports** list, click **Edit**, and then go to step 4.

3 Click the report you want to format, and then click **Edit**.

If you clicked **Project Summary** or **Base Calendar**, go to step 5.

4 Click **Text**.

5 In the **Item to Change** box, click the task or resource category whose text you want to format, for example, Critical Tasks or Overallocated Resources.

6 Select the font, font style, size, and color you want.

7 To underline the item, select the **Underline** check box.

8 To have the text category appear in color, select from the **Color** list.

Specify the Print Range and Number of Copies

Microsoft Project provides a number of printing options. For example, you can print only the pages within a certain range, say, pages 3 to 5. You can also specify the number of copies you'd like of the entire or partial report.

There are different procedures for specifying printing options for reports.

To specify the print range and number of copies for a report

1 On the **View** menu, click **Reports**.

2 Click the report type you want, and then click **Select**.

If you chose **Custom** as the report type, click a report in the **Reports** list, click **Print**, and then go to step 5.

3 Click the report you want to print, and then click **Select**.

4 Click **Print**.

5 To print all the pages in the view, under **Print Range** click **All**.

To print a range of pages, under **Print Range** click **Page(s)**. Enter the number of the first page in the range in the **From** box and the number of last page in the range in the **To** box.

6 In the **Copies** box, type the number of copies you want to print in the **Number of copies** box.

Creating or Modifying a Report

Each report shows a default set of information in its rows and columns. But sometimes you might want to print a report with a different set of information. Microsoft Project provides you with several ways to include exactly the information you want in each report. For instance, you can:

- Change the report name.
- Change the table in a task or resource report.
- Change the filter in a report.
- Modify a copy of a report.
- Create a report.
- Delete a report.

You can only change the appearance of text in the Base Calendar and Project Summary reports. You cannot change the information they contain.

Change the Report Name

Some predefined report names might not tell you clearly what kind of information is contained in the report. Or, if you modified a report, you might want to give it a name that reflects the new information it contains. In these situations, you can change the report name.

When you change a report name, you give the name to a copy of the original report. The copy, with the name you've given it, is added to the list of custom reports (in the Custom Reports dialog box). You do not change or delete the original report.

You cannot change the names of the Project Summary or Base Calendar reports.

To change the report name

1. On the **View** menu, click **Reports**.
2. Click the report type you want, and then click **Select**.

   If you chose **Custom** as the report type, click a report in the **Reports** list, click **Edit**, and then go to step 4.
3. Click the report you want to rename, and then click **Edit**.
4. Click the **Definition** tab.
5. In the **Name** box, type the new report name.

Change the Table in a Task or Resource Report

A *table* consists of a set of columns of related information. Each column displays a particular kind of information. A default table is attached to each task and resource report. For example, the Summary table is attached to the Completed Tasks report. To see other columns of information, you can apply a different table to the report. When you apply a different table to a report, the new table replaces the old table.

When you replace one table with another, you do not add information to or remove information from your project; you change only the project information displayed at the moment. Also, the list of tasks or resources on the report remains the same. Only the other columns of information change.

You cannot apply tables to crosstab reports or to the Project Summary or Base Calendar reports.

To change the table in a task or resource report

1 On the **View** menu, click **Reports**.

2 Click the report type you want, and then click **Select**.

If you chose **Custom** as the report type, click a report in the **Reports** list, click **Edit**, and then go to step 4.

3 Click the report you want, and then click **Edit**.

4 Click the **Definition** tab.

5 In the **Table** box, click the table you want to apply.

Change the Filter in a Report

A *filter* is a set of criteria for displaying a specific group of related tasks, resources, or assignments. A default filter is attached to each report. For example, the default filter for the Unstarted Tasks report is the Unstarted Tasks filter. If you want to show tasks or resources that meet a different set of criteria, you need to apply a different filter.

You can apply the filter that displays only those tasks or resources that share certain characteristics. For each filter, you can specify whether the filter displays only those tasks or resources that meet the filter criteria (and hides the tasks or resources that don't) or highlights the tasks or resources of interest in gray bands (while still displaying the other tasks or resources).

You can apply filters to task, resource, crosstab, and monthly calendar reports. You cannot apply filters to the Project Summary or Base Calendar reports.

To change the filter in a task or resource report

1. On the **View** menu, click **Reports**.
2. Click the report type you want, and then click **Select**.

   If you chose **Custom** as the report type, click a report in the **Reports** list, click **Edit**, and then go to step 4.
3. Click the report you want, and then click **Edit**.
4. Click the **Definition** tab.
5. In the **Filter** box, click the filter you want to apply.
6. To highlight filtered information, select the **Highlight** check box on the **Definition** tab.

Because Microsoft Project doesn't include any predefined monthly calendar reports, you must first create a monthly calendar report before you can apply a filter to it. When you create a monthly calendar report, you specify its default filter. Afterward, you can change its filter when you want to show a different set of tasks or resources.

To change the filter in a monthly calendar report

1. On the **View** menu, click **Reports**.
2. Click **Custom**, and then click **Select**.
3. In the **Reports** list, click the name of a monthly calendar report, and then click **Edit**.
4. In the **Filter** box, click the filter you want to apply.

Modify a Copy of a Report

The predefined reports that come with Microsoft Project are designed to include the information you're most likely to want in useful formats. However, if none of the predefined reports meets your information or format needs, but the report you want is similar to a predefined report, you can modify a copy of the existing report and save the modified version under a different name.

When you modify a copy of a report, the original predefined report remains unchanged. You can create a copy of any predefined or custom report. The copy you create is displayed in the Reports list of the Custom Reports dialog box.

To copy a report

1. On the **View** menu, click **Reports**.
2. Click **Custom**, and then click **Select**.
3. In the **Reports** list, click the report you want to copy.
4. Click **Copy**.

5 If you want to change the copied report's name, type a new name in the **Name** box.

6 If you're copying a task, resource, or crosstab report, specify the report content by entering the information you want in the appropriate boxes and selecting the options you want on the **Definition** and **Details** tabs.

If you're copying a monthly calendar report, specify the report content by entering the information you want in the appropriate boxes and selecting the options you want on the **Monthly Calendar Report Definition** dialog box.

Create a Report

The predefined reports that come with Microsoft Project are designed to include the information you're most likely to want and in useful formats. However, if the report you want differs significantly from existing reports, you can create a new report. When you create a new report, you base it on one of the four basic report types: task, resource, crosstab, or monthly calendar.

When you create a report, the new report is displayed in the Reports list of the Custom Reports dialog box.

To create a report

1 On the **View** menu, click **Reports**.

2 Click **Custom**, and then click **Select**.

3 Click **New**.

4 Select a report type, and then click **OK**.

5 If you're creating a task, resource, or crosstab report, specify the report content by entering the information you want in the appropriate boxes and selecting the options you want on the **Definition** and **Details** tabs.

If you're creating a monthly calendar report, specify the report content by entering the information you want in the appropriate boxes and selecting the options you want on the **Monthly Calendar Report Definition** dialog box.

Delete a Report

If you don't need a particular report, you can delete it. When you delete a report, you delete it from this project file only. A copy continues to be stored in the Microsoft Project global file, global.mpt. Deleting a report does not delete information from your project file.

You can delete any predefined or custom report using the Organizer. Deleting a report in this way removes it from the project file, but not from the global.mpt file.

To delete a report

1 On the **View** menu, click **Reports**.

2 Click **Custom**, and then click **Select**.

3 Click **Organizer**.

4 On the right side, in the list of reports available to the current project, click the report you want to delete.

   The left side of the Organizer lists reports that are available to all projects. Do not select a report from the GLOBAL.MPT list on the left unless you want to permanently delete it from Microsoft Project.

5 Click **Delete**.

6 Click **Yes** to confirm the deletion.

All predefined reports are listed in both the GLOBAL.MPT list and the project list. If you delete a predefined report, or any report, that's included in both files from the project file only, Microsoft Project will continue to display the report in the Reports list in the Custom Reports dialog box. Microsoft Project will remove a report from the Reports list only after it's deleted from both the GLOBAL.MPT list and the project list.

Part 5

Using Other Projects and Programs

As a project manager, it's likely that you juggle a multitude of responsibilities. You might manage several projects at one time, often using many of the same resources. You might also use a number of different tools to assist you in achieving your goals.

The information in Part 5 can help with both challenges. The two chapters in this part deal with using Microsoft Project to share information across multiple projects and multiple programs.

Chapter 17, "Managing Several Projects at Once," explains how Microsoft Project enables you to effectively organize, manage, and share resource and task information between multiple concurrent projects.

Chapter 18, "Sharing Project Information with Other Programs," explains how to exchange project information between different software programs. It discusses copying and pasting, linking and embedding, importing and exporting, and creating links to information in other files or on the Web.

17

Managing Several Projects at Once

If your situation is similar to that of many project managers, your biggest everyday challenge is juggling several projects at the same time. Your projects might share resources, start and finish at different times, and experience budget cuts, all at the same time. But Microsoft Project can help you keep track of all your projects, put resources where they're needed most, and give you the best possible chance of completing all of your projects on time and within budget.

One way to manage several projects at the same time is to insert several project files into one *consolidated project* file. Each inserted project is represented as a single task, similar to a summary task. You can open each project to view and edit its tasks, resources, and assignments, the same way you can when a project resides in a separate file.

By using a consolidated project file, you can display all your projects in the same window. In particular, you can quickly see which resources are working on which tasks and in which projects. You can review a single critical path across all the projects.

But consolidating projects is not the only help you get when you need to manage multiple projects. With Microsoft Project, you can also:

- Link tasks between projects, which is helpful when a task in one project is dependent on a task in another project.
- Create a resource pool to make it easy to share resources among projects. You can even level resources across multiple projects.
- Open separate project files all at once in a *workspace*, so that you can work with them at the same time even without the benefit of a consolidated project file.
- Create a project template, which contains the basic tasks that occur in many projects. Using the template, you can automate the creation of your projects.

While this chapter refers to consolidated projects, you might also be familiar with the concept of *master project* and *subprojects*. A master project is a type of consolidated project into which related projects, or subprojects, are inserted. The relationship between the master project and subprojects is analogous to that of a summary task and subtasks. A consolidated project can follow the multiple project/subproject model. A consolidated project can also simply be a file that is the repository for several projects unrelated except for the fact that they take place at the same time, are managed by the same person, or use the same set of resources.

Managing Several Projects in One Project File

Managing a number of projects simultaneously requires you to keep track of the progress, resources, and costs of each project. If each project is in a separate project file, you can focus on one project at a time, but you lose the big picture. Combine all those projects into one project, and you might end up with a huge file with hundreds of tasks, which can make it difficult to focus on one part at a time.

A better way to manage several projects at once is to consolidate them into one project file. To create a consolidated project file, you insert individual projects into one project file. In the Gantt Chart, each project is represented by a summary task that you can expand to show all the other tasks in the project. A consolidated project enables you to focus on one project and see an overview of all of your inserted projects at the same time. By default, each inserted project retains its link to its source file. When you revise the source file, the inserted project is revised also. Likewise, when you revise information in the inserted project, the source file is updated.

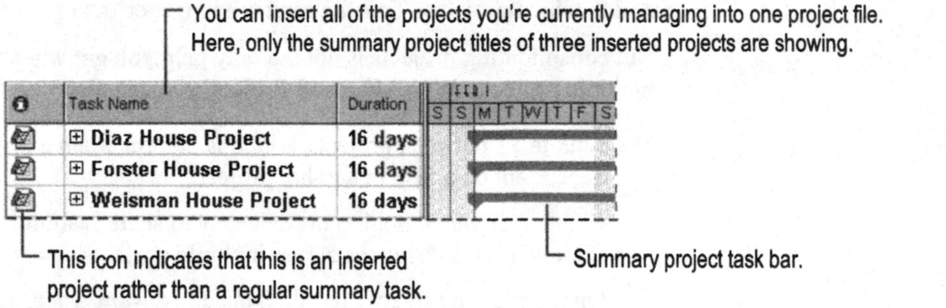
You can insert all of the projects you're currently managing into one project file. Here, only the summary project titles of three inserted projects are showing.
Task Name
Duration
S S M T W T F S
Diaz House Project
16 days
Forster House Project
16 days
Weisman House Project
16 days
This icon indicates that this is an inserted project rather than a regular summary task.
Summary project task bar.

Consider consolidating projects when:

- You break a large, complex project into smaller project phases, with each phase residing in a separate project file. That way, the manager of each phase can focus on his or her tasks and update those tasks as necessary. The manager of the whole project sees the phases as summary tasks in the consolidated project file.

- You want updates in related component projects of a larger project to be automatically reflected in the larger project.
- You're managing a number of separate projects and want to see an overview of them.
- You want to create reports that include information from several projects.

After you insert a project into a consolidated file, any changes you make to the source file appear automatically in the corresponding inserted project of the consolidated file, and vice versa. Format changes, however, are not updated between source and consolidated project files.

There are two ways to consolidate projects. You can customize as you consolidate your projects, which means you can specify the order of the inserted projects within the consolidated project.

If the projects you want to consolidate are already open in separate windows, you can use a quick method to consolidate them. When you use the quick method, Microsoft Project determines the order in which the inserted projects appear in the consolidated project file.

You can insert up to 1000 projects in a consolidated project file.

Consolidate Project Files in Specific Places

A consolidated project file contains projects that have been inserted into it. If the inserted projects are unrelated or only loosely related, their order in the consolidated project file might not matter to you. But, for example, if each inserted project represents a project phase, you probably want the inserted projects to appear at the correct outline level and in the correct order.

The simplest way to make sure that projects appear where you want them is to insert each project one at a time into a consolidated project. The reason: An inserted project inherits the outline level of the task or project that it's inserted under. In other words, a project inserted beneath a summary task will be indented one outline level with respect to the summary task. When you insert several projects at the same time, they'll appear at the same outline level and in the same location in the consolidated project. If that's what you want, fine. However even though you can change their order after you've inserted the projects, you won't be able to indent or outdent the inserted tasks with respect to each other; you'll only be able to do so with respect to the task they've been inserted under. To insert each project at a different outline level, you'll need to insert the projects one at a time.

You can insert a project into any location in an existing project. If you're creating a new consolidated project file—that is, inserting projects into an empty project file—you can insert the first project, expand it to show all of its tasks, then insert the next project into the first project at the outline level and in the location you want.

To insert a project file in a specific location in a consolidated project

1. Open a new or existing project file that you want to become the consolidated project.
2. On the **View Bar**, click **Gantt Chart**.
3. In the **Task Name** field, select where you want to insert the project.

   The inserted project will adopt the outline level of the surrounding tasks.
4. On the **Insert** menu, click **Project**.
5. In the **Look in** box, click the drive, folder, or Web location that contains the project files you want to insert.

   To insert several projects at the same time, they must reside in the same folder. You can, however, insert projects from one folder, then insert projects from another folder.
6. Hold down CTRL, and then click each project file you want to insert.
7. Click **Insert**.

   The projects are inserted into the consolidated file in the order that you selected them.
8. Repeat steps 3–7 for each folder that contains project files you want to insert into the consolidated project.

Consolidate Several Open Project Files at the Same Time

If you'd rather keep project files separate, you can set up a workspace. See "Open Several Project Files at Once with a Workspace" later in this chapter.

If you're managing several projects concurrently and you frequently have their project files opened at the same time, you might find it more convenient to consolidate those files into one project file. Microsoft Project provides a way to consolidate open project files quickly, without you having to insert them one at a time.

When you consolidate open project files, you can't specify the order or the outline location of each inserted project into the consolidated project. The projects are inserted at the same outline level in a new project file. You can, however, specify which of the open projects you want to consolidate.

To consolidate open project files

1. Open all the project files you want to consolidate.
2. On the **Window** menu, click **New Window**.
3. In the **Projects** list, click the project files you want to consolidate.

   Hold down CTRL, and then click each project file you want to insert.
4. To have the consolidated project appear in a view other than the one currently displayed, click a different view in the **View** box.

   Microsoft Project consolidates the projects in the order that they're listed in the **Projects** list.

Because each project is inserted into a new project file at the same outline level, you won't be able to indent or outdent the inserted projects with respect to each other. You can, however, insert a task above the topmost inserted project, then indent and outdent the inserted projects with respect to this task.

Delete the Link Between an Inserted Project and Its Source File

When you consolidate project files, the inserted files are linked to their source files by default. If you revise the source file, the change automatically appears in the corresponding inserted project. If you revise the inserted project, the change automatically appears in the corresponding source file. If you do not want a change in the source file to be reflected in the corresponding inserted project, or vice versa, you can break the link between them. The tasks, resources, and assignments in the inserted project become regular tasks, resources, and assignments, as if they were simply copied and pasted in.

To delete the link between an inserted project and its source project file

1 In the **Task Name** field, click the project summary task of the inserted project.

Task Information

2 Click **Task Information.**

3 Click the **Advanced** tab.

4 Under **Source project**, clear the **Link to Project** check box.

Organize the Inserted Projects in a Consolidated Project

After you insert a project into another project, you can indent, outdent, and move the inserted project. After you insert open projects into a new project file, you can change their order but you can't indent or outdent them. They are inserted at the same outline level. If you insert a task above the topmost inserted project, all the inserted projects can be indented with respect to that task.

In a consolidated project, an inserted project can behave as a normal summary task. For example, you can change the order of inserted projects by moving the inserted projects to different locations. When you move an inserted project, all of its tasks move with it, just like any summary task.

If you were to insert three projects into a new (empty) project file to create a consolidated project from scratch, you wouldn't be able to indent or outdent the inserted projects with respect to each other.

When you insert several projects at the same time into an empty project file, you can change their order but cannot indent or outdent them.

If you insert a task above the inserted projects, you can indent them with respect to this summary task.

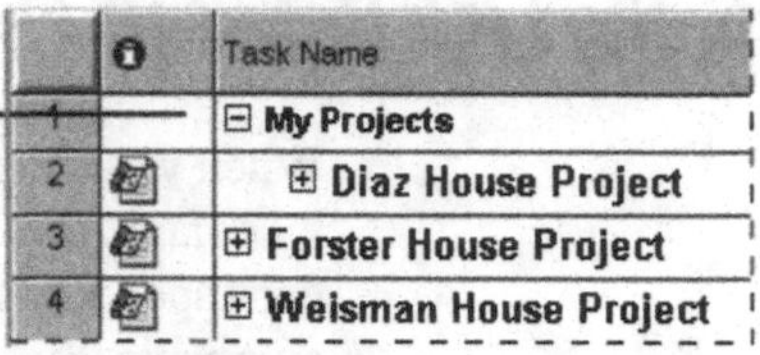

Because of this, instead of inserting projects into a completely empty file, it's best to insert one project at a time into an existing project, at the outline level and in the location you want.

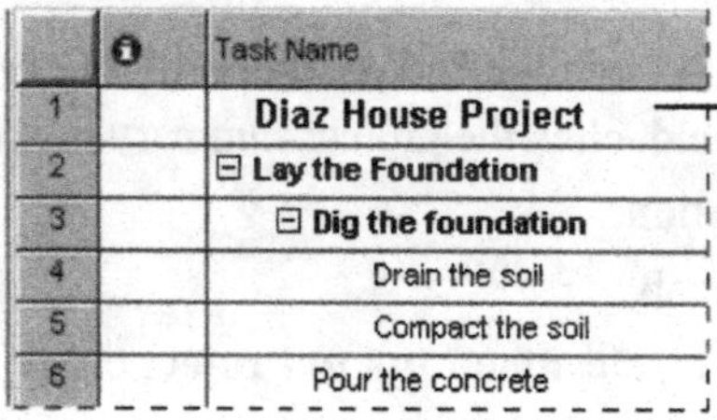

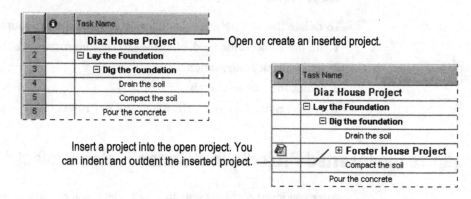

Open or create an inserted project.

Insert a project into the open project. You can indent and outdent the inserted project.

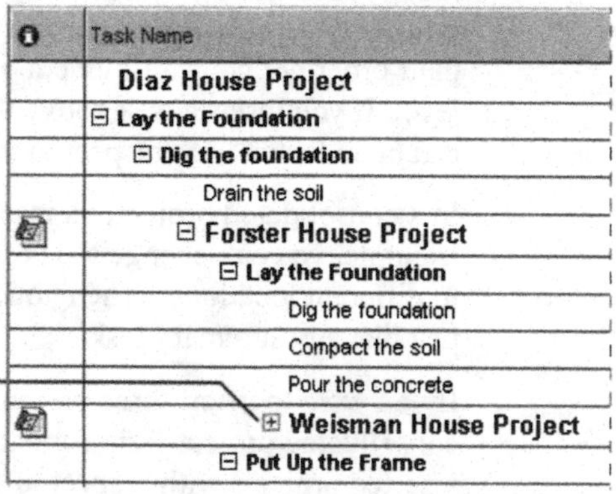

You can show the subtasks of the inserted project, then insert another project into it. You can have an inserted project within another inserted project.

In situations in which you can indent and outdent inserted projects, a project that's outdented with respect to a project below it becomes a *summary project*. The projects below a summary project become the subprojects of the summary project. Each summary project displays cumulative information about the projects beneath it.

For information about how to move, indent, and outdent an inserted project or to show or hide the tasks of an inserted project, see chapter 4.

Linking Tasks Between Projects

Suppose you're managing a house construction project. As you develop the project plan, it's clear that the roof can't be put on until the frame's been built. There's a dependency between these two tasks. You might show that dependency by linking the tasks with a finish-to-start (FS) link.

Let's say that, at the same time, you're managing the construction of a second house, but you only have enough roofers to work on one house at a time. In that case, work on the second roof can't begin until work on the first roof has been completed—two separate projects, but a task in the second project dependent on a task in the first project. When you're managing several projects, especially if they're related, dependencies between tasks from different projects are common.

With Microsoft Project, you can link tasks between projects. The tasks can be in completely separate projects or in projects that have been inserted into the same consolidated project file. The links between tasks in different projects work the same way as links do between tasks within the same project.

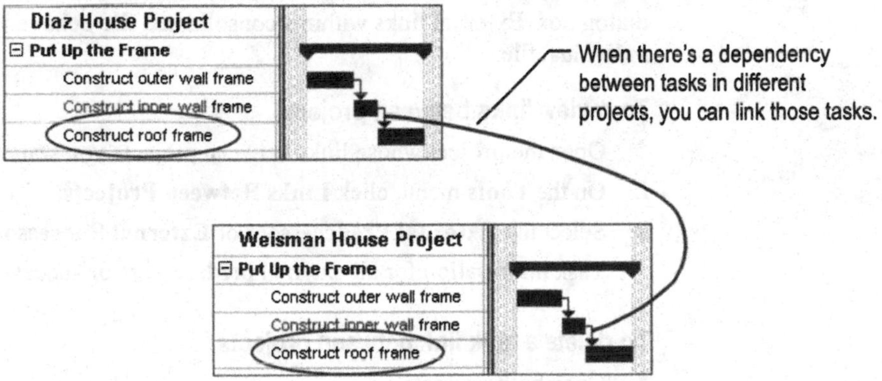

When you link tasks by using the following procedure, an FS dependency is established by default. You can, however, change the link to a start-to-start (SS), finish-to-finish (FF), or start-to-finish (SF) link, and you can also specify lead and lag time.

To link tasks between projects

1. Open both projects.
2. On the **Window** menu, click **New Window**.
3. Hold down CTRL, click the projects that contain the tasks you want to link, and then click **OK**.

4 On the **View Bar**, click **Gantt Chart**.

5 Click the predecessor task in one project.

6 Hold down CTRL, and then click the successor task in the other project.

Link Tasks

7 Click **Link Tasks**.

An FS task dependency is created. You can change this to a different type of task dependency.

8 Close the new window.

You don't need to save the project file that contains both projects. If you do save it, it will contain both projects and the link between them.

If the tasks you linked are not within a consolidated project, an external predecessor task is added to the project containing the successor task, and an external successor task is added to the project containing the predecessor task.

The predecessor and successor are shown in a different color (gray, by default) to indicate that they are externally linked tasks.

If you change any schedule information for an externally linked task, the next time you open the other project, the Links Between Projects dialog box notifies you of the change. You can then have Microsoft Project update your linked project.

If you are working with external links between projects in the same consolidated file, you won't see the tasks highlighted, and you won't see the Links Between Projects dialog box. External links within a consolidated file behave like regular links within an individual file.

To review links between projects

1 Open the project whose links between projects you want to review.

2 On the **Tools** menu, click **Links Between Projects**.

3 Select the **External Predecessors** or **External Successors** tab.

Task information for all external predecessors or successors are listed.

To delete a task link between projects

1 Open both projects.

2 On the **Tools** menu, click **Links Between Projects**.

3 Select the **External Predecessors** or **External Successors** tab.

All the external predecessors or successors are listed with their task ID, task name, and link type.

4 On the **View Bar** of either project, click **Gantt Chart.**

5 In the **Task** field of the **Links Between Projects** dialog box, click each task whose task you want to unlink, and then click **Delete Link**.

Calculate a Single Critical Path Across Multiple Projects

Whether you're working with a consolidated project or a single project, by default, Microsoft Project displays only one critical path—the one overall critical path that affects the consolidated project's overall finish date. In other words, rather than showing a separate critical path for each inserted project within the consolidated project, Microsoft Project shows the overall critical path for the entire consolidated project and all its inserted projects as if it were a single large project.

When you link tasks between projects in a consolidated project, seeing a single critical path becomes all the more interesting and useful.

Show a single critical path across multiple projects

1 Create a consolidated project file.

2 On the **Tools** menu, click **Options**, and then click the **Calculation** tab.

3 Select the **Inserted Projects Are Calculated Like Summary Tasks** check box.

To see individual critical paths for the inserted projects, clear this check box.

Sharing Resources Among Projects

The several projects you're managing simultaneously might use the same set of resources. You could add these resources to one project file at a time, but that's time-consuming. A more efficient method of sharing the resources among projects is to create a *resource pool.* A resource pool is a project file that contains a common set of resource information that you can share with other projects. Other projects link to this resource pool file to make its resources and their information available in those projects.

A resource pool file can be a regular project, including tasks, that happens to contain the resource information to be shared. The resource pool file can also be a project file dedicated to resource information only.

When you use a resource pool, you can:

- Quickly add resources to any project.
- Spend less time creating and updating resource lists. You create a resource pool once, and then share it with as many projects as you want. Also, by updating resource information in the resource pool, it is automatically updated in all the projects that share the pool.
- Share resources among many projects.
- Easily identify and resolve conflicts resulting from resources working on more than one project.
- Check resource usage and costs across all projects without opening each individual project file.
- Print reports about resource usage across projects.

You can share a resource pool among individual projects as well as among consolidated projects. You can also use a "real" project file, one that contains both tasks and resources, as your designated resource pool file.

A resource pool has a two-way link to the projects that share it. When you update information in the resource pool, you can update that information in all the linked projects. Likewise, if you update resource information in a project, you can update that information in the resource pool.

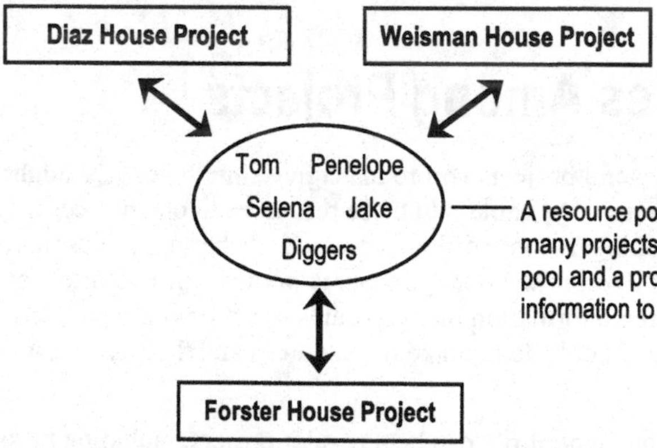

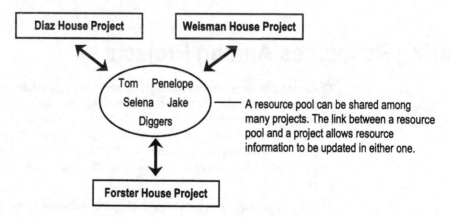

A resource pool can be shared among many projects. The link between a resource pool and a project allows resource information to be updated in either one.

When you add a new project to the group of projects that share a resource pool, that project might already contain resource information. In this case, resource information in the project is added to the resource pool. If there is resource information in common, and if there's a conflict between the two, then, by default, the information in the resource pool takes precedence. The resource pool is not overwritten by the resource information in the new project unless you specify otherwise.

For example, suppose you've just set up the Diaz House project to share the resource pool. If Richard Brooks, at $20/hour, is a resource in the Diaz House project and is not already in the resource pool file, his information is added to the resource pool. However, if there is already a Richard Brooks in the resource pool, and his cost information indicates $25/hour, then there's a conflict between common information, and the rate in the resource pool will take precedence over the rate in the Diaz House project.

Create and Share a Resource Pool

When you know that several projects will use the same resources, you can save time by entering task information only in those projects and information about all the shared resources in a separate file that contains resource information only. The project file that contains resource information only becomes the resource pool file. To share resources and resource information among several projects, you link the resource pool file to the project files.

To create and share a resource pool

1 Open a new project file.

2 On the **View Bar**, click **Resource Sheet**.

3 Enter information for each resource assigned to the projects that will share the resource pool.

Save

4 Click **Save**.

5 In the **File Name** box, type a name for the resource pool file.

6 Open the projects that will share the resource pool.

7 Switch to one of the open project files.

8 On the **Tools** menu, point to **Resources**, and then click **Share Resources**.

9 Click **Use Resources**, and then click the resource pool file in the **From** box, which lists all open project files.

10 Repeat steps 7–9 for each project that will share the resource pool.

The resources from the resource pool are added to the resource list in the project file.

Update Information in a Resource Pool

Whenever you open a project that shares a resource pool, you're prompted to also open the resource pool file. With the resource pool open, any task or assignment changes you make that affect the resource pool can be updated immediately. This is also the way you can see updated resource workload information.

However, you might share the resource pool with other project managers. If this is the case, you might all be updating information in your respective projects and the resource pool at the same time. To ensure that all the necessary changes are made and that no one's changes are overwritten by another's, you all open the resource pool as read-only. If you need to explicitly open the resource pool, use this procedure:

Open the resource pool

1 On the **File** menu, click **Open**.
2 Find the resource pool file, and then click **Open**.
3 In the **Open Resource Pool** message, specify whether you want to open the resource pool as read-only or read-write.

The only time you should open the resource pool as read-write is when making direct changes to resource information such as cost rates or units. If you open the resource pool as read-write, no one else can save any task, assignment, or resources changes to it.

When you open the resource pool as read-only, you can still update the resource pool with task and assignment information. When you're ready to update information to the resource pool, you can give the Update Resource Pool command. This quickly switches the resource pool from read-only to read-write, saves your changes, then switches it to read-only again, all in an instant.

To update information in a resource pool

1 Open the sharing project, along with the read-only resource pool.
2 Update task or assignment information in the project as needed.
3 On the **Tools** menu, point to **Resources**, and then click **Update Resource Pool**.

Resource information you updated in your sharing file is now available in the resource pool to update any other sharing project files.

If you're currently working with a sharing project file and want to update your resource pool with the latest updates that other project managers might have made recently, you can use the Refresh Resource Pool command.

To refresh resource pool information

1 Open the sharing project and the read-only resource pool.
2 On the **Tools** menu, point to **Resources**, and then click **Refresh Resource Pool**.

Set Leveling Priorities for Multiple Projects

For information about leveling, see "Use Microsoft Project Resource Leveling" in chapter 8.

If you're working with multiple projects in a consolidated project or linked files, and if you're using a resource pool across these multiple projects, you can use the Microsoft Project leveling feature to balance the workload among the resources across the multiple projects. To prepare for leveling, you can set project priorities to indicate the order in which the tasks in different projects are to be leveled in relation to one another.

To level across multiple projects, you must have a resource pool set up. Otherwise, resource John Smith in Project A is treated as a different resource than John Smith in Project B.

To set leveling priorities for multiple projects

1. On the Project menu, click Project Information.
2. In the **Priority** box, enter a priority.

   As for tasks, the default priority setting for projects is 500. The lowest priority is 0 and the highest is 1000, meaning "do not level."
3. Open the other projects that are consolidated with or linked to this project. Repeat step 2 to set their priorities.

For more information, see "Set Leveling Priorities" in chapter 8.

When you set leveling priorities for individual tasks as well as projects, note that project priority is considered before task priority. For example, a priority 0 task in a priority 501 project is considered a higher priority than a priority 999 task in a priority 500 project.

Open Several Project Files at Once with a Workspace

When you're managing several projects at the same time, you're probably working with their project files—the same project files—day after day. To work on those project files, you have to open them. If the projects are related, you could insert them into one consolidated project file. Then you'd just have to open one consolidated project file to work on all of your projects.

You can open project files independent of their workspace.

But if the projects aren't related, you might not want to insert them into a consolidated project file (although you can). You might prefer to keep the project files separate. When you create a *workspace*, you can automatically open a defined set of project files. You add the project files you want to the workspace. When you open a workspace, you open all the listed projects at the same time.

To create a workspace

1. Open all the files you want to include in the workspace.
2. On the **File** menu, click **Save Workspace**.
3. In the **File Name** box, type a name for the workspace file.
4. Click **Save**.

To open a workspace

Open

1. Click **Open**.
2. Find the workspace file, and then click **Open**.

   All the files in the workspace quickly open in Microsoft Project.

Creating Projects Using a Project Template

You can automate the creation of project plans by creating and using a project template. In a project template, you enter as much common task and resource information as possible, the kind of information that will likely be used in future projects. Then, when you need to create a project plan, you can do it faster by modifying a copy of the template, making only those changes that are specific to the new project.

Another advantage of using a template is that you can take advantage of previous experience, capturing which tasks and subtasks were required, how long they took, what types of resources were required, and so on.

The process for creating and using a project template is as follows:

- Create the project with the tasks, duration, dependencies, and other information you might want to include. You0 can go so far as to set up resource information, calendars, and make assignments.
- Save the project as a template file.
- When you have a new project that's similar to the template you created, open the template file.
- When you save the template, you're automatically prompted for a new filename, so you don't have to worry about changing the template accidentally.
- Modify the copy of the template to match your current project needs.

You can either create your own project template or adapt one of the predefined templates that comes with Microsoft Project.

Create a Project Template

You might create a template when you create and fine-tune your project. That's the point when the project is set to go, but you have not begun tracking yet. Or, you might create a template after you've finished a project as a way of capturing valuable historical data.

To create a project template

1. Create a project containing all the basic tasks.
2. On the **File** menu, click **Save As**.
3. In the **File Name** box, type the name you want for the template.
4. In the **Save as Type** box, click **Template**, and then click **Save**.

   By default, Microsoft Project specifies that the template be saved in the Templates folder. If you retain that default, the template will be available with the predefined Microsoft Project templates.

5 In the **Save as Template** dialog box, select any values you do not want to be saved with the template—for example, baseline values or resource rates.

Create a Project Based on Your Own Project Template

After you've created a project template file, you can use that template as the basis for your project plans. Each new project plan that's based on the template starts with the basic information you included in the template. For each project, you can revise, add to, or subtract from the basic information, according to the needs of the project.

To create a project based on your own project template

Open

Save

1 Click **Open.**
2 In the **Look In** box, select the folder that contains the template you want, click the template, and then click **Open.**
3 Change the details in the project.
4 Click **Save.**
5 In the **File Name** box, type a name for the project file, and then click **Save.**

   By default, the file is saved as a project file rather than a template.

   If PlanningWizards are on, the Planning Wizard dialog box will appear.
6 Click **Save Without a Baseline.**

If you saved the template in the Templates folder, you can find it easily. On the File menu, click New. On the General tab, click your template.

Create a Project Based on a Microsoft Project Template

In addition to project templates that you create, Microsoft Project comes with a set of predefined templates, designed for different industries and efforts:

- Commercial construction.
- Efforts.
- Infrastructure deployment.
- New business.
- New product.
- Residential construction.
- Software development.

If any of these are close to the type of project you're setting up, you can start with this project, then tailor it to your specific situation.

To create a project based on a predefined project template

1 On the **File** menu, click **New**.

2 Click the **Project Templates** tab.

3 Click the project template you want to use, and then click **OK**.

4 In the **Project Information** dialog box, enter the project start date, if different than today's date. Enter other project information as necessary, and then click **OK**.

5 Review the tasks, durations, and other task information, and revise them according to your specific situation.

Save

6 Click **Save**.

7 In the **File Name** box, type a name for the project file, and then click **Save**.

By default, the file is saved as a project file (rather than a template file).

If PlanningWizards are on, the Planning Wizard dialog box will appear.

8 Click **Save Without a Baseline**.

18

Sharing Project Information with Other Programs

To manage some projects, the only software tools you'll need are Microsoft Project and the project file that contains your project plan. But when those tools aren't enough, Microsoft Project has the ability to work with a number of other software programs. You might need to work with other software when:

- You want to use specialized programs to perform more calculations on project data than Microsoft Project can, then include the results in your project plan. For example, a spreadsheet program might be able to perform more complex cost calculations than Microsoft Project.
- A client or someone you work with does not have Microsoft Project or any other program that can open project files in a Microsoft Project file format. For example, a client who wants to see an electronic copy of your project plan might have only a database program.
- You want to include a portion of your project information in a file created in a program that doesn't support Microsoft Project file formats. For example, you want to include task information in a status report created in a word-processing program.
- You want to access project information that resides in another source, such as a Web site or another project file, from within your project plan.
- You want to archive, compare, or generate reports for several project files, which might best be accomplished in a database.
- You want to open a project file created with an older version of Microsoft Project.
- You want to jump from a task, resource, or assignment to a Web site or to a file on a server.

You can accomplish these tasks and others by sharing project information. When you share project information, you either include information from your project plan in another software tool or include information from another software tool in your project plan. A software tool can be either another project file or a Web site. It is most often another program, such as a spreadsheet, word-processing, database, personal information management, or project management program.

For information about sharing project information between people via e-mail, see chapter 10. For information about sharing project information between people via the Web, see chapter 11.

To share project information with other software tools, you can:

- Copy and paste project information.
- *Import* or *export* project information.
- Link or *embed* project information.
- Create *hyperlinks* to project information.

This chapter focuses on sharing project information so it can be viewed, edited, calculated, and stored in a variety of programs. Typically, the shared information consists of all or part of a project plan, though it can also be supplemental information that augments a project plan, such as a project management document hyperlinked from a Web site or a presentation linked from a presentation program.

Methods of Sharing Project Information

The method you use to share information depends on the amount, source, and format of the project information as well as how you want to edit the information in the destination program, file, or Web site. You can use the following methods to share project information.

To	Use
Copy small amounts of text or a graphic from one file and paste it into another file. Editing the information in the destination file does not change the source file.	**Copying and pasting.** Use the Copy command in one program and the Paste command in the other.
Quickly copy or move small amounts of information between two open files.	**Drag-and-drop editing.** Drag selected information to another file.
Open all or part of a file created in another program in Microsoft Project.	**Importing.** Use the Open command on the File menu.
Open all or part of a Microsoft Project file in another program.	**Exporting.** Use the Save As command on the File menu.

To	Use
Copy information from one file and paste it into another file in such a way that updates in either the source or destination file update the information in the linked file.	**Linking.** Use the Paste Link option from the Paste Special command on the Edit menu to paste the information as a linked object.
Copy information from one file and paste it into another file in such a way that it can be opened and edited from within the destination file independently of the source file.	**Embedding.** Use the Paste option from the Paste Special command on the Edit menu to paste the information as an embedded object.
Jump to information in another file, another part of the same file, or a Web site.	**Hyperlinks.** Use the Hyperlink command on the Insert menu.

Copying and Pasting Project Information

The amount of information you can copy or paste depends on the amount of memory your computer has and how easy it is to select the information.

When you want to insert small amounts of text or a graphic from Microsoft Project into another Windows program or vice versa, you can copy and paste that information. For instance, you can copy and paste Microsoft Project cells or columns of information into a word-processing or spreadsheet program, and copy and paste text, icons, or logos into Microsoft Project. You can also copy and paste information between the sheet views of different Microsoft Project files.

The process for copying and pasting information between two Microsoft Project files or between Microsoft Project and another Windows-based program is as follows:

1. Open the file that you want to copy from—that is, the *source file*.
2. Select the information you want to copy, and then choose the program's Copy command.
3. Open the file you want to paste the information to—that is, the *destination file*.
4. Select the location where you want the information to be inserted, and then choose the program's Paste command.

Copy Text from Another Program into Microsoft Project

You can copy text information created in another Windows-based program and paste it into a sheet view, such as the Gantt Chart, the Resource Sheet, or the Task Usage view. Text information can be either words or numbers and can consist of a single piece of calculated data, such as a cost calculated in Microsoft Excel, or it can consist of several cells, fields, or columns of information.

When you copy information from one field to another, the destination field must be able to accept the type of information that's been copied. For example, if the copied information is numerical, the destination field must be capable of accepting numerical data.

To copy text from another program to a Microsoft Project sheet view

1. Open the source program and the source file.
2. Select the text, noting the size, order, and type of the information.
3. Choose the program's **Copy** command.
4. Open the Microsoft Project file into which you want to paste the text.
5. On the **View Bar**, click the sheet view into which you want to paste the text.
6. If necessary, add or remove columns or apply a table with columns that match the order and type of the copied text.
7. If necessary, insert more rows to accommodate the entire text. Select the number of rows you're inserting, and then click **New Task** or **New Resource** on the **Insert** menu.

   Pasted rows replace existing rows. If you don't want to replace an existing row, be sure to paste copied information into a blank row.
8. To paste the text into new fields or rows, select the first field in the blank rows where you want the pasted information to begin.

Paste

9. Click **Paste**.

Copy a Graphic from Another Program into Microsoft Project

You can copy a graphic created in another Windows-based program, such as a logo or pie chart, and paste it into a Microsoft Project graphics area. Areas that can accept a copied graphic include a:

- Chart portion of a Gantt Chart.
- Header.
- Footer.
- Legend.
- Note.

To copy a graphic from another program to a graphics area

1. Open the source file that contains the graphic you want to copy.
2. Select the graphic.
3. Click the program's **Copy** command.
4. Open the Microsoft Project file into which you want to paste the graphic.

Paste

To insert a graphics file into a note, click

Insert Object.

To insert a graphics file into a header, footer, or legend, click

Insert Picture.

5 To paste the graphic into the **Gantt Chart**, click **Gantt Chart** on the **View Bar**, and then click **Paste**.
The graphic appears in the upper left corner of the visible chart area. Drag the graphic to position it where you want.

6 To paste the graphic into a note, double-click a task, resource, or assignment in a sheet view, click the **Notes** tab, and then press CTRL+V.

7 To paste the graphic into a header, footer, or legend, switch to the view in whose header, footer, or legend you want to include the graphic. On the **View** menu, click **Header and Footer**, and then click the **Header**, **Footer**, or **Legend** tab. Click the **Left**, **Center**, or **Right** tab. Press CTRL+V.

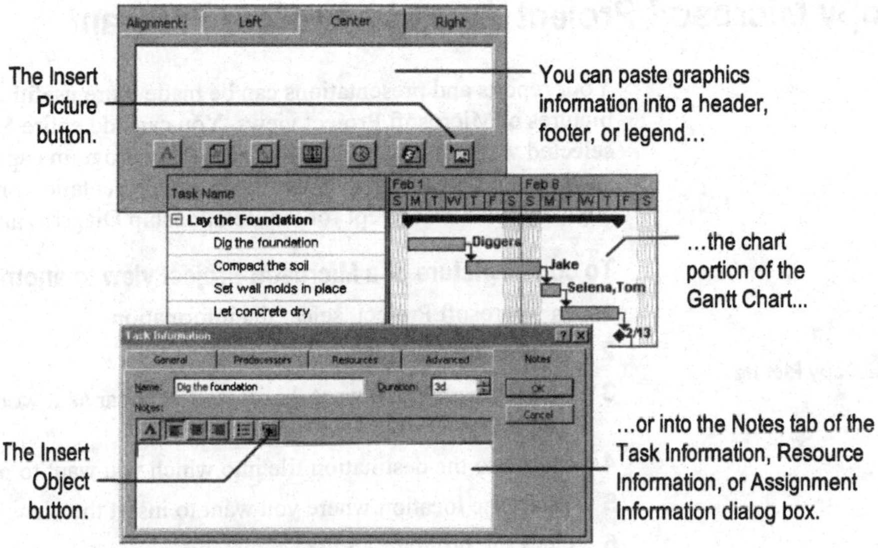

Copy Microsoft Project Text to Another Program

You can copy and paste fields or columns of information from your project into the file of another program. It's most convenient to copy text from a sheet view, such as the Gantt Chart, the Resource Sheet, or the Task Usage view.

Another program's field into which you paste text information might accept information of a certain type only. For example, some fields accept numerical information only; other fields accept words only. When you copy several fields of information, those fields must match the order and type of the fields into which you're pasting the information. For example, if you copy information from the Microsoft Project Task Name, Duration, and Start fields, you must paste the information into fields that accept alphabetic characters, numbers, and dates, in that order.

To copy Microsoft Project text to another program

1 In Microsoft Project, display the view and apply the table containing the text.
2 Select the text you want to copy.

Copy

3 Click **Copy**.
4 Open the destination program and the file into which you want to paste the Microsoft Project text.
5 In the destination file, select the location where you want to insert the text.
6 Click the program's **Paste** command.

Copy Microsoft Project Views to Another Program

Your reports and presentations can be made more useful and interesting by adding pictures of Microsoft Project views. You can add entire Microsoft Project views or selected view information as pictures in any program capable of displaying graphics, such as word processing, spreadsheet, and presentation programs. All views can be copied as pictures except for the Relationship Diagram and form views.

To copy a picture of a Microsoft Project view to another program

1 In Microsoft Project, select the information.

Copy Picture

2 Click **Copy Picture**.
3 Select whether you want the image to appear as it would on the screen, on a printed page, or as a GIF image file. Click **OK**.
4 Switch to the destination file into which you want to paste the information.
5 Select the location where you want to insert the view.
6 Click the program's **Paste** command.

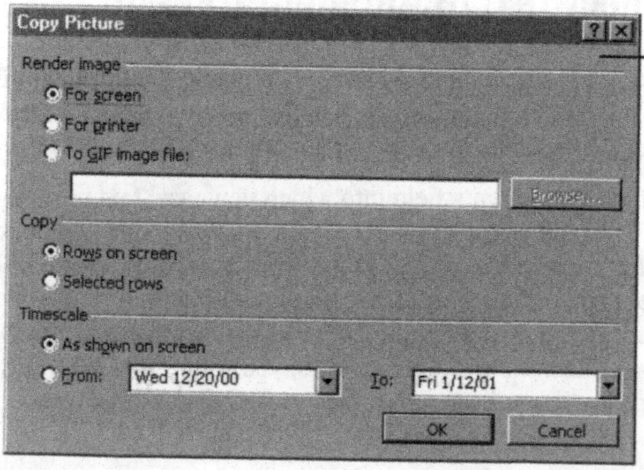

The Copy Picture dialog box provides options for copying the view the way you want.

Drag Project Information from One Program or File to Another

For more information about OLE, see "Linking and Embedding Project Information" later in this chapter.

You can copy information between Microsoft Project files or between a Microsoft Project file and a file in another program that supports object linking and embedding (OLE) by using *drag-and-drop editing*. This method works only when the drag-and-drop editing option is turned on in both programs.

If you drag information into a field, the copied information must be the type of information that can be entered into the field. For example, you can drag a number into the Microsoft Project Duration field, but not a letter. The copied information replaces the information in the field.

To turn on drag-and-drop editing in Microsoft Project, click Options on the Tools menu. Click the Edit tab, and then select the Allow cell drag and drop check box.

To drag project information between programs or files

1. Arrange the file windows so that both the source file and the destination file are open and visible.

   You must be able to see the information you want to drag as well as the location where you want to drop it.

2. Select the information, and then use the left mouse button to drag the information to the new location in the other file.

   To drag information from a Microsoft Project field, select the information, point to an edge of the field box (the cursor must be an arrow), then use the left mouse button to drag the information to the new location.

If you are using Windows 95 or later, or Windows NT 4.0 or later, you can drag the information to the open destination program even if it isn't visible. After you select the information in the source program, hold down the left mouse button, then drag the item to the destination program's button on the Windows task bar, which is usually located at the bottom of your screen. After a few seconds, the destination program will appear on your screen; while still holding the mouse button, you can drag the information where you want.

Importing and Exporting Project Information

Suppose you have a file, created in another program, that contains project information you want to use in your Microsoft Project plan. You can convert this file into a format that can be used by Microsoft Project by *importing* the file.

Likewise, you might have a Microsoft Project plan whose information you need to make available in another program. You can convert a Microsoft Project file into formats used by other programs by *exporting* the file.

When you import or export information, you convert most or all of the file in such a way that you can work with the information as if it were originally created in the destination program. While you can copy and paste information between programs, importing and exporting is often best for converting significant amounts of data between programs.

In addition, importing and exporting are often the best ways to share information with databases. For example, the only way to share project information with an SQL database (a database that uses the *structured query language*) is by importing or exporting the information. You can also store several projects together by exporting them to a single database. You can use the database to conduct cross-project analyses as well as to archive projects.

The process for importing and exporting project information is as follows:

1 Identify information in the source program that you'd like to open in the destination program.

  Usually, the information is contained in a file that has a particular *file format*, which tells you what type of information is in the file. The file extension after the file name indicates its file format. For example, .mpp is the file extension for Microsoft Project files, .xls is the extension for Microsoft Excel files, and .txt is the extension for generic text files.

2 Identify the file format of the information in the source program.

  Each program saves and stores files in a default file format. For example, the default file format for Microsoft Project files is MPP. The default file format for the source program is typically different than the default file format for the destination program. The import/export process basically converts a file from one file format to another.

3 Determine which file formats can be accepted by the destination program.

  Each program can open certain types of files only. Although each program has a default file format, many programs, such as Microsoft Project, can accept and open files with other file formats.

4 Convert the information from the file format of the source program to a file format that's compatible with the destination program.

  Programs do this for you automatically, either when a file is opened in the importing program or saved by the exporting program. If the source program can't convert a file directly into the destination program's default file format, it might be able to convert the file into one of the other formats that the destination program recognizes. If so, the destination program can convert the intermediate file format into the default format.

  When a file is converted from one format to another, the original file is not changed. Rather, a copy of the original file is converted to the target format.

5 Open the file in the destination program.

Using Microsoft Project, you can import and export entire files or selected parts of files, depending on the type of program you're working with. For example, an entire project file can be exported to a database but not to a spreadsheet program. When you import or export selected information only, and not an entire project, you must use an *import/export map* to match one field of information in Microsoft Project to the corresponding field in the destination program.

File Formats That Microsoft Project Can Import or Export

For information about saving project information as an HTML document, see "Publish Project Information to a Web Site" in chapter 14.

The default file format for Microsoft Project is the MPP file format. In addition to this, however, Microsoft Project can open and save project files in a variety of other file formats. For example, within Microsoft Project, you can open a Microsoft Access file that's in the MDB file format. You can save Microsoft Project information in the XLS file format, which can then be opened in Microsoft Excel. You can even save project information in HTML (Hypertext Markup Language) format to display that information on a Web site.

When you save project information to a non-Microsoft Project format—that is, anything other than MPP, MPX, or MPT—you can't save all the information in the project file. For example, if you save project information as a Microsoft Excel XLS file, the file can contain only information from Microsoft Project fields. An XLS file can't, for instance, contain information that reconstructs Microsoft Project views or formatting.

You can, however, import or export entire projects, including view and formatting information, to databases. For example, you can export an entire project to Microsoft Access by saving a project file in the Microsoft Project database file format, MPD, or in the Microsoft Access file format, MDB.

When you import or export an entire project using the MPP, MPD, or MDB file formats, you don't need an import/export map. When you import or export selected project information, such as for XLS, TXT, or HTM file formats, you must use an import/export map.

The following table summarizes the file formats you can use with Microsoft Project.

File format	Description
Microsoft Project file	The default standard file format for Microsoft Project files. With Microsoft Project 2000, you can open Microsoft Project 98 files and save to the Microsoft Project 98 file format. Uses the .mpp extension.
Microsoft Project database	The file format for sharing project information with databases. Uses the .mpd extension.
Microsoft Project template file	The file format for projects that contain information you're likely to include in future projects. Uses the .mpt file format.
Microsoft Project Exchange	An ASCII format used with other project management software and other programs that support MPX. While you cannot save project information to this MPX, you can import field data from the MPX 1.0, MPX 3.0, and MPX 4.0 file formats. Uses the .mpx extension.
Microsoft Access	The file format used by the Microsoft Access 8.0 database program. You can save an entire project or selected project information in this format. Uses the .mdb extension.
Microsoft Excel	The file format used by the Microsoft Excel spreadsheet program. You can export selected field information to this format, but not an entire project. Uses the .xls extension.
Microsoft Excel Pivot Table	The file format used by the Microsoft Excel spreadsheet programs for a Pivot Table. You can export field information to this format, but not an entire project. You cannot import from a pivot table format. Uses the .xls extension.
HTML (Hypertext Markup Language)	The format used by browser programs on intranets and the World Wide Web. You can export field information to this format, but not an entire project. You cannot import from an HTML file. Uses the .htm extension.
Text-only or ASCII	A generic file format used by word-processing and other programs. It is tab-delimited. You can export field information from a single Microsoft Project table to this format, but not an entire project. Uses the .txt extension.
System list separator (CSV)	A generic text format used by word-processing and other programs, where information is separated by a system list (comma-delimited) separator. You can export field information from a single Microsoft Project table to this format, but not an entire project. Uses the .csv extension.

About Import/Export Maps

The majority of the information you import or export is stored in fields. When you import or export selected project information, such as the information in the Task

Name, Duration, Start, and Finish fields, you need to ensure that the data from a field in the source program is inserted into the correct field in the destination program. You ensure that the fields from the two programs are correctly matched by using an *import/export map*.

For example, suppose you want to export information from the Microsoft Project Duration field. In the destination program, the field that contains duration information is called Length. Using an import/export map, you specify that the counterpart for the Duration field in the destination program is the Length field. This ensures that, upon export, the information from the Duration field will be inserted into the Length field.

Microsoft Project comes with a number of predefined import/export maps that you can use in many common situations. You can also copy and modify a map, or create one from scratch. An import/export map can contain any combination of task, resource, and assignment information and can be filtered to allow only specific tasks, resources, or assignments in the exported file. You can use the same map to import or export information. You can also use the same map for different programs with different file formats.

Create an Import/Export Map

If none of the existing import/export maps matches the Microsoft Project fields you want to the fields in the other program, you can create your own import/export map.

There are different procedures for creating an import/export map for importing data and creating one for exporting data. However, once you create an import/export map, you can use it for either importing or exporting data.

To create a custom import/export map for importing data

Open

1. Click **Open**.
2. In the **Files of Type** box, click the type of file you want to import—for example, a Microsoft Excel workbook or a text file.
3. In the **Look In** box, click the file you want to import.
4. Click **Open**, click the **Selective Data** tab, and then click **New Map**.
5. In the **Import/Export Map Name** box, enter the name you want.
6. Under **Data to Import/Export**, select the check boxes for the types of data you want to import.

7 In the options area, select any available options you want.

The title of the options area is different for each type of program you import from. For example, if you're importing data from Microsoft Excel, the options area is titled **Microsoft Excel Options**.

8 Click the tab for the type of data you want to import.

For example, if you selected the **Tasks** check box, click the **Task Mapping** tab.

9 In the **Source worksheet/database table name** box, click the worksheet or table name from which you're importing.

If you select a table, Microsoft Project fills the From column with all the fields from the table. Any table field that matches a Microsoft Project field name will be automatically matched to the Microsoft Project field.

10 For any unmapped field in the **To: Microsoft Project Field** column, select or enter the Microsoft Project field that you want to map to the corresponding table field from the other program.

11 In the **Method for incorporating imported data** box, click an option.

12 To save the map, click **OK**.

To create a custom import/export map for exporting data

1 On the **File** menu, click **Save As**.

2 In the **Save in** box, click the drive or folder in which you want to save the exported file.

3 In the **Save as type** box, select the type of file (the file format) that you'd like the exported file to be.

4 In the **File name** box, enter the name for the file you want to create.

5 Click **Save**, click the **Selective data** tab, and then click **New Map**.

6 In the **Import/Export map name** box, enter the name you want.

7 Under **Data to import/export**, select the check boxes for the types of data you want to export.

8 In the options area, select any available options you want.

The title of the options area is different for each type of program you import from. For example, if you're exporting data to a text file, the options area is titled **Text file options**.

9 Click the tab for the type of data you want to export.

For example, if you selected the **Task** check box, click the **Task Mapping** tab.

10 In the **From: Microsoft Project Field** column, select or enter the name of a Microsoft Project field that you want to export.

Microsoft Project automatically fills in the corresponding fields in the **To** column with default names for those fields.

11 To change a default field name in the **To** column, type the name you want.

12 Repeat steps 10 and 11 for each field you want to export.

13 To export certain tasks only, click a filter in the **Export filter** box.

14 To save the map, click **OK**.

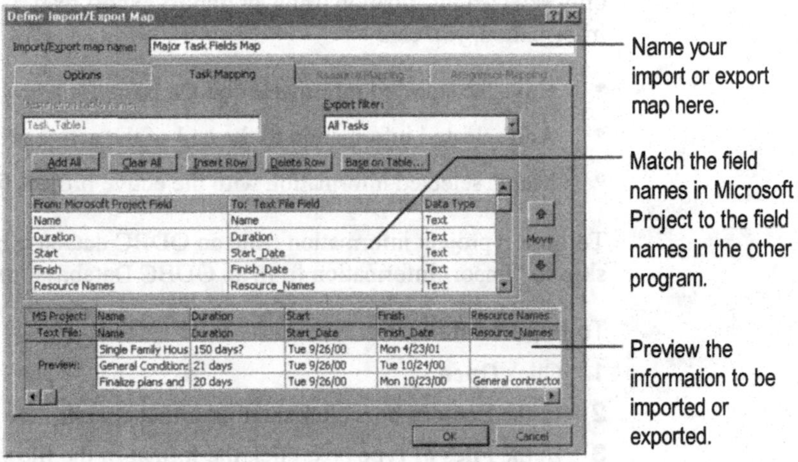

Name your import or export map here.
Match the field names in Microsoft Project to the field names in the other program.
Preview the information to be imported or exported.

Delete an Import/Export Map

If you no longer need an import/export map, you can delete it. Both predefined and newly created import/export maps are stored in the global file (Global.mpt), but they can be moved to, and stored with, a project file. You can delete an import/export map from the global file and from a project file.

To delete an import/export map

1 On the **Tools** menu, click **Organizer**.

2 Click the **Maps** tab.

3 To delete a map from the global file, click the map you want to delete in the **GLOBAL.MPT** list, and then click **Delete**.

To delete a map from a project file, click the map you want to delete in the project file list (on the right), and then click **Delete**.

Import Information into Microsoft Project

Important project information might sometimes be created, calculated, or stored in programs other than Microsoft Project or in plans created in previous versions of Microsoft Project. For example, you might have task and resource information in a database. Or, you might have created the project plan for a current project using Microsoft Project version 4.0. To use information created in other programs or in earlier versions of Microsoft Project in the current version of Microsoft Project, you can import it.

You can import an entire project from a database or a previous version of Microsoft Project to create a new project plan. From all other kinds of programs, you can import only selected information using an import/export map. If you import selected information, you can:

- Have the selected information be the basis for a new project file.
- Add selected information to the end of the active project file.
- Merge selected information with the active project file.

To import project information from an ODBC database other than Microsoft Access, skip to "Import Information from an ODBC Database into Microsoft Project" below.

To import data

Open

1 Click **Open**.
2 In the **Look in** box, click the folder that contains the file you want to import.
3 In the **Files of type** box, click the format of the file you want to import.

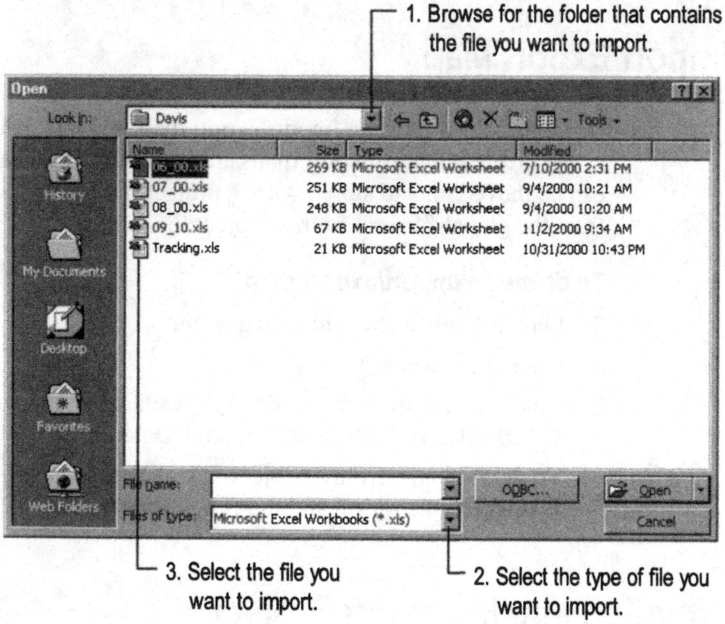

4 In the folder list, click the file you want to import, and then click **Open**.

If you're importing an entire project in the MPP, MPX, or MPT file format, Microsoft Project opens the file.

If you're importing selected project information or an entire project in a file format other than MPP, MPX, or MPT, the **Import Mapping** dialog box appears.

If you open a project file created in Microsoft Project version 4.1 or 4.0, you might see differences in the calculated values of some fields.

5 To import selected project information, click the **Selective data** tab, click an existing import/export map or create a new one, and then click **Open**.

See "Create an Import/Export Map" earlier in this section.

To import an entire project in a database that's in a file format other than MPP, MPX, or MPT, click the **Entire project** tab, and then select the project you want from the list.

Import Information from an ODBC Database into Microsoft Project

Open Database Connectivity (ODBC) is an information exchange standard for databases. Database programs that support ODBC can exchange information with one another.

Microsoft Access is a database program that supports ODBC, but Microsoft Project uses the same basic procedure for importing information from Microsoft Access that it uses for other kinds of programs. If you want to import information from any other ODBC database, use the following procedure.

To import project information from an ODBC database

Open

1 Click **Open**.

2 Click **ODBC**.

3 To use a file data source, click the **File Data Source** tab, and then enter the file name or browse for one in the **Look in** box.

To define a new data source for any installed driver, click **New**, then follow the instructions for defining a new data source.

4 Click the **Machine Data Source** tab, click the machine data source that contains the data you want to import, and then click **OK**.

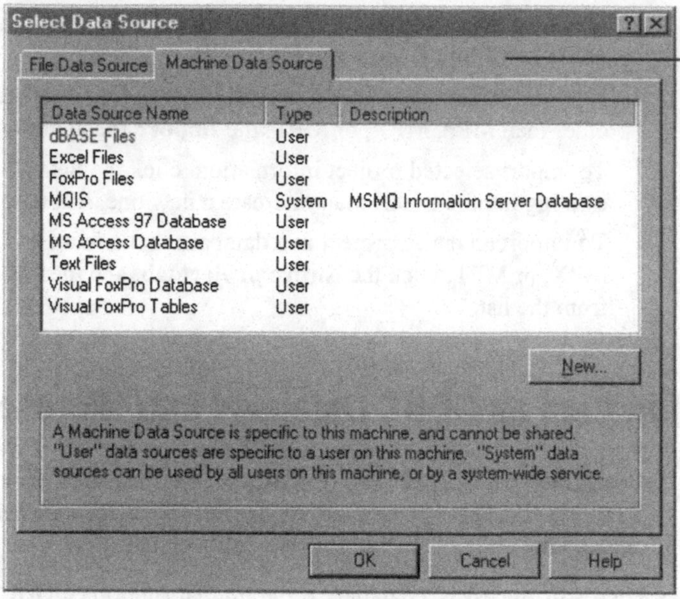

Use the Select Data Source dialog box to import information from or export information to an ODBC database.

5 If you need to log on to the ODBC data source that you selected, enter your logon ID, password, and any other information that might be required, and then click **OK**.

6 To import a complete project from the database, click the **Entire project** tab, and then click the project you want to import in the **Project name** box.

  To import only some of the data into your project, click the **Selective data** tab. In the **Import/export map** box, click the name of the map you want to use for importing your data, define a new map, or edit an existing map.

7 Click **Open**.

Export Microsoft Project Information to Another Program

Sometimes you might need to open some or all of your project plan in another program, or even in a Web site. For example, a client who wants to see your project plan might not have Microsoft Project. But perhaps the client has Microsoft Access or Microsoft Excel. Or, maybe you want to use another program to store project files or calculate project data. In such situations, you can export project information from Microsoft Project.

You can export an entire project to a database. You can export selected information using an import/export map to spreadsheet, word-processing, and project management programs as well as to databases. You can also export project information to an HTML document for posting on an intranet or the World Wide Web.

To export project information to an ODBC database other than Microsoft Access, skip to "Export Microsoft Project Information to an ODBC Database" below.

To export project information

1 On the **File** menu, click **Save As**.
2 In the **Save in** box, click the folder in which you want to save the exported file.
3 In the **File name** box, enter the name of the exported file.
4 In the **Save as type** box, click the format in which you want to export the file, and then click **Save**.

   If you're exporting an entire project in the MPP, MPX, or MPT file format, Microsoft Project saves the file.

   If you're exporting selected project data or an entire project to a file format other than MPP, MPX, or MPT, the **Export Mapping** dialog box appears.
5 To export an entire project (if you're exporting to a database, for example), click the **Entire project** tab, then enter the project you're exporting in the **Project name** box.

   To export selected project data, click the **Selective data** tab. In the **Import/export map** list, click the name of the map you want to use for exporting your data, define a new map, or edit an existing map.
6 Click **Save**.

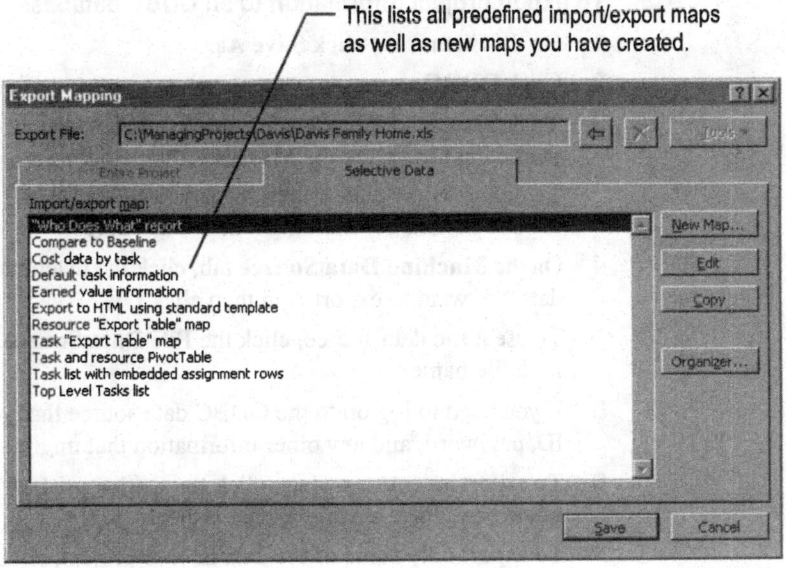

Export Microsoft Project Information to an ODBC Database

While Microsoft Access is a database program that supports ODBC, you can export information to Microsoft Access the same way you do for other kinds of programs.

You can export project information to ODBC databases, such as Microsoft SQL Server and other programs that provide drivers with ODBC Level 1, to access their data files.

When you export to a database, Microsoft Project automatically makes the following changes to the names of Microsoft Project fields so that they are compatible with database field-naming conventions:

- Periods are deleted.
- Spaces are replaced with underscores.
- Forward slashes "/" are replaced with underscores.
- The percent sign "%" is replaced with the word "Percent".
- "Start" is changed to "Start_Date".
- "Finish" is changed to "Finish_Date".
- "Work" is changed to "Scheduled_Work".
- "Group" is changed to "Group_Name".

To export project information to an ODBC database

1. On the **File** menu, click **Save As**.
2. Click **ODBC**.
3. To display the defined machine data sources for any ODBC drivers installed on your computer, click the **Machine Data Source** tab.

   To define a new data source for any installed ODBC driver, click **New**, then follow the instructions for defining a new data source.
4. On the **Machine Data Source** tab, click the machine data source that contains the data you want to export, and then click **OK**.

   To use a file data source, click the **File Data Source** tab, and then enter or browse for a file name.
5. If you need to log on to the ODBC data source that you selected, enter your logon ID, password, and any other information that might be required, and then click **OK**.
6. To export an entire project, click the **Entire project** tab, and then, in the **Project name** box, enter a name for the project.

   To export only some of the data in your project, click the **Selective data** tab. In the **Import/export map** box, click the name of the map you want to use for exporting your data, define a new map, or edit an existing map.
7. Click **Save**.

If you want to perform cross-project analyses or simply want to archive your projects efficiently, you can store several projects in a single database.

To store several projects in a single database

1. Open a Microsoft Project file that you want to store in a database.
2. On the **File** menu, click **Save As**.
3. In the **Save in** box, click the folder that contains the database in which you want to store the project file.
4. In the folder list, click database name, and then click **Save**.
5. In the dialog box, click **Append**.
6. Click the **Entire project** tab, and then enter the name of the project you want to export in the **Project name** box.
7. Click **Save**.

Linking and Embedding Project Information

Project information can consist of text and pictures created in Microsoft Project and in other programs. When you want to include project information in one program that's been created in another program, you can *link* or *embed* the information, or *object*. You can link and embed objects between any two programs that support *object linking and embedding (OLE)* technology.

With OLE technology, you can insert an object from another program into your Microsoft Project plan, then either activate the source file (linking) or a special set of editing tools (embedding) from within the project plan to edit the inserted object. You can also link or embed objects from Microsoft Project to other programs. By linking or embedding, you get the combined power of the program that's providing the object with the project management features of Microsoft Project.

Link an object if you want the changes made to the object in the source program to be updated wherever the object exists. Create the object once and link it to multiple places. Update it once, and it's updated in each place where you've linked it. The object is stored in the source file only, and your project plan (or destination file) contains only the name and address, or *path*. You need to make sure that the source file is always available to the project file so the link isn't broken. Linking results in a smaller file than if you actually included the object in the project plan, such as by copying or embedding it.

Embed an object if you want the changes you make to the object in the destination file to be independent of the changes you make to the original object in the source file. When you embed an object, updating the original object does not automatically update the embedded object, as there's no link between the two. The object itself is included in the destination file. While embedding objects in a file can make that file large, you don't have to keep track of where the source file is, because the two files are not connected. You can open and edit the object within the destination file.

When you link or embed, text objects can be linked to sheet views. Objects, including graphics, can be placed in any graphics area, such as:

- The chart portion of a Gantt Chart.
- Headers, footers, and legends of printed views and reports.
- Notes boxes in the Task Information, Resource Information, and Assignment Information dialog boxes.

Link or Embed Project Information from Other Programs

From another program into Microsoft Project, you can link or embed:

- Text information.
- Graphics.
- An entire file.

Link or Embed Text Information from Another Program

Other programs might contain text information you want to include in a project plan. Examples of text information are project costs and other values calculated in a spreadsheet program and task documentation stored in a word-processing program.

If you update the information regularly and want the updates to appear in each file that contains the information, you can link the text information as an object in the sheet view of one or more project plans.

If you want to be able to edit the information within Microsoft Project without affecting the source file, embed the information instead. Embedding text information in a sheet view has the same effect as a simple copy and paste operation between programs.

The type of information that you link or embed within a sheet view must match the type of information already in the view that receives the text. For example, you can link numerical information to the Duration field, but not alphabetical information.

To link or embed text information into a Microsoft Project sheet view

1. Open the source file.
2. Select the object, noting the size, order, and type of the information.
3. Choose the program's **Copy** command.
4. Open the Microsoft Project file in which you want to create the link.
5. On the **View Bar**, click the sheet view in which you want to create the link.

6 If necessary, add columns or create a new table to make the view compatible with the order and type of information in the object.

7 If necessary, add rows to the table to accommodate the entire object. Select the number of rows you're inserting, and then click **New Task** or **New Resource** on the **Insert** menu.

Remember that pasted rows replace existing rows. If you don't want the incoming object to replace existing rows, be sure to add the correct number of new blank rows.

8 Select the field where the upper left cell of the linked information should begin.

9 On the **Edit** menu, click **Paste Special.**

10 To create an embedded object, click **Paste.**

To create a linked object, click **Paste Link.**

11 In the **As** box, click a format.

For example, to paste the information as text, click **Text Data.**

To embed information in Microsoft Project, click Paste.

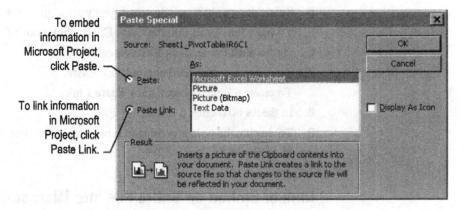

To link information in Microsoft Project, click Paste Link.

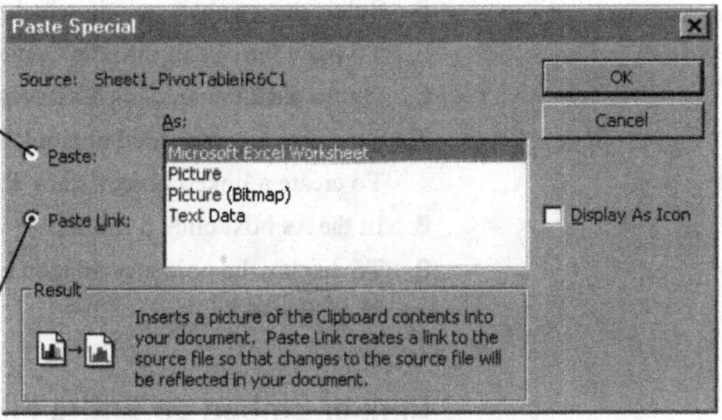

Linked text information displays a gray marker in the lower right corner of each field.

Link or Embed Graphics into Microsoft Project

Pictures can be invaluable in your project. For instance, a pie chart added to the Gantt Chart might take the place of several paragraphs in a status report. At the least, pictures can make printed views and reports more useful and compelling. When you want to include a picture from another program in one or more project files, you can link or embed the picture.

When you link a picture, the picture resides only in the source program. The Microsoft Project file to which it's linked just contains the path to the source file. If the picture in the source file is updated, the picture is automatically updated everywhere it's linked.

When you embed a picture, there's no link between the source file and the picture in the destination file. Updating the picture in the source file will not update the picture in the destination file. However, you can edit the picture from within Microsoft Project.

You can link or embed a selected picture to a Gantt Chart only. If you paste a selected picture into any other Microsoft Project graphics area, such as a note, header, footer, or legend, it will be pasted into your project file as a *static* (uneditable) picture, just as if you had simply copied and pasted the graphic.

Alternatively, you can insert an entire graphics file and link the file to the source. See "Link or Embed an Entire File into Microsoft Project" below.

To link or embed a selected graphic into Microsoft Project

You can link or embed only those graphics created in programs that support OLE.

1 Open the source file for the graphic.
2 Select the graphic.
3 Choose the program's **Copy** command.
4 Open the Microsoft Project file in which you want to create the link.
5 Select the graphics area in which you want to create the link.
  To paste the object into the Gantt Chart, click **Gantt Chart** on the **View Bar**.
6 On the **Edit** menu, click **Paste Special**.
7 To create an embedded object, click **Paste**.
  To create a linked object, click **Paste Link**.
8 In the **As** box, click a format.
9 To display the object as an icon representing the source program, select the **Display as Icon** check box.

Link or Embed an Entire File into Microsoft Project

Sometimes an entire file created in another program is important enough to include in a project plan. For example, you can include a presentation about your project right in the Gantt Chart. Double-click the presentation object; if it's linked to the source program, you can start the presentation. You can also link or embed entire spreadsheets and word-processing documents into your project plan.

In addition, if you want to link a graphic from another program—in your footer or a task note, for example—you can do so by bringing in the entire graphics file.

If you link the file, any changes to the source file appear in the inserted file. If you embed the file, changes to the source file do not appear in the inserted file.

Microsoft Project treats each inserted file as a graphic. Therefore, you can link or embed entire files in Microsoft Project graphics areas only, such as the Gantt Chart or a note. You can link or embed multiple files to a selected task, resource, or assignment.

To link or embed an entire file into Microsoft Project

1 Open a Microsoft Project file and select the graphics area into which you want to insert the file.

2 To insert the file in the Gantt Chart, click **Object** on the **Insert** menu.

Insert Object

To insert the file in a task, resource, or assignment note, double-click a task, resource, or assignment on a sheet view. Click the **Notes** tab, and then click **Insert Object**.

3 Click **Create from File**.

4 In the **File** box, enter the path and file name of the file you want to insert or click **Browse** to locate and select the file.

5 To embed the file, clear the **Link** check box.

To link the file, select the **Link** check box.

6 To display the file as an icon, select the **Display as Icon** check box.

If you do not select the Display As Icon check box, the entire contents of the file are displayed in the graphics area.

Link or Embed Information from Microsoft Project

As the main program you use to manage projects, Microsoft Project might be the source of information for other programs you use to control specific aspects of the project. For example, you might feed cost information from Microsoft Project to a spreadsheet file so that the spreadsheet program can perform complex cost calculations. You might include the latest look at the Gantt Chart in a status presentation you give every week. You can also link or embed information from one Microsoft Project file to another Microsoft Project file.

If you want the information in other programs to be updated each time you update it in Microsoft Project, you can link the information. Linking is especially useful if you include the Microsoft Project information in several files. Then, by updating the information once in Microsoft Project, you can update it in every file in which it's linked.

If you don't want the information in other programs to be updated, you can embed the information. When you embed information, you can edit project information from within the other program.

You can link or embed project information:

- From Microsoft Project to another program.
- From one Microsoft Project file to another.

Link or Embed Microsoft Project Information in Another Program

You can link and embed entire views or selected information from views. However, you cannot link or embed graphics created in Microsoft Project into other programs.

For specific information about copying Microsoft Project objects into another program, see the documentation for that program.

To link or embed Microsoft Project information in another program

1 On the View Bar, click More Views.

2 In the **Views** list, click the view that contains the information you want to copy, and then click **Apply**.

Copy

3 Select the information you want to paste in the other program, and then click **Copy**.

To copy an entire sheet view, such as the Gantt Chart, the Resource Sheet, and the Task Usage view, click the blank button in the upper left corner of the view, above the ID field, and then click **Copy**.

To copy the Network Diagram, the Resource Graph view, or the Calendar view, you don't need to select anything. Simply display the view, then click **Copy**.

4 Open the program and file into which you want to paste the Microsoft Project information.

5 Select the location for the object.

6 Click the program's **Paste Special** command.

To embed the object, click the program's **Paste** option.

To link the object, click the program's **Paste Link** option, and then click the option to link the object as a Microsoft Project object.

If you link or embed an entire Microsoft Project view into another program, the portion of the view that actually appears in the destination program depends on how that program scales or crops the view.

Link or Embed Information Between Microsoft Project Files

You can create links to information between Microsoft Project files as well as to information from different areas within a single project file. You can also create multiple links to one object. You can create links to text only—between one sheet view and another—not to graphics.

To link or embed project information between or within project files

1 Open the project file containing the text.

2 On the **View Bar**, click the sheet view that contains the text you want to link, and then select the text.

Copy

3 Click **Copy**.
4 Open the project file in which you want to create the link.
5 On the **View Bar**, click the sheet view in which you want to create the link.
6 If necessary, add columns or create a new table to make the view compatible with the order and type of information in the object.
7 If necessary, add fields to the table to accommodate the entire object.

   If there is not enough room, information already in the view might be replaced by the incoming object.
8 Select the field where the upper left cell of the linked information should begin.
9 On the **Edit** menu, click **Paste Special**.
10 To create an embedded object, click **Paste**.

   To create a linked object, click **Paste Link**.

Linked text information displays a gray marker in the lower right corner of each field.

Change Linked and Embedded Objects

As your project progresses, you'll need to update the information you've entered in your project plan, such as task durations and start dates. You might also need to update information you've linked to or embedded in your plan.

You can:

For information about updating information in a source file, see the documentation that came with the source program.

- Update linked information by updating the information in the source file.
- Edit embedded information (which is independent of the source program).
- Cancel the link to linked information.

Edit Objects Embedded in a Microsoft Project File

Embedded objects can be edited within the Microsoft Project file using the tools of the source program. These tools appear when you double-click the object. Because they are not linked to the source file, your edits to the embedded object do not affect the source file.

To edit information embedded in a Microsoft Project file

1 Open the Microsoft Project file that contains the embedded information you want to edit.
2 Double-click the object.

3 Edit the object using the source program commands.

4 On the **File** menu of the source program, click the program's equivalent of the **Exit and Update** command.

Cancel the Link to an Object in a Microsoft Project File

Information that you've linked to your project plan gets updated whenever the source file is updated. If you want linked information to be independent of the source file, you can cancel the link between the source file and the project file. Even when the link is canceled, the information remains in your project file.

After you cancel the link to text information you've inserted into a sheet view, you can edit that information the same way you edit information you've entered manually. However, if you cancel the link to a graphic in a graphics area, the object becomes a static picture; you cannot edit it.

To cancel the link to an object

1. Open the Microsoft Project file that contains the link you want to cancel.
2. On the **Edit** menu, click **Links**.
3. In the **Links** list, click the link you want to cancel.
4. Click **Break Link**.

Hyperlinking from a Project File to Another Location

Other Microsoft Project files, files created in other programs, and Web sites might contain good supplemental information to your project. Examples of such information include project status reports, marketing documents, and project management tips. You can access these kinds of information and many others by inserting *hyperlinks* in your project plan.

A hyperlink is text or an icon that you can click on to open another file or to jump to a Web site. The destination can be almost any file, such as another Microsoft Project file, a word-processing document, a spreadsheet, or a database, or any Web site on an intranet or the World Wide Web. For example, you might have a link to a page on your company's intranet or to the Web site of a consultant who's on your team.

Any number of project plans can have a hyperlink to the same file or Web site. Updates to the destination file or Web site show up immediately in each hyperlinked plan.

Insert a Hyperlink

When you want quick access to supplemental information, you can insert a hyperlink to that information. You can insert a hyperlink to a Web site on an intranet or the World Wide Web, or to another file on a server, including another Microsoft Project file. You associate a hyperlink with a particular task, resource, or assignment in a sheet view.

A hyperlink connects your project plan to a Web site or file the way a phone number connects you to a particular person or organization. A phone number contains information that puts your call on the correct path to someone's telephone. Likewise, a hyperlink contains information that puts you on the correct path to a particular Web site or file.

A path to a Web site uses front slashes (/), while a path to a file on your computer or a network server uses back slashes (\).

To specify the path to a Web site on an intranet or the World Wide Web, use the following convention:

http://www.<site name>/<file name>

To specify the path to a file on your computer, use the following convention:

<folder name>\<subfolder name>\<file name>

To specify the path on a network server, use the following convention:

\\<server name>\<share name>\<folder >\<subfolder >\<file name>

Be sure to include the full path of the destination file in your project file, and make sure there is indeed a destination file located at the hyperlink address.

To insert a hyperlink from a task, resource, or assignment in a sheet view

To view hyperlink addresses, display the Hyperlink table in a sheet view.

Insert Hyperlink

1 Open the project file in which you want to create the hyperlink.
2 In a sheet view, select the task, resource, or assignment to which you want to associate the hyperlink.
3 Click **Insert Hyperlink**.
4 In the **Type the file or Web page name** box, enter the address of the destination file.
  If you're linking to a file on your computer or network, under **Browse for**, click **File.**
  If you're linking to a file on the web, under **Browse for**, click **Web Page**.
5 If you want a friendly name to show for this link, type it in the **Text to display** box.

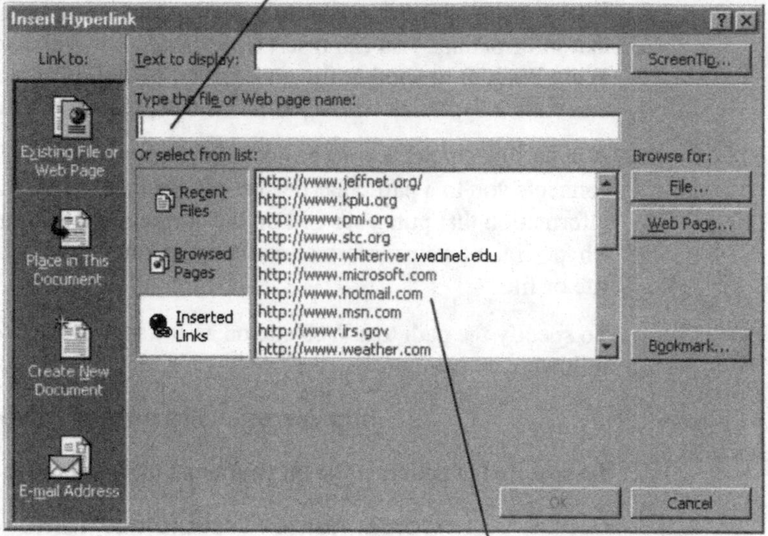

Perhaps it would be useful to access more than one Web site or file from a task, resource, or assignment in your project plan. For example, both a word-processing document and a Web site might contain important information about a resource. If that's the case, then you can insert as many hyperlinks as you want to associate with the resource.

To insert multiple hyperlinks for a task, resource, or assignment

1 In a sheet view that contains the task, resource, or assignment, click the task, resource, or assignment.

 **Task Information**

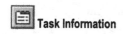

2 Click **Task Information, Resource Information**, or **Assignment Information**.

3 Click the **Notes** tab.

4 In the **Notes** box, enter the addresses of the files to which you want to create hyperlinks. Add a space between each address, or enter each address on a separate line by pressing ENTER after you enter an address.

To enter the location of a file, such as on a computer or a network, type:

file:\\<*path*>\<*filename*>

For example, file:\\computername\folder\filename

To enter the location of a Web site, type:

http://<*URL*>

For example, http://www.filename.com

Hyperlink

When you insert a hyperlink in the **Notes** tab of the Task Information, Resource Information, or Assignment Information dialog box, the hyperlink icon appears in the **Indicators** field of the task or resource for which you inserted the hyperlink.

Go to a File or Web Site Using a Hyperlink

When you want to display the file or Web site associated with a task, resource, or assignment, you can jump to the appropriate hyperlink. The method you use depends on whether you inserted the hyperlink with the Hyperlink command on the Insert menu or with the Notes tab in the Task Information, Resource Information, or Assignment Information dialog box.

To follow a hyperlink inserted with the Hyperlink command

1 Switch to a sheet view that contains the task, resource, or assignment to which you've added the hyperlink.

2 In the **Indicators** field, click the hyperlink icon.

Hyperlink

To follow a hyperlink inserted in the Notes tab

1 Switch to the sheet view that contains the task or resource to which you've added the hyperlink.

2 In the **Indicators** field, double-click the Note indicator.

Note

3 In the **Notes** box, click the hyperlink you want to follow.

You can use the Web toolbar to move around or access web pages. The Web toolbar appears when you insert your first hyperlink. To show or hide the Web toolbar, on the **View** menu, point to **Toolbars**, then click **Web**.

Copy, Paste, or Move a Hyperlink

After you've hyperlinked a task, resource, or assignment to a file or Web site, you might find it useful to hyperlink other tasks, resources, and assignments to the same file or Web site. Instead of creating a new hyperlink for each additional task, resource, or assignment, you can copy, paste, or move the existing hyperlink.

To copy, paste, or move a hyperlink

1 Switch to a sheet view.

2 On the **View** menu, point to **Table**, and then click **Hyperlink**.

3 In the **Hyperlink** field, select the task, resource, or assignment whose hyperlink you want to copy or move.

To select the field, click a field next to the hyperlink, then use the arrow keys to move into the **Hyperlink** field. If you click the hyperlink in the Hyperlink field, you will jump to the listed file or Web site.

4 If the hyperlink contains information in the **SubAddress** field, you need to also select the **Address** and **SubAddress** fields so that all three fields are selected.

To select multiple fields, click a field next to the **Hyperlink** field, hold down SHIFT, and then use the arrow keys to select all necessary fields.

Copy

Cut

5 To copy the hyperlink, click **Copy**.

To move the hyperlink, click **Cut**.

6 In the **Hyperlink** field, select the task, resource or assignment to which you want to add the hyperlink.

Paste

7 Click **Paste**.

Change the Destination of a Hyperlink

Suppose you've added a hyperlink to a task, resource, or assignment, then the file or Web site location changes. You can change the path within the hyperlink so that it connects the task, resource, or assignment to the new location.

To change the destination of a hyperlink

1 In a sheet view, select the task, resource, or assignment that contains the hyperlink.

Insert Hyperlink

2 Click **Insert Hyperlink**.

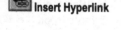

3 In the **Type the file or Web page name** box, enter the new destination address.

Delete a Hyperlink

A hyperlink has outlasted its usefulness when it connects a task, resource, or assignment to outdated or irrelevant information. For these and similar reasons, you can delete the hyperlink.

The method you use for deleting a hyperlink depends on whether you inserted the hyperlink with the Hyperlink command on the Insert menu or with the Notes tab in the Task Information, Resource Information, or Assignment Information dialog box.

To delete a hyperlink inserted with the Hyperlink command

1. Switch to a task, resource, or assignment sheet view as appropriate.
2. On the **View** menu, point to **Table**, and then click **Hyperlink**.
3. In the **Hyperlink** field, select the task, resource, or assignment that contains the hyperlink you want to delete.

   To select the field, click a field next to the hyperlink, and then use the arrow keys to move into the field.
4. Press DELETE.

To delete a hyperlink inserted in the Notes tab

1. Switch to a task, resource, or assignment sheet view as appropriate, and then select the item containing the hyperlink.
2. Double-click the **Notes** icon.

   Note
3. In the **Notes** box, select the entire text of the hyperlink.
4. Press DELETE.

Part 6

Customizing Microsoft Project Tools

Microsoft Project is like a desk filled with tools that help you perform project management tasks. Two kinds of tools come with Microsoft Project: tools that enable you to enter, display, or print project information, such as views, reports, tables, and filters; and tools for performing the many detailed tasks required to manage projects and work with project files, such as menus and commands, toolbars and buttons, and forms and dialog boxes.

Part 6 describes how to customize menus, toolbar buttons, forms, and more, so you can work with Microsoft Project as efficiently as possible. It also covers custom fields, along with the value lists, formulas, and graphic indicators you can use with them. It explains how you can automate repetitive tasks with macros. Finally, you'll learn how to copy, move, or delete tools from one project to another using the Organizer.

Part 6 consists of a single chapter, chapter 19.

For information about how to customize views, reports, tables, and filters, see Part 4.

19

Customizing Microsoft Project

When you work with Microsoft Project, you use various sets of tools, including menus and menu commands, toolbars and toolbar buttons, and forms and custom fields in which you enter project information. Microsoft Project's many tools are designed and organized to fit the preferences of a majority of users.

But maybe you have special requirements. Perhaps you have a unique method of working that calls for a different organizational scheme of tools. Possibly you've devised shortcuts that you want to automate and set up in your own way. For example, maybe it would be more convenient for you if the toolbar button that opens project files were on the right side of the Standard toolbar instead of the left side, or if the Details command were on the View menu instead of the Format menu.

If some tools aren't organized in a way that enables you to work as efficiently as possible, you can reorganize them. But that's not all you can do. You can also:

- Show or hide the View Bar and toolbars.
- Add commands to menus.
- Create custom menus.
- Add a button to a toolbar.
- Change the image on a toolbar button.
- Move toolbars where you want them.
- Create custom forms for entering and editing project information.

In addition, you might have certain fields of task, resource, or assignment information that you want to customize. You can customize cost, date, number, text, and other types of fields. To these custom fields, you can add lists of set values to choose from, formulas to perform calculations, and graphical indicators to provide visual cues in your project.

If you frequently perform a series of repetitive actions in Microsoft Project, you can automate it by recording them in a macro. Macros can help you automate complex tasks.

You can share toolbars, menus, fields, macros, and other tools you create with other project files by using the Microsoft Project Organizer. You also use the Organizer to delete and rename tools you've made.

Creating and Customizing Menus and Commands

A menu is a set of commands that have related functionality. For example, the Edit menu consists of commands for editing task and resource information. Each command performs a specific action. On the Edit menu, the Copy Cell command copies a piece of information, the Paste command inserts copied or cut information into a cell, and so on.

However, the default menu structure might not suit you. For instance, you might want commands grouped differently, or you might want to create a new menu. To customize menus and menu commands, you can:

- Add a command to a menu.
- Delete a command from a menu.
- Create a command.
- Create a menu.
- Delete a menu.
- Reset a menu bar.

The following illustration shows you some of the ways you can customize menus and menu commands.

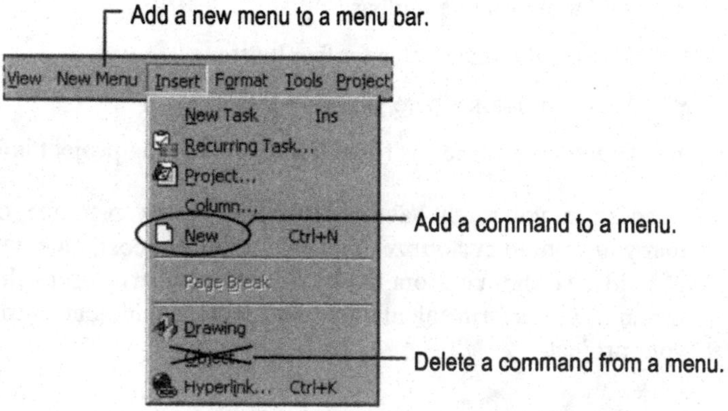

When you create or modify commands or menus, Microsoft Project saves them in your global file, Global.mpt. Any other project files you open on your computer using that global file will contain the new tools.

Set Personalized Menu Preferences

When you first install Microsoft Project, the menus are relatively short of commands. They're all there; it's just that some of the more infrequently used or specialized commands are hidden until you use them. When you click the double arrows at the bottom of a short menu, the full version of the menu appears with all the available commands. When you choose a command that was previously hidden, it becomes a part of your short menu. This helps you automatically tailor your menus to the way you work.

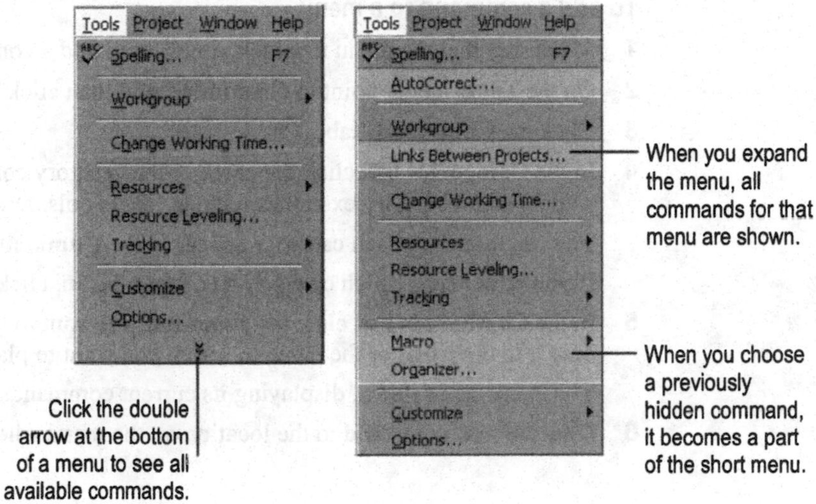

You can change how these personalized menus work. You can:

- Always show the full menus.
- Have the full menu expand after the short menu is displayed for a few seconds.
- Reset your menus to the default short menus.

To change personalized menu settings

1 On the **Tools** menu, point to **Customize**, and then click **Toolbars**.
2 Click the **Options** tab.
3 If you want full menus to always show, clear the **Menus show recently used commands first** check box.

4 If you want short menus and also want the full menus to show after a few seconds, select the **Menus show recently used commands first** and the **Show full menus after a short delay** check boxes.

5 To return to the default short menus, erasing your command usage data, click **Reset my usage data** then click **Yes**.

Add a Command to a Menu

A command performs a specific action, such as deleting a task, displaying a dialog box, or running a macro you've created. If a menu doesn't have a command you want, the command might be on another menu, or it might be a custom command that hasn't yet been added to any menu. If the command exists, you can add it to any menu you want.

To add a command to a menu

1 Make sure that the menu to which you want to add a command is displayed.

2 On the **Tools** menu, point to **Customize**, and then click **Toolbars**.

3 Click the **Commands** tab.

4 In the **Categories** list, click the name of the category containing the command you want to add. Category examples include File, Tools, Drawing, and All Forms.

   The commands in each category appear in the **Commands** list on the right side.

   If you're not sure which category a command is in, click **All Commands**.

5 In the **Commands** list, click the command you want to add to the menu, and then drag it to the name of the menu in which you want to place it.

   The menu drops down, displaying its current commands.

6 Drag the new command to the location on the menu where you want it.

Delete a Command from a Menu

A menu might contain built-in or custom commands you don't use. You can save scanning time when selecting commands by paring a menu to just those commands you do use. You can delete unused commands from any menu.

To delete a command from a menu

1 Make sure that the menu bar from which you want to delete a command is displayed.

2 On the **Tools** menu, point to **Customize**, and then click **Toolbars**.

3 Click the **Commands** tab.

4 On the menu bar, click the menu command you want to delete, and then click **Modify Selection.**

If necessary, drag the **Customize** dialog box to the side to see the button.

5 Click **Delete.**

Create a Menu Command

Microsoft Project provides dozens of built-in menu commands to help you perform dozens of project management tasks, but if none of the existing commands has the functionality you want, you can create your own command.

You can place a new command on any toolbar or menu, then assign any Microsoft Project command, macro, or form to the command. Be aware that you should assign functionality to a new command before you edit its image (if you give it an image). Assigning functionality after you edit the image will remove any modifications you made to the image.

To create a menu command

1 Make sure that the menu bar to which you want to add a new menu command is displayed.

2 On the **Tools** menu, point to **Customize**, and then click **Toolbars.**

3 Click the **Commands** tab.

4 In the **Categories** list, click **All Commands.**

The command will probably have a default function associated with it, but you can change that function.

5 In the **Commands** list, click the command you want to add to the menu, and then drag it to the name of the menu in which you want to place it.

The menu will drop down, displaying its current commands.

6 Drag the new command to the location on the menu where you want it.

7 Click **Modify Selection,** and then click **Assign Macro.**

In the Command box, you'll see the default functionality of the command

8 In the **Command** box, click a command, macro, or custom form whose functionality you want to assign to this command, and then click **OK.**

In the **Command** box, commands, macros, and custom forms are listed together in alphabetical order. Macros are preceded by "Macro" and custom forms are preceded by "Form."

When you click a command, macro, or form, the new functionality replaces the old.

9 In the **Name** box, type the command name.

10 In the **Description** box, type the text you want displayed in the status bar when the pointer pauses over the command. Click **OK.**

To change an existing image or create a new image, click Modify Selection, then click Edit Button Image.

Create a Menu

Microsoft Project provides a number of standard menus, each one grouping a set of related commands. But maybe you'd like to speed your work and create a menu that contains those commands you use most frequently.

If you've created new menu bars, you have more than one menu bar to work with.

To create a menu

1 Make sure that the menu bar to which you want to add a new menu is displayed.
2 On the **Tools** menu, point to **Customize**, and then click **Toolbars**.
3 Click the **Commands** tab.
4 In the **Categories** list, click **New Menu**.
5 In the **Commands** list, drag **New Menu** to the location you want on the menu bar.
6 Click **Modify Selection**, and then type the name of the new menu in the **Name** box.

You can now add commands to the menu as described earlier in this section.

Delete a Menu

A menu bar might contain built-in or custom menus you don't use. To pare a menu bar to those menus you do use, you can delete the unused menus from the menu bar. You can delete any menu from any built-in or custom menu bar.

To delete a menu

1 Make sure that the menu bar that contains the menu you want to delete is displayed.
2 On the **Tools** menu, point to **Customize**, and then click **Toolbars**.
3 Click the **Commands** tab.
4 Click the menu you want to delete.
5 Click **Modify Selection**, and then click **Delete**.

Reset a Menu Bar

When you create, modify, or delete menus and menu commands, you're modifying the menu bar that contains those menus and menu commands. To restore a menu bar to its original configuration, you can reset it.

When you reset a menu bar, Microsoft Project deletes custom menus and menu commands that you've added, adds menus and menu commands that you've removed, and restores all modified menus and menu commands to their original state. To save custom or modified menus before you reset a menu bar, you can move the menus onto a built-in or custom toolbar. After you reset the menu bar, you can move them back.

To reset a menu bar

1. On the **Tools** menu, point to **Customize**, and then click **Toolbars**.
2. Click the **Toolbars** tab.
3. In the **Toolbars** list, click the menu bar you want to reset.
4. Click **Reset**.

Creating and Customizing Toolbars and Buttons

A toolbar is a set of toolbar buttons that either have related functionality or are frequently used together. Toolbar buttons are visual representations of commands. While menu commands are hidden until you click a menu, toolbar buttons are always displayed with their toolbar. Therefore, a toolbar button is often a shortcut to a command. You don't have to pull down a menu to get to it.

Microsoft Project provides you with 13 built-in toolbars, two of which, the Standard toolbar and the Formatting toolbar, are displayed by default. If the built-in toolbars or toolbar buttons don't meet your needs, you can customize them in a number of ways. For example, you can:

- Show or hide a toolbar.
- Move a toolbar.
- Add a button to a toolbar.
- Remove a button from a toolbar.
- Create a toolbar button.
- Create a toolbar.
- Change the image on a toolbar button.
- Reset a toolbar.

The following illustration shows some of the ways you can customize toolbars and toolbar buttons.

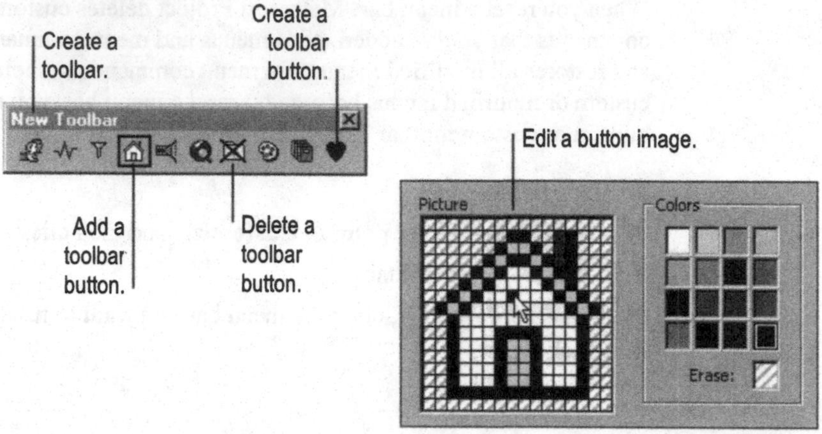
Create a toolbar.
Create a toolbar button.
New Toolbar
Edit a button image.
Add a toolbar button.
Delete a toolbar button.
Picture
Colors
Erase:

You can also show and hide the View Bar, which enables you to display some of the more commonly used views by choosing icons that represent those views.

When you create or modify toolbars or toolbar buttons, Microsoft Project saves them in your global file. Any other project files you open on your computer that use that global file will contain the modified toolbars and toolbar buttons.

Show or Hide a Toolbar

By default, Microsoft Project displays the Standard toolbar (which has buttons such as Save, Open, Copy, Link Tasks, and Assign Resources) and the Formatting toolbar (which has buttons and other tools such as Indent, Outdent, Font, Bold, and Filter). The buttons and other tools on these toolbars can help you perform many of the basic tasks you need to perform with Microsoft Project. Sometimes, however, you might need to use tools that are on other toolbars. Conversely, you might no longer need a toolbar that's displayed, so you can hide it to increase the work area. You can display any number of toolbars.

To show or hide a toolbar

- On the **View** menu, point to **Toolbars**, and then click the toolbar you want to show or hide.

Move a Toolbar

A toolbar you display for the first time appears beneath the toolbars that are already displayed. You can, however, drag a toolbar to a different toolbar row or to any other screen location.

To move a toolbar to any location from the toolbar row

- At the left side of a toolbar that's in a toolbar row near the top of the screen is a light gray vertical bar. Position the pointer over this bar, and then drag the left side of the toolbar to the location you want.

You can position the toolbar along the top, left, or right edges, as long as the Windows toolbar is not also positioned there.

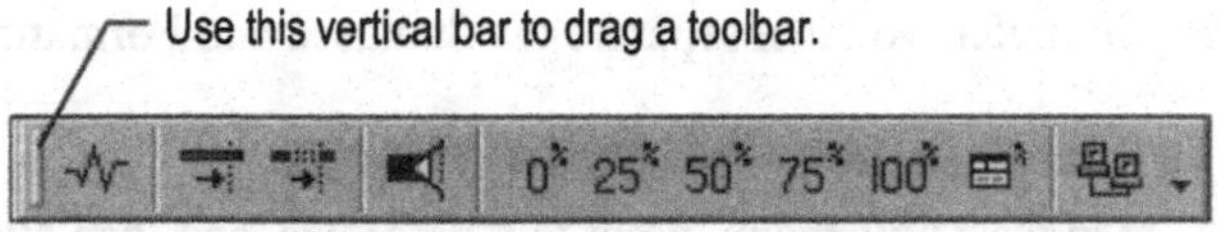
Use this vertical bar to drag a toolbar.
0%
25%
50%
75%
100%

To move a toolbar from the middle of the work area to the toolbar row quickly

- Double-click the toolbar's title bar.

Show or Hide the View Bar

The View Bar, located on the left side of the screen, displays icons that represent the most commonly used views. To display any of these views quickly, you can click its image on the View Bar. While the View Bar is displayed by default, you can also hide it.

To show or hide the View Bar

- On the **View** menu, click **View Bar**.

Set Personalized Toolbar Preferences

When you first install Microsoft Project, the Standard and Formatting toolbars are relatively short of toolbar buttons and combined onto a single row. All thc tools are available, but the infrequently used or specialized commands are hidden until you use them. When you click the double right arrows on the right side of either the Standard or Formatting toolbar, you see the rest of the buttons available for the toolbar. When you click a tool that was previously hidden, it becomes a part of the short toolbar. This helps you automatically tailor your toolbars to the way you work.

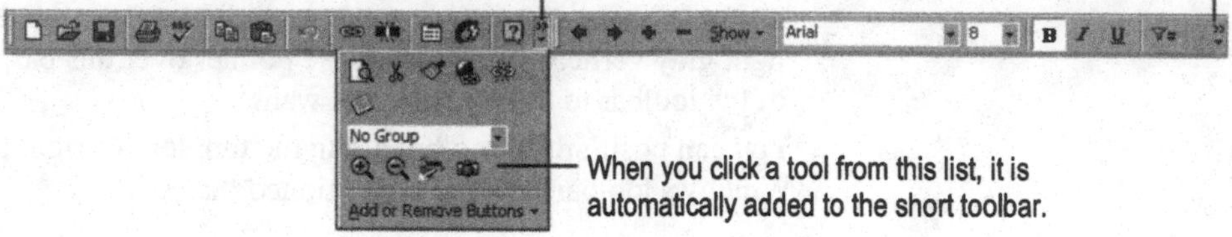
More Standard toolbar buttons.
More Formatting toolbar buttons.
Show
Arial
8
No Group
Add or Remove Buttons
When you click a tool from this list, it is automatically added to the short toolbar.

If you prefer, you can separate the Standard and Formatting toolbars into two rows.

To change personalized toolbar settings

1 On the **Tools** menu, point to **Customize**, and then click **Toolbars**.

2 Click the **Options** tab.

3 To view the Standard and Formatting toolbars in a single row, select the **Standard and Formatting toolbars share one row** check box.

  If you prefer to have them fully displayed on two rows, clear this check box.

Add a Button to a Toolbar

If a toolbar doesn't have a button and associated function that you want, the button might be on another toolbar, or, it might be a button that exists but has not yet been added to any toolbar. Such buttons tend to have highly specialized functions. If the button exists, you can add it to any built-in or custom toolbar you want.

To add a button to a toolbar

1 Make sure that the toolbar to which you want to add a button is displayed.

2 On the **Tools** menu, point to **Customize**, and then click **Toolbars**.

3 Click the **Commands** tab.

4 In the **Categories** list, click the name of the category that contains the command and button you want to add to the toolbar.

  If you're not sure which category the command is in, click **All Commands**.

5 In the **Commands** list, click the command you want, and then drag it to the toolbar on which you want the button displayed.

Remove a Button from a Toolbar

A toolbar might contain built-in or custom buttons you don't use. To pare a toolbar to those buttons you do use, you can delete unused buttons from any toolbar.

To remove a button from a toolbar

1 Make sure that the toolbar from which you want to delete a button or tool is displayed.

2 On the **Tools** menu, point to **Customize**, and then click **Toolbars**.

3 Click the **Commands** tab.

4 On the toolbar, click the button or tool you want to delete, and then click **Modify Selection**.

5 Click **Delete**.

Change the Image on a Toolbar Button

If you think a button should have a different image, one that's more meaningful to you, or if you've changed the button's command and want to give it an image that matches its new function, you can change the button's image.

Microsoft Project provides more than 100 images to choose from for your custom button images. You can apply an image as is. If you want, you can modify its appearance by using the Microsoft Project Button Editor.

To change the image on a toolbar button

1 Make sure that the toolbar that contains the button you want to modify is displayed.

2 On the **Tools** menu, point to **Customize**, and then click **Toolbars**.

3 Click the **Commands** tab.

4 On the toolbar, click the button you want to modify, and then click **Modify Selection**.

5 Point to **Change Button Image**, and then click the image you want.

Edit the Image on a Toolbar Button

If the image on a toolbar button is close to what you want but just needs a little tweaking, you can edit the image. When you edit the image on a toolbar button, you can change its colors one pixel at a time, and you can move the image to a different position on the button.

To edit a button image

1 Make sure that the toolbar that contains the button you want to edit is displayed.

2 On the **Tools** menu, point to **Customize**, and then click **Toolbars**.

3 Click the **Commands** tab.

4 On the toolbar, click the button you want to modify, and then click **Modify Selection**.
5 Point to **Edit Button Image**.
6 Make the changes to the button image.

Reset a Toolbar Button

You can modify a toolbar button's appearance and functionality. If you've modified a toolbar button and want to restore it to its original appearance and functionality, you can reset it.

To reset a toolbar button

1 Make sure that the toolbar that contains the button you want to reset is displayed.
2 On the **Tools** menu, point to **Customize**, and then click **Toolbars**.
3 Click the **Commands** tab.
4 On the toolbar, click the button you want to reset, and then click **Modify Selection**.
5 Click **Reset**.

Create a Toolbar Button

Microsoft Project provides dozens of built-in toolbar buttons to help you perform dozens of project management tasks quickly, but if none of the existing toolbar buttons has the functionality you want, you can create a toolbar button.

You can place a new toolbar button on any toolbar or menu, then assign any Microsoft Project command, macro, or form to the button. Be aware that you should assign functionality to a new button before you edit its image. Assigning functionality afterwards will remove any modifications you made to the button's image.

To create a toolbar button

1 Make sure that the toolbar to which you want to add the button is displayed.
2 On the **Tools** menu, point to **Customize**, and then click **Toolbars**.
3 Click the **Commands** tab.
4 In the **Categories** list, click **File**.
5 In the **Commands** list, drag any button onto the toolbar. This will be the placeholder for the new button.
6 Click **Modify Selection**, and then click **Assign Macro**.

The **Command** box displays the default command for the placeholder button you dragged onto the toolbar.

7. In the **Command** box, click a macro, command, or custom form whose functionality you want to assign to the new button. Click **OK**.

   In the **Command** box, commands, macros, and custom forms are listed together in alphabetical order. Macros are preceded by "Macro" and custom forms are preceded by "Form."

   When you click a command, macro, or form, its functionality replaces that of the placeholder button.
8. In the **Name** box, type the command name. This will become the button's ToolTip.
9. In the **Description** box, type the text you want displayed in the status bar when the pointer pauses over the button. Click **OK**.
10. To change an existing image or create a new image, click **Modify Selection**, and then click **Change Button Image** or **Edit Button Image**.

Create a Toolbar

Microsoft Project provides you with a number of standard toolbars, each consisting of a set of toolbar buttons. But maybe you'd like to speed up your work and create a toolbar that contains those buttons you use most frequently.

To create a toolbar

1. On the **Tools** menu, point to **Customize**, and then click **Toolbars**.
2. Click the **Toolbars** tab.
3. Click **New**.
4. In the **Toolbar name** box, type a name for the new toolbar, and then click **OK**.

   The new toolbar is displayed in the work area.
5. Add buttons to your custom toolbar as described in "Add a Button to a Toolbar" above.

   You must add buttons starting from the left side a new toolbar. After you've added two or more buttons to a new toolbar, you can add buttons between buttons.

Delete a Toolbar

If you no longer need a toolbar, you can delete it. You can delete any built-in or custom toolbar from any project file. You can delete custom toolbars from the global file, but you can't delete built-in toolbars from the global file.

To delete a toolbar

1 On the **Tools** menu, point to **Customize**, and then click **Toolbars**.
2 Click the **Toolbars** tab.
3 In the **Toolbars** list, click the name of the toolbar you want to delete, and then click **Delete**.

Reset a Toolbar

When you create, modify, or remove toolbar buttons, you're modifying the toolbar that contains those buttons. To restore a toolbar to its original configuration, you can reset it.

When you reset a toolbar, Microsoft Project deletes custom toolbar buttons that you've added, adds buttons or other tools that you've removed, and restores all modified buttons to their original state. To save any custom or modified buttons before you reset a toolbar, you can move the buttons onto a built-in or custom toolbar.

To reset a toolbar

1 On the **Tools** menu, point to **Customize**, and then click **Toolbars**.
2 Click the **Toolbars** tab.
3 In the **Toolbars** list, click the name of the toolbar you want to reset, and then click **Reset**.

Creating Your Own Forms for Project Information

Forms are windows in which you enter information about selected tasks or resources. Dialog boxes are examples of forms.

You can create your own forms to enter the information that you're interested in. For example, if you want to add specific project information to selected tasks—for example, percent work complete and task start dates—you can create a custom form containing the % Complete and Start fields. The information you enter in the form will be added to the selected tasks.

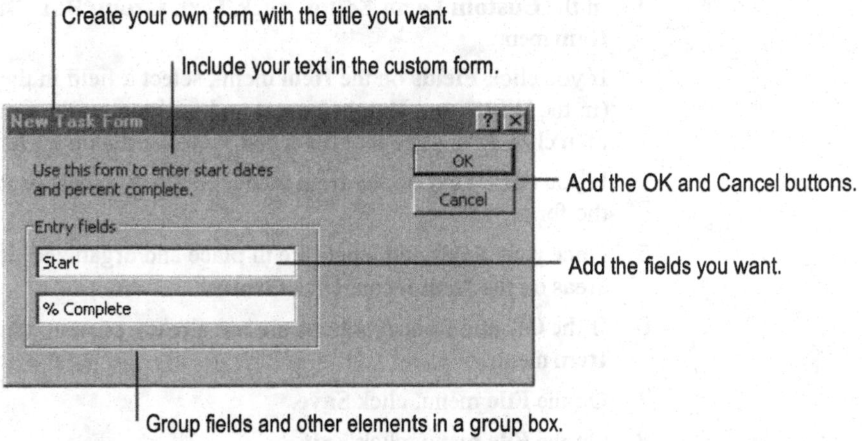

You can work with custom forms in a number of ways. You can associate the form with a new menu command, a new toolbar button, and include it as part of a macro operation.

Create a Custom Form

When you create a custom form, you can add:

- Text, as a title or to explain or describe something on the form.
- A group box, which can visually bundle related text, buttons, and fields.
- Fields—that is, project information fields such as the % Complete field, the Resource Name field, and the Baseline Cost field.
- The OK and Cancel buttons.

For information, see "Sharing Custom Tools Using the Organizer."

Any custom forms you create are stored only in the active project file. However, you can make them available to other project files using the Organizer.

To create a custom form

1 On the **Tools** menu, point to **Customize**, and then click **Forms**.
2 Click **Task** or **Resource**, and then click **New**.
3 In the **Name** box, type the name of the new custom form, and then click **OK**.

4 In the **Custom Form Editor**, click **Text, Group Box, Button**, or **Fields** on the **Item** menu.

If you click **Fields** on the **Item** menu, select a field in the **Field** box, specify its size (in the **Width** and **Height** boxes) and position on the form (in the **X** and **Y** boxes), then click **OK**. (The 0 of the x and y axes is the upper left corner of the form.)

If you click **Text** on the **Item** menu, enter any labels or instructions you want on the form.

5 Once your fields and labels are in place and organized, if you want to group related areas on the **Item** menu, click **Group**.

6 If the OK and Cancel buttons are not already present, click **Button** on the **Item** menu.

7 On the **File** menu, click **Save**.

8 On the **File** menu, click **Exit**.

To move a component in a form, drag it within the form.

To change the size of a component, drag the top, bottom, or side border. You can change the size of the entire form the same way. To change the size of a component so that it maintains its current proportions, drag a border corner.

To edit a component, double-click the component to display the Item Information dialog box.

Use a Form You've Created

To use a form you've created, you need to display it. You can either choose it from the Forms menu or associate the form with a custom menu command or toolbar button.

To use a form you've created

1 Select the task or resource whose information you want to update with your form.

2 On the **Tools** menu, point to **Customize**, and then click **Forms**.

3 Click **Task** or **Resource**, click the form you want to display, and then click **Apply**.

4 Enter the information in the form.

You can add your form to a menu or toolbar. See "Add a Command to a Menu" or "Add a Button to a Toolbar" earlier in this chapter. You can find your new form in the Categories list under All Forms.

Using and Enhancing Custom Fields

A Microsoft Project field contains one piece of project information about tasks, resources, or assignments. Examples of fields are Duration, Overtime Rate, and Actual Work. The standard set of Microsoft Project fields contain predefined pieces of information.

However, there's also a set of custom fields that you can define for your own purposes. For example, you might want to include employee IDs as part of resource information. You can define one of the Number custom fields as your custom Employee ID field.

The names, formats, and quantities for custom fields are:

- Cost1-10.
- Date1-10.
- Duration1-10.
- Finish1-10.
- Flag1-20.
- Number1-20.
- Outline Code1-10.
- Start1-10.
- Text1-30.

You can define the title for the custom field. For example, you can identify the Date1 field to show as "Status Date." You can also:

- Write your own formulas, including references to other Microsoft Project fields, to be calculated as part of the field, with the result being displayed in the field.
- Create a list of values for a custom field to ensure fast and accurate data entry.
- Display a visual indicator, rather than text or numbers, in a custom field. This can help you see at a glance when the data in that field meet certain criteria, such as when resources are overallocated or a deadline is missed.

For more information, see "Using Custom Outline Codes" in chapter 4.

A major category of custom fields is the outline code. With outline codes, you can create a hierarchical structure of codes for tasks or resources. For example, you can associate your organization's cost codes with your project data. Once you create the codes in these fields and apply the codes to your project data, you can filter, sort, and group your project data based on these outline codes. These can help you see entirely different angles of your project information that are relevant to the operation of your project and your organization.

See "Creating Your Own Forms for Project Information" earlier in this chapter.

You can display custom fields in any sheet view, such as a Gantt Chart, Resource Sheet, or Task Usage view. You can also display custom fields in the Network Diagram or Descriptive Network Diagram. You can even add custom fields to custom forms that you create. Custom fields appear in dialog boxes that operate on fields, such as Filter Definition, Box Styles, Table Definition, Group Definition, and Define Import/Export Map.

Create a Custom Field

When you first create a custom field, you simply rename an existing custom field, such as Date3 or Flag5.

To rename a custom field

1. On the **Tools** menu, point to **Customize**, and then click **Fields**.
2. Click **Task** or **Resource**.
3. In the **Type** box, click the type of custom field you want to define—for example, Cost or Number.
4. In the list, click the custom field you want to use—for example, Cost1 or Number3.
5. Click **Rename**, type a new name for the field, and then click **OK**.

To add a custom field to a sheet view

1. On the **View Bar**, click the sheet view in which you want to add a custom field.
2. Click the column to the right of where you want the new custom field to be inserted.
3. On the **Insert** menu, click **Column**.
4. In the **Field name** box, click the custom field.

   The custom field is in alphabetical order as you renamed it.

Calculate Data in a Custom Field

You can make formulas and their calculations an integral part of a field's definition. The formula can refer to other Microsoft Project fields. The result of the formula is displayed in the field. This can be useful for special cost calculations, date comparisons, counts, and other operations.

In task field calculations, formulas can reference any other task field. Likewise, in resource field calculations, formulas can reference any other resource field. Whenever new data are entered, or when Microsoft Project recalculates values referenced by these formulas, the results in the custom fields are dynamically updated.

To create a formula for a custom field

1. On the **Tools** menu, point to **Customize**, and then click **Fields**.
2. Click **Task** or **Resource**, and then click the type of custom field you want to customize in the Type box.
3. In the list, click the field to which you want to add a formula.
4. Under **Custom attributes**, click **Formula**.
5. Under **Edit formula**, enter the formula you want to apply to the custom field. Use any of the following techniques to help build your formula.

   Click **Field**, point to the type of field you want, then click the name of any field you want to reference in the formula.

   Click **Function**, point to the type of function you want, then click the name of the function you want to use in the formula.

   In the row of buttons representing a standard set of operators, click any operator buttons you need to build your formula. Your formula can operate on referenced fields, functions, or data you enter.

   Type the formula in the **Edit formula** box.

Create a List of Values for a Custom Field

You can define the list of values a custom field can contain, so you and other users of the project can just pick from the list. The *value list* appears as a drop-down list in the custom field. You can limit the entry into this field to those in your original value list only, or you can set the field to accept new values.

For example, you can rename Text3 "Supervisor" and create a list of supervisor names to be associated with resources in your project. Whenever you encounter your custom Supervisor field in Microsoft Project, you can simply pick from the list rather than retype the supervisor's name repeatedly for each resource.

To create a value list for a custom field

1. On the **Tools** menu, point to **Customize**, and then click **Fields**.
2. Click **Task** or **Resource**, and then click the type of custom field you want to customize in the **Type** box.
3. In the list, click the field to which you want to add a value list.
4. Under **Custom attributes**, click **Value List**.
5. In the **Value List** dialog box, click the **Value** field in a row, and then type an item that should appear in the value list.
6. If you also describe the item in the **Description** field, that description appears next to the value itself in the drop-down list you see when entering data in the field.

7 To enter another value, select the next row, and then repeat steps 5 and 6 until you finish entering values.

8 If a value in the list should be the default value for the field, click the value, select **Use a value from the list as the default entry for the field** check box, and then click **Set Default**.

9 To determine whether new values can be added to the list during data entry, click the options you want under **Data entry options**.

Display Graphic Symbols in a Custom Field

If you want to be able to discern specific information at a glance in your project, you can define a custom field with a graphical indicator. These indicators can help alert you to potential problems or let you know when tasks, resources, or assignments are progressing as expected.

For example, you can define a custom field to indicate when a resource has worked more than a specified amount of overtime, or when the cost for an assignment has exceeded the budget.

You set up the criteria, or tests, for when the graphical indicator should appear. This process is similar to setting filtering criteria. If the task, resource, or assignment matches the criteria you set, the graphical indicator appears. If not, the field remains blank.

You can set up multiple criteria for different graphical indicators to display in the same field. A set of graphical indicators is included with Microsoft Project. These indicators include colored circles, boxes, flags, faces, and more.

To specify criteria for displaying graphical indicators in a custom field

1 On the **Tools** menu, point to **Customize**, and then click **Fields**.

2 Click **Task** or **Resource**, and then click the type of custom field you want to customize in the **Type** box.

3 In the **Fields** list, click the field in which you want to display a graphical indicator, and then click **Graphical Indicators**.

4 Under **Indicator criteria for**, click whether the graphic should apply to summary or nonsummary rows.

5 In the **Test for** field, click the test you want to apply to the custom field—for example, **is greater than** or **equals**.

6 In the **Value(s)** field, type or select the value that the test should compare to the value in the custom field.

7 To compare a value in the custom field with the value in another field, click the name of that field in the **Value(s)** field.

To compare the value in the custom field with specific data (such as 25) or a range of data (such as 25,50), type the data in the **Value(s)** field.

8 Repeat steps 5 and 6 for each additional test you want to apply to the custom field.

Move Up

Move Down

9 Arrange the rows in the order you want the tests applied to the data in the custom field.

Click the **Move Up** or **Move Down** buttons to rearrange the rows.

Automating Your Tasks Using Macros

Doing the same task over and over again in Microsoft Project can become tedious, especially if that task requires you to press a number of keys. You can replace most of those keystrokes by recording them in a macro. A *macro* is a small program that consists of a recorded series of keystrokes or mouse clicks. When you record a macro, you determine which keystrokes it includes, and in what order, by performing those keystrokes one last time. The next time you want to perform the task that requires those keystrokes, you simply run the macro and let it do the work.

Microsoft Project provides you with a number of ways to work with macros. For example, you can:

- Record a macro.
- Run a macro.
- Interrupt a macro while it's running.

You can record a macro and perform other actions with macros without knowing any programming whatsoever. However, you can get even more out of macros if you know how to program with Visual Basic for Applications (VBA). Find information about VBA in Microsoft Project Help Reference.

Record a Macro

To create a macro, you record the keystrokes and mouse clicks for the task sequence.

To record a macro

1 On the **Tools** menu, point to **Macro**, and then click **Record New Macro**.

2 In the **Macro name** box, enter a name for the macro.

You must use a letter as the first character of the macro name. The other characters can be letters, numbers, or underscore characters. The macro name can't contain spaces or be a word that Microsoft Project reserves as a keyword.

3 In the **Store macro in** box, click the location where you want to store the macro. You can store the macro in the active project file only or in the Global file. If you want the macro to be available to the other projects that use the Global file, click **Global File**.

4 Type a description of the macro—its purpose or other information—in the **Description** box.
5 Click **OK**, and then perform the series of actions you want to record.
6 On the **Tools** menu, point to **Macro**, and then click **Stop Recorder**.

Run a Macro

When you run the macro you've created, Microsoft Project quickly performs the task for you, saving you time.

To run a macro

1 Open the project that contains the macro.
2 On the **Tools** menu, point to **Macro**, and then click **Macros**.
3 Select the macro you want to run from the **Macro name** list.
4 Click **Run**.

Sharing Custom Tools Using the Organizer

When you create a custom toolbar, menu, custom field, macro, form, or other tool that you find particularly useful, you might want to use it in other project files. To make custom tools available to other files, use the Organizer.

The Organizer is a dialog box in which you can copy various Microsoft Project tools from one project file to another. You can also delete and rename those tools in the Organizer. In the Organizer, you can copy, delete, and rename forms, views, calendars, toolbars, tables, reports, menu bars, filters, modules (macros), fields, and more.

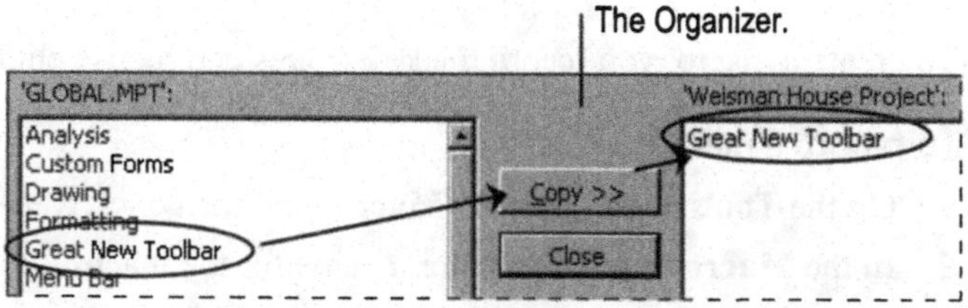

When you modify or create menu bars, menus, commands, toolbars, buttons, and macros, the new or modified tools are saved in the global file, Global.mpt. These tools will be available in any project file that uses the Global.mpt file in which the tools are stored. Global.mpt is like a common reservoir of tools for the project files on one computer—that is, if you create a custom tool in one project file on your computer, it's likely that the tool will appear in all other project files on your computer.

However, custom forms and custom fields are saved only with the project file in which you created them. To share a custom form or field with other project files, you can copy it to Global.mpt or to one project file at a time.

Copy a Custom Tool from One Project File to Another

To copy a custom tool from one project file to another, especially custom forms and files, both the project file where the tool resides and the project file to which you want to copy the tool must be open. By default, tools for the current project and the Global.mpt file are listed.

To copy a custom tool from one project file to another

1 On the **Tools** menu, click **Organizer**.

2 Click the tab named with the category that contains the kind of tool you want to copy—for example, **Forms** or **Fields**.

3 In the list on the right side, click the custom tool you want to share.

4 In the **Available in** box on the left side, click the project into which you want to copy the custom tool. By default, Global.mpt is selected. Click **Copy**.

Delete or Rename a Custom Tool

To rename or delete a custom tool, you can access the tool in the Organizer. Before you can rename or delete a custom tool that resides in a specific project file, you need to open that file.

To delete or rename a custom tool

1 On the **Tools** menu, click **Organizer**.

2 Click the tab named with the category that contains the kind of tool you want to delete or rename—for example, **Toolbars**.

3 In an **Available in** box, display the file that contains the tool you want to rename or delete.

   That file might be the Global.mpt file, or it might be a specific project file.

4 In the list that contains the tool, click the tool you want to rename or delete.

   To rename a project tool, click **Rename**, and then type a new name for the tool.

   To delete a project tool, click **Delete**.

Glossary

A

Accrual method The method for determining the point at which resource costs and fixed costs for tasks are charged to a project. You can incur costs at the start or finish of a task, or prorate them throughout the duration of the task.

Actual Information that indicates real progress on scheduled tasks. Actual information can be collected and entered on start dates, finish dates, percent complete, duration, cost, and so on.

Assignment A task that's been given as work to a resource.

Assignment delay The difference between a task start date and an assignment start date.

Assignment units The percentage of time a resource has to devote to a specific assignment, based on the resource's working time calendar. Assignment units are specified when a resource is assigned to a task. See also *Max units*.

Assumption An educated guess of factors expected to be true for the sake of planning a project. For example, you might assume that the cost of a particular material will stay the same during a project.

AutoFilter In a sheet view, a filter that enables you to filter tasks or resources quickly based on a criterion in a specific column. Each column has an AutoFilter associated with it.

Availability See *Resource availability*.

B

Base calendar A kind of calendar template that shows the working days and hours for a group of resources (such as a department or a shift). The project calendar, resource calendars, and task calendars are based on a base calendar you choose or create.

Baseline A snapshot of original scheduled project information that you can save and compare with actual information as your project progresses. If you set a baseline after you develop your project plan, you can track progress throughout the project.

Bottom-up method The project planning technique in which you list all possible tasks first, then organize them into phases.

C

Calculated field A field whose value is calculated and entered by Microsoft Project based on values in other fields. If you change a value in one of those other fields, Microsoft Project automatically recalculates the value in the calculated field.

Code mask The format you set up to specify the numbering scheme for your custom work breakdown structure. For example, you can set a code mask to assign WBS codes such as TJ-1067c.

Collapsing Hiding the subtasks of summary tasks in a task outline so that only the summary tasks are visible.

Combination view A view that contains two views in a split screen. The view in the lower pane displays detailed information about the tasks or resources selected in the upper pane. The Task Entry view is an example of a predefined combination view.

Consolidated project file A project file into which other project files have been inserted. Each inserted project is represented as a single summary task, which can be expanded for the details. A consolidated file enables you to manage multiple projects from one project file.

Constraint A restriction you place on a task's start or finish date. For example, you can specify that a task must start on a certain date or start no earlier than a certain date. See also *Limitations*.

Consumption rate See *Fixed consumption rate* and *Variable consumption rate.*

Contour A specific distribution of work that indicates the shape of an assignment over time. The default contour, "flat," distributes the same number of hours of work per day. You can apply different contours to different assignments.

Cost The total cost of a task, resource, assignment, or project.

Cost rate table A matrix for specifying up to 25 rate levels for the same resource and the date each rate will take effect. Used for increases or decreases in salary, or different pay for different kinds of jobs.

Criteria Traits that distinguish one set of tasks or resources from all others. In a filter, for example, criteria determine which tasks or resources are displayed or highlighted. You also specify criteria for grouping, sorting, and so on.

Critical path The sequence of tasks that has the latest finish date in a project. The critical path determines the project finish date. If any task in the critical path is delayed, the project finish date will also be delayed.

Critical task A task that, if delayed, delays the project finish date. All critical tasks are part of the critical path. By default, a critical task has zero slack time.

Crosstab report A report that shows information about tasks or resources broken down by time period. Tasks or resources make up the rows, and information in the columns is shown by time period.

Current date line On the Gantt Chart view or the Resource Graph view, a vertical dotted line that indicates the current date.

Custom field A type of field in which you can enter information you define. For example, you can have Number1 contain employee numbers, or Text3 contain department responsibility. You can set up formulas, value lists, and graphical indicators for custom fields.

Custom outline codes See *Outline codes.*

D

Database The central storage area of all project information in Microsoft Project. When you display a view, you're looking at a portion of the information contained in the database.

Date constraint See *Constraint.*

Deadline A date indicator in your schedule that reminds you of an important date but does not set an inflexible constraint.

Default value A predefined value that Microsoft Project automatically inserts into a field. The default value might be a typical one that suits the majority of users, thus saving time.

Delay The amount of time inserted between tasks, usually to resolve resource overallocations. Delay is the difference between the scheduled start date and the assignment start date.

Dependency A condition that specifies the start or finish of one task relative to the start or finish of its predecessor task. For example, if two tasks are linked with a finish-to-start dependency, the condition is that one task can start only after its predecessor task is completed. Same as *Link.*

Destination file A file, sometimes in another software program, into which you are pasting, exporting, embedding, or linking project information. See *Source file.*

Details Sets of related information that display detailed task, resource, or assignment information in a special view format other than a table such as the Resource Graph and Network Diagram.

Diagram view A view that displays project information graphically, with each task represented by a box or node. Examples include the Network Diagram and Relationship Diagram.

Divider bar The vertical bar that separates the two portions of a view in the Gantt Chart, Resource Graph, Resource Usage, and Task Usage views.

Drag-and-drop editing A method for changing project information using the mouse to drag information from one location to another.

Duration The length of time it takes to complete a task during normal working hours. When each task's duration is included in a project, Project can start to calculate the schedule. To express a duration that stretches across nonworking time, use elapsed duration.

E

Earned value A project tracking method that determines whether tasks are on budget and on schedule based on actual costs incurred and actual progress to date. For example, if a task that's 50% complete has incurred 70% of its planned cost, the task would be said to be behind schedule.

Effort-driven scheduling The default scheduling method used by Microsoft Project to calculate duration, work, and assignment units. With effort-driven scheduling on, you increase or decrease a duration by removing or adding resources to a task.

Elapsed duration A task duration that includes nonworking time. Used when task duration needs to span a continuous period of time.

Embedding A method for copying information between two files, especially between files created in different programs. When you embed information, the information retains its separateness in the destination program. You can edit embedded information by using tools that are the same as or similar to the editing tools in the source program, even though the information does not retain a link to the source file.

Entered field A field in which you enter information, either by typing or selecting. See also *Calculated field*.

Estimated duration A task duration that is an estimate rather than confirmed. Estimated durations are marked with a question mark.

Expanding Showing the subtasks of summary tasks in a task outline.

Exporting Transferring and converting information from Microsoft Project to another program, such as a database or spreadsheet program, and in a format compatible with the destination program, such as MPD, or XLS, or TXT.

F

Field A cell or box in a view that contains a particular kind of information about a task resource, or assignment. In a sheet view, for instance, a field is the intersection of a row and a column.

File format The particular traits of a file that allow it to be opened in a particular program. Each program can open files that are in certain formats only. Each format is indicated by a specific file extension. For example, Microsoft Project can open files in the MPP, MPX, MPT, CSV, and several other file formats.

File name The name of a file, which usually consists of a given name and a file extension. For example, project.mpp could be the name of a file created in Microsoft Project. In Microsoft Project, a valid file name can have up to 255 characters, consist of any combination of letters or numbers, and can include the following characters: ! @ # $ % & ( ) - _ { } ' ~

Filter A tool that uses a set of criteria that tasks or resources must match for them to be displayed or highlighted. See also *AutoFilter*, *Criteria*, and *Interactive filter*.

Fixed consumption rate The usage calculated for a material resource when the amount of material is to remain constant even if the task duration should change. See also *Variable consumption rate*.

Fixed cost A cost, usually associated with a task rather than a resource, that doesn't change regardless of the task duration or how much work a task requires.

Fixed-duration task A task whose duration remains constant if work or assignment units change. See *Task type*.

Fixed-work task A task whose work remains constant if duration or assignment units change. See *Task type*.

Fixed-units task A task whose assignment units remain constant if duration or work change. This is the default task type. See *Task type*.

Flexible constraint A constraint that does not tie a task to a date and allows Microsoft Project to move the task when the schedule changes. The flexible constraints are As Soon As Possible and As Late As Possible. See also *Moderate constraint* and *Inflexible constraint*.

Font A family of characters—letters, numbers, and symbols—that share a particular look.

Font style Any extra characteristics added to a font, such as bold, italic, or underlining.

Footer Text that appears at the bottom of every printed page. Examples of footer information are page numbers and current date.

Form A type of view in which you can enter, edit, or view detailed task or resource information, usually in boxes. Examples include the Task Form and Resource Form.

Free slack The amount of time a task can slip without delaying the finish date of another task.

G

Gantt bar A horizontal rectangular bar in the chart portion of the Gantt Chart view. Each Gantt bar represents a task and typically includes information representing duration, start date, finish date, percent complete, and assigned resources.

Gantt Chart A view that displays a table of task information in its left half and a bar chart showing a task schedule in its right half. Examples include the default Gantt Chart and the Tracking Gantt.

Global file The Global.mpt file, which contains the Microsoft Project tools such as views, calendars, forms, fields, reports, tables, filters, toolbars, menus, macros, and options settings. Typically, all the project files created on the same computer share the same Global.mpt file.

Goal One of the objectives you want to achieve in a project. Project goals articulate the purpose of the project.

Graph A view, such as the Resource Graph, that displays project information graphically.

Graphics area Any area in Microsoft Project into which picture information from another program can be inserted. The graphics areas in Microsoft Project are the bar chart portion of the Gantt Chart view, notes, headers, footers, legends, and the Objects box in form views.

Gridlines The horizontal and vertical lines that appear in most Microsoft Project views. By separating pieces of information or sections of a view, gridlines make it easier to read a view. Gridlines can be formatted, displayed, and hidden.

Grouping Collecting certain tasks or resources together according to criteria you choose—for example, milestones, duration, or incomplete tasks.

H

Header Text that appears at the top of every printed page. Examples of header information are project name, company logo, and the project start or finish date.

Hyperlink A specialized string of text in a file or Web site that contains the address of another document. When you click a hyperlink, your computer displays the destination document. The address of the destination document is either a URL address or a UNC address. Hyperlink text is usually distinguished by color.

I

Importing Transferring and converting information from another program, such as a database or spreadsheet program, to Microsoft Project.

Import/export map A table that specifies parallels between corresponding fields of information in two programs for the purpose of importing or exporting information.

Indenting In a task outline (such as on the Gantt Chart view), moving a task to a lower outline level by moving it to the right. Also known as demoting. When you indent a task, it becomes a subtask of the task above it that's at the higher outline level. See also *Outdenting* and *Outline*.

Indicators Icons in the Indicators column that serve as flags to important information about tasks or resources, such as constraints, deadlines, and notes. When you point to an indicator, the task or resource information is displayed.

Inflexible constraint A constraint that ties a task to a date. If the schedule changes, the task's start and finish dates remain unaffected. The inflexible constraints are Must Start On and Must Finish On.

Inserted project A project file that's inserted into another project file to create a consolidated project file.

Interactive filter A filter that displays a dialog box into which you enter the filter criteria, such as a resource name or a range of dates. In the filter menu, interactive filters are listed with an ellipsis after the name.

Interim plan A set of current task start and finish dates that are saved with a project file. Saving interim plans periodically and comparing them with the baseline plan can help you track project progress. You can save up to ten interim plans.

Internet A global computer network whose most visible component is the World Wide Web (WWW).

Intranet A computer network that resembles the Internet but exists only within an organization. An intranet may or may not be connected to the Internet.

L

Lag time The amount of waiting time added between the completion of a predecessor task and the start of its successor task.

Lead time The amount of overlap between a predecessor task and its successor. The amount of overlap is the lead time; it represents the amount of time that the successor is worked on before its predecessor task is completed.

Legend An explanatory list that appears on every page of a printed chart or diagram view, such as a Gantt Chart or Calendar view. Typically, a legend explains the meaning of symbols in the view. You can add information in the legend box, such as the project file name, logo, and more.

Leveling Eliminating resource overallocations by either delaying or splitting tasks that have overallocated resources assigned to them. You can do this yourself or use the Microsoft Project leveling feature.

Leveling delay The amount of time between the scheduled start of a task and the time when work should actually begin on the task. Leveling delay is added to resolve resource overallocations.

Limitations Constraining factors that affect your project—for example, a specific deadline or a fixed budget.

Link A dependency between tasks that specifies the start or finish conditions of a task relative to the start or finish of another task. For example, if two tasks are linked with a finish-to-start link, the condition is that one task can start only after its predecessor task is completed. Same as *Dependency*.

Link line On the Gantt Chart and Network Diagram views, a line that links one task to another and shows the type of dependency between the tasks—for example, finish-to-start or finish-to-finish.

Linking Can refer to one of two actions. When scheduling tasks, it refers to establishing a dependency between tasks. When including an object from one program in another program (object linking and embedding), it refers to establishing a connection between programs.

Lookup table A list of preset values defined in a list box so users don't have to type them in each time the field is encountered. Used in outline codes and in other custom fields. Also known as a *Value list*.

M

Macro A small program that consists of a recorded series of keystrokes or mouse clicks to help you automate a specific repetitive task. With Visual Basic for Applications (VBA), you can create more complex macros.

MAPI The acronym for Messaging Application Programming Interface. This is the standard programming interface proposed and supported by Microsoft for exchanging electronic mail messages.

Master project A type of consolidated project into which related projects, or subprojects, are inserted. The relationship between the master project and subprojects is analogous to that of a summary task and subtasks. See *Consolidated project*.

Material consumption See *Fixed consumption rate* and *Variable consumption rate*.

Material resource Consumable supplies that are used in the performance on a task. Examples include concrete, steel, and soil.

Max units The specification of how much time a work resource has to devote to the project in relation to what is considered full time for the resource, as established in the resource's working time calendar. See also *Assignment units*.

Microsoft Project Central The Web-based companion product to Microsoft Project used for exchanging messages, managing task lists, and viewing the overall project for resources and other individuals over your organization's intranet or the World Wide Web.

Milestone A major event, such as the completion of a project phase or major deliverable, that indicates project progress. In Microsoft Project, a milestone is used as a marker and typically has a duration of zero.

Moderate constraint A constraint that allows Microsoft Project to move the task when the schedule changes, within loose date guidelines. The moderate constraints are Finish No Earlier Than, Finish No Later Than, Start No Earlier Than, and Start No Later Than. See also *Flexible constraint* and *Inflexible constraint*.

N

Network Diagram A view that graphically displays tasks and relationships as a set of nodes and connecting lines.

Noncritical tasks Tasks that can be delayed a day or more before the project finish date without delaying the project finish date.

Nonworking time Those periods of time when resources don't work. Examples of nonworking time are weekends, holidays, and vacations. Defined in the project, resource, and task calendars.

Note A memo regarding a task, resource, or assignment that you can enter in the Notes tab of the Task Information dialog box, the Resource Information dialog box, or the Assignment Information dialog box.

O

Object In object linking and embedding (OLE), text or graphics information from one document that's inserted into another document. The documents can be created by the same program or by different programs. A single object can be inserted into many documents. The object may or may not remain linked to its source program. If it's linked, then modifying the object in the source program modifies all inserted instances of the object also.

Object linking and embedding (OLE) The technology for sharing information between programs or files by linking or embedding it. When you link information, you insert the information into one or more destination documents, but the information remains linked to the source program. Updating the information in the source program updates it in the destination documents. When you embed information, you can also insert the information into one or more destination documents, but the information is not linked to the source program. You can, however, edit embedded information in a destination document by using editing tools associated with the source program.

Objects box An area of a form view into which you can link or embed objects, such as text or pictures from other programs.

Organizer A tabbed dialog box, accessible via the Tools menu, in which you can copy custom views, tables, filters, fields, macros, toolbars, menus, and so on from one project file to another. You can also rename and delete custom tools.

Outdenting In a task outline (such as on the Gantt Chart view), moving a task to a higher outline level by moving it to the left. Also known as promoting. See also *Indenting* and *Outline*.

Outline A list of tasks, arranged in a hierarchical relationship, showing some tasks subordinate to other tasks. The subordinate tasks, called *subtasks*, are indented with respect to the other tasks, called *summary tasks*.

Outline codes Outline codes are custom tags that share specific characteristics and a specific hierarchy. Tasks and resources can be organized and viewed according to these outline codes to review the project from different points of view.

Outline level The position a task occupies in the outline hierarchy. A task at outline level 1 occupies the highest outline level. All tasks below this task are subordinate to it. A task indented just once is at outline level 2, a task indented twice is at outline level 3, and so on.

Outline number A number used to indicate a task's level in the outline hierarchy. By default, outline numbers aren't displayed.

Overallocation The result of assigning more hours of work to a resource within a certain time period than the resource has available to work in that time period.

Overtime The number of hours of work performed by a resource beyond the resource's usual hours of availability.

P

Password A combination of characters that you can enter to display a project or to log in to Microsoft Project Central.

Path The address to a particular file, either on a computer, a network, or Web site. The path often contains a server name, folder name, and file name.

Per-use cost A cost that's incurred only at the point when a resource is used.

PERT analysis A process for determining a probable schedule from best-case, expected-case, and worst-case task durations.

PERT chart See *Network Diagram.*

Phase A group of logically related tasks required to complete a major step in a project.

Plan A model of your project that you use to predict and control progress. It includes a schedule and the task, resource, and cost information required to manage a project effectively.

Point The unit of measurement for text size. The size of this text is 10 points. A 72-point character is 1 inch high.

Predecessor task A task on which another task depends. A predecessor task must start or finish before its successor task can start or finish.

Priority When you level overallocated resources, the place you give to a task in the leveling order. To level resources, you might prefer that low-priority tasks get delayed first. If delaying low-priority tasks doesn't resolve overallocations, Microsoft Project will delay higher-priority tasks.

Product scope The features and functions to be included in goods or services being developed by the project. Sometimes referred to as a product specification.

Progress bar On the Gantt Chart view, a horizontal line drawn in the center of a Gantt bar to indicate the percent that a task is complete.

Progress line On the Gantt Chart view, a vertical zigzagging line that represents the degree to which tasks are ahead or behind schedule.

Project A one-time endeavor that ends with a specific accomplishment, such as the development of a unique product or service.

Project calendar A calendar of working and nonworking times used by the entire project. It initially determines how all tasks and resources are scheduled. The default project calendar is the Standard calendar.

Project finish date The latest date on which you want your project to end. If you enter a project finish date, Microsoft Project schedules backward from this finish date.

Project management The defining, planning, scheduling, and controlling of the tasks that must be completed to achieve your project goals.

Project model A representation of the way a real project proceeds in the real world.

Project scope A statement that articulates the work that must be done to deliver the product or service with the specified features and functions. The project scope determines which tasks do and do not need to be performed to satisfy the product scope and achieve the project goals. See *Product scope*.

Project start date The date on which you want your project to start. If you enter a project start date, Microsoft Project schedules tasks forward from this date. By default, the project start date is the date you create your project.

Prorated cost A cost incurred gradually over time as a task progresses.

R

Rate table A matrix for specifying up to 25 pay rates for the same resource and the date each rate will take effect. Used for increases or decreases in salary, or different pay rates for different kinds of jobs.

Recurring task A task that occurs repeatedly and, usually, at regular intervals during the course of a project. An example of a recurring task is a weekly status meeting.

Report A detailed account of a particular aspect of a project that can include task, resource, assignment, calendar, or cost information, or some combination of these. Microsoft Project supplies 29 predefined and formatted reports, grouped into categories, that are designed to be printed.

Resource allocation The assignment of resources to tasks in a project.

Resource availability The exact dates when work resources are available to your project and their max units at those times.

Resource calendar A calendar showing the working and nonworking times for an individual resource, including vacation and personal days. Microsoft Project uses calendar information to calculate task schedules.

Resource group A set of resources that's usually grouped by job type and given a group name.

Resource leveling See *Leveling*.

Resource list A list of the resources available to be assigned to tasks in a project. A resource list can include people, equipment, and materials.

Resource pool A project file that usually contains a common set of information on resources that are shared with multiple projects. A resource pool is linked to the project files that share it.

Resource view A view that displays resource information. Examples of resource views are the Resource Sheet and the Resource Graph.

Resource A person, piece of equipment, material, facility, or service required to complete tasks in a project.

Roll up On the bar chart of the Gantt Chart view, displaying subtask Gantt bars on summary task Gantt bars.

Routing Using your MAPI e-mail system to send a project file to several people to review and return to you. You can have the file routed from one person to the next, or you can have a copy sent to all recipients at once.

S

Scaling Increasing or decreasing the size of the printed image on a page.

Schedule A plan showing the sequence, start dates, finish dates, and durations of tasks in a project.

Scheduled The current planned value, based on actuals entered to date and work remaining. You can see scheduled information for work, cost, duration, and more. See *Baseline* and *Actual*.

Scope The quantity, depth, or quality of work being undertaken in a project. See *Product scope*.

Server A computer set up to be the central source of information or services for other computers.

Sheet view A view that includes a table portion of information, arranged in columns and rows. Examples of sheet views include the Resource Sheet and the Task Usage view.

Slack The amount of time a task can slip before it delays another task (free slack) or the entire project (total slack). Also referred to as *float time*.

Slippage The difference between a task's scheduled start or finish date and its baseline start or finish date, when the scheduled dates occur later than the baseline dates.

Sorting Arranging tasks or resources in an order based on a particular set of criteria. For example, you can sort tasks by duration or by start date.

Source file A file, sometimes in another software program from which you are pasting, exporting, embedding, or linking project information. See *Destination file*.

Split task A task in which work is interrupted, then begins again. On the Gantt Chart view, the Gantt bar for a split task appears with gaps in it. Tasks are often split to resolve resource overallocations or to reschedule tasks in progress.

Status date A date that you set and use as a reference point from which to measure project progress.

Subproject A project that's inserted into a master project to which the subproject is related in a hierarchical structure. See *Master project*.

Subtask A task that's indented under and is part of a summary task. Subtasks are the steps that complete the summary task.

Successor task A task whose start or finish date depends on the start or finish date of another task. A successor task can't start or finish before its predecessor task has started or finished.

Summary project In a consolidated project, a project outdented in relation to another project below it to indicate a hierarchical relationship between the projects. Like a summary task, a summary project rolls up summarized information from its subprojects.

Summary task In a task outline (such as on the Gantt Chart view), a task that's at a higher outline level than the tasks beneath it, often representing a major task or phase. A summary task rolls up and summarizes the information of its subtasks.

T

Table A set of fields arranged in columns and rows of related information about tasks, resources, or assignments. Tables appear in sheet views. You can apply different tables to display different sets of information in the same sheet view.

Task One of the specific, concrete activities that need to be completed to achieve project goals. A task is typically associated with a duration, cost, and resource requirement.

Task calendar A set of working and nonworking times assigned to a task that can be different than the project calendar or the resource calendar of assigned resources.

Task dependency See *Dependency*.

Task duration See *Duration*.

Task list A list of all the tasks required to achieve project goals.

Task sequence The order in which your project tasks are to be done. Once you set the task sequence, you can start to link tasks to indicate the type of dependency they have with each other.

Task type One of three types of tasks in which either assignment units, work, or duration is held fixed when you edit units, work, or duration, while one of the other two quantities varies.

Task view A view that displays task information. Examples of task views are the Gantt Chart and the Network Diagram.

Template A generic project that contains basic project information that's likely to be used in other projects. You can create projects faster by basing them on an existing template, then modifying the new project files.

Timephased An even distribution of a quantity, such as costs, work, or units, over the task duration.

Timescale An axis or line divided into evenly spaced time intervals. Timescales on the Gantt Chart, Resource Graph, Resource Usage, and Task Usage views enable you to see events over time or breakdowns of information per time period—for example, hours worked per day.

Top-down method The project planning technique in which you identify and enter major project phases first, then enter the milestones and tasks within each phase. You continue breaking tasks into smaller and smaller units until you reach the level of detail you want.

Total cost The total cost of a task, resource, or assignment over the life of a project.

Total slack The amount of time a task can slip without delaying the project finish date.

U

UNC Universal Naming Convention. UNC addresses are used to identify the locations of files that reside on network servers.

Underallocation The condition that exists when a resource is assigned to work fewer hours than that resource has available during a particular time period.

Units See *Assignment units* and *Max units*.

URL Uniform Resource Locator. A URL is the name or location of a site on the Internet. URLs are used in HTML documents to specify the destination of a hyperlink.

Usage view A special combination view consisting of a sheet view on the left and a timesheet view on the right. In these views, you can see tasks with assignments (Task Usage view) or resources with assignments (Resource Usage view).

V

Value list A list of preset values defined in a list box so users don't have to type them in each time the field is encountered. Used in outline codes and in other custom fields. Also known as a *lookup table*.

Variable consumption rate The usage calculated for a material resource when the amount of material is based on time—that is, if the task duration changes, the amount of material used changes correspondingly. See *Fixed consumption rate*.

Variable cost A cost that changes, generally by increasing, over time. For example, the cost of a resource who gets paid an hourly rate is a variable cost.

Variance The difference between scheduled information and baseline information. Variances alert you to potential problems in your schedule that might need corrective action.

View An organized format for displaying, entering, and editing project information. Views collect and display task, resource, or assignment information. Categories of views are Gantt charts, usage views, graph and diagram views, sheet views, and form views. You can print most views.

W

Web browser A program that enables you to locate and display information on the World Wide Web. In Microsoft Project Central, workgroup members use their Web browser to display and respond to their workgroup messages as well as view aspects of the entire project.

Web server A computer that processes requests from other computers that want to display a Web site. A Web server can also contain Web sites.

Web site Any location on the World Wide Web or an intranet that's formatted in HTML and is accessible from a Web browser.

Work The amount of time or effort required by an assigned resource to complete a task. For example, if two resources each work 8 hours to complete a task, the task is said to have 16 hours of work.

Work breakdown structure WBS. A tree-type structure, much like an organizational chart for tasks, based on deliverables. Tasks are grouped according to deliverables that are the result of every phase, subphase, and task.

Work contour See *Contour*.

Work package The lowest level of a work breakdown structure that represents the point at which actual work is done, resources are assigned, for the outcome of a specific deliverable.

Work resource The people and equipment that accomplish the work or a task. See *Material resource*.

Workgroup A set of resources, and their manager, who work on the same project and exchange task status information through the same electronic communications system.

Workgroup messages Special Microsoft Project messages used by workgroup members and the workgroup manager to exchange task status information. Includes the TeamAssign, TeamUpdate, and TeamStatus messages.

Working time The time periods specified in a base project, resource, or task calendar during which work can occur.

Working time calendar A generic name for base, project, resource, and task calendars. A working time calendar stores working and nonworking time.

Workspace A tool that enables you to open a number of project files at the same time. A workspace consists of a list of project names linked to the project files you specify. You add the project files you want to the workspace. When you open a workspace, you open all the listed projects at the same time.

World Wide Web The most visible component of the Internet, the World Wide Web consists of innumerable Web sites.

Index

A

B

D

J

K

L

M

N

O

P

R

T

U

V

W

X